JESUS AND THE
SPIRAL OF VIOLENCE

Popular Jewish Resistance
in Roman Palestine

Richard A. Horsley

Harper & Row, Publishers, San Francisco

Cambridge, Hagerstown, New York, Philadelphia, Washington
London, Mexico City, São Paulo, Singapore, Sydney

FIRST EDITION

Library of Congress Cataloging-in-Publication Data
Horsley, Richard A.
    Jesus and the spiral of violence.
    Includes index.
    1. Jesus Christ—Political and social views.
2. Judaism and state—History. 3. Violence—
Religious aspects—Judaism. 4. Government, Resistance
to—Religious aspects—Judaism. 5. Jews—History—
586 B.C.–A.D. 70   I. Title.
BS2417.P6H67 1987   220.9′5   86-45811
ISBN 0-06-254448-9

87 88 89 90 91 HC 10 9 8 7 6 5 4 3 2 1

Contents

Acknowledgments

I would like to express appreciation to a number of friends for stimulation, critical insights, and patient assistance in this project. Sandra Washburn, Jim Tracy, Sue Rivers, Brian Riley, and Jack Reynolds all contributed to the analysis and critical discussion of some of the materials dealt with in Part Two. Similarly, Anna Ortiz, Chris Motta, and Mary Malone provided stimulation and insights in a highly productive series of conversations about several aspects of Jesus' practice and preaching. Stephen Mott and Howard Kee gave me valuable critical response to the initial draft of Parts One and Two. Max Myers, Carol Robb, and Michael LaFargue provided helpful critical discussion of the ethical implications of some of Jesus' teachings. Special appreciation goes to Jim Tracy for a critical reading of the whole manuscript and for numerous helpful suggestions and to Jim Pasto and Diane Bergen for research assistance, critical reading, and other processing of the whole. Justus George Lawler's critical response to and suggestions for the presentation of the material, finally, have been invaluable. Partial support for the completion of the research and writing was provided by the University of Massachusetts, Boston, through a reduction in teaching responsibilities for the spring term, 1986, and an Educational Needs grant.

Introduction

The issue of violence has traditionally been treated in an individualistic and abstract way in New Testament studies. It has been taken for granted, for example, that Jesus' "love command" is a general, even absolute, principle pertaining to individual behavior.[1] The context in which Jesus uttered the "command" and in which the modern person applies the command have not been important factors. As Third-World church leaders and theologians have been explaining to Europeans and North Americans for some time, however, the question of violence does not begin with the individual agent. For violence is often structured into the social-historical situation in which the individual lives. In order to understand the concrete situation in which first-century Palestinian Jews, including Jesus, were placed historically, the issue of Jesus and violence clearly requires a more complex and comprehensive approach than we have previously pursued.[2]

The historical situation of first-century Jewish Palestine, including Jewish resistance to Roman rule, has, of course, been seriously investigated. The results of archaeological explorations and dramatic discoveries of new documents such as the Dead Sea Scrolls have considerably broadened and deepened our knowledge of late second Temple Palestine.[3] Much of the earlier reconstruction of the social-political history of Palestinian Jewish society, however, seriously underestimated the complexity of the society, particularly the potential differences in interest and outlook between the priestly aristocracy, who controlled the society as client rulers for the Romans, and the mass of peasants (90–95% in any traditional agrarian society), who were taxed to support the aristocracy. Moreover, it has been assumed that we can speak intelligibly of something called "Judaism" on the basis of a few documents produced by literate individuals and groups who comprised a tiny stratum somewhere in the middle of the social structure.[4] Yet even our literary sources feature dramatic social conflicts. Hence it is clearly necessary to deal more adequately with the complexity and conflict in ancient Palestinian Jewish society.

In particular, the modern scholarly concept of "the Zealots" has badly oversimplified and distorted our understanding of Jewish resistance to Rome and has skewed our treatment of Jesus as well. Despite the warnings of a few distinguished American scholars, the view that at the time of Jesus there existed a widespread religious–political movement of national liberation called "the Zealots" became enshrined in important handbooks and dictionaries in the field.[5] According to the usual scholarly construct, the Zealot party is the same as the "Fourth Philosophy" founded by Judas of Galilee in opposition to enrollment for the tribute imposed along with direct Roman rule in 6 C.E., and its members, whom Josephus called interchangeably "sicarii" and "brigands," agitated for Jewish liberation until they finally provoked the massive Jewish revolt in 66. This view has served important functions, both theologically and politically. As the supposed fanatical advocates of violent revolution against the Romans, "the Zealots" served as a convenient foil over against which to portray Jesus of Nazareth as a sober prophet of a pacific love of one's enemies. Theologians and biblical scholars could then ward off any implication that Jesus had advocated any sort of active resistance to the established order.[6] "The Zealots," leaders of a Jewish people supposedly united against Roman domination, served equally well as a historical precedent for the Zionist cause or for the modern Jewish state fighting for its survival against hostile neighbors. The ancient fortress of Masada, where supposedly the last remaining band of Zealots held out valiantly against the Roman siege and finally committed mass suicide rather than "surrender" to the alien conquerors, became a rallying symbol for modern Israel: "Masada shall not fall again!"[7]

Unfortunately for these studies and for the concerns of their authors, "the Zealots" as a movement of rebellion against Roman rule did not come into existence until the winter of 67–68 C.E.—that is, until the middle of the great revolt. The recent move to less specific labels such as "resistance fighters" or "the activist element,"[8] however, does not change the fact that there is simply no evidence for an organized movement of violent resistance that agitated for armed revolt from 6 to 66 C.E. Jewish reaction to Roman rule was far more complex than the old "Zealots" concept allowed, and social unrest took a variety of social forms.[9] It is obviously necessary to reexamine the view that Jewish Palestine was a hotbed of violent resistance during the time of Jesus.

The whole debate of "Jesus and the Zealots" was thus misconceived.[10] If there is no historical reality behind the modern scholarly construct of "the Zealots," many of those discussions were not only tilting at windmills but were distorting the ministry of Jesus as well. Once the "Zealots" or any other "resistance movement" is removed from the discussion of Jesus and the question of violence, however, we must begin a fresh analysis of Jesus' ministry as well as of the situation in which he worked.

Along with views of "the Zealots" there are a number of other important assumptions and distortions that we must avoid or cut through in order to make a more concrete and precise approach to Jesus in the context of his society and movement. It will be necessary to deal with these problematic assumptions and scholarly generalizations in greater detail in the following chapters. Yet it might be useful at the outset to briefly remind ourselves that the Palestinian Jewish people at the time of Jesus did not deal in such abstractions as "the individual" and did not have a "religious" sphere of life separate from the political and economic dimensions of their common life.

I. THE IMPERIAL SITUATION AND THE SPIRAL OF VIOLENCE

1. The Imperial Situation of Palestinian Jewish Society

The Jews of Jesus' day were a subject people. Ever since the fall of Jerusalem to the Babylonian armies in 587 B.C.E., Jewish society had been subject to one imperial regime after another. The Babylonians destroyed the original Temple of Solomon, deported the ruling class to Babylon, and thus brought the Davidic dynasty to an end. When the Persians conquered Babylon in 540 B.C.E., they reversed the Babylonian imperial policy by allowing the Judean and other indigenous ruling classes to return to their native countries. Although the Persian empire thus appears relatively benign in our sources, most of which were produced by the governing elite, Judea remained a subject territory.

Alexander the Great and his Macedonian armies, who conquered all territory from Greece to Egypt and India in the 330s B.C.E., did not simply bring yet another foreign political rule but imposed a cultural imperialism as well. The little out-of-the-way territory of Judea, relatively isolated from the cosmopolitan currents of communication and trade, did not come immediately under the sway of the new Hellenistic cultural and political forms. Indeed, the Jewish aristocracy's attempt to implement a Hellenizing "reform" in 175 B.C.E. touched off the massive popular Maccabean revolt (after 168) that asserted the independence of Judean society once again.

Yet the tiny country ruled now semi-independently by the Maccabean or Hasmonean high priests was still part of a larger imperial system. As the Hellenistic empire of the Seleucids declined, the Romans exerted their influence and finally conquered the whole eastern Mediterranean, including Palestine, in 63 B.C.E. Thereafter, whether through the Herodian client kings or the collaborating Jewish priestly aristocracy, the Romans controlled affairs in Jewish society. Jesus was crucified by the Romans, and it was the Romans who placed the Pharisees (become rabbis) in control of Palestinian Jewish society after the Jewish revolt of 66–70. Thus, both Christianity and Rabbinic Judaism began under Roman imperial rule.

In the fields of biblical studies and Jewish history there has been a tendency to interpret biblical and other material on the assumption that we could deal with Jewish society by itself. There has also been the understandable tendency in biblical interpretation and study of religion to concentrate on the cultural dimension of history. Some have cautioned that Jewish phenomena of the second Temple period must be understood as part of a larger cosmopolitan whole—Hellenistic civilization in the eastern Mediterranean.[1] To the extent that such appeals have been heeded, however, adjustments have been made principally in the area of cultural history, particularly in examining the influence of "Hellenism."

Because Palestinian Jewish society was a constituent part of successive empires throughout the second Temple period, however, it was involved in something similar to what in modern times has been called a "colonial situation."[2] The particular structure of this "colonial" or "imperial situation" influences the orientation and actions of both "colonizer" and "colonized" and particularly the relations between them. It is important to recognize that relations between the dominant empire and the subject people are full of tension and conflict and cannot possibly be comprehended simply in terms of "culture contact" or "acculturation." If Jewish society had been occupied and exploited for only a short time, it would be less important to take the "imperial situation" into account. However, in a case such as ancient Judea, where the people had been ruled by one empire after another for a period of centuries, we must consider the antagonism and conflicts resulting from the prolonged forcible subjugation of a proud people by the dominant imperial regimes.

For example, such a society may have been almost continually in circumstances of crisis. To use only the most dramatic manifestations of the endemic tensions and conflicts between imperial domination and subjugated Judean society—that is, violent rebellion—late second Temple and New Testament times were framed by three of the major popular revolts in antiquity. In the Maccabean revolt, beginning in 168–167 B.C.E., the Judeans successfully rebelled against the Hellenistic empire of the Seleucid regime in Syria and against their own assimilationist, "Westernizing" aristocracy. Then twice within seventy years, in 66–70 and in 132–135 C.E., Palestinian Jews rose in prolonged popular rebellion against Roman domination and, in the revolt of 66–70, against their own priestly aristocracy as well. Between the Maccabean revolt and the anti-Roman revolts, moreover, there were several lesser Jewish popular rebellions against the imperial power or against their own semi-independent rulers or both: a rebellion against Alexander Jannai, popular resistance to the Roman conquest of Judea by Pompey in 63 B.C.E., prolonged popular rebellion and "civil war" during the great Roman "Civil War" in the 40s B.C.E., popular resistance to Herod's conquest of his realm as the client ruler for Rome in 38–37, and an outbreak of popular rebellion in every major district of Herod's kingdom at the latter's death in 4 B.C.E.

There was resistance and even rebellion in certain other subject societies in antiquity. The conflict and turmoil created in Palestinian Jewish society, however, was unusually intense and the "colonial situation" more volatile than elsewhere in Hellenistic-Roman antiquity. We must consider, finally, that these frequent armed rebellions were only the most violent manifestations. Underlying these highly visible rebellions were the continuing tensions and conflicts in which the more violent outbursts were rooted. It thus seems obvious that we should consider the principal aspects of the *imperial situation* in which the Judean people lived during the second Temple period.

DOMINATION BY FOREIGN EMPIRES

The relation between empire and subject people is one of power. Generally the imperial regime establishes domination initially by military force, often aided appreciably by technological superiority.[3] Domination is often maintained, however, by economic and cultural means. The relations between master and subject can thus be conveniently understood in terms of three interrelated but analytically separable dimensions: the economic, the political, and the cultural. Whereas some interpreters of modern colonialism have overemphasized the economic aspect, the tendency in biblical studies, with their focus on cultural-religious phenomena, has been to underemphasize or ignore the economic dimension. It is important to consider all dimensions and their interrelationship.

Pacification, domination, and development of a subject country is carried out in the interests of the imperial society. Modern colonizers sought trade and markets as well as materials. Economic exploitation by ancient empires, while including trade and materials, concentrated primarily on demanding tribute for the benefit of the dominant ruling groups. Development, in the form of cities, roads and aqueducts—all constructed with forced labor—was primarily in the interest of the imperial rulers and of their local upper-class allies. In order to extract its tribute from the primarily agricultural producers, the empire required a staff of tax collectors. The ostensibly "political" administration also basically served the purpose of economic exploitation. Even where cultural forms and psychological habits of dependency had been established, the country had to be held down—by occupying troops or by credible threat of military violence. Of course some areas were occupied not only for direct economic exploitation, but for their strategic importance in maintaining imperial control of other peoples or in protecting an uncertain frontier.

As we have noted, the Jews were subject to a succession of imperial regimes throughout the second Temple period, except for a brief interlude of about two generations when they were semi-independent under the Hasmonean high priests. If the legacy of the Babylonian conquest was the termination of the Judeans' existence as an independent people, along with the destruction of Jerusalem and of the original Temple, the legacy of the Persian empire was the reconstruction of Judea as a subject Temple-community under the imperially guaranteed authority of the high priesthood.

Alexander the Great's imperial successors, particularly the Ptolemies in Egypt and the Seleucids from Syria eastward, imposed Hellenistic political and cultural forms in addition to the usual exaction of tribute. The Ptolemies, who ruled Judea along with the rest of Palestine from 301 to 200, instituted an unusually efficient imperial bureaucracy that proved highly effective in the economic exploitation of Palestine as well as Egypt. The ubiquitous operation of the hated "tax" and "toll-collectors" (*telōnes* in Greek) dates from Hellenistic times. For both the Ptolemies and the Seleucids (the latter took control of Palestine in 200), Judea was probably more important strategically as a link in their frontier defenses against each other than as a source of economic exploitation. Ptolemaic presence and, initially, Seleucid rule in Judea were primarily military and economic. In contrast to what was done in other areas, neither the Ptolemies nor the Seleucids imposed Hellenistic political forms directly on traditional Judean society. As the Seleucids' power became overextended, however, they became more desperate for funds and encouraged and then forcibly imposed the Hellenization of Judea through the Jerusalem ruling class. This Seleucid shift in imperial policy with regard to Judea proved fateful for subsequent Judean and Western religious history, for it led eventually to the successful Maccabean revolt.

The unusually predatory and oppressive treatment of the Jews by the Seleucid empire is vividly portrayed in the vision of four beasts recounted in Daniel 7. The first three beasts, representing the Babylonian, the Medean, and the Persian empires respectively, were fearsome enough. The bear, for example, "had three ribs in its mouth between its teeth; and it was told, 'Arise, devour much flesh.' " However, the fourth beast—the Hellenistic empire(s)—was "terrible and dreadful and exceedingly strong, and it had great iron teeth; it devoured and broke in pieces, and stamped the residue with its feet. It was different from all the beasts that were before it . . ." (Daniel 7:5, 7).

As the power of the Hellenistic empires declined, Rome easily dominated instead. Pompey "pacified" the eastern Mediterranean in 64–63 B.C.E. Augustus, the winner of the battle of Actium in 37 B.C.E., finally imposed the imperial *pax Romana,* which was to remain until its decline in late antiquity. As for the earlier empires, Judea probably held more of a strategic than an exploitative economic value for Rome. Tribute was nevertheless taken without fail; in Rome's eyes, nonpayment was tantamount to rebellion. Besides the tribute, Rome also collected numerous tolls. The "tax collectors" mentioned in the Gospels were probably the collectors of these tolls (and were apparently underling Jews working for the principal government tax agents). Under Roman rule, particularly under Rome's client King Herod, there was considerable "development" in the country, including Herod's rebuilding of the Temple and the construction of an aqueduct under the Roman governor Pontius Pilate. This "development," however, far from benefiting the ordinary people, was funded by the products taken from them in the form of taxes, tithes, and tribute. To hold the pacified people in check, the Romans depended on a relatively small occupying military force stationed primarily in Caesarea on the coast. But this force was backed by the well-known threat of overpowering retaliation in the event of serious trouble or resistance—as the Jews discovered on several occasions (in 63 and the 40s B.C.E., and especially in 66–70 and 131–135 C.E.).

The development of cultural and psychological mechanisms of domination and dependency (which supported imperial domination) included religious forms along with "civilization" through language and education. The modern Christian mission enterprise is not historically unprecedented. Ancient Near Eastern empires had long ago imposed their "gods" on subject peoples. The Old Testament is full of such stories. In modern colonial situations, "less sophisticated societies interpreting the impact of the West in their own categories, came to the conclusion that the superiority of the White man was so great that it must derive from quite supernatural sources. The White man clearly did not work. There must be some mystical secret."[4] In ancient Hellenistic and Roman empires, however, it was the *more* "sophisticated" (both the imperial courts and the aristocratic class in the subject cities and peoples) who interpreted the cosmically symbolized order and welfare brought to the world as due to the divine powers of the emperor.[5] The Romans appear to have been unusually cautious in dealing with Judea. Although they expected a daily sacrifice for the emperor in the Jewish Temple in Jerusalem, they generally respected the Jews' special sensitivity regarding "emperor worship." The points at which Roman officials were not sensitive, however, became occasions for some dramatic events (as we shall see in Part Two).

SUBORDINATION AND CRISIS FOR THE SUBJECT SOCIETY

Control of a subject society has often been exercised through an already-existing indigenous ruling class or dominant aristocracy. The imperial regime compromised members of such a class by giving them a serious economic stake in the imperial system of domination. Often such nominally "indirect" systems of government "involved as much control over and manipulation of, the 'traditional' authorities . . . as any system of 'direct' rule."[6] Indirect rule had another advantage. It provided a bridge of legitimation that enabled an empire to divide and rule. Popular resentment was deflected onto the local officials or aristocracy, while the imperial rulers remained more remote, less directly evident and involved.[7] Whether the system of government worked through imperial officials or indigenous aristocracy, the net effect on the subject society was the elimination of political participation by the people. All depended upon powerful control by the elite.[8] In these and other respects, the position and role of the Judean priestly aristocracy or of the Herodian client "kings" was typical of a colonial situation.

Whereas the Babylonians had deported the Judean ruling class, the Persians established a priestly aristocracy and, initially, returned the remnants of the Davidic family to power.[9] The high priesthood and an apparatus of "priestly" government centered in the rebuilt Temple soon completely eclipsed the Davidic family as the Persians' client rulers. The two Jewish leaders who played the major role in the reconstitution of Judean society, Ezra and Nehemiah, held their authority and power as officers of the Persian emperor. This double role, however, was also true of the high priesthood once it was securely established. That is, the very representative of the Jewish people and their mediator with God was also the representative of the Persian imperial regime. From the Persian imperial viewpoint it made sense to sponsor both the restoration of "the House of the God who is in Jerusalem" and its attendant priesthood. The populace of Judea thus could focus their loyalty and worship on the God of Israel in Jerusalem —and of course bring their tithes and taxes in due season to the Temple, i.e., to the high-priestly officers, who in turn would render loyalty and tribute to the Persian court.

This same imperial arrangement of ruling through the priestly aristocracy remained in effect basically until the destruction of the second Temple, with the exception of the period of rule by Herodian client kings.[10] The Hellenistic empires, Ptolemies and Seleucids, both governed Judean society and apparently collected tribute through the Judean high priesthood. Indeed, the office of high priest itself became a virtual dynasty in the control of the same Zadokite family from the sixth to the second century. In 175 B.C.E., however, a strong Hellenizing faction of the aristocracy, with the cooperation of the Seleucid king Antiochus IV Epiphanes, carried out a successful coup and instituted a great *reform* that transformed Jerusalem into a Hellenistic *polis*. In Judea "indirect" imperial rule was effective only so long as the client aristocracy had credibility as representatives of the people. When the usurping Hellenizing aristocracy attempted to transform the social-political order into the forms of the dominant Hellenistic civilization, the popular resentment was directed initially against them. Then when the emperor intervened directly and attempted to suppress the resistance, a widespread revolt erupted against Seleucid rule as well as against the apostate priestly aristocracy.

Following the successful Maccabean revolt, the Hasmonean high priests exerted some autonomy. Although their rule was conditional on Seleucid tolerance, they were able to play the Seleucids off against rapidly expanding Roman influence in the East. When the Romans finally took direct control of the eastern Mediterranean in 63 B.C.E., they also delegated rule of Judean society to the (Hasmonean) high-priestly regime. Following the devastating Roman and Judean civil wars in the 40s, in which rival Hasmoneans battled for control of the country, the Romans entrusted the rule of Jewish Palestine to the ambitious young opportunist Herod as client king. After conquering the country with the help of Roman troops, Herod set up an intensely repressive regime (37–4 B.C.E.). While posing as "king of the Jews," he instituted Roman-Hellenistic political and cultural forms, with mercenary troops manning his elaborate security apparatus. Because he maintained surveillance and tight control over the people, no serious opposition could effectively emerge. He also replaced the priestly aristocratic families who had held hereditary power since the Maccabean revolt, installing his own creatures in office. Thus, effective political participation of the people came to an end, even at the level of the aristocratically dominated high council, the Sanhedrin.

Upon the death of Herod the Great in 4 B.C.E., the Romans installed his sons in power: Antipas in Galilee, who ruled as tetrarch until 36 C.E., and Archelaus in Judea and Samaria. When the latter proved unsatisfactory as client king, Rome set up a system that combined "direct" and "indirect" rule. Ultimate authority was placed in the hands of a Roman governor, resident ordinarily at Caesarea. But domestic Jewish affairs were left to the priestly aristocracy again. From 6 to 66 C.E. four principal families dominated the society, with the office of high priest, in effect, alternating among them. The priestly aristocracy also dominated the Sanhedrin or high council throughout this period. Partially because of the awkward combination of Roman governor and Jewish priestly aristocracy, Roman control of Jewish Palestine was not as tight as it had been under Herod. But with all matters of importance in the hands of the high priests and the Roman governor, there was no legitimate channel for political participation by the people.

Such political decay in a "colonized" society was simply the most visible aspect of the extreme crisis in which prolonged imperial domination placed a subject people. Effects of imperial exploitation also began to break down the traditional social-economic infrastructure on which the society was based. Most fundamental and significant for its impact in other ways was the economic pressure brought on the peasantry for taxes and tribute and participation in an increasingly monetarized economic life. Rising indebtedness of the peasants led to loss of their land that was the base of their economic subsistence and of their place in the traditional social structure. Thus the traditional village-based social structure as well as the traditional economic structure began to break down. The peasantry in subject societies have typically experienced some degree of dispossession of land, destruction of the economic unity of the family, and disruption of traditional custom-regulated local social-economic relationships. Generally the native "bourgeoisie," or rather in the ancient world the native aristocracy (including newcomers) increased their landholdings as well as power in society, while formerly proud and independent peasant producers lost their self-respect along with their land and status as they became sharecroppers, day laborers, or simply vagabonds.[11] Imperial subordination thus creates or exacerbates the social-economic divisions within the subject society.

Under the Davidic monarchy, before Judean society was placed in the imperial situation, the prophets had bitterly protested the economic exploitation of the peasantry by the ruling class.

The Lord enters into judgment with the elders and princes of his people: "The spoil of the poor is in your houses. What do you mean by crushing my people, by grinding the face of the poor?" (Isaiah 3:14–15)*

The king, however, always had a concrete economic interest in protecting the productive base of his country and had the monarchy to help reinforce his moral or ideological motivation as protector of the "fatherless" and the "widow." Once the society was subject to a foreign empire, however, the Judean aristocracy, kept in power by, and responsible primarily to, their imperial overlords, had no corresponding interest and motive. Apparently they simply exploited the people for their own benefit, as well as for that of the empire—whether under the Persians, the Hellenistic regimes, or the Romans. Already by the time Nehemiah arrived to reorganize Judean affairs after 450 B.C.E., he found serious decay in basic social-economic relations: the wealthy and powerful were using indebtedness to weaken and subordinate the desperate peasants.

There arose a great outcry of the people . . . For there were those who said, "We have to pledge our sons and daughters to get grain, that we may eat and keep alive." There were also those who said, "We are mortgaging our fields, our vineyards and our houses to get grain because of the famine." And there were those who said, "We have borrowed money for the king's tax upon our fields and our vineyards; . . . some of our daughters have already been enslaved; . . . (and) other men have our fields and our vineyards." (Nehemiah 5:1–5, RSV adapted)

---

*All Bible quotations are from the Revised Standard Version unless otherwise noted.

Here is a classic picture of economic pressure on the peasantry for tithes and tribute, a pressure leading to increasing indebtedness that results in debt bondage and eventual loss of the family inheritance of land. But along with the economic decline of the peasantry went the decay of the traditional village-based social structure. Nehemiah's reform, the restoration of some sort of Mosaic covenantal law, must have done something to stem this decay; for the fourth-century B.C.E. Greek traveler Hecataeus found in Palestine a surprising situation (apparently unusual in his experience) in which ordinary people still had rights to their own land. A similar check to such social-economic decay may also have been one result of the Maccabean revolt. We can well imagine that the rebelling peasantry would have reclaimed their land lost or threatened with loss by indebtedness. Moreover, the expansionist policy and wars of the Hasmoneans would also have extended the territory open to the Jewish population.

With the Roman conquest, however, came a shrinking of available territory and a general shortage of land. Herod in particular intensified the economic exploitation of the people. In addition to supporting his elaborate regime and lavish court, he embarked on extensive building projects and made a name for himself in the Empire for his astounding munificence to the imperial family and to Hellenistic cultural causes such as athletic games, the whole funded by taxing his people. The intense economic pressure on the peasant producers continued under the Roman governors and Jewish high priests; the people struggled under a double burden of taxation: tithes and other dues paid to the Temple and priests as well as tribute and other taxes to Rome.[12] It is not difficult to imagine the resultant exacerbation of social-economic divisions within Palestinian Jewish society. The Galilee portrayed in the Gospels is a society of the very rich and the very poor.[13] Jesus' parables in particular give us illuminating insights into the social-economic conditions resulting from generations of intense economic pressure: heavily indebted peasants who cannot possibly avoid loss of their land or their freedom, tenant farmers and innumerable day laborers who have already forfeited their land or who must supplement their living by hiring themselves out. Over against the declining peasantry stands a class of wealthy absentee landowners who employ stewards to run their estates. Moreover, there is no love lost between the very wealthy and the desperately poor and threatened tenant farmers (see especially Matthew 18:23–33; 20:1–15; Luke 16:1–13; Mark 12:1–9). In fact, Luke's version of the parable of the pounds (Luke 19:11–27) is a miniature word-picture of the very imperial situation that had brought about a severe decline of social-economic conditions for the Jewish people and an intensification of the divisions within the society: A "nobleman" goes into a far country to receive "kingly power"; his servants (officials) meanwhile dramatically expand his capital, apparently by making usurious loans; but his people, having focused their resentment on him (not on the "far country"), are opposed to his ruling over them.

Simultaneous with and perhaps partly resulting from the perceived threat to the traditional social order and its sanctions, especially in situations of indirect rule, there was a tendency to "freeze" the social order, to inhibit change in the name of conformity with "immemorial custom."[14] This "freezing" of the social structure in the name of sacred tradition indicates how cultural domination aided political domination. The native aristocracy, legitimated in their position by tradition while themselves assimilating new cultural forms from the dominant imperial culture, perpetuated the traditional cultural forms as a way of keeping their people subordinated to the system as a whole. All the while, of course, the *culturally* productive groups were busy adjusting the tradition to the requirements of the "colonial situation" and of its impact on their society.

The very origins of second Temple Jewish society and religion can be understood in this light. Although Ezra, Nehemiah, and the high priests owed their power to their position as officers of the Persian empire, they and the "Priestly writers" of early postexilic times reconstructed and virtually *established* a religious tradition as a way of legitimating the "restored" Jewish social-political order. The priestly aristocracy's attempt at Hellenizing reform illustrates how, when they abandoned the sacred cultural traditions—even though they made no change in the actual social structure—they suddenly lost legitimacy in the eyes of the people. The Hasmoneans, who rode the Maccabean rebellion into power, far from claiming to be messianic kings (which would have been a departure from second Temple cultural tradition), immediately restored the traditional high-priestly regime with themselves as the new incumbents. However, the compromises and outright violations of tradition that they made in pretending to restore sacred customs (as well as in reestablishing social-economic stratification) did not sit well with some other priests and intellectuals among their former allies, the Hasidim (pious ones). The Dead Sea Scrolls provide vivid witness that to those who had hoped for a more egalitarian and revitalized social outcome of the revolt, the Hasmonean "Wicked Priests" simply reverted to the same old "frozen" stratified social order, while legitimating themselves by a putative restoration of traditions. Similarly, throughout the decades of more direct Roman rule in the first century C.E., the high priests appealed to sacred tradition to legitimate the preservation of the social structure as it stood, even though they themselves were not from the traditional Zadokite families.

POPULAR RESISTANCE AND RENEWAL

Colonized people, however, do not always cooperate. In a situation of tension, antagonism, and conflict with their traditional culture, with even their own sacred land visibly threatened, the subject people produce movements that attempt to adjust or to renew their traditional way of life. Indeed, the crises into which "colonized" societies are drawn often manifest themselves first "in the modification or disappearance of institutions and groups"[15] and even in the appearance of new groups and social patterns. As the old social structure comes under pressure, some social relationships persist even when the overall structures within which they previously functioned disintegrate, while new relationships may appear as a result of social conditions arising from imperial domination. Close attention to the specific conditions of this ordeal of subordination helps elucidate the processes of rejection or adaptation and the new patterns of behavior resulting from the destruction of the traditional social order. Attention to these "colonial" conditions and the processes of adaptation and renewal, moreover, can help elucidate the "pressure points" or "resistance points" of the subject people.[16]

Considering the structure of an imperial situation, we would expect that certain strata would be more likely to resist or to rebel or to attempt to renew the traditional way of life. Especially in a situation of indirect rule, the dominant aristocracy would have a substantial stake in maintaining the status quo. Even "middle strata" (those with some education or some regular contact with the imperial society and influenced by the imperial ideology) typically would make significant adjustments and find themselves a role in the colonial system. The resentment of such self-aware members of the subject society may well be rather intense; but they are in a position to have a more "realistic" sense of the actual imperial power relationship and therefore to hold to a more "conservative" stance. Villagers, however, who are more insulated from direct contact with the imperial system and its ideology are more likely to attempt to restore the old way of life or even to develop what might appear as "social revolutionary" notions.[17]

The "resistance points" at which numbers of Jewish people reacted against the imperial situation or some particular manifestation of it, and the various popular protests of renewal movements that took shape among the people, will form the subject of Part Two. Attempts will be made there to relate the protests and renewal movements to the social conditions resulting from the imperial situation, such as the decay of the traditional local social-economic structure. At this point it seems highly pertinent simply to recognize that the groups or sects or "philosophies" that we have usually looked upon as the most typical and important in Palestinian Jewish society in the late second Temple period were, in effect, all products of the imperial situation.

The Pharisees, the Sadducees, and the Qumran community were all products of and responses to the crisis into which Jewish society had been drawn during its subjection to dominant empires. Our consideration must begin with a serious caveat, however. Except for the Qumran community, from which we have the extensive Dead Sea Scrolls and archaeological remains, we have meager and unreliable evidence for these groups. We are much less certain of their social profile, characteristics, and social roles than we were a few decades ago. Our picture of the Pharisees in particular will surely be revised—and, we hope, become more distinctive—as the result of research and analysis still underway.[18]

We can conclude that at some point in the postexilic period there emerged a type of "sage" or "scribe" not totally subordinate to though still somewhat dependent on the high priesthood, and highly dedicated to both individual and social practice of the Mosaic Torah. At some point also they appear to have associated in brotherhoods, although even with the later Pharisees the use of the term "party," with its connotations of political organization, may be misleading. Now, in traditional societies the ruling class generally extracts its surplus and governs through "retainers" of various sorts, such as the military, tax collectors, and "bureaucrats," among whom skills of literacy and keeping of records, traditions, and laws are of special importance.[19] Judea may have been somewhat unusual insofar as it was governed by both the Temple, headed by the high priesthood, and the Torah. This made literacy and the role of scribes and interpreters-lawyers-teachers of the Torah especially important. Thus, while the scholars may have been supported by the high-priestly establishment, they would likely have developed some degree of independence and leverage over against the high priests. Moreover, as we might expect of professional scholars and teachers of the Torah, they would also have developed considerable personal loyalty or devotion to the traditions of which they were the guardians. Thus in an imperial situation in which the ruling class had become compromised by collaborating with the imperial regime, the scribes and scholar-teachers would not necessarily do likewise, but might be inclined to resist for personal as well as "professional" motives.

The most likely time when such scholar-teachers would have asserted greater independence from the high priesthood was during the Hellenizing reform, as the priestly aristocracy became more remote from the people who lived predominantly in the villages of Judea, while the "retainers" still functioned locally as teachers or sages knowledgeable in the now-threatened sacred traditions.[20] At the outbreak of the Maccabean revolt we find a group called the *maskilim* (Daniel 11:33). Perhaps the *maskilim* were simply one such association of "sages." The pre-Maccabean apocalyptic visions in Daniel 7–12 and the revelations in early sections of 1 Enoch must have originated from such circles of intellectuals.

According to one widely accepted hypothesis of the origins of the community at Qumran, a large group of Hasidim, hoping for just social-economic relations to emerge out of the Maccabean revolt, were disillusioned by the mundane climax brought about by the "Wicked Priest," i.e., the Hasmonean leadership of Jonathan and Simon. Persisting in their more apocalyptically informed expectations, they withdrew into the wilderness to "prepare the way of the Lord"; i.e., they carried out a new exodus and formed a new covenantal community in strict adherence to the Torah.[21]

Other groups of intellectual leaders devoted to the practice of the Torah, whom we have often referred to as Pharisees, may also have developed from the Hasidim or similar earlier groups. Instead of withdrawing to the wilderness when the Hasmoneans reverted to the old patterns of domination, the "Pharisees" attempted to influence or pressure the Hasmonean high priests to observe the Mosaic Law according to their own more progressive, popularly oriented interpretation. The "Sadducees" may have originated as the priestly aristocratic "party" of strict and conservative literal interpretation of the written Mosaic Law (written Law only) in opposition to the Pharisees. Against Alexander Jannai, the Pharisees led an open rebellion, and many Pharisees and others were killed or exiled as a result. Jannai's wife and successor, however, placed the Pharisees in positions of political influence. The Pharisees apparently opposed Herod in some sense and refused to sign his loyalty oath. Perhaps it was their exclusion from political influence under Herod that began their withdrawal from more active political involvement. During the first century C.E. they appear to have been reduced basically to brotherhoods devoted to rigorous study and practice of the (Mosaic) Torah.

Most important to realize is that in response to the conditions created by the imperial situation of a widening gulf between the remote priestly aristocracy and the threatened peasantry, there emerged a small semi-independent *intellectual* but not economic middle stratum, however small, devoted to the preservation of the traditional way of life, oriented toward popular concerns, and eager to influence, even willing to offer resistance to, the ruling aristocracy. The development of changes in the character and social rule of the Pharisaic or similar groups, moreover, is directly related to the particular changes in the constellation of forces in the imperial situation of Jewish history during the second Temple period. The important final stage in this development, of course, was the emergence of the Pharisees as the client rulers of Jewish society following the destruction of Jerusalem, including the Temple, and the termination of the priestly arisocracy in the great Revolt of 66–70.

In sum, contrary to whatever inclinations some may have to find a stable and "traditional" social order and religious tradition, the imperial situation in which the Palestinian Jewish people were living entailed tension and conflict. Structural-functionalist social science has been especially influential in Anglo-American scholarship. Yet it is based on the assumption of a stable social system that undergoes certain tensions and adjustments while it is maintained basically intact. The colonial or imperial situation, however, requires by its very structure of dynamic tensions and conflictual relationships a more historically conscious and dialectical approach.

2. The Politics of Violence

TOWARD AN ADEQUATE CONCEPT OF VIOLENCE

Without much reflection on the word, we tend to understand violence as an overt, direct physical act of injury or destruction. This is the way dictionaries usually treat the terms "violence" and "violent." In the last decade or so, however, "violence" has been the subject of much debate and critical reflection. In terms of both etymology and/or a basic sense of values, violence is related to the Latin *violare,* "to violate." Thus, "whatever 'violates' another, in the sense of infringing upon or disregarding or abusing or denying that other, whether physical harm is involved or not, can be understood as an act of violence. The basic overall definition of violence would then become *violation of personhood.*"[1]

However, once we begin reflecting upon our basic sense of values and the "real" world of social-political affairs, it is virtually mandatory to keep expanding and deepening our understanding of "violence." For example, what differentiates "violence" from "force"? Some might hold that "force" is exercised by the established government in maintaining public order and national defense, whereas "violence" is the proper label for physical violation of public order and security. But what of the government of a totalitarian dictatorship? In that case its use of "force" is "illegitimate." Hence it would be preferable to have the *legitimacy* of force as a principal criterion: "force" is legitimate, but "violence" is illegitimate. The term "violence" is thus not only descriptive but also evaluative or normative. Furthermore, "legitimacy" depends upon the will or at least the tacit approval of those on behalf of whom the force or power is used. "Force seems to be properly used only in the context of legitimate power and right and as a means to the achievement of communal ends."[2] By contrast, violence would then be the illegitimate or unauthorized use of power against the will or desire of others. Thus a legitimate government would be using *force* to restrain and eliminate criminal abuse and harm to its citizenry. And similarly, citizens would be using *force* and not violence in acting to overthrow an illegitimate government that had been using violence and not force against its subjects.[3]

It is becoming evident, once we begin reflection, that the reality of violence extends well beyond the direct, personal, and physical. There is also psychological or spiritual violence—for example, when one person consistently belittles or harangues another. Acts that impair other persons' dignity or integrity, demeaning them or causing them to betray themselves or their comrades, are spiritually violent.[4] Violence, physical or psychological, moreover, can be indirect as well as direct, as when one leaves others in circumstances that in some way violate their personhood. Whether direct or indirect, moreover, violence may be covert as well as overt.[5] Of course "covert" violence may not be very hidden to its victims. Through analysis of and reflection upon the complex network of social interaction and conflicts in which we live, supposedly social agents could and should become increasingly aware of the potential violence they actually do. Nevertheless, the concept of "covert violence" may prove to be an important critical tool simply in bringing us to admit the reality of violence that we cause but about which we remain unaware because of our own interests and ideology.

Extensive and widespread violence is done to people largely in indirect ways, and "covertly" as well as overtly, in what has come to be called "institutional" or "structural violence." War and other systematic corporate actions of killing and destruction are only the most obvious overt examples of institutionalized violence. As Thomas Merton noted

We also have to recognize that when oppressive power is thoroughly well-established, it does not always need to resort openly to the "method of beasts" because its laws are already powerful—perhaps also bestial—enough. In other words, when a system can, without resort to overt force, *compel* people to live in conditions of abjection, helplessness, wretchedness that keeps them on the level of beasts rather than of men, it is plainly violent. To make men live on a subhuman level against their will, to constrain them in such a way that they have no hope of escaping their condition, is an unjust exercise of force. Those who in some way or another concur in the oppression—and perhaps profit by it—are exercising violence even though they may be preaching pacifism. And their supposedly peaceful laws, which maintain this spurious kind of order, are in fact instruments of violence and oppression.[6]

Merton's explanation here expresses views that are of long standing in the tradition of Christian reflection on social-political affairs. St. Thomas Aquinas stated in unequivocal terms that unjust laws "are acts of violence rather than laws."[7]

This understanding of structural violence, of course, is rooted in attention to concrete historical conditions. "If people are starving, when this is objectively avoidable, then violence is committed and if that starvation is an effect of the existing social and financial system, then we have structural violence or alternatively violent structures."[8] Or, to borrow another example, "When one husband beats his wife there is a clear case of personal violence, but when one million husbands keep one million wives in ignorance there is structural violence." Institutionalized violence has thus become built into the very structure of a society, being manifest "as unequal power and consequently as unequal life chances."[9] A 1972 World Council of Churches consultation on violence and social justice declared that structural violence is present "when resources and powers are unevenly distributed, concentrated in the hands of a few who do not use them to achieve the possible self-realization of all members, but use parts of them for self-satisfaction for the elite or for purposes of dominance, oppression, and control of other societies or of the underprivileged of that same society."[10] Structural violence, finally, can cause heightened overt personal violence. Structural injustice can be so dominating that resentment is allowed no outlet against the source of injustice. Overt interpersonal violence can thus become virtually "institutionalized" within the system as people's anger explodes against others caught in the same situation.

In attempting to understand the escalation of overt violence in the "neocolonial" situations of the 1960s (i.e., the struggle between peoples of the "Third World" and their oppressive governments backed by "First World" governments and corporations), Dom Helder Camara,

Archbishop of Recife in northeastern Brazil, pointed to a three-stage "spiral of violence." The first stage he describes is *injustice*, or basically the structural violence described above. "Look closely at the injustices in the underdeveloped countries, in the relations between the developed world and the underdeveloped world. You will find that everywhere the injustices are a form of violence, . . . the basic violence."[11] As Brown observes, this is "the subtle, institutional destruction of human possibilities that is around us all the time, but is often not apparent to those who are comfortably situated."[12] "This established violence, however," writes Camara, "attracts violence No. 2, *revolt,* either of the oppressed themselves or of youth, firmly resolved to battle for a more just and human world . . . Certainly there are . . . from country to country, variations, . . . degrees, nuances in violence No. 2, but generally in the world today the oppressed are opening their eyes."[13]

In its own way, the Presidential Commission investigating the Causes and Prevention of Violence in the U.S. was aware of the relation between what Camara calls violence No. 1 and violence No. 2, between injustice and what people ordinarily think of as violence: "To make violence unnecessary, our institutions must be capable of providing justice for all who live under them. . . . Violence has usually been the lava flowing from the top of a volcano fed by deeper fires of social dislocation and injustice. . . ."[14] Finally, observes Camara, "when conflict comes out into the streets, when violence No. 2 tries to resist violence No. 1, the authorities consider themselves obliged to preserve or reestablish public order, even if this means using force; this is violence No. 3. Sometimes, the logic of violence leads them to use moral and physical torture."[15]

Viewed from a broad historical perspective, however, revolt does not appear to be the principal initial or direct response to injustice in concrete sequences of events. In situations where revolts eventually erupt, the oppressed have usually tried less extreme forms of protest and resistance to the injustices to which they have been subjected. It seems necessary, therefore, to adapt Camara's scheme somewhat in order to deal adequately with the dynamics of imperial situations both of the past and of modern "neocolonial" situations, expanding the stages from three to four. Historically, once a particular situation has been developing, three or all four stages or levels of violence may be present simultaneously. Many historical cases, however, appear to have developed according to the following four stage sequence.

The *first stage* is the same as Camara's: *injustice* or structural violence. In many contemporary neocolonial situations the ruling groups of the subject society cooperate with First World governments, banks, or giant international corporations in fostering and benefiting from exploitation of their countries and people. These neocolonial alliances maintain in power the political regimes—often military rule—and economic structures that further their own interests. Such "internal colonialism" thus creates a situation of structural violence for the indigenous people.

The *second stage,* the reaction against injustice or structural violence, is that of *protest and resistance.* In fact, such resistance to institutionalized violence is often not itself violent. Protest is often carried out through mass demonstrations or through the spontaneous outcries of a "mob" —which may appear as riots to the ruling class even when they involve no violence other than verbal. A method of resistance to exploitation and violence typical of traditional peasantries was to avoid as much as possible any dealings with their rulers and exploiters. Another was to protect their fellow peasants from what they considered unjust seizure and punishment by hiding them and supporting them. Resistance is also often carried out through efforts toward local self-help and cooperation. The Black Panther Party provides a fascinating example from recent United States history. By the time it issued the statement of its Program in 1972, the Black Panther Party (long persecuted by local police and the national administration) was proclaiming its own revolutionary rhetoric, some of which it derived from the Declaration of Independence. But the Party had originated in the Oakland, California, Black community as a self-help organization sponsoring such programs as breakfast for poor children.[16] In the recent history of El Salvador and elsewhere, we are familiar with attempts at local farming cooperatives by those being forced off their traditional lands.[17] A final example of nonviolent resistance is the strike, which did not originate in the modern labor movements.

Some protest and resistance, of course, assumed more violent forms.

One form of individual self-help in peasant societies has been social banditry. The bread riots of early modern times were a minimally violent form of protest. Sometimes initially nonviolent protest demonstrations have gotten violently "out of control." A deliberately violent form of anticolonial resistance in modern times has been terrorism, such as that practiced against the British by EOKA on Cyprus and by Irgun Zvi Leumi in Palestine.[18]

The main points about this stage in the "spiral of violence" are that protest and resistance short of outright revolt may be the first and more typical reaction to injustice or structural violence, and that this resistance as often as not takes nonviolent forms.

Whether the resistance and protest are violent or nonviolent, however, they are usually taken as a challenge to the ruling groups, which respond with violence. The *third stage* of the spiral of violence thus involves *repression* by the established holders of power. At the milder end of a spectrum of repressive violence we might place its psychological or spiritual forms. What Marcuse called "repressive tolerance," the way in which government officials announce that dissent is even valuable (yet will not change their "necessary" policies) and personal intimidation, provide a few examples.[19] Traditional organized religion can be used to advantage in repression. For example, the victims of injustice can be continually reminded that any misfortune is due to their own sinfulness. In the middle of the spectrum come, e.g., economic sanctions such as loss of jobs or destruction of homes or of animals or food sources. Also in the middle of the spectrum of repressive violence are persecution and harassment. To use Brown's example of the Black Panthers again, because they were apparently threatening to the local Oakland authorities, the police harassed their members, some of whom then felt goaded into more vigorous protest and resistance. The Black Panthers were then singled out for surveillance and harassment by federal authorities as well.[20] At the more physically brutal (but also psychologically effective) end of the spectrum of repressive violence are such forms as selective tortures and killings, used partly as examples to others, or the "disappearance" of representative people. On a more massive scale are invasions with troops and tanks or planes as in Prague and the Dominican Republic in 1968, Budapest in 1956, or Guatemala in 1954.[21]

Ruling groups perhaps expect that they can put an end to resistance and conflict by repressing it with sufficient violence. Repressive violence, however, does not end the conflict and resistance, but merely suppresses it or drives it underground.[22] Repression thus drives the spiral of violence to its *fourth stage,* that of *revolt,* where a large number of people will no longer passively bear the violence of injustice and/or repression. Revolt, moreover, is not necessarily violent, or it might involve minimal violence in the form of armed insurrection, as in the overthrow of the Shah in Iran. On the other side of the spectrum, popular revolts can be violent outbursts of long pent-up resentment against the oppressive ruling groups. Historically most popular revolts have been spontaneous eruptions. One important reason for the longer-lasting success of modern popular revolts is their greater degree of preparation and organization by revolutionary organizations.

(One might argue that counter revolution mounted by former ruling groups, often with the help of an outside imperial power, constitutes a fifth stage. Functionally, of course, following successful counter-revolution, the spiral of violence is returned to the stages of resistance and repression, from which the spiral may escalate again to revolt.)

Lest we think this spiral of violence is only a modern phenomenon, it is worth noting at least briefly that it can be found at a number of key points in the Old Testament. In some cases it is questionable whether it is possible to reconstruct historical events behind the biblical narrative. But it is striking how the biblical narrative and the broad pattern of historical development follow the same sequence of stages as the spiral of violence observed in modern neocolonial situations.

In Exodus, the paradigmatic story of liberation, for example, the initial situation is one of blatant oppression, the structural violence of forced labor for the "Hebrews." The Egyptians made their lives "bitter with hard service" so that they "groaned under their bondage, and cried out for help" (Exodus 1:13–14; 2:23–24). The Hebrew midwives, however, resisted the Pharaoh's oppressive program to hold the Hebrews in check. Moses and Aaron carried the people's protest directly to

Pharaoh. The latter, of course, responded to their appeals with repression: "Let heavier work be laid upon the men . . ." (Exodus 5:9), which brought upon his realm, in turn, the wrath of God in a series of plagues (Exodus 7–11). Finally, resolved to bear their condition no longer, the Hebrews, along with a further "mixed multitude," simply revolted. Called by the God of liberation and organized by Moses, they fled their oppression in Egypt and witnessed the destruction of the pursuing forces of oppression.

Once the Davidic monarchy had been firmly established over the Israelite clans and tribes, Solomon sharply intensified the exploitation of the people. Besides the heavy tribute taken in kind to support the royal religious and military establishment, Solomon imposed upon Israelites the hated forced labor from which their ancestors had fled in order to build his royal temple, luxurious palaces, and military fortifications (1 Kings 5–7;9). Although the regime maintained a tight domestic security (through such means as those very fortifications), there must have been some resistance or protest, symbolized by the figures of Jeroboam and Ahijah the Shilonite (as can be discerned through the somewhat cryptic, as well as retrospectively schematized, narrative in 1 Kings 11:26–40). Solomon's internal security system was already repressive enough. Yet, when the Israelites elders protested their "heavy yoke" and "hard service" to Solomon's son and supposed successor, Rehoboam and his young advisers responded with plans to intensify the repression (1 Kings 12:1–14). The Israelites thereupon declared their independence and stoned the royal emissary, significantly the taskmaster over forced labor, Adoram. "So Israel has been in rebellion against the house of David to this day" (1 Kings 12:16–24).

In the newly independent kingdom of (Northern) Israel, however, the spiral of violence repeated itself. Although the Israelites violently resisted the establishment of a dynasty in the north for the first few generations of their independence from Judah, Omri and his son Ahab (and his Canaanite wife Jezebel) succeeded in "stabilizing" the monarchic state. Grandiose building programs for the new capital as well as general royal aggrandizement (1 Kings 19) necessarily intensified the exploitation and dispossession of the people. The stories about the exploits of the prophet Elijah (especially in 1 Kings 18–19) provide windows upon both popular *resistance* to the oppressive rule of Ahab and the violently *repressive* measures taken by Ahab and Jezebel who "cut off the prophets of Yahweh" (1 Kings 18:4) to hold the resistant people in check. Indeed the repression was so severe at times that the prophets had to hide, and Elijah fled for his life. As the story reports next, however, Yahweh's response to the oppression and repression was to commission Elijah the prophet to "anoint" a new king over Israel, i.e., to catalyze a revolt. Although Elijah did not live to carry out the anointing himself, his successor Elisha finally did touch off the revolt led by Jehu against the Omride monarchy (2 Kings 9).

The spiral of violence leading up to the Maccabean revolt brings us more into an imperial situation like that of the Jewish people at the time of Jesus. Under the Ptolemies and Seleucids there was intense exploitation of the Judean peasantry to support both the imperial tribute and the high-priestly regime. The imposition of new foreign cultural and political forms by the Hellenizing aristocracy provoked the apparently violent resistance by the Hasidim and others.[23] The response to this popular Jewish resistance by the emperor Antiochus Epiphanes, however, could not have been a more total and severe repression: the abolition of the traditional law, customs, and religious practices under threat of death, i.e., a systematic and violent persecution. This repressive violence in turn helped touch off widespread rebellion, guerrilla warfare, and a prolonged war of attrition between the Seleucid armies and the Jewish liberation forces.

THE SPIRAL OF VIOLENCE IN JEWISH PALESTINE

Recognition of the reality of structural violence (and colonial situations) requires us to broaden the ways in which we have often dealt with the question of violence in the New Testament and ancient Jewish history. That is, it is no longer possible to understand the issue of violence in the New Testament only in narrow, direct, personal, physical terms—such as the slap in the face (Matthew 5:39) or the thieves in the Good Samaritan story—and to abstract the issue from concrete social-historical circumstances. It would appear obvious that any discussion of violence in the New Testament or in Jewish society in late second Temple times must begin by recognizing the realities of structural violence and the escalating spiral of violence in Roman-dominated Jewish Palestine.

INSTITUTIONALIZED INJUSTICE

In broad general terms the situation in Jewish society had been determined by imperial conquest. The Romans, of course, had their self-legitimating ideology of "defending their friends and allies" and of bringing "civilization" and "peace" to the rest of the world. But their imperial conquests were carried out by massive use of violence, with whole populations either slaughtered or enslaved (30,000 at one time from Tarichaeae in 52 B.C.E., *Ant.* 14.120; *War* 1.180). Not surprisingly, the imperial regime was hardly legitimate in the eyes of the conquered.

There arose up against them a man that was alien to our race.
The lawless one laid waste our land so that none inhabited it;
They destroyed young and old and their children together.
Being an alien the enemy acted proudly. (Psalms of Solomon 17:9,13,15)

Particularly the rule of Herod, who had conquered the land with Roman troops and governed through intimidation, can hardly have been legitimate in the eyes of his Palestinian Jewish subjects.

The final "pacification" of Palestine by Herod and the Romans, moreover, left the ordinary people deprived of any legitimate political participation and the social-economic infrastructure in decline. The victims of the violence of the imperial situation were suffering from poverty, hunger, and despair (Luke 6:20–22). Many peasants, having been forced off their land, had become day laborers hoping for work (Matthew 20). The pressure came from the double burden of taxation, the many dues for the cultus and priests, and the tribute to Rome. Neither the Romans nor the Jewish aristocracy were about to forgo their income by reducing their demands. Instead they collaborated in the effective exploitation of the largely peasant producers.[24]

Instrumental in maintaining the structure of violence that perpetuated or exacerbated the injustices were some of the sacred traditions through which Jewish society was governed. The high-priestly aristocracy both concurred in and profited by the oppressive structures of the imperial situation—and preached pacifism to the people (Josephus, *Ant.* 18.3; *Ant.* 20.120–124; *War* 2.315–324; 2.237). Certain sections of the sacred Torah itself were instrumental in maintaining the priestly aristocracy's privileged position and in holding the peasantry in conditions of worsening poverty. Since Persian times the social position of the priestly aristocracy had been legitimated in the scriptures (Exodus 28–29, 39; Leviticus 8–10; Numbers 16–18; and Nehemiah 10:32–39). More importantly, the Torah legitimated their effective control and use of the tithes and other Temple dues. "The differences in the legal requirements concerning the tithe payable to the officials of the cultus on the produce of the field and tree (Numbers 18:20–32; Leviticus 27:30–32; Deuteronomy 14:22–26) resulted in their being interpreted as directing *two* tithes."[25] Not surprisingly the high-priestly party, the Sadducees, did not want any progressive "interpretation" of the scriptures, such as the more popularly oriented Pharisees might have offered. Of course, even the interpretations of the Law offered by "scribes and Pharisees" seemed oppressive to the ordinary people: "Woe to you lawyers also! for you load men with burdens hard to bear, and you yourselves do not touch the burdens with one of your fingers" (Luke 11:46; Matthew 23:4). If legal interpretations by the Pharisees and other lawyers seemed oppressive, however, how much more "structural" were the demands of the priestly aristocracy legitimated by the Torah itself. One of Thomas Merton's points is directly applicable: "Their supposedly peaceful laws, which maintain this spurious kind of order, are in fact instruments of violence and oppression."[26] The very Temple of the Lord was the center of the system. To critically aware people, however: "My House shall be called a house of prayer for all the nations! But you have made it a den of robbers" (Mark 11:17 and parallels).

In modern colonial and neocolonial situations, as the "system" makes it impossible for peasants any longer to make a living off their land, then the moneylenders, banks, large landowners, and large international corporations use legal means to buy their land or find other means to force them off the land and into further poverty and dependency.[27] A similar if much less extensive and rapid process was apparently taking place through quasi-legal means in ancient Jewish society under Roman domination. The process of increasing indebtedness under the pressures for tithes and tribute led to the growth of the large landed estates of the Herodian families and of the priestly aristocracy who were probably themselves often the creditors.[28] Ironically, moreover, the very measure taken by Pharisees to alleviate the pressure on the peasantry worked over the long run to exacerbate the problem of indebtedness and loss of land by the former freeholding peasant families. According to the Torah, debts were supposedly canceled every seventh year. Practically, creditors were reluctant to risk losing their "capital" by making loans in the years immediately preceding the sabbatical year. To make loans easier to obtain, Hillel (and/or his tradition) created the legal device of the *prosbul,* which enabled the creditor to avoid the literal requirement of the sabbatical cancelation of debts.[29] Loans may have been more easily obtainable, but once peasant families fell into the whirlpool of indebtedness, they now had no sabbatical protection to aid their recovery. In the modern colonial situation "the influence of European cultures" results in "the destruction of the indigenous cultural basis."[30] Again, something similar was apparently happening in ancient Jewish society, as is illustrated in the *prosbul* ruling of Hillel. The traditional, religiously sanctioned laws protecting the economic position of the peasantry were effectively vitiated precisely through the attempts of the progressive "native intellectuals" to adjust their traditions to the realities of the imperial situation. The structural violence rode roughshod right over the very traditional mechanism designed originally to prevent the development of structurally based injustices.

It is possible to view the overt direct interpersonal violence within Jewish society as rooted in and caused by the broader structural violence of the imperial situation. The continuing conflict between Jews and Samaritans is yet another instance of where the imperial power uses the principle of "divide and conquer." A major flare-up of violence mentioned by Josephus illustrates how these subject peoples directed their frustrations at each other rather than at the imperial oppressors. When some Samaritans attacked and killed some Galileans on pilgrimage to a festival in Jerusalem, and when the Roman governor Cumanus did not move to punish the offenders, numbers of Galilean and Judean villagers, with brigand heroes at their head, sacked some Samaritan villages in retaliation. The feud then escalated to include the ruling aristocracy of both Jews and Samaritans, whom the Romans expected to control their respective peoples. In the imperial situation, of course, the intergroup violence only brought down official violence on all heads. The Roman response to such a situation was massive military action and the crucifixion of all common people who had taken part, and a rendering of accounts from the respective aristocracies. The colonial structures that maintained injustice were enforced by the threat and the occasional use of imperial military violence.

An example of the interpersonal conflicts among the Jewish common people locally might be found in the parable of the unmerciful servant, although using this parable as evidence depends upon one's view of how realistic these metaphoric "slices of life" in the parables are. In any case, as we will discuss further below, many of the sayings of Jesus presuppose that Jewish peasants in local situations were at one another's throats: angry enough to refuse needed loans, to take one another to court, even to kill one another.

Given the society's religious-political background in the Mosaic covenant thinking, it is easy to understand how the covenantal sanctions —if you do not keep the laws you will receive curses—could have been interpreted in such a way that if one appears to be cursed with misfortunes, one has sinned against the Law and God. Nevertheless, the idea that one's misfortunes, sickness, poverty, etc., are the result of, or the just punishment for, sin is a case of inflicting psychological or spiritual violence. To foster the religious idea that sin is the principal cause of suffering is simply "blaming the victims" of structural violence. Judging from some of the stories of Jesus' healings (see especially Mark 2:1–12 and parallels), this was a prominent and firmly rooted belief in first–century Jewish society.

Other Jewish religious beliefs of the late second Temple period also indicate a certain kind of spiritual violence corresponding to the more political-economic aspects of the structure of oppression. At the level of the common people, the belief in and the reality of demonic possession was a vivid expression of distress. With a certain assumption of psychoanalytic license, one might suggest that it would have been dangerous for the people to focus too directly on the actual political-economic causes of their distress. In any case, their misery and its symptoms were not comprehensible without the belief that superhuman, demonic forces were at work. In a sense such beliefs were also a "protest against distress." That is, it was unacceptable to the people to believe that the sole cause of their distress was their own sinning; Demonic agents were responsible. Belief in demons at least allowed them not to blame only themselves.

At the more sophisticated level of the literate intellectuals at Qumran, the people's distress and the political conflicts of the situation were placed in the broader spiritual context of the transcendent struggle between God and Satan, between the Prince of Light and the Prince of Darkness, between the power that violated personal integrity and destroyed social justice and the power that could restore both self and society. The spiritual dualism expressed in the Dead Sea Scrolls and elsewhere in Jewish culture at the time was rooted in the very concrete dualism of the people's lives, threatened as they were by alien and destructive forces.

PROTEST AND RESISTANCE

Much of Palestinian Jewish history of the first century C.E. involved protest and resistance against Roman oppression and provocations. In Part Two we will examine several of the major events in a series of *nonviolent* popular Jewish protests and a resistance movement. At this point in illustrating the second stage in the spiral of violence we will examine only cursorily some instances of nonviolent protests and renewal movements along with a few phenomena of violent resistance.

Marx theorized in now-famous phrases that *"religious* distress is at the same time the *expression* of real distress and the *protest* against real distress. Religion is the sigh of the oppressed creature, the heart of a heartless world, just as it is the spirit of a spiritless situation. . . . It is the *fantastic realization* of the human essence because the *human essence* has no reality."[31] Not only is this function of religion illustrated in certain Palestinian Jewish religious phenomena in the late second Temple period, it is possible to discern in the imperial situation of Roman Judea how this function of religion is rooted in concrete historical experience.

In the case of Palestinian Jews, the sacred scriptures were far more than what we think of today as "religious." The biblical books contained also their "constitution" and their history as a people. The principal festivals of the society, moreover, included not simply celebrations of the annual natural-agricultural cycle, but celebrations of the principal events through which God had given the people freedom from oppression. Under Roman rule, Palestinian Jewish society, or rather the ruling class, had the authority to govern its internal affairs according to the Torah, adjusted of course to the imperial situation. The society, however, was obviously not independent of foreign oppression. Hence, when the Jews celebrated the festival of Passover in commemoration of liberation from Egypt, the freedom celebrated was necessarily in *fantasy* form, there being no actual freedom.

It may not be so surprising, therefore, that Passover was a time when the underlying tensions of the imperial situation came to the surface, this may also help us better understand the rather cryptic reports about incidents at Passover time in our sources.

When the festival called Passover was at hand . . . a large multitude from all quarters assembled for it. [The Roman governor] Cumanus, fearing that their presence might afford occasion for an uprising, ordered a company of soldiers to take up arms and stand guard in the porticoes of the Temple so as to quell any uprising that might occur. This had been in fact the usual practice of previous procurators of Judaea at the festivals. (*Ant.* 20.106–107; cf. *War* 2.223–224)

Similarly, in the Gospels, the chief priests are eager to arrest Jesus and kill him, but they are uneasy, saying, "Not during the feast, lest there be a tumult of the people" (Mark 14:2; Matthew 26:5). Why are the Roman authorities and the Jewish high priests anxious about a "tumult" or "uprising" during the Passover festivals? The reason becomes clearer once we set the celebration of liberation in juxtaposition with the structural oppression of the imperial situation. Since the Jews no longer had their own freedom (human essence having "no reality"), given the imperial situation, there remained only the celebration of liberation in religious fantasy ("the fantastic realization of human essence"). The annual Passover celebration, however, was not simply "the sigh of the oppressed creature." It was also "the *protest* against real distress."

The rest of the Passover incident under Cumanus that Josephus narrates vividly illustrates how the protest already expressed religiously in the Passover celebration of liberation could erupt into explicit protest by an excited mob, given the slightest provocation. The Jews no longer having actual freedom, the celebration had become the last line of defense of their human dignity. Offenses against their religious forms and sensitivities could not be taken lightly. When a soldier on the Temple porticoes exposed himself to the multitude below, the crowd exploded in protest ("It was not they only who had been insulted, but it was a blasphemy against God") and directed their enraged outcry at Cumanus. The governor quickly resorted to violent suppression.

Cumanus, fearing a general attack upon himself, sent for reinforcements. When these troops poured into the porticoes, the Jews panicked and turned to flee from the Temple and escape into the town. But such violence was used as they pressed round the exits that they were trodden under foot and crushed to death by one another. (*War* 2.226)

Thousands perished, and the festival was turned into mourning for the whole people. As we will examine more closely in chapter 3, there was more than one such protest at Passover time.

The popular prophetic movements of the mid first century C.E. constituted another type of nonviolent protest against the imperial situation of domination and oppression.[32] Like the Passover festivals, the prophetic movements were both expressions of and protests against real distress, and they sought liberation in fantasy form. Also, as in the Passover festival, the memory of past liberation informed the religious fantasy. The prophetic movements went further than the Passover celebrations, however, in attempting to *realize* their fantasy of liberation. Josephus gives us the impression that several such prophetic movements—which he despises and denigrates—emerged while Judea was under the direct rule of Roman governors such as Pilate and Felix.

Impostors and deceivers called upon the mob to follow them into the desert. For they said that they would display unmistakable signs and wonders done according to God's plan. (*Ant.* 20. 167–168)

He provides some detail on only three of these movements: one under Pilate among the Samaritans in which a prophet led his followers up to Mt. Gerizim to recover the sacred vessels left there by Moses, and two among the Judeans (both of which are also mentioned in Acts).

When Fadus was governor [44–45 C.E.], a charlatan named Theudas persuaded most of the common people to take their possessions and follow him to the Jordan River. He said he was a prophet and that at his command the river would be divided and allow them an easy crossing. (*Ant.* 20.97–98; Acts 5:36) [During the time of Felix, 52–60] a certain man from Egypt arrived at Jerusalem saying he was a prophet and advising the mass of the common people to go with him to the Mount of Olives, which is just opposite the city. . . . He said that from there he wanted to show them that at his command the walls of Jerusalem would fall down, and they could then make an entry into the city. (*Ant.* 20.169–170; *War* 2.261–262; cf. Acts 21:38)

From Josephus's descriptions we can discern that these movements follow a common pattern. The prophets and their followers apparently believed that God was about to accomplish a new act of liberation similar to one of the great historical acts of liberation in the past, e.g., the exodus led by Moses through the parted waters and out into the wilderness, and the battle of Jericho led by Joshua by means of the miraculous collapse of the city walls. The anticipated deliverance was also conceived of as the implementation of God's design or eschatological *plan* (*raz* in Hebrew, or *mysterion* in Greek) as revealed to the prophet, an idea familiar from apocalyptic literature such as Daniel and the Dead Sea Scrolls (Daniel 2:17–30; 1QS 3–4).[33] The prophets and their followers, convinced that the time had now come for God to liberate them anew, went out to participate in the action themselves; i.e., they *acted out* their *fantasy*. These movements, of course, are not protests in any ordinary sense. Their most distinctive feature is the lack of a critical, realistic sense of the concrete political situation. These prophets and their followers, caught up in an "apocalyptic" frame of mind, are acting precisely out of a *fantasy* that God is about to deliver them from reality.

A form of violent protest and resistance to the oppression of the Jewish people under Rome was the endemic social banditry. The brigands mentioned at several points by Josephus have often been misunderstood as organized and religiously motivated Jewish freedom fighters, "the Zealots." The *lestai* referred to by Josephus, however, were not guerrilla fighters but rather ancient Jewish social bandits.[34] While bandits are "prepolitical" and are not revolutionaries, though they can become such, they do resist the dominant oppression. Besides resisting injustice personally, they become the occasion for other peasants to resist those in power. In times of severe economic crisis, of course, banditry risen to epidemic proportions may well reflect "the resistance of entire communities or peoples against the destruction of its way of life."[35]

Many brigands were in origin simply peasants who refused to submit. In the face of some injustice done to themselves or to relatives or neighbors, they risked the route of resistance and outlawry as preferable to meek submission. Once declared by the authorities to be outlaws, bandits often took it upon themselves to "right wrongs," to "take from the rich and give to the poor." In his reports of brigands Josephus provides no detail about individual origins or exploits, such as that on the ancient Italian bandit Bulla Felix, who is reported to have declared, "Tell your masters that if they would put a stop to banditry they must feed their slaves" (Dio Cassius 77.10). Nonetheless, since social banditry is so consistent from society to society and from period to period in peasant societies, perhaps we could posit similar individual protests or righting of wrongs by Jewish brigands.[36]

In Roman Palestine, Jewish bandits were more important as symbols and as occasions for resistance by the peasants who supported and protected them. The brigand is a symbol of resistance to injustice as well as a champion of justice in his righting of wrongs for the poor villagers with whom he remains in close contact. Moreover, brigands provide the occasions for supportive peasants to resist the authorities themselves. Josephus provides some examples of this. After Hezekiah and his men had been killed by the young Herod (who had been delegated as governor in Galilee by his father Antipater, the chief minister of the high priest Hyrcanus II), the kinsmen of the brigands journeyed to

Jerusalem, and "every day in the Temple they kept begging the king and people to have Herod brought to judgment in the Sanhedrin for what he had done" (*Ant.* 14.159, 167–168; cf. *War* 1.204–209).

A second case is a less active protest but a more general popular resistance. After some brigands robbed an imperial servant, the villagers in the area apparently protected them. "Cumanus [the governor] thereupon sent troops around the neighboring villages with orders to bring up the inhabitants to him in chains, reprimanding them for not having pursued and arrested the brigands." Evidently the peasants were prepared to take the consequences of harboring the outlaws (*War* 2.228–229; cf. *Ant.* 20:113–114). A summarizing comment by Josephus somewhat later in his narrative gives us some indication about just how widespread this protection of, and resistance on behalf of, the brigands must have been among the Jewish peasantry.

Felix took prisoner Eleazar [ben Dinai], the brigand chief, who for twenty years had ravaged the country, with many of his associates. . . . Of the brigands whom he crucified, and of the common people who were convicted of complicity with them and punished by him, the number was incalculable. (*War* 2.253)

There is even evidence that the Judean common people looked to brigand bands for leadership in taking vengeance and restoring justice —which to their minds could hardly be expected from the Roman or high-priestly government.[37] When the Samaritans attacked the Galilean pilgrims in the incident already mentioned, the Roman governor was slow to intervene. Failing to receive justice from the Roman governor, the Jewish peasants "invited the assistance of Eleazar son of Deinaeus, a brigand who for many years had had his home in the mountains," to help lead a retaliatory expedition into Samaria (*Ant.* 20.118–121; *War* 2.232–235).

We should not overemphasize the effectiveness and seriousness for the imperial regime of the resistance offered by active social banditry and peasant collaboration. Social bandits constitute at most a modest protest against an established order. Of course, the closer the brigand comes to the ideal symbol of a champion of the oppressed, the more the authorities may view him as a threatening revolutionary. The social bandit, however, simply "rights wrongs." "He does not seek to establish a society of freedom and equality."[38] Even in situations in which they are adopted as leaders of massive peasant revolts and lead more serious attacks upon the government, they generally are not revolutionaries; they do not have "any programme except that of sweeping away the machinery of oppression."[39]

Very seldom does social banditry lead to more serious popular rebellion. This has happened only in conjunction with two related developments. First, having escalated to widespread proportions, the bandit groups would have to be joined by more massive popular resistance. Second, the prevailing social orientation would have to become intensely "millennarian" or "apocalyptic"; i.e., masses of people would have to become convinced that the time has come for establishing the new world, the world of freedom, community, and equality.[40] When this happens—as apparently it did in Palestinian Jewish society in 66 C.E.—then banditry flows into and becomes peasant revolt.[41] Prior to the mid 60s C.E., however, Jewish social banditry was simply one form among others of resistance to the oppression structured in the imperial situation.

We can make one final important point in connection with banditry spreading through Judea and Galilee during the first century C.E. In the structure of oppression that was effecting a decline of the Jewish peasantry, we can discern how the system was generating its own opposition in the spiral of violence. Economic pressures placed many peasants in desperate circumstances. Many were driven off their land and, having become a surplus rural population, were forced to find some other source of livelihood. A connection with the escalation in banditry seems obvious. The Roman governors' attempts to suppress the increasing banditry, however, served only to bring more of the peasantry into active resistance to the regime and to lessen what legitimacy the ruling class still had in the people's minds. The structural violence of injustice and oppression in Roman Palestine was thus sowing the seeds both of resistance and eventually of its own susceptibility to more genuine revolutionary challenge.

The only protest that was both politically conscious and violent in form was the terrorism carried out in the 50s and 60s C.E. by those known as the Sicarii. The name "dagger men" came from the weapons they used: "they employed daggers, in size resembling the scimitars of the Persians, but curved and more like the weapons called by the Romans *sicae*" (*Ant.* 20.186). Josephus frequently refers to the Sicarii as "brigands." It is clear from one specific statement, as well as from several contexts, however, that the Sicarii were "another form of brigands" (*War* 2.254) operating in clandestine fashion in Jerusalem, as distinguished from ordinary brigands who operated in the countryside, openly supported by the peasants (cf. *War* 2.253). If we read carefully what Josephus says about their activities, they appear to be somewhat similar to modern anticolonial terrorists (rather than to a revolutionary party).[42]

The Sicarii engaged in two types of terrorist activity: assassination and kidnapping. They began their selective assassinations at some point in the 50s C.E.

But while the countryside was thus cleared [of brigands], a different type of bandits sprang up in Jerusalem, the so-called *sicarii,* who murdered men in broad daylight in the heart of the city. Especially during the festivals they would mingle with the crowd, carrying short daggers concealed in their clothing, with which they stabbed their enemies. Then when they fell, the murderers would join in the cries of indignation and, through this plausible behavior, avoided discovery. The first to be assassinated by them was Jonathan the High Priest. After his death, there were numerous daily murders. (*War* 2.254–256)

It is worth noting that the principal (perhaps the only) victims of the Sicarii were important members of the high priestly aristocracy. Drawing on analogies from modern terrorist tactics, we may surmise that the Sicarii were carrying out *selective* assassinations for their "demonstration" effect, i.e., their wider reverberation among both the ruling class and the ordinary people. Targets were chosen who had a maximum of political and/or religious symbolic value as representatives of the structure of power and domination. Perhaps the Sicarii deliberately inaugurated their terrorism with the assassination of *the* symbol of the high-priestly aristocracy's collaboration with the Romans, the (former) High Priest Jonathan, who wielded great power in Roman Judea.

Apparently the assassination of such symbolic figures from among the ruling aristocracy was both a punishment for previous exploitation of the people and a warning against their future ill treatment of the people and collaboration with Rome. The selective assassinations would also have signaled to the common people the vulnerability of their ruling elite.

The kidnapping by the Sicarii was probably more of a pragmatic tactic. During festival time under the governorship of Albinus (62–64 C.E.)

the Sicarii entered the city by night and kidnapped the secretary of the [Temple] Captain Eleazar, the son of the High Priest Ananias, and led him off in bonds. They then sent to Ananias saying that they would release the secretary to him if he would induce Albinus to release ten of their numbers who had been taken prisoner. Ananias under this constraint persuaded Albinus and obtained the request. This was the beginning of greater troubles; for the brigands contrived by one means or another to kidnap some of Ananias' staff and would hold them in continuous confinement and refuse to release them until they had received in exchange some of the *sicarii*. (*Ant.* 20.208–210)

The kidnappings appear to be simply an expedient method to extort the release of some of their own number who had been taken prisoner.

The overall purpose and strategy of the Sicarii must be deduced from interpretation of their actions in the context of the imperial situation and the particular social-historical conditions of the 50s C.E. If there was some continuity between the earlier Fourth Philosophy (see chapter 3) and the Sicarii, then perhaps the latter were also motivated by some of the same ideology, i.e., exclusive loyalty to One God and an intense passion for freedom. The Fourth Philosophy, however, had focused its opposition on the tribute to Rome, whereas the Sicarii focused exclusively on the Jewish high-priestly aristocracy. Josephus mentions no action by the Sicarii against the Romans.

Comparison and contrast with modern terrorist groups may be useful at this point. Modern anticolonial terrorist groups struggling against a colonial power presuppose the existence of modern mass media and rapid communications between the colony and the dominant imperial society. The aim of the "demonstration effect" of their terrorism, therefore, has been to convince the government and people of the dominant society that the costs of maintaining their rule by violent repression will be intolerable. The Sicarii faced a somewhat different situation and therefore had a different strategy. They may well have aimed ultimately at the elimination of Roman rule from Jewish Palestine. Their strategy focused on the Jewish ruling groups, particularly the priestly aristocracy. This is only what we would expect in a rationally calculated strategy, for the Romans ruled in Palestine, as elsewhere in the empire, primarily through an indigenous aristocracy who collaborated in the imperial situation. Thus the obvious way to resist the system, especially as it affected the Jewish people themselves, was to attack the Jewish ruling groups. By means of attacks on selected key figures they demonstrated the vulnerability of the high priestly regime and stimulated intense anxiety among ruling circles.

Since the terrorism of the Sicarii is the only case (for which we have evidence) of violent resistance deliberately planned, we should attempt to understand the possible circumstances and reasons why at least this one group of Jews took this form of action. From the late 40s on, social-economic conditions and the political situation declined seriously and steadily in Jewish Palestine. The severe drought and famine of the late 40s dramatically exacerbated the already-severe economic conditions for the peasantry. There was no abatement, however, in the heavy exploitation by the ruling groups. Politically, a whole series of protests over various Roman provocations had resulted only in administrative errors, inconsistency, and intransigence. The Sicarii may well have decided the situation was no longer tolerable. Anticolonial resistance groups often find all ordinary "legitimate" channels of political expression denied to themselves and other "natives" by the colonial regime or by its client government. For those who have decided the situation has become intolerable, therefore, terrorism may appear as the only means left through which to resist. Moreover, for a group that is small in numbers and lacks an organized base among the common people, terrorism may be the only form of resistance it is capable of carrying out. Resistance focused against their own priestly aristocracy must have seemed the most effective way to cry out for relief.

Their choice of terrorism indicates finally that the Sicarii were not a revolutionary group leading a revolt. They were small in number, with no broader base among the people in villages and towns. Their surreptitious assassinations were more of a harassment than a revolutionary threat to the high-priestly regime and the Romans. Because of the anxiety they created, however, they clearly contributed to the escalation of the spiral of violence by evoking violent repression by the threatened rulers.

REPRESSION

The Romans not only conquered their subject peoples with massive use of violence, they also maintained the *pax Romana* by terror, i.e., by the threat and (when resisted) the use of further massive violence.[43] In pacified areas the Romans relied less on large occupying armies than on forceful persuasion. Both during the conquest and periodically thereafter as necessary, the subject peoples were given vivid lessons in what the consequences would be of opposing Roman rule, such as the enslavement of 30,000 Jews in the district of Tarichaeae (southwest shore of Sea of Galilee) in 52 B.C.E. (*Ant.* 14.120; *War* 1.180). At times, even the slightest resistance such as a delay in payment of tribute became the occasion for brutal reprisal. For example, in 43 B.C.E., as Cassius was plundering Syria, northwestern Judea bore some of the brunt of his deliberate and systematic violence.

Worst of all was his treatment of Judea, from which he exacted seven hundred talents of silver. . . . But [when they were too slow in delivering up their apportionment] the officials of the other cities [toparchy capitals] along with all the inhabitants themselves, were sold as slaves, and at that time Cassius reduced to slavery four towns: Gophna, Emmaus, Lydda, and Thamma. (*Ant.* 14.272–275; *War* 1.219–220)

When the Romans had to reconquer an area that had rebelled, they became unusually brutal. Following the insurrections that burst forth at the death of Herod, for example, Varus, with his legions and auxiliary troops from the neighboring "allies," provided the needed object lesson to the stiff-necked Jews.

Varus . . . sent a detachment of his army into the region of Galilee . . . [that] routed all who opposed him, captured and burnt the city of Sepphoris and reduced its inhabitants to slavery. . . . [From Samaria] he advanced to Sappho, another fortified village, which they likewise sacked, as well as all the neighboring villages which they had encountered on their march. The whole district became a scene of fire and blood. . . . Emmaus [whose inhabitants had been enslaved less than forty years earlier], the inhabitants of which had fled, was burnt to the ground by order of Varus, in revenge for the slaughter of Arius and his men. [After entering Jerusalem] Varus now detached part of his army to scour the country in search of the authors of the insurrection. . . . The most culpable in number, about 2,000, he crucified. (*War* 2.66–75; *Ant.* 17.288–295)

Very clearly the extensive destruction, slaughter, enslavement, and mass crucifixions were intended to strike terror into the hearts of the Jewish subjects.

As the Romans' client king, Herod intensified the atmosphere of repression. From the start the Jews apparently hated Herod's rule—as an instrument of foreign domination, as politically and economically oppressive, and as a Hellenizing threat to their own culture. Having become acutely aware of the people's hatred after a foiled plot on his life, Herod "decided to hem the people in on all sides lest their disaffection should become open rebellion" (*Ant.* 15.291). "Several measures for security he kept thinking up from time to time, and he placed garrisons throughout the entire nation so as to minimize the chance of [the Jews] taking things into their own hands . . ." (*Ant.* 15.295). The impressive fortifications at Masada are but one example of the many massive fortresses he constructed throughout the land to ensure his security.

In addition, Herod maintained an army of foreign mercenaries, a secret police, and a spy network throughout the country.

He took away any opportunities they might have [for agitation]. . . . No meeting of citizens was permitted, nor was walking together or being together permitted and all their movements were observed. Those who were caught were punished severely, and many were taken, either openly or secretly, to the fortress of Hyrcania, and there put to death. Both in the city and on the open roads there were men who spied upon those who met together. . . . Those who obstinately refused to go along with his [new] practices he persecuted in all kinds of ways. He demanded an oath of loyalty . . . to his rule. (*Ant.* 15.366–368)

Not without reason did the sages Shemaiah and Avtalion advise their students to "love work and hate mastery, and make not thyself known to the government" (Avot 1.11).[44]

To help reinforce the general context of repression through the threat and occasional exercise of massive and systematic physical violence, the Romans employed a more subtle method on the Palestinian Jews in particular. The latter were unusual in the ancient world for having a religious-historical tradition focused on freedom from foreign domination or domestic oppression. Instead of totally outlawing or suppressing the Palestinian Jews or their "religion," as Antiochus Epiphanes had unsuccessfully attempted, the Romans "tolerated" the Jews' exercise of their traditional rites and belief. This toleration itself, however, was probably repressive in its effect; for its effect would have been to interiorize and spiritualize what had traditionally been comprehensive or total (social-economic-political-religious) in its scope and operation. That is, the Romans allowed the exercise of Jewish religion so long as it took no form other than mere cultic celebration, personal belief, and the reinforcement of local social order. The minute it became more collective in its expression and had political implications, the Romans intervened with renewed physical repression. The presence of the Roman troops on the Temple porticoes provides a vivid example of this enforced limitation of Jewish religious celebration.

This repressive tolerance was not without its effects on Palestinian Jews. For example, blocked in their social-political exercise of the Torah, the Pharisees focused on personal piety and purity in their brotherhoods.[45] Another result was to reinforce the focus on sin as the cause of individual and collective suffering. This in turn reinforced the importance of the sacrifices necessary to atone for sin—which, of course, were controlled by the ruling priestly aristocracy. Given the actual structure of the imperial situation, therefore, the Roman toleration of the limited exercise of Jewish religious traditions became a repressive reinforcement of the basic structural violence and oppression.

The general Roman practice was to respond to Jewish protests, no matter how cautious, nonviolent, and apparently nondisruptive of the public order, with sharply repressive military violence, as we will observe in Part Two. There were some notable exceptions, as we will also observe. But brutal military response was typical, as is illustrated by the Roman governors' attack on the nonviolent prophetic movements.

Fadus did not permit [Theudas and his followers] to reap the fruit of their folly, but sent against them a squadron of cavalry. These fell upon them unexpectedly, slew many of them and took many prisoners. Theudas himself was captured, whereupon they cut off his head and brought it to Jerusalem. (*Ant.* 20.98)

[Similarly Felix], setting out from Jerusalem with a large force of cavalry and infantry, fell upon the Egyptian and his followers, slaying four hundred of them and taking two hundred prisoners. (*Ant.* 20.171; cf. *War* 2.263)

In response to protest, even in fantasy form, the Romans reinforced the structural violence of oppression with further overt institutionalized violence.

Although Roman practice was to keep an imperial monopoly on the use of violence in Judea, both the Herodians and the principal high-priestly families eventually spawned their own private forces. They may, on occasion, have used these private bands against each other. Primarily, however, they used them against the lower priests and ordinary people in repressive, even predatory, actions. They meanwhile turned the Roman governor's head the other way with liberally provided bribes. In the key passage in the *Jewish War* Josephus appears to be softening the implications of ruling class violence and the passage is misleadingly translated in the Loeb edition (*War* 2.274–276). But clearly it is the powerful figures among the ruling groups *(dynatoi)* who "secured immunity for their seditious practices" by bribes to the governor and who, "towering above their own bands of followers, employed their bodyguards to plunder peaceable citizens" (*War* 2.274–275). Josephus gives a clear picture of the repressive effects:

The result was that the victims of robbery kept their grievances, of which they had every reason to complain, to themselves, while those who escaped injury cringed to wretches deserving of punishment, through fear of suffering the same fate. In short, none could now speak his mind, with tyrants on every side. (*War* 2.276)

Josephus provides further detail in the *Antiquities*. While holding the governor Albinus and the reigning high priest at bay with munificent gifts,

> Ananias had servants who were utter rascals and who, rallying the most reckless men, would go to the threshing floors and take by force the tithes [meant for the regular] priests; nor did they refrain from beating those who refused to give. The [other] high priests were guilty of the same practices as his servants, and no one could stop them. So it happened at that time that those of the priests who in olden days were maintained by the tithes now starved to death. (*Ant.* 20.206–207; cf. the parallel or doublet in 20.181)

> [Moreover] the Herodians Costobar and Saul also on their own part collected gangs of villains. They themselves were of royal lineage and found favor because of their kinship with [king] Agrippa, but were lawless and quick to plunder the property of those weaker than themselves. (*Ant.* 20.214)

The effects of the repression on the people is also remembered in the Talmud:

> Woe unto me because of the house of Baithos;
> woe unto me for their lances!
> Woe unto me because of the house of Hanin (Ananus); . . .
> Woe unto me because of the house of Ishmael b. Phiabi,
> woe unto me because of their fists.
> For they are high priests and their sons are treasurers
> and their sons–in–law are Temple overseers,
> And their servants smite the people with sticks! (Pes. 57a)

In dealing with the numerous brigands active in the countryside, the Roman governors not only took action against the brigands themselves but also intimidated and punished the villagers suspected of protecting the outlaws. The effect of such repressive violence was clearly to bring more people into opposition to the Roman-imposed order. In the incident when governor Cumanus sent out troops to exact vengeance for the robbery of an imperial servant and to punish the villagers for not having pursued and arrested the bandits (*War* 2.228; *Ant.* 20.113–114), the effect was further to escalate the conflict. When a soldier tore and burned a copy of the Torah [scroll] in the course of sacking one of the villages, "the Jews were roused as though it were their whole country which had been consumed in flames . . . and hurried in a body to Cumanus at Caesarea" (*War* 2.230). When Felix captured and crucified not only numbers of brigands but also large numbers of peasants suspected of complicity with them, the effect was simply to define more and more peasants as opponents of the regime or to provoke them into opposition.

Another of the three open conflicts under Cumanus provides a further illustration both of how the Romans relied upon violence to enforce their rule and of how brutal repression escalated rather than reduced the spiral of violence (*War* 2.232–246; *Ant.* 20.118–133). This major conflict began in the incident mentioned above of the Samaritan attack on some Galilean pilgrims journeying to Jerusalem. The hostility between Jews and Samaritans escalated, and appeals were made to the governor to intervene; but Cumanus was inexplicably preoccupied with other matters. Only when masses of Jews, frustrated at his failure to execute justice, mounted a sizeable retaliatory expedition into Samaria did Cumanus finally intervene—with massive military force. With thousands of troops, cavalry, and infantry "he marched out against the Jews and, in an encounter, slew many, but took more alive" (*Ant.* 20.122). The initial failure to act and then the heavy-handed suppression had provoked widespread resistance. Although some of the Jewish people heeded the high priests' remonstrances to withdraw peaceably, "many of them, emboldened by impunity, had recourse to banditry, and raids and insurrections broke out all over the country" (*War* 2.237–238). When the matter came on appeal to Quadratus, the legate of Syria, he sent the principal leaders of both the Jewish and the Samaritan aristocracies to Rome for a hearing at the imperial court (presumably for not having restrained their people as expected by their Roman overlords) and simply had all the prisoners taken by Cumanus crucified.

The case of the Sicarii provides a final illustration of the interaction and escalation between resistance and repression in the Roman imperial situation. As was noted above, the Sicarii did not attack the Romans directly but instead attacked their own Jewish aristocratic leaders who were collaborating in the imperial rule of Judea. Judging from Josephus's reports, the Roman governors had apparently been successful in capturing some of the "dagger men." The Sicarii, however, having learned how to exploit the selfish interests of the high-priestly families, and using some "forceful suasion" of their own, were able to engage the Roman regime in a cyclical game of assassination-arrest-kidnapping-release. In the imperial situation of mid-first century Jewish Palestine, opposition to injustice and to violent domination evoked violent repression by the Romans. But the repression resulted only in wider and more intense opposition by the Jews that in turn brought more repressive violence by the Romans.

REVOLT

The usual historical experience is that the spiral of violence ends with repression. This is not at all to suggest that repression puts an end to conflict. On the contrary, the tensions and conflicts inherent in an imperial situation remain, and repression builds up resentment even if oppressed people do not dare to protest, let alone rebel. One result of such a tightly repressive and controlled situation, which we are familiar with in second Temple Jewish society, was the sense among many people that the situation was in the control of Satan and that one's own personal disintegration was due to demonic possession.

At times, however, the spiral of violence does move into a fourth stage, that of *revolt.* In modern times such revolts have tended to result from a critical analysis of the situation, painstaking political organizing, and careful planning by revolutionary groups. But before modern times this was usually not the case. Ancient revolts, even sizeable ones, were almost always the result of spontaneous actions on the part of the peasantry in economically deteriorating and politically volatile situations. The Maccabean revolt was perhaps unusual for ancient times insofar as it may have been prepared by the attempts of certain groups such as the Hasidim to organize resistance to the Hellenizing reform carried out by the high-priestly ruling groups. But there is no evidence that any of the other popular rebellions later in second Temple times were even partly the result of deliberate organizing activity.

There are three dramatic cases of widespread popular revolt against the oppressive and repressive imperial situation in late second Temple times: in 4 B.C.E., 66–70 C.E., and 132–135 C.E. Two of them provide a significant "framing" for our picture of the ministry of Jesus of Nazareth, for they came roughly thirty-five years before and after his ministry, respectively. Both illustrate how the spiral of violence in Roman Palestine could escalate into massive popular rebellions. These revolts can be seen as the outcome both of the cumulative effects of long-standing oppression and repression and of an intensified spiral of violence in the immediately preceding months or years. After the foregoing general survey of the spiral of violence in Roman Palestine there is no need to review the deeper roots of these Jewish revolts. However, it may be useful to observe how in each case the eventual revolt flowed out of a particular sequence of oppression, resistance, and repression.

The Insurrections of 4 B.C.E.:

The brutal and hated tyrant Herod died in 4 B.C.E.. In a public audience after his funeral, his son Archelaus promised the people that he would be kinder than his father (*Ant.* 17.201–204). Sensing a somewhat more receptive hearing from Archelaus than they had ever had from Herod, the people in Jerusalem began voicing their grievances, calling for a reduction in the yearly tribute, the abolition of special Herodian taxes, and the release of Herod's political prisoners (*Ant.* 17.204–205; *War* 2.4). The brutal and sometimes vicious treatment of the people by the Herodian regime was still vivid in the people's mind because of the recent martyrdom of a group of distinguished teachers and their students. These protesters had dared to pull the Roman eagle down from the Temple portal and had been burned alive by Herod (*Ant.* 17.149–167; *War* 1.648–655; and see further in chapter 3). Hence the crowds also called for the punishment of Herod's officials responsible for such brutal repression, and in particular the removal of the high priest recently appointed by Herod (*Ant.* 17.206–208; *War* 2.5–7). Archelaus's lukewarm response to these demands and his exhortations of restraint only served to fan the ardor of protests. The size of the protesting crowds, moreover, was multiplied by the thousands of people coming into the city for Passover celebration, with its inherent connotations of liberation from oppressive alien rule. Panicking at the possibility of open revolt, and dependent on the Romans for confirmation of his succession to his father's rule, Archelaus sent in a cohort of troops to restrain the leaders of the protest. Infuriated, the crowd rushed upon the soldiers and stoned most of them to death, according to Josephus, after which the people simply returned to their Passover sacrifices. Archelaus thereupon unleashed his entire army, including the cavalry.

The soldiers, falling unexpectedly upon the various groups of people busy with their sacrifices, slew about 3000 of them and dispersed the remainder among the surrounding hills. The heralds of Archelaus followed and ordered everyone to return home; so they all abandoned the festival and departed. (*War* 2.11–13; *Ant.* 17.215–218)

Nor did the military repression end when Archelaus departed for Rome to receive his anticipated confirmation as client king. Varus, the legate of Syria, moved into Judea immediately with three legions. After a few weeks he departed for Antioch, believing he had suppressed most of the disturbance, and leaving Sabinus, an imperial procurator, in charge with one of the three legions. Not content to leave any pockets of resistance, Sabinus used the regular troops to harass the stubborn Jews. He had also armed "a large number of his own slaves" and "used them as terrorists, thereby goading and disturbing the Jews to the point of revolting" (*Ant.* 17.252–253; *War* 2.40–41).

When widespread revolt finally erupted it was not centrally coordinated. Besides the conflict in Jerusalem, there were uprisings in every major section of the countryside: Galilee, Perea, and Judea. It is impossible from Josephus's reports to tell just when the revolts in the countryside erupted in earnest, although they cannot have been far behind or ahead of the pitched fighting that began during the Pentecost festival in Jerusalem in late May, 4 B.C.E. The rebels in and around Jerusalem, like those in the various country districts, were largely peasants. The population of the country districts, of course, was almost exclusively peasant, there being no real cities and only a few small towns that served as district capitals. Josephus also indicates that those who besieged and fought against the Roman troops in Jerusalem were from the countryside. On the arrival of Pentecost (harvest festival), "A countless multitude had flocked into Jerusalem from Galilee, Idumea, from Jericho, and from Perea beyond the Jordan, with the native population of Judaea being preeminent both in numbers and ardor" (*War* 2.43; *Ant.* 17.254). Moreover, Jerusalemites later disclaimed any responsibility for the outbreak of hostilities (*War* 2.73; *Ant.* 17.293). Josephus's narratives clearly indicate that those who besieged and fought back against the Roman troops, far from being city residents, were "encamped" at three major points around the city: to the north, south, and west of the Temple itself (*War* 2.44,72; *Ant.* 17.255,292).

It is somewhat unclear how and exactly when open fighting began in Jerusalem. Josephus gives the impression that the harassment and raids by Sabinus's men had produced a volatile situation. "It was not the customary ritual so much as indignation which drew the people in crowds to the capital" (*War* 2.42). The people coming in from the country also encamped where they did in order to "invest the Romans on all sides" and hold them under siege (*War* 2.44; *Ant.* 17.255). It was the anxious Sabinus, however, who initiated the actual fighting. After urgent appeals to Varus to send immediate reinforcements, Sabinus signaled his soldiers to attack. The Jews held their own against the trained legionaries by hurling missiles down from the Temple porticoes and because of their fanatical bravery in hand-to-hand combat. The Romans, however, set fire to the Temple porticoes, overcame the largely unarmed Jews, and broke through to plunder the Temple treasury (*War* 2.46–50; *Ant.* 17.257–264). This only inspired the Jews to fiercer resistance. They surrounded the palace in which the Roman forces had taken refuge and threatened to set it afire and to kill all within unless they promptly withdrew. Although most of the Herodian royal troops deserted to the rebels, the Roman legion and the crack Sebastian infantry and cavalry, 3,000 strong, held out. The Jews pressed the siege, assaulted the fortress, and "told the men ready to change sides not to interfere now that at least they had the opportunity to recover their country's liberty" (*Ant.* 17.265–267; *War* 2.51–54).

Meanwhile the three major popular revolts, in each of the major outlying districts—Galilee, Perea, and Judea—all assumed the same social–religious form, that of a popular messianic movement.[46] In his accounts Josephus repeatedly uses phrases such as "aspire to the kingship," "be acclaimed king," "don the diadem," and act "like a king" with reference to the leaders of these uprisings (e.g., *War* 2.55,61–62; *Ant.* 17.273–274,278). In Palestinian Jewish parlance, key terms of which Josephus studiously avoids in writing for a predominantly Hellenistic–Roman audience, the equivalent would be a popularly acclaimed or "anointed" (*messiah,* in Hebrew) king. These popular revolts and their leaders, however, should not be understood in terms of the fulfillment of the Jewish expectation of *the Messiah.* Standardized Jewish expectation of a "Messiah" did not crystalize until much later (well after the Jewish revolt of 66–70).[47] There is little or no evidence for what even literate groups such as the Pharisees believed about the anointed figure (see, e.g., Psalms of Solomon 17), let alone for what the common people may have been thinking. Through Josephus's accounts of these uprisings, however, we can discern concrete popular movements that acclaimed their leaders as kings. Perhaps the people's recent experience of a "king" who proved to be an illegitimate tyrant had left them eager to have a truly legitimate leader from their own ranks. Earlier biblical history, moreover, may have informed the participants in these movements. The stories about Saul, David, Jeroboam, and Jehu were paradigms of Israelite leaders who, acclaimed as popular "anointed" kings by their followers (and by God, through a prophet), had led the people in successful rebellion against oppressive rulers.

In any case, these popularly acclaimed "kings" and their movements apparently quickly took charge of their respective areas of the countryside and *governed* for a few weeks or even, in the one case, for a much longer period of time—until the Roman legions or Archelaus's troops were able to reconquer their territory. In Galilee, the leader was the son of the famous popular hero, the brigand-chief Hezekiah, whom Herod had killed early in Herod's rise to power (*War* 2.56; *Ant.* 17:271–272). This Judas (not the same as the founder of the Fourth Philosophy, Judas of Galilee, ten years later)[48] armed his "large number of desperate men" from the arsenal in the royal palace at Sepphoris. In Perea the "mighty warrior" Simon, a former royal servant who was proclaimed king, led his followers against the royal palaces and estates of the wealthy. In the palace at Jericho in particular, they took back "the goods that had been seized from the people and stored there" (*War* 2.57–59; *Ant.* 17.273–277).

The popular revolt and kingship in Judea was apparently the most serious and long-lasting. Its leader, Athronges, a "mere shepherd," placed his four brothers each at the head of an armed band. "Anthronges himself put on the diadem and held a council to discuss what things were to be done. . . . This man kept his power for a long while, for he had the title of king and nothing to prevent him from doing as he wished." He and his people vigorously attacked both Romans and Herodian forces, "towards both of whom they acted with a similar hatred." On one occasion near Emmaus they surrounded an entire Roman company engaged in carrying grain and arms to the legion (in Jerusalem ?). "This kind of [guerrilla] warfare they kept up for a long time and caused the Romans no little trouble." It was not until months later that Archelaus was able to capture the last brother and bring this popular revolt in the Judean countryside to an end (*Ant.* 17.278–284; *War* 2.60–65).

The Revolt of 66–70

The massive Jewish revolt of 66–70 was deeply rooted in the long-range spiral of oppression, resistance, and repression. More immediately it arose from a rapid escalation of a particular spiral of violence in the period immediately preceding the outbreak. Our principal source, Josephus, even appears to be aware of the "causal" sequence of repression and revolt. We may question his ability to know the very intentions of the Roman governor Florus (64–66 C.E.), but Josephus clearly believes that one of the principal causes of the revolt in 66 was the unprecedented violence unleashed by the arrogant Roman governor Florus (*War* 2.280–283). As we follow Josephus's narrative of the sequence of events leading up to the outbreak of the revolt, we can observe illustrative instances of how first Florus and then the Jewish client rulers (both priestly aristocracy and Herodians) attempted to repress or otherwise contain the vehement protests of the Jewish people, and how that repression provoked the protesters into outright rebellion.

When some Jews loudly protested against Florus's plans to make an extraordinary extraction of funds from their Temple treasury, Florus came to Jerusalem with troops to accomplish his objective forcibly. When the ruling groups could not deliver the protesters, he had his soldiers sack the upper market area, plundering houses and killing their residents, and he had those arrested in the ensuing melee scourged and crucified, including some high ranking persons (*War* 2.293–308). The Jewish high priests succeeded in calming the crowds, only to see them abused once again (*War* 2.321–326). When they cried out once more in protest, the troops were upon them. This time, however, they fought back, blocking Florus and his troops from taking control of the Temple and the Antonia fortress. Florus retired from the city, leaving the priestly aristocracy in charge with a cohort of troops (*War* 2.331–332).

The high priests who had already been attempting to mediate and keep the peace then welcomed king Agrippa II to assist them in their efforts to hold the populace in check. Agrippa's way of treating the Jews, as described by Josephus, could almost be described as psychological repression. He may have been genuinely indignant at Florus's brutality (says Josephus), but he "diplomatically turned his resentment upon the Jews whom at heart he pitied, wishing to humiliate their pride and . . . to divert them from revenge" (*War* 2.337). The chief priests and other leaders, "being men of position and, as owners of property, desirous of peace, understood the benevolent intention of the king's reprimand" (*War* 2.338). The ordinary people, on the other hand, pressed for a protest to Nero. Agrippa and the high priestly officers, however, insisted upon submission to the Roman system regardless of Florus's abuses, and proceeded to collect the overdue tribute. The exasperated populace thereupon "heaped abuse upon the king and formally proclaimed his banishment from the city" (*War* 2.405–407). Shortly thereafter, according to Josephus, the group of militant priests insisted upon stopping the sacrifices for the emperor, "which laid the foundation for the war"; other insurgents took such actions as the capture of the fortress at Masada. What ensued in Jerusalem itself was virtual class warfare, the priestly aristocracy and Herodians appealing to both Florus and Agrippa for troops to crush the revolt, while the populace, apparently mostly ordinary people along with a few high-ranking priests such as Eleazar, attacked the aristocracy in their upper-city strongholds. The insurgents further burned the archives to destroy debt records, attacked the Antonia and killed the Roman garrison, and captured and killed high-priestly leaders such as Ananias (*War* 2.408–441).

By the end of the summer the rebellious Jews had driven from the country all the Roman troops sent in to restore order. It was a year before Rome reconquered Galilee, and it took four years before Roman legions, after a prolonged siege, finally retook and destroyed Jerusalem. Shortly after the Jews' initial success in driving the Romans from Jerusalem and much of the rest of the land, a high-priestly junta was able to assume control in Jerusalem. Its members pretended to lead the revolt while playing for time to negotiate a settlement. Popular forces from outside Jerusalem, however, persisted in resistance, fleeing for refuge into the fortress city of Jerusalem when their areas were recaptured by Roman troops. By the end of 68 these popular groups, initially the Zealots (proper) from northwestern Judea, then the Idumeans and the followers of Simon bar Giora, had forced out the moderate junta. All these principal groups of combatants who persisted against the overwhelming military forces of the Romans were largely peasant forces from various areas of the countryside. Two of these groups deserve further attention because of the distinctive form they gave to part of the widespread popular revolt.

The emergence of the Zealots in the winter of 67–68 illustrates how the tactics employed by Rome in reconquering the country created further opposition by the Jewish peasants.[49] As the Roman armies moved into northwestern Judea after retaking Galilee, they systematically devastated villages and either slaughtered or enslaved the occupants (*War* 4.130; cf. 4.419–439). Many of the peasants apparently fled rather than be enslaved or killed, and formed bands of brigands. Then, as the Romans advanced further, several of these brigand-bands seeking a more secure fortress fled into Jerusalem. In Jerusalem they formed a coalition called "the Zealots" (*War* 4.128–138,161). Their very presence in the city, as well as their eagerness to fight back against the Roman reconquest and especially the attack against particular Herodians, was a threat to the high-priestly junta that had controlled affairs in Jerusalem since the autumn of 66 (*War* 4.138–150). Before long the Zealots moved to establish an alternative government. They selected occupants of the high-priestly offices *by lot* (i.e., in popular egalitarian fashion) and according to the biblical traditions of legitimate Zadokite lineage, as opposed to choosing from the ruling high-priestly families, who came to power as creatures of Herod and appointees of the Romans. The high-priestly forces attacked the Zealots and drove them into the Temple fortress for refuge. The Zealots, however, appealed to other popular forces from Idumea to rescue them (*War* 4.138–161,193–207,-224–235). The high-priestly junta could never thereafter effectively retake control of the city. The Zealots, however, were not a very large coalition. Moreover, apparently because of their egalitarian ideals, they insisted upon collective leadership and hence were never cohesively united around a single strong leader. In the final resistance to the Roman siege, they were thus less important than other groups, particularly that of Simon bar Giora.

Simon was a popularly acclaimed king, his followers in effect another popular messianic movement like those led by Judas, Simon, and Athronges after the death of Herod.[50] Simon bar Giora himself had been active in the initial stages of the revolt in 66 but Ananus and the high-priestly junta had ousted him from Jerusalem as too popular and militant. When Ananus was killed in the struggle with the Zealots and Idumeans, Simon "withdrew to the hills where, proclaiming liberty for slaves and rewards for the free, he gathered around him villains from every quarter" (*War* 4.508). This beginning is only the first of several parallels between Simon's rise to leadership and that of David, the brigand leader who had become the prototypical "messiah" a millennium earlier (see 1 Samuel 22:2). Proclaiming the restoration of the people's individual and collective liberty, Simon built his strength in villages of the hill country until he was strong enough to operate also in the plain. Impressed by his "career of unbroken success" even "men of standing" joined his movement. "His was no longer an army of mere serfs or brigands, but one including numerous citizen recruits, subservient to his command *as to a king*" (*War* 4.509–510; cf. 5.309). He consolidated his rule both in the province of Acrabatene and, like David, in the hill country of Judea extending down into Idumea (*War* 4.511). Simon was able to enter Jerusalem when the desperate high-priestly group invited him in to help them against the Zealots (*War* 4.566–577). Thereafter, he and his followers held effective control of most of the city except the Temple area, which the Zealots still held. Like the Zealots and Idumeans, Simon and his followers were suspicious of the high-priestly families and other wealthy or formerly powerful figures and brought many of them to trial for collaborating with or planning to desert to the Romans (*War* 5.420–441,527–533). When finally the Romans captured and destroyed Jerusalem, they took Simon prisoner to Rome, where they ceremonially executed him as *the* enemy leader—in effect, as the one who had functioned as king of the Jews (*War* 7.26–36, 116–157).

II. POPULAR JEWISH NONVIOLENT RESISTANCE

3. From Rebellion to Tax-Resistance: Protests by Groups of Intellectuals

Jewish resistance against Roman domination and against the imperial situation in general was far more complex and varied than has ordinarily been recognized. Not only must the imperial situation in Palestine be grasped with considerably more attention to particular effects and relationships, but the Jewish protests and resistance groups must be understood with considerably more precision. The several movements of various forms that have been misunderstood as part of one sizeable and long-standing "Zealot" movement or linked with the "Zealots" (i.e., the Zealots proper, the Sicarii), various bands of brigands, and both the popular prophetic and the popular messianic movements, have all recently been analyzed in terms of their social-historical context and distinctive social forms.[1]

Besides these movements, however, there was a variety of other resistance, some of which has already been mentioned in chapter 2. These other phenomena were not movements with distinctive forms, but more ad hoc responses to particular incidents or situations. Since these other protests have not previously been examined together or placed in the context and perspective of continued Jewish resistance to Roman domination, it is necessary to do so here in order to complete a more adequate and comprehensive picture of Jewish resistance to Roman rule.

Such protests are of particular relevance to the issue of violence in the context of the imperial situation of Jewish Palestine because they were basically nonviolent. Thus an examination of these other popular protests provides a fitting way of illustrating that, contrary to the picture often evoked of Palestinian Jewish society as being a hotbed of revolutionary violence, the people resisted their unacceptable situation with considerable patience and discipline. As was noted above, for seventy years, from 4 B.C.E. to 66 C.E., the Jewish people, with the exception of the Sicarii, engaged in a series of nonviolent protests of different sorts, despite the often-violent response by the Romans. Our analysis will proceed according to the participants, treating protests by groups of "intellectuals" in this chapter and both the Jerusalem "crowd" and more widespread popular protests in the next chapter. Also, the protests led by the scholar-teachers occurred earlier and prior to the time of Jesus, while with one exception the protests by the urban mob and the peasants occurred later, shortly after the ministry of Jesus.

THE HERITAGE OF ACTIVE RESISTANCE BY INTELLECTUALS

Intellectuals such as teachers and priests, either as individuals or as leaders of larger groups of people, have often been in the forefront of resistance against oppression and the exercise of violence by illegitimate authority. This has been true especially when domestic oppression and/or foreign domination have threatened the traditional way of life of which intellectuals see themselves as the representatives or guardians. This is certainly true of Jewish history in the late second Temple period: much of the sustained opposition to Herodian and Roman rule came from groups of intellectuals.

The role of Jewish intellectuals in resistance to imperial domination had a long history prior to the time of Jesus. Indeed, the role of intellectuals in resistance appears to have been more prominent, vigorous, and organized under the Hellenistic empires and the Hasmonean regime than under Roman and Herodian domination. Because our sources are so fragmentary and difficult to decipher, it is impossible to write a history of such resistance. Partly because of the influence of Josephus's terminology there has been a tendency to think of most of the teachers or sages of Hasmonean and early Roman times as belonging to the Pharisees. Similarly, there has been a tendency to think of Palestinian Jewish intellectuals of Hellenistic times as belonging to a well-defined group of the Hasidim or "pious ones," from which both the Pharisees and the "Essenes" were somehow descended.[2] However, it is unlikely that all scholars, teachers, or "pious ones" belonged to some organized group, let alone to the same "party" or "sect." Our knowledge (through the Dead Sea Scrolls) of the highly organized residential community at Qumran, with its dominant scribal-priestly leadership, provides a useful contrast with other teachers and sages who may have been, say, Pharisees or, earlier, Hasidim. Such intellectuals, for example, could not have supported themselves simply by being teachers. They must have played other roles in society as well. Indeed, precisely in order to explain how such scholars-teachers-scribes-lawyers were supported economically it helps to conceive of them as among the "retainers" through whom the society was governed (as was noted in chapter 1).[3] Jerusalem, as the only city and (with the Temple and high priesthood) the center of the society's political, economic, and religious life, would have been the only place where scholar-teachers in any number would have concentrated and would have been the center of communications for others ordinarily resident in small towns.[4]

Our fragmentary sources provide evidence of at least two groups of intellectuals who resisted the Hellenizing reform and the Antiochean persecution of the 160s B.C.E. under the Seleucids. The last vision in the Book of Daniel refers to *maskilim,* "wise teachers" who steadfastly resisted the Hellenizing attempts to abolish the Mosaic Law and to institute pagan reforms.

And those among the people who are wise shall make many understand, though they shall fall by sword and flame, by captivity and plunder, for some days. When they fall, they shall receive a little help. And many shall join themselves to them with flattery; and some of those who are wise shall fall, to refine and to cleanse them and to make them white, until the time of the end, for it is yet for the time appointed. (Daniel 11:33–35)

Indeed, the Book of Daniel was probably produced by one or more of these very *maskilim* or wise teachers, not simply for their own edification, but to help others understand the oppression and persecution in broader apocalyptic perspective. Their purpose was thus apparently to help "the people who know their God" to "stand firm and take action" (Daniel 11:32) in a situation where they were being forcibly compelled to violate the Covenant. As a result of their steadfast resistance, many of the wise were being martyred for their faith. In Daniel 10-12 such martyrdom is understood in broad apocalyptic perspective. The motivation for active and steadfast resistance, besides an unshakable attachment to the Torah, was the conviction that God was finally about to realize his historical purpose.

"Your people shall be delivered. . . . And many of those who sleep in the dust of the earth shall awake, some to everlasting life, and some to shame and everlasting contempt. And those who are wise shall shine like the brightness of the firmament; and those who turn many to righteousness, like the stars for ever and ever." (Daniel 12:1-3)

The *maskilim* believed not only that their people would experience deliverance but also that if they suffered they themselves would be restored to life in glorious fashion. This hope, nurtured by apocalyptic visions such as those in Daniel 7, 8, 9, and 10-12, enabled them to persevere in their resistance to the Antiochene persecution.[5]

The textual evidence is not sufficient to enable us to determine for certain whether the *maskilim* were committed to nonviolence either as a principle or as a method of resistance, or were simply resisting in a way natural to intellectuals committed to the traditional way of life and awaiting the (violent) action of God, who they believed would eventually liberate them from their Hellenistic and Hellenizing oppressors.[6]

The second principal grouping of intellectuals who actively resisted the Hellenizing reform and persecution were, depending on how one reads the sources, either the Hasidim as a scribal group or the scribal leadership among the broader Hasidim group.[7] Which ever way we reconstruct the "Hasideans," the references in 1 and 2 Maccabees provide evidence of intellectuals active in resistance to Seleucid oppression and persecution.

In 2 Maccabees 14:6 the term "Hasideans" is used for the rebellious Jews in general who are fighting against the Seleucid forces, and Judas Maccabeus ("the hammer") is their leader. First Maccabees, a court history written to legitimate and glorify the origins of the Hasmonean dynasty (i.e., Judas's family), surely minimizes the importance of the Hasidim, many of whom later (as Qumranites or Pharisees) apparently opposed the Hasmoneans' consolidation of power. First Maccabees, however, cannot obscure the fact that the Hasidim, right from the start of the revolt, fought shoulder to shoulder with the Maccabees. "Then there united with them a company of Hasideans, mighty warriors of Israel, everyone who offered himself willingly for the law" (1 Maccabees 2:42). Again it is most natural, especially considering the likelihood that 1 Maccabees is minimizing the importance of the Hasidim, to read this as a reference to the Jews generally who fought the Seleucids. The idea that the Hasidim were a party of scribes is suggested only by 1 Maccabees 7:12–13. A group of scribes is mentioned in 1 Maccabees 7:12 as prepared to negotiate with the Seleucid officer and the new high priest Alcimus. Although certain translation of 1 Maccabees 7:13 is virtually impossible, one possible meaning of the sentence is that these scribes "were the first of the Hasidim among the Israelites" to seek peace. Thus, it may well be that not all Hasidim were scribes; yet it is clear that a large number of scribes were prominent among the Hasidim. In any case, even if in this reading of the sources the Hasidim were not a party of scribes but a broader grouping that included scribal leaders, the texts still indicate that a number of scribes were involved in active and in this case violent resistance to Seleucid tyranny.

In Tcherikover's reconstruction, the Hasidim were the scribal leaders of the people.[8] Indeed, on this reconstruction it is likely that the scribal Hasidim had actually begun the rebellion before the rise to prominence of the "Maccabees" by driving the usurping pro-Seleucid high priest Jason out of Jerusalem. This Hasidic rebellion would have been what then provoked Antiochus Epiphanes to intervene and impose the systematic persecution that in turn led to the wider revolt eventually led by Judas. But the Hasidim remained an important element among the forces fighting against the Seleucids and cooperated with the "Maccabean" leaders, as is clear from the use of the term "Hasideans" in 2 Maccabees 14:6 and as acknowledged even by 1 Maccabees (2:42).

The motivation of the Hasidic resistance appears to have been both a devotion to the Torah, as indicated in 1 Maccabees 2:42, and a sharpened sense of God's imminent liberating action. Although the apocalyptic visions collected in the Book of Daniel do not stem from the Hasidim, the early Enoch literature may well provide a glimpse of the apocalyptic perspective of this party of scribes. Certainly the "Animal Apocalypse" (1 Enoch 85–91, and probably the "Apocalypse of Weeks," 93:1–10 and 91:11–17 as well) "is addressed to the crisis that led to the Maccabean revolt" . . . and "affirms a militant role for the righteous."[9] The authors of these apocalypses were presumably scribes, just as Enoch himself, in the "Book of Watchers" is a "scribe of righteousness" (1 Enoch 12:4). These apocalypses directly criticize the Temple and the Jewish rulers. The "Animal Apocalypse" in particular implies that "the lambs" had begun armed struggle and been defeated by "the ravens" prior to the rise of Judas the Maccabee, who was one of "the sheep" (1 Enoch 90:9). Such features in the early Enoch literature are similar to Tcherikover's reconstruction of the Hasidim as a scribal party.[10] Even if we understand "Hasidim" as a term used more generally for the Jews who resisted Hellenization and fought the Seleucids, we can still conclude that this apocalyptic literature was produced by scribes responding to the crisis of Hellenization and engaged actively in armed resistance. The "revelation" contained in the literature thus provides an understanding of history as still under divine control.[11] The assurance that God was about to bring judgment against the wicked idolaters and oppressors and to reward the faithful would have provided support for the active resistance by scribes and others.

Two particular misconceptions regarding the Hasidim should be dealt with briefly. There is no textual basis for the assumption frequently found in historical reconstructions of the Maccabean revolt that the people who refused to fight on the Sabbath, and who were therefore easily massacred by the Seleucid troops, were Hasidim (1 Maccabees 2:29–38). Secondly, there is no solid evidence that the Hasidim were fighting for a narrower, more exclusively "religious" goal than were the Maccabeans. There is no reason to suppose that some of the Hasidic scribes were naïve enough to believe that the restoration of a legitimate Aaronid to the high-priestly office itself was a sufficient basis for them to end their armed opposition. This supposition has been based on 1 Maccabees 7:8–17:

The king . . . sent Bacchides and the godless Alchimus, whom he established as High Priest . . . who sent messengers to Judas and his brothers with treacherous proposals of peace. But these did not trust them. . . . Nevertheless a commission of scribes presented themselves before Alcimus and Bacchides, to sue for just terms. The first among the Israelites to ask them for peace terms were the Hasideans, who reasoned like this, "This is a priest of Aaron's line . . . he will not wrong us." He did in fact discuss peace terms with them and gave them his oath, "We will not attempt to injure you or your friends." They believed him, but he arrested sixty of them and put them to death in one day.

The text says nothing of the aims of the Hasidim in seeking to negotiate peace. It is possible that they were attempting to mediate a settlement that would avoid further bloodshed and devastation. Their slaughter, moreover, need not be explained as the result of intellectuals' naïveté (as hinted in the text). The treachery of Alcimus and the brutal tyranny of the Seleucid officers are sufficient explanation. The more complete version of these events in 2 Maccabees 14 provides a very different picture of such negotiations.[12] Nicanor, not Bacchides, and Alcimus negotiated with Judas himself, not with the Hasidim, and Judas accepted their terms, married, settled down, and led a normal life. Such a negotation and settlement by Judas would hardly have suited the purpose of the author of 1 Maccabees, the court history legitimating the Hasmonean dynasty, who deflected any naïveté and premature settlement away from Judas and onto the shoulders of Hasidic scribes who may well have been involved in the negotiations along with Judas. Little stock can be placed in the text of 1 Maccabees 7:8–17 other than the indication that at least some of the Hasidim were scribes.

Thus, although the evidence is fragmentary, it is possible to discern that groups of intellectuals were prominent in the resistance, including armed rebellion, to Hellenistic encroachments. In the crisis of Hellenizing reform led by members of the priestly aristocracy and of systematic attempts to suppress the Jewish Torah and traditional way of life, scribes and teachers, apparently in at least two different groupings, led resistance in various ways. They apparently saw their own roles in terms of discerning the will and action of God, not simply for personal enlightenment, but in order to "help to make many understand" that God was still in control of history and that there was hope for deliverance from an otherwise impossible situation of persecution. By cultivating and disseminating such revelation they would have encouraged "many" others to resist Hellenization and Seleucid tyranny. The *maskilim,* moreover, set personal examples of resistance by their willingness to be martyred for their loyalty to the law and for their persistent faith in God's redemption. Indeed, it is likely that scribes and other intellectuals had taken the lead well before Judas the Maccabee came on the scene. The Maccabean revolt was apparently organized and motivated as much by scribal-intellectual leadership as it was led militarily and "charismatically," in guerrilla warfare, by Judas Maccabeus. From the time of the most extreme threat to the traditional Jewish religion and society there emerged a strong heritage of resistance led by groups of intellectuals.

It is increasingly evident that we know far less about the Pharisees prior to 70 C.E. than previously assumed.[13] It does seem clear that under the Hasmonean dynasty the Pharisees were more directly and influentially involved in social-political affairs. They apparently functioned as scribes-lawyers-teachers, i.e., as "retainers" who established certain regulations for the people and "passed onto the people certain regulations handed down by former generations and not recorded in the Laws of Moses" (*Ant.* 13:296–297; 408). Josephus refers to them several times as a group with some coherence and as being several thousand strong.

Within a generation of the Hasmoneans' consolidation of high-priestly power the Pharisees stood in active opposition to the Hasmonean regime. Their opposition probably began already under John Hyrcanus (134–104 B.C.E.), although in the Talmud (b Quid. 66a) a story told about their break with Alexander Janneus is very similar to the story Josephus tells of their break with Hyrcanus (*Ant.* 13.288–298). It is certain that they were prominent in the popular opposition to Hyrcanus's son, the brutal Alexander Janneus. Josephus says that in several years of virtual civil war, Jannai killed nearly 50,000 of his Jewish subjects (*War* 1.91) and that the Pharisees suffered many injuries at his hands (*Ant.* 13:402–403). It is likely that Pharisees were among the 800 captives he crucified and among the 8,000 "of the hostile faction" that "fled beyond the pale of Judea" toward the end of his reign (*War* 1.97–98; *Ant.* 13:380–383). In a dramatic political reversal

Jannai's widow and successor, Alexandra Salome, brought the Pharisees into participation and perhaps into dominance in her government. Once in power they "freed [political] prisoners, recalled exiles," and attempted to purge their old opponents (*Ant.* 13:409–410).

If the Pharisees had provided successful political opposition under Jannai and had shared a certain degree of political power under Alexandra Salome, however, their role as a direct political force came to an end during the reign of Herod.[14] The Pharisees' decline as an effective political force illustrates one of the principal features of the imperial situation sketched in chapter 1. Similarly, viewing the Pharisees in the context of the imperial situation, particularly as it worked through the client kingship of Herod, illuminates the special dilemma in which they were placed. As an imperial administration or a client regime takes effective control of a subject society, the traditional opportunities for political participation are closed off to the people. With his extensive security forces, Herod, besides preventing any organized resistance, denied virtually any political influence to the people through legitimate traditional channels; they could not even meet in small groups without surveillance.

Yet it would go against the evidence in Josephus to conclude that the Pharisees as a group or other scribes-scholars-teachers no longer played any role at all in the politics of Jewish Palestine. They were still several thousand strong. And they were still capable of coordinated action. "When the whole Jewish people affirmed by an oath that it would be loyal to Caesar and to the king's government, these men, over six thousand in number, refused to take this oath," writes Josephus in his second report of the matter (*Ant.* 17.42). According to his earlier report, Herod "also tried to persuade Pollion the Pharisee and Samaias and most of their disciples to take the oath, but they would not agree to this." Yet in contrast with the other Pharisees whom Herod fined when they refused, Pollion and his followers were not punished because of Herod's gratitude at the realistic advice they had earlier given the Jerusalemites to open the gates to Herod rather than suffer more destruction and bloodshed (*Ant.* 15.370 and 15.3–4; cf. 14.172–176). Moreover, at least some of the Pharisees were involved at high levels in a court intrigue encouraging a rival claimant to the kingship (*Ant.*

17.43). Herod's execution of the Pharisees who plotted against him in this case, like his fining of the Pharisees who refused his loyalty oath, indicates that Herod had not already simply killed or exiled the Pharisees or purged them completely from participation in governing the society. He had rather left to the Pharisees and other scribes or teachers some of their traditional functions in domestic Jewish societal affairs as "retainers" of the high-priestly administration.

Two important steps taken by Herod, however, had vitiated the Pharisees' influence on politics at the higher levels. Herod replaced the Hasmonean priestly aristocracy with new high-priestly families of his own choice and under his own influence, and they in turn determined policies that the Pharisees would have been expected to implement. Herod also imposed another, more powerful and more important level of government above that of the Temple high-priestly apparatus, i.e., his own royal administration staffed with his own Hellenistic (non-Jewish) officers or "servants." The combination of a number of the features of this new arrangement in the imperial situation of the Temple-state as a client kingship would have left the Pharisees and other scribe-scholars in an acute dilemma. In order to continue to have any role in society, they had to acquiesce in the new arrangement. They were surely realistic enough to understand the actual power relations (note the realistic advice to the Jerusalemites by Pollion and Samaias to submit to Herod's conquest), yet their actual power and influence were drastically diminished—by an illegitimate client king! Hence, as is illustrated by their court intrigue to replace Herod, many of them would have been sitting uneasy in an ambiguous situation, eager to find an opportunity to change it.

A somewhat similar situation prevailed under Antipas in Galilee and the Roman governors in Judea (and later in Galilee as well) in the first century C.E. The Gospels give the distinct impression that the Pharisees, scribes, and lawyers are still functioning as representatives ("retainers") of the Temple-government in dealings with local affairs. Yet Herod Antipas in Galilee and the Roman governors in Judea surely relativized and diminished their authority and were virtually impervious to their influence while determining the policies they were expected to mediate. They must have been torn between maintaining what role and local influence they still held, and being resentful at the alien domination that had diminished their own traditional role and broader influence in Jewish society.

TORAH SCHOLARS AND HEROD'S GOLDEN EAGLE

In the most dramatic episode of protest by a group of intellectuals against Herodian-Roman rule, two famous sages inspired their students to tear down the golden eagle that Herod had erected over a portal of the Temple (*War* 1.648–655; *Ant.* 17.149–167). It was hardly "an insurrection of the populace" (*War* 1.648). But because it happened as Herod lay dying, the protest reverberated with considerable "demonstration value" among the people during the chaotic period in which power was being transferred to Herod's successors.

The protest was a conspiracy among the two teachers and their students. The two sages, Judas, son of Sariphaeus/Sepphoraeus, and Matthias, son of Margalothus/Margalus, are described as "the most learned of the Jews and unrivalled interpreters of the ancestral laws." In both accounts Josephus uses the term *sophistai* for the teachers, which surely does not have any negative connotations of "sophists,"[15] but the more positive one of "sages" or "doctors." One might surmise that most learned interpreters of the Law were Pharisees and that for apologetic reasons Josephus avoided mentioning that these protest-leading teachers were Pharisees, especially in the *Antiquities* (in which he is supposedly making a case for the Pharisees' being entrusted with the domestic government by the Romans).[16] This is unlikely considering Josephus's almost casual comment that a Pharisee was the cofounder of the Fourth Philosophy along with Judas of Galilee. Surely not all distinguished scribes and Torah scholars were Pharisees. There was also probably more than one school of interpretation (as symbolized perhaps by the rabbinic projection backwards of the rival schools of "Hillel" and "Shammai").[17] Josephus suggests that these two scholars were working in concert. He surely exaggerates the number of actual students who were "attending their lectures on the laws," but perhaps they had a wider following in addition to the young men who regularly spent time with them in studying the Torah.

The scholars' concern about Herod's violation of the Torah's provisions clearly was not new. They had previously reproached Herod on these matters, according to Josephus. Reports of the king's declining health, however, provided the occasion for bolder expression of that concern. "This was the fitting moment to avenge God's honor and to pull down those structures which had been erected in defiance of their fathers' law" (*War* 1.649).

The scholarly conspirators focused their protest on the "great golden eagle" that "the king had erected over the great gate of the Temple, as a votive offering and at great cost" (*Ant.* 17.151). The Torah, of course, forbade the setting up of images or the making of dedications in the likeness of any creature. The great golden eagle over the Temple gate, however, was also apparently symbolic of Herod's general practices in his vast building programs and other cultural projects. In one of his passages on Herod's cultural program Josephus himself appears to be complaining about the degree to which the king had "departed from the native customs and through foreign practices gradually corrupted the ancient way of life" (*Ant.* 15.267).

For in the first place he established athletic contests . . . in honor of Caesar and he built a theatre in Jerusalem, and after that a very large amphitheatre in the plain, both being spectacularly lavish but foreign to Jewish customs. . . . All round the theatre were inscriptions concerning Caesar and trophies of the nations which he had won in war, all of them made for Herod of pure gold and silver. . . . Foreigners were astonished at the expense . . . but to the natives it meant an open break with the customs held in honor by them. For it seemed glaring impiety to throw men to wild beasts for the pleasure of other men as spectators. . . . But more than all else it was the trophies that irked them [for they believed] that these were images surrounded by weapons . . . against their national custom. . . . (*Ant.* 15.267–276)

Josephus links the earlier conspiracy to assassinate Herod with the Jews' anxiety over these violations of their sacred traditions. It is important to keep in mind not only that the tremendous cost of these buildings and projects was borne by the Jewish people through heavy taxation, but that the decorations and activities kept the Jews constantly aware of their subjection to Rome as well. This lends credibility to Josephus's report that the scholars Judas and Matthias were concerned about Herod's more general violations of which the golden eagle was a symbol and that they wanted their disciples to "pull down all the works built by the king in violation of the laws of their fathers" (*Ant.* 17.150).[18]

The scholars and their disciples appear to have undertaken the protest out of a dual motivation. They acted primarily in defense of their ancestral laws (*Ant.* 17.152; *War* 1.650). Such dedication might only be expected from those who had devoted their lives to the study and practice of the Torah. Linked with the defense and possible death on behalf of the Torah was their anticipation of reward. In the *Antiquities,* Josephus portrays this in Hellenistic language derived from earlier Greek ideals of heroism: a "virtue *(arete)* acquired in death" and the "winning of eternal fame and glory, . . . praise from those now living, . . . and memorable examples to future generations" (*Ant.* 17.152). In the parallel passage in the *War,* however, Josephus allows us to discern that the scholars and their disciples were acting out of some sort of expectation of resurrection. He states this initially in terms of the Hellenistic terminology of immortality of the soul, but he then adds the phrases "and an eternally abiding sense of felicity" (*War* 1.650). That Josephus, despite his Hellenistic terminology, is referring to expectation of resurrection as a motive of the protesters can be determined by noting (a) the currency of belief in the resurrection in Jewish Palestine, (b) its prominence in contemporary martyrological stories of bold encounters of martyrs with the tyrants about to kill them, and (c) the recurrent importance of the hope of resurrection as an answer to a concrete situation (and not simply as a generalized belief). Each of these is worthy of analysis.

(a) Belief in some form of resurrection or resurrected life was clearly current in Palestinian Jewish society, whether among the Jews generally or among scribal-intellectual circles in particular. Despite his use of Hellenistic terminology of immortality and eternal fame, Josephus has given indications at several points of the more distinctive Palestinian Jewish idea of an afterlife as resurrection. For example, in his description of the Pharisees he says they believe both "that souls have power to survive death" *and* "that there are rewards and punishment under the earth for those who have led lives of virtue or vice"—seemingly a clear allusion to resurrection, judgment, and some sort of resurrection-life (*Ant.* 18.14). In other passages he evidently alludes to the resurrection in terms of a reincarnation of the soul (*War* 2.263; 3.374). Most striking in connection with the motivation of the scholars and their disciples in the golden-eagle incident is Josephus's statement about the Jews' belief that to those who observe the laws and, if they must need die for them, willingly meet death, God has granted a renewed existence and in the revolution of the ages the gift of a better life (*Ag. Apion* 2.218). The "eternally abiding sense of felicity" in Josephus's golden-eagle report would appear to be some sort of resurrection-life similar to that alluded to in "rewards under the earth for the virtuous" and "renewed existence" and the "gift of a better life."

(b) Yet another indication of the scholars' expectation of resurrection as a part of their motivation for possible martyrdom is Josephus's portrayal of their encounter with the tyrant Herod after the destruction of the golden eagle. Josephus must have been familiar with typical Jewish martyrological stories. A prominent motif in these is the bold encounter of the martyrs with the tyrant who is about to torture and kill them for their persistent adherence to the Torah. In 2 Maccabees 7, for example, one or another of the seven brothers says repeatedly, "We are ready to die rather than transgress the laws of our fathers. . . . I will not obey the king's command, but I obey the command of the law that was given to our fathers through Moses. . . . I, like my brothers, give up body and life for the laws of our fathers" (2 Maccabees 7:2,30,37). In both of his reports of the golden eagle, Josephus includes this typical motif of the bold confession before the tyrant (Herod) and the explicit declaration of disobedience to the king's command because of loyalty to the Law: "Nor is it at all surprising if we believe that it is less important to observe your degrees than the laws that Moses wrote as God prompted . . . (*Ant.* 17.159; cf. *War* 1.653).

In some of the Jewish martyr stories the reward is exaltation. Other martyr stories such as 2 Maccabees 7 clearly anticipate a risen life for those who die on behalf of the Law: "You accursed wretch, you dismiss us from this present life, but the King of the universe will raise us up to an everlasting renewal of life, because we have died for his laws" (2 Maccabees 7:9). Josephus's account of the protest by the scholars and their disciples makes the same connection with the anticipated resurrection:

"Who ordered you [to cut down the golden eagle]?" asked Herod.
"The Law of our fathers."
"And why so exultant, when you will shortly be put to death?"
"Because after our death we shall enjoy greater felicity." (*War* 1.653)

Of course, one might be tempted to dismiss this evidence as indicating that Josephus is simply using a familiar and typical motif in his portrayal. Yet a comparison with his portrayal of the scene between Herod and those who had conspired to assassinate him is telling. In his portrayal of that earlier conspiracy, in which he also does not mention the involvement of scholars or teachers, no mention is made of any reward of life after death for the conspirators, although they too are dying in defense of their communal customs (*Ant.* 15.281,288). Hence it is reasonable to conclude that Josephus's report about the golden-eagle protest reflects the particular dual motivation of the scholarly martyrs: to defend the traditional law and, if martyred, to be resurrected as reward for their devotion.

(c) In earlier apocalyptic texts such as Daniel 11–12, Jubilees 23, or the Assumption of Moses 10, the hope of resurrection was an answer to a specific problem in a concrete situation. Jews such as the *maskilim* of Daniel 11:33–35 were dying "precisely because they had willfully chosen to obey the Torah. . . . Resurrection to life . . . was an answer to this problem."[19] Far from being removed from concrete historical situations, such apocalyptic literature was rooted in them. "The friends of the people who composed and read these apocalypses had died in persecution. Perhaps these people themselves faced the real possibility of violent death. God would vindicate them."[20] Belief in the resurrection supposedly later became simply a standard belief unrelated to particular circumstances.[21] However, even if the resurrection had already become a standard component of general Jewish expectations by Herodian times, there is no reason why the belief could still not function as an inspiring motive for protest and resistance in particular concrete circumstances. Thus it is reasonable to conclude that, as with the *maskilim* in the Book of Daniel, it was their hope of resurrection as well as their dedication to the Torah that enabled Judas, Matthias, and their disciples to risk certain death in their protest against Herod.[22]

As a protest, the chopping down of the golden eagle from atop the main Temple gate is impressive, given Herod's tight security measures. It is evident that the whole event was deliberately conceived and carefully planned as a nonviolent protest. The very number of those arrested, forty young men, indicates how extensive the group was that planned the action. Those who carried out the action could not have been any more aggressive and bold in their defiance of Herod and his practices. Yet they did not offer armed resistance to the military force sent to apprehend them, but "courageously awaited the attack" (*Ant.* 17.157). The scholars Judas and Matthias and their disciples must have undertaken the demonstration as a symbolic act of disobedience and challenge to the Herodian regime. The object (the golden eagle) and the location (the Temple's main gate) were not only highly central and visible, but were symbolic of the conflict between the Jewish people and their alien rulers as well.[23] Indeed, to have the eagle over their own Temple gate was a constant visible reminder of their subjection. Thus cutting down the eagle was no simple matter of individual youthful heroics, but a carefully considered and planned action symbolic of a more general protest against Herodian rule.

Did the scholars and their disciples also intend to touch off more general popular resistance to the dying Herod with their highly visible and dramatic symbolic act? There is no direct evidence for this; yet this was certainly the effect of their action and of their resultant martyrdom at the hands of the tyrant. Herod himself, of course, responded to the protest with brutal severity, having the scholars and their students burned alive (*War* 1.655; *Ant.* 17.167). The memory of the recent dramatic protest and martyrdom was still quite vivid in the people's mind when Archelaus prepared to replace his deceased father as client king. Lamentation over the fate of the protesters quickly became a central motivating force in the popular demand to Archelaus, not simply for reduction of taxes and liberation of political prisoners but also for the ouster of Herodian officials responsible for their oppression.

[There began] a lamentation over the fate of those whom Herod had punished for cutting down the golden eagle from the gate of the Temple . . . mourning . . . in honor of the unfortunate men who had in defense of their country's laws and the Temple perished on the pyre. These martyrs ought, they clamoured, to be avenged by the punishment of Herod's favorites, and the first step was the deposition of the High Priest whom he had appointed, as they had a right to select a man of greater piety and purer morals. (*War* 2.5–7)

In both their protest and their own martydom the scholars and their disciples became symbols for further popular protest against the Herodian client kingship.

THE FOURTH PHILOSOPHY AND ROMAN TRIBUTE

Because of the modern scholarly construct of "the Zealots," the importance of the group that Josephus labels "the Fourth Philosophy" (the others being Pharisees, Sadducees, and Essenes) has been greatly exaggerated and the texts referring to its founders have been seriously misread. In their "founding" of an "intrusive fourth philosophy" in 6 C.E., Judas of Galilee and Saddok the Pharisee are seen as beginning the Zealot movement and agitating for armed rebellion against Rome. Although there is no evidence for either of these claims, they are found repeatedly in the scholarly literature of New Testament studies and in Jewish history. The resultant historical distortions can be illustrated by a particularly blatant example of such misconception and misinterpretation:

The coming of God's reign [according to Judas and Saddok] depended on human "revolutionary activity.". . . . This cooperation between God and the "true Israel" took place in the form of a "holy war," which had to be conducted by means of guerrilla warfare, a situation like the beginnings of the Maccabean rebellion. The Zealots had their bases in the numerous caves in the desert of Judah, whence they launched attacks upon the settled regions where they found support among the oppressed rural population. The guerrillas retreated once more into the desert after their surprise attacks, frequently leaving the Jewish peasants to bear the vengeance of the Roman occupation troops. . . . Individual groups later advanced as far as Jerusalem, where they executed summary justice and kidnapped high-placed personalities in order to extort the release of prisoners. The ultimate goal was to stir up a general popular rebellion against Rome, which was seen as the prerequisite for God's intervention.[24]

None of the previous paragraph is historically true; there is simply no extant evidence to support any of these assertions. Certainly none of these statements is true either of the Zealots proper, who did not originate until the middle of the Jewish revolt, i.e., in 67–68, or of the Fourth Philosophy started by Judas and Saddok. Hengel has simply lumped together, under the modern concept of the Zealot movement, a number of disparate incidents and the activities of quite different groups, such as brigand bands and the terrorist Sicarii. Yet similar misreadings of the sources is found in much of the scholarly literature, from tendentious translations and notes in the Loeb edition of Josephus to articles in encyclopedias. Even those who are aware that the evidence does not accord with a single "Zealot movement" nevertheless describe Judas and Saddok as having issued "a call for armed revolt" and "involved the Jewish body politic in uprising." "They maintained adamantly that it was essential to come out openly in war against Roman rule and also to compel those who disagreed with them to join the struggle."[25] Our first step in dealing with the greatly misunderstood Fourth Philosophy and its founders must be to deal critically with those Josephus passages that constitute our principal evidence and to sort out the misreadings and misleading concepts.

A principal factor contributing to the misunderstanding of the Fourth Philosophy as starting the Zealot movement and as advocating armed revolt has been the frequent failure to read critically Josephus's harangue about what he sees as the effects of the Fourth Philosophy's views, but not as the activities of its members. In his only reference of any length to Judas of Galilee and the Fourth Philosophy, Josephus connects them with subsequent developments. He accuses them of having "sowed the seed of every kind of misery which so afflicted the nation" later, of having "filled the body politic with tumult, and planting the seeds of those troubles which subsequently overtook it" (*Ant.* 18.6,9). These seeds and tumult, however, far from being any sort of "armed rebellion," are their ideas: "the novelty" of their philosophy, which Josephus claims was "an innovation and reform in [the Jewish] ancestral traditions" (*Ant.* 18.9).

Josephus does portray the miseries and troubles that later sprouted from these "seeds" with considerable flourish: "wars, brigand raids, assassinations of prominent leaders, civil strife, attacks by the enemy, famine," and finally the siege and devastation of Jerusalem and the Temple by the Romans. All of these seem to be allusions to events during the revolt of 66–70 that represent the activities of various groups, including the Roman army. None of the illustrations is recognizable as an *action* of the Fourth Philosophy. At no point in this digression (*Ant.* 18.6^b–9) is Josephus describing the supposedly violent actions of Judas, Saddok, and their followers. The point of his harangue is that their *philosophy* had contributed to subsequent troubles, chiefly because of its effect on the young.

Indeed, in this passage Josephus does not blame the later revolt directly on Judas and his followers, as is often supposed.[26] He simply complains about the effects of their ideals, including their passionate devotion to freedom. The passage concludes by blaming the Roman governor for the outbreak of the revolt: "The folly that ensued began to afflict the nation after Gessius Florus . . . had by his overbearing and lawless actions provoked a desperate rebellion against the Romans" (*Ant.* 18.25). Nowhere in the whole passage (*Ant.* 18.4–10,23–24) is there a claim that members of the Fourth Philosophy engaged in any armed revolt. Nor is there any statement that could be construed as evidence that the Fourth Philosophy continually agitated for revolt against Rome.

Another factor in the misunderstanding that Judas and the Fourth Philosophy advocated armed revolt has been the assumption or claim that Judas of Galilee is identical with Judas, the son of Hezekiah, who was leader of the popular insurrection in Galilee following the death of Herod.[27] Josephus, however, says nothing to suggest such an identification, and there are insuperable chronological difficulties that would make Judas well over 50 years of age in 6 C.E. and his own sons either sired when he was very old or themselves very old when active later. Josephus, in fact, makes it very clear that Judas, son of brigand-chief

Hezekiah, was one of the popularly acclaimed kings in 4 B.C.E., whereas Judas of Galilee was a scholar. Thus there is no basis for attributing the armed revolt of the one Judas in 4 B.C.E. to the other Judas in 6 C.E.

Yet another factor (often used with the one just discussed) that has contributed to the misunderstanding of Judas of Galilee as a leader or advocate of armed revolt is the conclusion that Judas was part of a dynasty of "messianic" leaders of resistance that included Menahem, the "messianic pretender" among the Sicarii who participated briefly in the beginning of the Jewish revolt in the summer of 66 C.E.[28] That Judas was the father or grandfather of Menahem, who helped lead the revolt until he was assassinated, does not mean that Judas himself engaged in or advocated revolt. Similarly, although there was continuity between the leadership of the Fourth Philosophy (the "scholar" Judas) and the leadership of the later rebel group, the Sicarii (the "scholar" Menahem), this does not mean that the members of the Fourth Philosophy favored or engaged in violent activities.

A final factor that has contributed to the misunderstanding of Judas of Galilee as having led an armed revolt is the translation of some principal texts mentioning him. The word *apostasis* and its variations, used both in the Josephus and in the Acts 5:37 accounts of Judas, has a meaning both broader and a good deal more ambiguous than the English "rebellion" or "revolt."[29] Thus the translation of Acts 5:37 in the Revised Standard Version, that Judas "drew away some of the people after him," or in the Jerusalem Bible, that Judas "attracted crowds of supporters," is surely more appropriate than that in the New English Bible (perhaps shaped according to the "Zealots" concept), that Judas the Galilean "induced some people to revolt under his leadership." Similarly, it should be clear that Josephus's account does not necessarily indicate that Judas led a "revolt."

A closer, more critical reading of the principal evidence thus indicates that Judas and the Fourth Philosophy were not the beginnings of any organized movement of anti-Roman agitation called the Zealots and that they may not have been involved in or even advocated rebellion at all. Once we have laid aside these misconceptions of modern scholarship, we can take a closer look at the principal description Josephus provides of Judas, Saddok, and their followers.

A certain Judas, a Gaulanite from the city of Gamala, in league with the Pharisee Saddok, pressed hard for resistance. They said that such a tax assessment amounted to slavery, pure and simple, and urged the nation to claim its freedom. If successful, they argued, the Jews would have paved the way for good fortune; if they were defeated in their quest, they would at least have honor and glory for their high ideals. Furthermore, God would eagerly join in promoting the success of their plans, especially if they did not shrink from the slaughter that might come upon them. . . . Judas the Galilean established himself as the leader of the fourth philosophy. They agree with the views of the Pharisees in everything except their unconquerable passion for freedom, since they take God as their only leader and master. They shrug off submitting to unusual forms of death and stand firm in the face of torture of relatives and friends, all for refusing to call any man master. (*Ant.* 18.4–5,23)[30]

Josephus's characterization here and elsewhere makes it clear that we are dealing with a group of intellectuals who have particular ideas that can be compared and contrasted with those of other "philosophies" among the Jews. In other references (*War* 2.118 and 2.433) Josephus describes Judas as a *sophistes,* i.e., a scholar-teacher trained in interpretation of the Torah, like Judas and Matthias, who inspired the tearing down of the golden eagle. Judas's cofounder Saddok, as a Pharisee, was also probably a scholar-teacher.

To describe people such as Judas and Saddok simply as "intellectuals" or scholars, however, is misleading as well as incomplete. Such characterizations in Hellenistic Greek as well as in modern English do not adequately convey their social-political concerns and roles. All of the other "philosophies" or "factions" originated not only as groups that had particular ideas and distinctive ways of interpreting the Torah, but as interest groups or "parties" striving to realize particular religious-political policies.[31] The Pharisees and Sadducees had earlier contested for political power and influence under the Hasmoneans. The Essenes (whom most now understand as the same as the Dead Sea Community at Qumran) were so intent on their own religious-political policies that they left the larger society to found their own community and polity. Of course, groups such as the Pharisees and Judas's followers could appropriately be characterized as "philosophies" (but not "parties") insofar as they no longer exerted much political influence in the imperial situation governed from above by imperial officials and client rulers. Precisely because of their exclusion from any effective political role, of course, some of the scribes and scholars must have desired ardently to put their religious-political convictions into practice.

Using for comparison the Pharisees, with whom they shared most ideas, according to Josephus, we should probably imagine Judas, Saddok, and their followers not as an organized political party or a widespread movement, nor simply as a few intellectuals teaching distinctive ideas. Rather they are likely to have been a relatively small association of teachers and others who had come together in response to the sudden imposition of direct Roman rule and the concomitant tax-registration.

That they were not merely a religious "philosophy" appears to be precisely why Josephus and others found them problematic in Roman-dominated Jewish society. Modern interpreters have treated Judas and his followers in terms of their principal "views," "axioms," "propositions," or "extreme freedom ideology."[32] Yet even Josephus, who otherwise characterizes this as an innovative "philosophy," provides indications that more than "views" and "propositions" were involved. In the following discussion, which proceeds according to ideas that can be isolated only for analytical purposes, it should be kept in mind that Judas and his followers did not simply teach, but attempted to realize their ideals in response to the particular problem posed by the Roman census.

"They agree with the views of the Pharisees in everything except their unconquerable passion for freedom," says Josephus. To be in favor of freedom for the Jewish people would not have been unusual in Jewish society at the time. Even the priestly aristocracy, who benefited greatly from the imperial system in which they collaborated, might have preferred to be independent of their Roman overlords. It is not surprising that the idea of freedom "recurs frequently" in Josephus's narratives of the tense social-political history of the Jews under Roman domination when we consider the content of Jewish historical-religious tradition. A people whose constitutive event was its liberation from subjection in Egypt, celebrated annually at Passover, whose hopes focused on the fulfillment of God's promise to their ancestors of being a great nation with land of their own, was bound to entertain ideas of freedom precisely in a continuing situation of imperial domination. Whether the terminology of freedom reflects the actual yearnings of concrete groups or is ascribable to Josephus's historiography, many of the groups and individuals he describes shared this ideal: the popular prophetic movements at mid-century, the Sicarii, who became active in the late 50s and 60s, priestly insurrectionaries in the summer of 66, Galileans resisting Roman reconquest in 67, the Zealots proper in 68, or the Jews generally in the tense months of early 66 (among other texts: *War* 2.259–260,264,443;4.95,272,348–349). The ideal of freedom was thus not distinctive of the "Fourth Philosophy," but it was understandably an ideal that they would have shared with other Jews who took their sacred traditions seriously.

Josephus sees their "unconquerable passion for freedom" closely linked with their conviction that God was "their only leader and master" (cf. *War* 2.433). The idea that God was the real ruler of Israelite society is one of the most prominent, overarching ideas in late second Temple Jewish literature as well as in the Bible itself. It is the very assumption and dominant theme of the Mosaic Covenant, of the oracles of the prophets, of most of the historical books in the Bible. Prayers and psalms (such as Psalms of Solomon 17) begin and end with a declaration of the kingship of God in the life of the people. There are variations with regard to how direct, immediate, and exclusive God's rule was portrayed. Nevertheless, there is considerable agreement from text to text that God was the true lord and master of the Jewish people. Even the kingship of David had been a compromise, and a future anointed king would be only an agent of the true, divine King. Throughout the biblical traditions and apocalyptic literature there are sharp objections to and condemnations of unjust and alien rulers. Thus it should not be surprising that even Josephus, who was beholden to his Roman patrons, could not help but indicate at points that the true Jewish polity as given by Moses was a "theocracy," which placed "all sovereignty and authority in the hands of God," (*Ag. Apion* 2.164–165) and that the God-given "laws" were their "masters" *(despotas)* and God their true "ruler" *(hēgemōn)* (*Ant.* 4.223). It is striking, moreover, that Josephus, in these passages in his apology *(Ag. Apion)* and in his account of Moses in the *Antiquities,* uses exactly the same terms of God and God's law as he does in reference to the supposedly completely innovative, unprecedented, and intrusive Fourth Philosophy. Thus even in Josephus it is clear that the Fourth Philosophy shared with Palestinian Jews generally, as well as with the Pharisees, its idea of God as the true ruler.

Another of their basic ideas, according to Josephus, was that, as they themselves took action to claim their freedom, God would be helping or concurring in that same action (*Ant.* 18.5). Again, this is not an idea distinctive to the Fourth Philosophy (and in this case, Josephus does not suggest it is). In Josephus's awkward Hellenistic philosophical terminology, how does one reconcile fate and free will? The more complex Jewish understanding of human action and history was not easily susceptible of restatement in Hellenistic concepts. But the Fourth Philosophy would appear to have been similar to beliefs of the Pharisees here as in other ideas. As Josephus explained, in a seeming contradiction, the Pharisees believed that "to act rightly or otherwise rests, indeed, for the most part with men, but that in each action Fate cooperates" (*War* 2.163). Rabbi Akiva (who favored the Bar Kokhba rebellion, 132–135) is cited to similar effect: All is foreseen, and free will is given (*Avot* 3.19). Biblical literature, of course, was filled with illustrations of how God effects liberation or takes other actions, but only through the actions of people. God led the Hebrews out of Egyptian slavery through the organizing leadership of Moses and the flight of the Hebrews themselves. God worked justice in the society through the people's obedience to his righteous will as delineated in covenantal law. Some Palestinian Jews at the time may well have been passively waiting for God to take some amazing action. Reportedly some contemporaries of Jesus were looking for clearly observable *signs* of the time of salvation (Luke 17:20). However, the adherents of the Fourth Philosophy were not at all unusual in their understanding that the rule of God actually worked through a human cooperation with God's action.

It thus appears that the three principal ideas that both Josephus and modern scholars find distinctive of the Fourth Philosophy were common views in Palestinian Jewish society of the time and were shared by the Pharisees and other identifiable groups. What was distinctive about Judas and his group was not their ideas or principles so much as their seriousness about those ideas. As Josephus explained, they were ready to die for their beliefs. It has been argued on the basis of two speculative comparisons, both of which attempt to go behind Josephus's portrayal of the group in Hellenistic philosophical terminology, that it was an imminent eschatological orientation that caused adherents of the Fourth Philosophy to be so unusually adamant about their beliefs. That is, the sole lordship of God was for them not so much present reality and actual demand as an imminent eschatological kingdom in preparation for which Judas supposedly preached repentance in charismatic or prophetic style, much as did John the Baptist or Jesus of Nazareth.[33] Similarly, they understood freedom as the final deliverance of Israel at the end time in a way resembling the supposedly eschatological deliverance concept of the popular prophets and their movements.[34]

As we begin to appreciate more the differences in form, viewpoint, and degrees of intensity among the various Jewish groups working for some sort of renewal in their society, it makes less sense procedurally to draw direct analogies from group to group. The friction between Jesus of Nazareth and the "scribes and Pharisees," for example, should make us cautious about viewing a scholar such as Judas and his concerns in terms of a John the Baptist. Similarly, the anticipation of deliverance *(eleutheria)* through God's new miraculous actions that would resemble those of the original exodus and conquest appears to have been distinctive of the popular prophetic movements. Hence it is not good historical method to ascribe such a fantastic orientation to one portrayed as a "scholar" by Josephus, simply because such fantasies occur elsewhere in Jewish society at the time.

In fact, there is no need to proceed only by analogy with other groups in this case because there is an indication of their orientation in Josephus's account and there are other groups of scholars-teachers to make comparisons with. To return to a previously-cited passage: "If successful, they argued, the Jews would have paved the way for good fortune; if they were defeated in their quest, they would at least have honor and glory for their high ideals" (*Ant.* 18.5). As usual Josephus has used Hellenistic terms ("honor and glory") in his portrayal of their "high ideals." With our historical imagination somewhat informed by biblical prophecies and contemporary Jewish apocalyptic literature, however, we may legitimately discern behind Josephus's "[paving] the way for good fortune" a hope for liberation from Roman rule that would bring a renewed society of peace and justice, a "new heaven and a new earth" in which

They shall not build and another inhabit; they shall not plant and another eat; for my chosen shall long enjoy the work of their hands. (Isaiah 65:17,22)

Similarly, their "honor and glory" would likely have been a resurrection like that expected by previous scholar-teacher martyrs such as the *maskilim* in Daniel 12:1–3 (and the other Judas and Mattathias, who inspired their disciples to cut down the golden eagle).

The most striking and distinctive aspect of the Fourth Philosophy was neither its ideas nor its supposedly eschatological orientation, but its insistence on the concrete practice or realization of its ideals. In fact, the best evidence for the ideals of its adherents comes from their behavior in concrete situations. Their unconquerable passion for liberty and their conviction that God was their sole leader and master were manifested (says Josephus) in their actions.

They shrug off submitting to unusual forms of death and stand firm in the face of torture of relatives and friends, all for refusing to call any man master. . . . Most people have seen their unwavering conviction under such circumstances . . ., their contempt for suffering pain. (*Ant.* 18.23–24)

This is surely our best indication of what was so distinctive about the Fourth Philosophy and why it was so objectionable to Jewish collaborators such as Josephus.

The adherents of the Fourth Philosophy did not keep their passion for freedom and commitment to the sole lordship of God confined to the fantasy realm or to an indefinite future. Rather, they insisted upon the concrete realization of Jewish liberty and the rule of God. Thus they were willing to submit to death and to suffer the torture of relatives and friends if only they could "avoid calling any man master." Perhaps some, even many, Jews could keep Caesar and God on separate planes or in separate categories, with the "religious" or "spiritual" differentiated from the "political" or "mundane." Judas of Galilee, however, "upbraided the Jews for recognizing the Romans as masters when they already had God" (*War* 2.433). The Fourth Philosophy was a revival of the earlier Israelite (biblical) sense that God was the ruler of its life in all dimensions, exclusively and uncompromisingly. Its followers refused to "spiritualize" or "compromise" in order to avoid outright conflict with the imperial situation in Jewish Palestine.

The Fourth Philosophy emerged as a response to the replacement of client kingship with direct Roman rule over Judea. One might wonder why, when Judea had already been subject to Roman rule and tribute for over two generations (and before that to other empires for centuries), suddenly a group would emerge insisting on freedom and the sole rule of God. The harshness of Herodian client kingship, continued by Archelaus, may well have been a factor, provoking as it did a high level of critical resentment against the Roman imperial situation generally. The deposing of Archelaus would have provided an occasion of change in which the discontented could voice their concerns. Herod's building projects, and in particular his construction of temples dedicated to Augustus throughout his realm, remained as visible reminders of Roman overlordship.[35] As Josephus commented at one point, "One can mention no suitable spot within his realm which he left destitute of some mark of homage to Caesar" (*War* 1.407).

The crucial factor, however, was surely the fact that this was the first time in second Temple history that the Palestinian Jews had been subject to *direct* foreign imperial rule. Previously the dominant empire had always ruled Judea through the Jewish high priesthood or, in the case of Herod and his sons, through client kings. This meant that the native Jewish aristocracy had formed a buffer between the imperial power and the Jewish people. Even when it came to the imperial tribute, it could be understood as paid to the high priesthood or to Herod, who then rendered tribute to the imperial treasury. With the imposition of Roman provincial rule through a governor, the Roman imperial domination became direct, and the assessment for taxation made this only too evident to everyone in the society. Moreover, the memories of previous special levies of taxes through temporary direct Roman intervention could have intensified the Judeans' anxieties in 6 C.E. For example, as was noted in chapter 2, when the Jews were slow in rendering up a special levy of taxes to Cassius, he had subjected and enslaved the population of the four leading district towns of Gophna, Emmaus, Lydda, and Thamna (*War* 1.271–275; *Ant.* 14.218–222). Suddenly the whole society was about to be subjected permanently to direct Roman rule and taxation. As Josephus indicates, "The Jews were shocked to hear of the registration of their property" (*Ant.* 18.2).

When we turn, finally, to the actual resistance activities of Judas, Saddok, and company, Josephus's passing references make the movement appear far less ominous and revolutionary than in his principal accounts. At the beginning of his major account of the group (*Ant.* 18:4–10,23–25) Josephus writes that Judas and Saddok "pressed hard for resistance" or ("led a defection") and "urged the nation to claim its freedom." The shorter principal account in the earlier *War* makes it sound less like an exhortation to rebel. When Coponius was sent as governor (no mention of the tax-assessment!),

a Galilean named Judas was urging his countrymen to resistance, reproaching them if they submitted to paying taxes to the Romans and tolerated mortal masters after serving God alone." (*War* 2.118)

The other two occasional references to Judas make his activity sound even less omnious:

Judas called the Galilean, a skillful teacher, who in the old days under Quirinius, had reproached the Jews for recognizing the Romans as masters when they already had God. (*War* 2.433)
Judas persuaded not a few Jews to refuse to enroll themselves when Quirinius was sent as censor to Judea. (*War* 7.253)

As was noted above, there is simply no basis in these texts for the conclusion that Judas led any sort of rebellion. Judging from these reports it is more easily imaginable that Judas, Saddok, and others were engaged in teaching or preaching against the tax-assessment. On the basis of the brief reference in *War* 7.253 we could imagine that they had also been "organizing" people against the assessment. At most, however, their action was organized "tax-resistance," in which they persuaded people to refuse to cooperate with the Roman census. Such action would have to be characterized as "nonviolent noncooperation" in modern terms. To the established imperial order, however, even nonviolent noncooperation was serious resistance.

It seems a far cry from the Hasidim who as "mighty warriors of Israel" had fought against Seleucid troops and war elephants to the Fourth Philosophy, whose adherents encouraged their fellow Jews not to cooperate with the Roman census. Along with the Torah scholars Judas, Matthias, and their students, however, Judas of Galilee and his followers stand in a long tradition of Jewish scribal-scholarly resistance to tyranny and oppression. The form of the intellectuals' resistance to the Hellenizing "reform" backed by Antiochus Epiphanes varied from martyrs' exemplary adherence to the outlawed Torah under conditions of persecution to full-fledged participation in guerrilla war against the Seleucid armies. Resistance to the point of rebellion was continued by the Pharisees and others against the arrogant and tyrannical practices of Alexander Jannai.

In their daring removal of the golden eagle from the Temple gate as Herod lay dying and in their subsequent execution, Judas, Matthias, and their students revived the tradition of scholarly martyrdom. The Fourth Philosophy's resistance to the tribute, as Rome imposed its direct imperial rule in Judea, stood potentially more in the revolutionary tradition of the Hasidim. The scholar Judas and the Pharisee Saddok and others apparently organized the people for collective resistance to the imperial government. But the Fourth Philosophy stopped short of active rebellion. There is no indication in the sources, moreover, that Judas and Saddok organized or left behind an organized, longer-lasting movement of armed resistance to Rome. Fifty years later some other intellectuals, probably in utter frustration at the deteriorating circumstances of the people, inaugurated terrorist activities against their own collaborationist high priests. But the Fourth Philosophy of 6 C.E. was a nonviolent, nonrevolutionary resistance to enrolling for the Roman tribute.

4. Popular Mass Protests

THE JERUSALEM CROWD

Riots by the Jerusalem "crowd" were an important form of protest against the imperial situation. As we saw in chapter 2, the Romans took the possibility of riots seriously, especially at festival times, even though scholars have not paid much attention to such protests. Of course, biblical scholars and Jewish historians are not alone. Until recently, historians have taken little heed of popular protests in general or of urban crowds in particular. The earlier work of Taine and G. LeBon was highly tendentious, dismissing the "mob" as criminals, vagrants, and social misfits.[1] More recently, however, the emergence of social history and the work of Hobsbawm, Thompson, and especially Rudé have revealed the importance of the "urban mob" or "the crowd" in preindustrial societies.[2] From their ground-breaking studies of the crowd in preindustrial France, England, and Italy, particularly in eighteenth-century Paris and London, we may be able to gain some clues regarding the importance of mass protests in ancient Jerusalem.

The urban crowd did not simply represent an irrational and spontaneous venting of resentment, rage, or frustration. "The classical mob expected to achieve something by its riot. It assumed that the authorities would be sensitive to its movements."[3] Often it may even have expected some sort of concession or official remedy for its grievance. This should not be surprising. In a time before the emergence of popular democratic forms such as elections, town meetings, or political parties, the crowd's protest or "riot" was one of the few forms through which the people could express their concerns.

Indeed, the "mob" was not simply a casual collection of people united for some ad hoc purpose but was in a recognized sense a permanent entity, even though seldom permanently organized as such.[4] Far from the rioters being merely criminals and riffraff, the crowd exercising its protest was composed of the ordinary people of the city, the urban poor of settled abode and trade.[5] As Rudé says, they ". . . were rarely vagrants, rarely had criminal records of any kind, generally had settled abodes, and tended to be respectable working men rather than slum dwellers or the poorest of the poor."[6] As typical members and representatives of the ordinary people, the "mob" expressed genuine interests and concerns of the urban poor, such as simple hunger if the price of bread was too high or if all the grain was sold abroad by speculators.[7]

The activities of the urban crowd "were always directed against the rich and powerful (though not necessarily the official head of the state or city)."[8] Rudé finds in city riots the expression of class interest, "a class hostility of the poor against the rich."[9] When violence erupted and damage was done—generally only to property—"it was strictly discriminating and was directed against carefully selected targets."[10] It is important to recognize that a riot can be an expression of class conflict of poor against the rich and powerful without being directed against the king or state or church. The king was usually revered as the very symbol and fount of justice and as the father and protector of his people. The mob's protest would focus on the powerful ones or officials who were deceiving the king even as they were abusing his faithful subjects.[11] Hobsbawm makes another important point closely related to this: "There was a group of towns in which 'the mob' was of particular importance and developed a peculiar sub-political complexion of its own: the classical preindustrial metropolis—normally a capital—living on a resident court, state, church, or aristocracy."[12] In such cities, "it is the business of the ruler and his aristocracy to provide a livelihood for his people."[13] Thus a special symbiosis may prevail between rulers and the urban poor, especially those dependent on the economy of an administrative capital, royal court, or religious center.

Once we recognize that ordinary people had genuine interests of their own that were not the same as, and may have been in conflict with, those of the wealthy and powerful, it is possible also to realize that the protesting crowd's motives were likely to have been complex. Besides an overt motive that may be immediately obvious, there may have been underlying motives and beliefs that could even have been the dominant ones. The shortage or the high price of bread may have been the occasion for popular outcries that were concerned also with other, broader issues. "Again, strikes, food riots, and peasant movements, even when the prevailing issues were purely economic, might take place against a political background that gave them a greater intensity or a new direction."[14] For example, in a situation of gross injustice, inaction by the authorities might have been a precipitating factor that brought the protesting mob together, while its deeper motives were rooted in the people's basic concern about particular injustices or intolerable circumstances.[15]

Amidst these multiple motives it is difficult to sort out the "political" factors from economic and other concerns. Hobsbawm finds a striking "political lag" of the city mob behind the countryside, particularly in the Italian "court" cities.[16] Rudé finds that the typical eighteenth-century riot in London was a social protest attached to a political cause.[17] The protesting urban crowd was capable of assimilating greater political awareness from organized political groups. In eighteenth-century Paris and London, respectively, the *parliament* and the Common Council became the political educator of the *menu peuple* ("lower orders").[18] Also, more politically aware professional people might join a protest started by the common people and might provid articulation and leadership for its concerns.[19]

Although urban mobs may have achieved a degree of political consciousness and direction, they were not usually revolutionary in intent or effect (until Paris in 1789). "The riots were not directed against the social system."[20] The crowd and its protests "functioned" to the extent that the threat of perpetual rioting kept rulers somewhat attentive to the concerns and grievances of their subjects, especially of those subjects dependent directly or indirectly on the court or capital for their livelihood. So long as the traditional concept of order was not replaced by some new political ideal, the common people protesting abuses in the system usually remained loyal to the authorities. The protesting urban crowd, however, might make a revolution disguised as a counterrevolution if the traditional order was threatened, either from outside or by the ruler's laxity in tolerating more than the expected level of poverty and injustice. As Hobsbawm suggests,

" 'legitimism' may cover a mass revolt against the injustices of the new order," . . . for "as soon as the injustices and sufferings of the people are laid *directly* at his door . . . an unjust king is the negation of kingship."[21] Ordinarily, however, the urban crowd's protests were far from being any serious threat to the established order.

It is worth noting, finally, that "riots" can run out of control for several days. The authorities, even with military forces, may be unable to contain them for a time. For example, in London both the Wilkite riots (1760s and 1770s) and the Gordon riots (1780s) went on for more than a week before the authorities were able to suppress them, and then only with savage violence. Several similar examples of sustained protest activity by crowds occurred in eighteenth-century French cities.[22]

Familiarity with this comparative material from eighteenth–century European cities makes us more sensitive to parallel aspects of protests by the crowds in first-century Jerusalem. Josephus's narratives and the passion narrative of the Gospels indicate that the crowd or mob was a regular feature of life in ancient Jerusalem. A "counter-revolution-ary" action by the Jerusalem crowd had been one of the key factors in the escalation of events toward the Maccabean revolt (2 Maccabees 4:39–42). Similarly, a riot by a festival crowd had been one of the key events in the intensification of conflict between Alexander Jannai and his people (*Ant.* 13.372). Thus it is not surprising to find the Jerusalem crowd playing an important role at key points in the events narrated by Josephus and in the final events of Jesus' ministry as portrayed in the Gospels.

Our exploration here will concentrate on two events in particular: the Jerusalem crowd's protest to Archelaus following Herod's funeral in 4 B.C.E. and the crowd's protest of a provocative action by a Roman soldier under Cumanus (governor, 48–52 C.E.). Other references can be used to flesh out the context and background. There are important and interrelated reasons for concentrating on these two protests. Both were outbursts that, in the views of the rulers at least, raged "out of control," the one in 4 B.C.E. apparently for several days. Yet they were also both apparently nonviolent until the crowds were attacked and provoked by official show of force. Finally, both occurred or at least reached their climax during the Passover festival, which may be of interest for comparison with the crowd that was active during the final days of the ministry of Jesus.

Josephus repeatedly writes of the Jerusalem populace/multitude/ crowd *(dēmos, plēthos, ochlos)*. He uses the different Greek words almost interchangeably. This word usage is an important piece of evidence that the social-political structure of Jerusalem in the period of Roman domination was not similar to that of a Greek city *(polis)*. Tcherikover critically examined such evidence and concluded that, far from using "technical" political language in a consistent sense about Jerusalem and its people, Josephus uses terms very loosely. He also found that the polity of Jerusalem had not been reformed to accord with the standard Greek city, with "council" *(boulē, koinon)* and "assembly" *(ecclē-sia)*.[23] It was rather still an "Oriental" city, divided basically between the ruling class, i.e., the royal court and priestly aristocracy, on the one hand, and the rest of the populace, on the other.[24] Jerusalem along with the rest of Judea was governed by the royal or the high-priestly administration, including the Sanhedrin. So far as we know there was no established or legitimate vehicle through which the ordinary people could express their concerns, except the outcry of the crowd. As the political channels through which the Pharisees and others had previously found expression were closed off by the client king or imperial administration, the crowd as a vehicle of popular expression probably would have become all the more important.

Ancient Jerusalem was thus similar to what Hobsbawm describes as a "court" city. As the capital it was the only large Jewish city in Palestine, and it was also the religious center for worldwide Jewry. A large percentage of the city's population was economically dependent directly or indirectly on the political-religious administration and other religious apparatus centered in the Temple, and/or on the earlier Herodian royal administration. Hence there would have been a symbi-otic relationship (however tense at times) between client king or high-priestly establishment and the bulk of the populace. There is evidence, moreover, that the rulers in the city were sensitive to their role in providing employment or livelihood for the populace. During the prolonged drought and famine of 35/34 B.C.E., for example, the other-wise highly exploitative Herod went to considerable effort to supply grain from Egypt to the Jerusalemites (*Ant.* 15.299–308). Another illustration is the decision by the Jerusalem authorities, with the concurrence of King Agrippa II, to provide work paving the city with white stone for the several thousand workers who became unemployed when construction of the Temple was complete (*Ant.* 20.219–222).

It is not surprising, therefore, to find Josephus portraying Archelaus as eager to communicate with the crowd after his father Herod's funeral, as he anticipated becoming their ruler himself. Of course, since his tenure as the Romans' client king depended on his ability to rule effectively, he had additional motivation "to show himself kinder to them [the people] than his father had been" (*Ant.* 17.201–203,205; *War.* 2.3). At the outset, at least, Archelaus appeared sensitive to the concerns of the Jerusalem crowd. But as the protest escalated he became brutally repressive. The Roman governors, who lacked the symbiotic relationship of native ruler or ruling aristocracy with its people, were frequently insensitive and even provocative. The most extreme example was Florus, whose callous brutality touched off the great revolt in 66 C.E., according to Josephus (*War.* 2.277–283,293–332; see the end of chapter 2). Pontius Pilate came a close second, as we will see. In their own way, however, the Roman governors also took the crowd in Jerusalem seriously, especially at festival time when the Jerusalemites were joined by thousands of pilgrims from the towns and villages. Cumanus accordingly posted a cohort of troops on the porticoes of the Temple at Passover, as "had the previous procurators [governors] of Judea at the festivals" (*Ant.* 20.106–107; *War.* 2.223–224; cf. Mark 14:2).

The Jerusalem crowds appear to have been composed of the common people, the urban poor—except, as noted, at festival time. Josephus, who tends to label the participants "rebels," mentions no particular leadership from any special quarter such as the Pharisees or ordinary priests, in any of his reports of crowd activity. In the escalating outcry against Florus in 66, the ruling aristocratic groups were desperately attempting to disperse and/or calm the crowd; hence they were clearly not part of it (*War* 2.315–316,320–324). In the protest directed toward Archelaus one has even more of a sense of the crowd as the mass of the urban poor clamoring against their treatment by their rulers. This crowd in 4 B.C.E. even insisted on the removal of the most hated officials, particularly the high priest recently appointed by Herod (*Ant.* 17.204–207; *War* 2.4–7). That the participants in the first stage of the protests in 4 B.C.E. were urbanites, not peasants, is further evident from the type of taxes they objected to (*Ant.* 17.205; see below). In the second stage of these protests, of course, the composition of the crowd changed somewhat as people streamed in from the countryside for the Passover festival. The protest to Cumanus also occurred during the Passover; hence the crowd was probably composed of peasants and other pilgrims as well as the urban poor.

Even in the midst of this class conflict and despite the recent experience of Herod's tyranny one can discern the symbiosis of the Jerusalem crowd with its "king." The multitude was looking to Archelaus, its anticipated next king, as the symbol and dispenser of justice in the context of the traditional order. It apparently expected him to respond with some sort of remedial action. It is more difficult to discern what the crowd may have expected from the Roman governors, as in the outcry over the blasphemous insult by the Roman soldier under Cumanus. Judging from Josephus's report (*Ant.* 20.108) that the more vocal among the multitude were quick to cry out against Cumanus himself, perhaps they were simply moved by a sense of outrage.

The concerns of the Jerusalem crowd, like those of eighteenth-century European mobs, were clearly complex. In the protests to Archelaus, assuming we can trust Josephus's accounts, the crowd expressed some very basic economic and political grievances.

Some cried out that he should lighten the yearly [tribute] payments that they were making. Others demanded the release of the prisoners who had been put in chains by Herod—and there were many of these, and they had been in prison for a long time. Still others demanded the removal of the taxes that had been levied upon public purchases and sales and had been ruthlessly exacted. (*Ant.* 17.204–205; cf. *War* 2.4)

The crowd, however, was driven by the general hardships experienced under the Herodian tyranny. As we have seen, the recent martyrdom of those who had torn down the golden eagle vividly symbolized Herodian brutality and became the rallying cry of protesters.

They began a lamentation, bewailing the fate of those whom Herod had punished for cutting down the golden eagle from the gate of the Temple. ... There were piercing shrieks, a dirge directed by a conductor, and lamentations with beating of the breast which resounded throughout the city; all this in honor of the unfortunate men who, they asserted, had in defence of their country's laws and the Temple perished on the pyre. (War 2.5–6)

Parallel to eighteenth-century urban "riots" or social protests having become attached to political causes, the particular economic grievances and general frustration over Herodian tyranny had become attached to the religious-political cause. The martyrdom of the revered teachers and of their students was the symbol; the intense resentment over the prolonged Herodian abuses was the deeper motive (see further Ant. 17.211). It was articulated explicitly in the religious-political terms of the Jewish Law.

They demanded that they be avenged by Archelaus through the punishment of those men who had been honored by Herod, and that first of all and most publicly he remove the High Priest appointed by Herod and choose another man who could serve more in accordance with the Law and purity. (Ant. 17.207)

The motives of the spontaneous protest under Cumanus appear on the surface of things to be outrage over the insulting gesture by the Roman soldier.

On the fourth day of the festival, one of the soldiers uncovered his genitals and exhibited them to the multitude—an action which created anger and rage in the onlookers, who said that it was not they who had been insulted, but that it was a blasphemy against God. (Ant. 20.108)

The Jews had recently experienced extreme economic hardship, however, during the severe drought and famine of the late 40s. Hence we may suspect that a crowd composed of rural folk along with the urban poor at the festival celebrating their forefathers' liberation would have been unusually sensitive to any infringement on their religious celebration, the last bastion of their self-respect as a people now perpetually subject to foreign rule.

The Jerusalem crowd appears to have had an unusually high level of political awareness, even if it was not what one would nowadays call "revolutionary." Perhaps the Jews' experience of sharp Hellenistic and then Roman subjugation in recent generations, along with their periodic attempts to liberate themselves, had left a heritage of sharper political awareness. Although Josephus's reports of the protest under Cumanus give little or no indication of this, his more extensive narratives of the protests to Archelaus indicate that the crowd was critically aware of what concrete political-economic steps they wanted taken. They knew precisely how Herodian rule had been more than usually exploitative and repressive. Josephus also suggests that the "mob" in 4 B.C.E. produced its own leadership, who then continued to agitate the crowd and guide its focus and flow.

Yet by no means were the demands and actions of the Jerusalem crowd under either Archelaus or Cumanus revolutionary. The crowd made no challenge to the system, but simply to its abuses exemplified in tyranny or insult. In both cases the crowd initially appealed to (and not against) the ruler or governor himself to correct the abuses. When the rulers failed to act and the protest intensified, moreover, there was apparently no "radicalization" toward ousting the ruler, let alone rejecting the system. Indeed, in both cases there seems to have been long-continuing communication between the protesting crowd and the rulers until the rulers resorted to repression.

Nor was either of these urban protests especially violent. In the protest to Cumanus, Josephus mentions only in the *War,* not in the *Antiquities,* that some rebellious persons from the people "hurled stones at the troops" (*War* 2.225). Otherwise it was the massive show of military force by Cumanus that was responsible for the self-destructive panic of the crowd. Under Archelaus the prolonged protest had proceeded quite nonviolently until Archelaus panicked and sent in troops. Thus provoked, the infuriated crowd then rushed and stoned the soldiers, at which point Archelaus "sent out his whole army," which slaughtered the protesters (*Ant.* 17.215–218; *War* 2.11–13). In 4 B.C.E. the crowd kept up a nonviolent protest for several days before being provoked into a violent response to violent repression.

Although not itself a revolutionary challenge to the client kingship and imperial rule, the Jerusalem crowd's protest to Archelaus became a bridge to more revolutionary activity by the mass of peasants in the countryside, and prior to that by thousands of peasants who flooded into Jerusalem at the feast of Pentecost a few weeks after the Passover "riot" to besiege the hated Roman troops sent in to maintain order (*Ant.* 17.254–268,269–285; *War* 2.39–54,55–65; see end of chapter 2). In this sense the Jerusalem crowd's protest in 4 B.C.E. was a precursor of the crowd's massive protest against the abuses of Florus in the summer of 66, which helped to touch off widespread revolt in the countryside as well as in the city. Even in these cases, however, before the crowds were provoked by military attacks ordered by the rulers, their activities were no more than a sustained nonviolent outcry to the rulers against the abuses and injustices that they felt were no longer tolerable.

POPULAR PROTESTS

Most remarkable of all Jewish nonviolent resistance to Roman rule were the massive popular demonstrations that occurred just before or shortly after the ministry of Jesus. Among the issues evident in these protests, the most obvious is the consistently nonviolent character of Jewish resistance.[25] It is also noteworthy that these other protests assumed a form that went beyond the spontaneous riots of the Jerusalem crowd. Furthermore, a closer scrutiny of these popular protests raises serious questions about the traditional scholarly picture of the whole Jewish nation united in solidarity against the Roman abuses, with the priestly aristocracy or Herodian princes supposedly representing the concerns of the whole people.[26]

PROTESTS OVER THE ROMAN ARMY STANDARDS, THE AQUEDUCT, AND THE TORAH SCROLL

Ordinarily the Romans were careful to take into consideration the special religious sensitivities of the Jews in their administration of affairs in Palestine.[27] Toward the middle of the first century, however, several actions by the Romans provoked angry outbursts from the Jewish people. The first two major popular protests were responses to provocations by Pontius Pilate, who appears in Josephus's reports as a very different character from the one portrayed in the Gospels. The first provocation must have occurred shortly after Pilate took up his duties in Judea.

Pilate, being sent by Tiberius as governor to Judea, introduced into Jerusalem by night and under cover the images of Caesar which are called standards (c.f., "that were attached to the military standards; for our Law forbids the making of images..." *Ant.* 18.55). This proceeding, when day broke, aroused immense excitement among the Jews; those on the spot were in consternation, considering their laws to have been trampled under foot, as those laws permit no image to be erected in the city; meanwhile, stirred by indignation of the townspeople, the people from the countryside came together in crowds. Hastening after Pilate to Caesarea they implored him to remove the standards from Jerusalem and to uphold their ancestral practices. When Pilate refused, they fell prostrate around his residence and for five whole days and nights remained motionless in that position. On the ensuing [sixth] day Pilate took his seat on his tribunal in the great stadium and summoned the multitude. With the apparent intention of answering them, he gave the arranged signal to his armed soldiers to surround the Jews. Finding themselves in a ring of troops three deep, the Jews were struck dumb at this unexpected sight. Pilate, after threatening to cut them down if they refused to admit Caesar's images, signalled to the soldiers to draw their swords. Thereupon the Jews, as by concerted action, flung themselves in a body on the ground, extented their necks, and exclaimed that they were ready to die than to transgress the Law. Astonished at such intense devotion [*deisidaimonia*] Pilate gave orders for the immediate removal of the standards from Jerusalem. (*War* 2.169–174, adapted from the Loeb ed.; cf. *Ant.* 18.55–59)

Pilate himself was surely not the indecisive figure portrayed in the Christian Gospel tradition who let himself be manipulated by the Jewish high-priestly leaders and who washed his hands of important decisions. In his later account, the *Antiquities* (although not in the earlier *Jewish War*), Josephus suggests the provocation was intentional, "a bold step in subversion of the Jewish customs," a break with the practices of previous governors who used troops with standards that had no such images when they entered Jerusalem (*Ant.* 18.56). This event, moreover, must have occurred toward the beginning of Pilate's governorship in Judea, and may well have been inspired by the anti-

Jewish policy of Sejanus, Tiberius's close adviser in the years shortly before his death in 31 C.E.[28] On the other hand, the provocation may have been an unwitting action on the part of a newly appointed governor inadequately acquainted with the special sensitivities of the Jews. Like regular Roman legions, each unit of the auxiliary troops ordinarily stationed in Judea carried its own special standards (*sēmeia* in Greek, *signum* in Latin). On the standards of a legion or cohort of troops would have been images symbolic of its origins and occasionally of the emperor. Both kinds of images would have held religious and even cultic significance.[29] In other areas of the empire, however, there was great tolerance and pluralism in religious matters. Hence Pilate may simply have been sending to Jerusalem the military unit he had assigned for duty there without realizing the implications the standards would have held for this particular subordinate society.[30]

In both reports of the incident Josephus explains that it was concern over the violation of their laws that motivated the Jews to protest. Indeed, the mere presence of images of animals, let alone of Caesar, on the standards would have been a violation of key stipulations of the Decalogue (Exodus 20:4; Deuteronomy 5:8) and other passages in the Torah (Deuteronomy 4:16). Moreover, opposition to idolatry was a long-standing tradition in Jewish prophetic and sapiential teaching. The prohibition of any representation of living things was prominent even in Hellenistic Judaism (e.g., Philo, *de Gig.* 59; *de Ebr.* 109; *de Decal.* 66–67). Laws dealing specifically with images in the city of Jerusalem itself would hardly have been necessary, although some sages may well have formulated oral Torah concerning the holy city.[31]

The simple violation of their laws, however, would not appear to have provided motivation sufficiently intense to rouse masses of Jerusalemites and country people to such serious and prolonged protest. They had lived with such violation of their laws for more than a generation under Roman and Herodian rule. For example, the people had apparently put up with the golden eagle over the gate of the Temple for some time before the sages, believing Herod on the verge of death, finally exhorted their students to tear it down.[32] Similarly, although both the Jerusalem authorities and Galilean commoners finally took action to destroy the animal representations in the palace built by

Herod Antipas once the revolt had erupted in 66 C.E., they had tolerated such representations for decades (*Life* 65–66). It is apparent, then, that more than the simple violation of the Torah must have been involved as motivation for such a massive and prolonged protest.

It has been suggested that the religious significance of the standards and of the images attached may also have been a factor in the Jewish reaction.[33] That is, the images were not simply violations of the Torah, but held religious significance for the Roman soldiers that supposedly threatened or challenged the Jews' religious sensitivities. The standards and their images were *numina,* representative of the divinity of the unit that bore them. The comment of the later Christian writer Tertullian holds for the Roman army generally: "Among the Romans the whole of the soldier's religion is to venerate the standards, swear by the standards, set the standards before all the gods" (*Apology* 16.8 Loeb ed.). Thus the standards would have been objects of veneration for the soldiers as a regular part of the army's religion.[34] (Of course, one may also wonder just how aware the ordinary Jews were of the religious rites of the troops.) Bothersome and irritating as this may have been for the Jews, however, it is evident that they had put up with other actions and symbols of pagan worship in their midst for decades without such vociferous protests. As Josephus explained, from the time of Herod the Great there were temples and cultic representations of Caesar at numerous places throughout the land. Under the Roman governors, moreover, sacrifice for the emperor was conducted in the Jewish Temple. Objectionable as both the violation of the Torah and the observance of pagan religious rites were to the Jewish people, these may not be sufficient explanations of the massive protest against the standards.

The scope and intensity of the popular protest may be more understandable if the people took the soldiers' entry into Jerusalem with standards and images as a direct challenge to the ultimate sovereignty of their God. This insult would have seriously compounded the others: violation of the Torah and alien religious symbols.[35] Since the garrison in Jerusalem was quartered either in the Herodian palace, which was close to the Temple, or in the Antonia fortress, which immediately overlooked the Temple courtyard, the images of Caesar would have been brought into close and threatening proximity to the sacred precincts, *the* places holy to God. We can better appreciate the potential challenge to Jewish devotion to God by looking ahead to what happened in 70 C.E. in a religiously symbolic celebration of the final Roman conquest of Jerusalem. "The Romans, now that the rebels had fled to the city and the sanctuary itself and all around it were in flames, carried their standards into the Temple court and, setting them up opposite the eastern gate, there sacrificed to them, and with rousing acclamations hailed Titus as *imperator*" (*War* 6.316). This action held ominous religious-political significance: "the divinities of the legion [and of Caesar!] have conquered the God of the Jews, and in token of their triumph receive the soldiers' homage in God's sacred precincts."[36]

The intensity of the Jewish reaction to the army standards is more comprehensible if understood in a parallel connection. That is, the vivid visible representation of the Roman military sovereignty over the Jews in close proximity to the Temple was a direct and highly threatening challenge to their God, the symbol of their ultimate loyalty and their hope for eventual freedom from the Romans. That there was a strong anti-Roman motive in the protest may also be indicated by the overly strong emphasis in Josephus's narratives on the Jewish multitude's concern about the violation of its customs. As both apologist for the Jews and friend of his patron, the Roman imperial court, Josephus apparently attempted to conceal the anti-Roman aspect of the protest by emphasizing the Jews' concern about their ancestral traditions.[37]

The demonstration against the provocative entry into Jerusalem was clearly a popular protest. In the *Jewish War* Josephus refers explicitly to the crowds of "people from the countryside," who can hardly have been gentry. Even without that explicit reference, however, we could deduce with a high degree of certainty that this was a popular protest. Josephus makes no mention either of members of the priestly aristocracy (or of Herodians, for that matter) nor of scholar-teachers as being involved. This cannot simply be explained as Josephus's avoidance of such references for apologetic reasons, for as we have seen, he does not hesitate to mention the sage-teachers or Pharisees who led the earlier protests against the golden eagle and the Roman tribute. Moreover, not only would such spontaneous and demonstrative behavior be uncharacteristic of the Jewish aristocracy; it would also be highly out of character for a Roman governor to treat native aristocrats in the cavalier manner in which Pilate treated these demonstrators. That the later governor Florus threatened to harm and even killed members of the Jewish aristocracy was utterly shocking to upper-class Jews such as Josephus. Only common people were handled so brutally. If the native aristocracy failed to control their people, they were sent to give account of themselves in Rome, as when the Syrian legate Quadratus sent members of both the Judean and the Samaritan aristocracy to Rome (along with the governor) after the border conflicts under Cumanus (*War* 2.232–244). The Jewish demonstrators whom Pilate threatened with such violence were almost certainly common people.

The protest also appears to have been spontaneous in origin yet disciplined in execution. Word of the entry of troops with images of Caesar into Jerusalem apparently spread quickly through the country-side (*War* 2.170). One might surmise that most of those aroused must have come from northwestern Judea, perhaps from along the route that the Roman cohort had just taken in their march to Jerusalem under orders from the newly appointed governor. It is unusual, in the annals of protests, for demonstrators to travel so far. The demonstrators were especially impressive for their discipline in maintaining their vigil in orderly and nonviolent fashion. There must have been no serious flare-up of violent outrage, or Pilate would have sent in the military to terminate the demonstration around his official residence. It is extremely difficult for any group of demonstrators to sustain its morale and to avoid falling back into the usual pattern of fear about repression, which results in submission—which in turn would result in a continuation of the objectionable action.[38]

When Pilate had the demonstrators suddenly surrounded by his troops with arms at the ready, the Jews' response surprised Pilate himself. Summoning an even higher degree of fearlessness and discipline than in the previous five days and nights, the protestors offered their necks to the soldiers' drawn swords in solidarity of passive resistance.[39] Rather than follow through with a bloody massacre, Pilate ordered the images removed from Jerusalem. In this case, at least, the highly disciplined and sustained nonviolent popular protest was successful. The objectives of the protesting crowd had been limited. The demonstration had never posed a serious threat to the governor. And by making the concessions they demanded, Pilate both maintained his authority and restored public order.[40]

A very similar popular protest over twenty years later under Cumanus (48–52) provides an exemplary illustration of popular nonviolent Jewish response to an intensification of the spiral of violence by the Romans. When some Jewish brigands attacked an imperial servant and his baggage train near Bethhoron, Cumanus sent troops on a punitive expedition into the nearby villages "with orders to bring up the inhabitants to him in chains" for not having pursued the bandits (*War* 2.228–229; *Ant.* 20.113–114). In the course of sacking one of the villages, a soldier destroyed a Torah scroll.

On first announcement of the news [the Jews] hurried in a body to Cumanus at Caesarea, and implored him not to leave unpunished the author of such an outrage on God and on their Law. The governor, seeing that the multitude would not be pacified unless they obtained satisfaction, thought fit to call out the soldier and ordered him to be led to execution through the ranks of his accusers. On this the Jews withdrew. (*War* 2.230–231)

As with the demonstration against the Roman standards, this protest over the destruction of the Torah was a spontaneous and widespread outcry by the common people, with no apparent involvement on the part of any high-priestly leadership. In contrast to the recent Roman violent reprisal against the peasant villages, in the course of which the outrage had occurred, the popular protest was disciplined and nonviolent. The fact that Josephus made no comment on how long the demonstration was sustained before Cumanus executed the offending soldier probably means that it lasted only a short while. For whatever reason, Cumanus, in contrast to his behavior in two other cases mentioned by Josephus, gave the protesters satisfaction.

A second major popular protest against action by Pilate was less successful because immediately and brutally suppressed by the governor. This protest was provoked by Pilate's use of the Temple treasury. The shorter of Josephus's two accounts says:

On a later occasion he provoked a fresh uproar by expending upon the construction of an aqueduct the sacred treasure known as *Corbonas;* the water was brought from a distance of 400 furlongs [200 in *Ant.* 18.60]. Indignant at this proceeding, the populace formed a ring round the tribunal of Pilate, then on a visit to Jerusalem, and besieged him with angry clamour. He, foreseeing the tumult, had had interspersed among the crowd a troop of his soldiers, armed but disguised in civilian dress, with orders not to use their swords, but to beat any rioters with cudgels. He now from his tribunal gave the agreed signal. Large numbers of the Jews perished, some from the blows which they received, others trodden to death by their companions in the ensuing flight. Cowed by the fate of the victims, the multitude was reduced to silence. (*War* 2.175–177)

In both accounts, Josephus indicates that the crowd was protesting Pilate's use of funds from the Temple treasury for construction of the aqueduct. It is not immediately obvious why people should be so incensed over this expenditure of Temple resources for a project potentially serving the common good. Temple funds derived from taxation of the people and gifts had traditionally been used for projects that benefited Jerusalemites generally, as well as for support of the cultic functions of the Temple establishment.[41] For example, Temple funds had been used to fund the reconstruction and repairs on the Temple begun by Herod and continued for several decades after his death. When work on the Temple was finally completed in the early 60s, the treasury supplied funds to have part of the city paved with stones (*Ant.* 20.219–222). (This is another indication that the Temple was not simply a religious institution but, equally important, a political and economic one.) The Temple funds, moreover, were under the oversight and perhaps the supervision of the Roman governors during the first few decades of direct Roman rule (from 6 to 41 C.E.) and thereafter were under the supervision of Rome's client rulers such as Agrippa II, who had to approve the expenditure for the paving of the city.[42] Thus Pilate may not have been completely unprecedented or out of line with Roman policy in his appropriation of Temple funds for such a public project as the aqueduct. The Roman governors in the early decades, moreover, had in their keeping in the Antonia fortress the sacred vestments worn by the high priest in the major cultic celebrations (*Ant.* 18.90–94). Hence the appropriation of Temple funds may have been viewed as an extension of the Roman oversight of Temple affairs generally.

In any case, just as the governors' jurisdiction over the sacred vestments necessarily involved close cooperation between the governor and the Jewish high-priestly leaders, so this appropriation of Temple funds involved the cooperation of the high priests, in particular the Temple treasurer(s).[43] If Pilate had stepped in to seize Temple funds against the strong objections of the high-priestly establishment, Josephus would have been reporting an incident of a very different kind. Though some high priests may have cooperated reluctantly, Pilate and the officiating high priest, Caiaphas, must have been on generally good terms: both served relatively long terms in office—unlikely if they had run into serious conflict with each other. Thus it may not be altogether obvious why the Jewish people should become so agitated over Pilate's procedure in this case of the aqueduct.

Probing Josephus's reports a bit further, however, may somewhat elucidate the crowd's concern. In the earlier *Jewish War,* though not in the later *Antiquities,* Josephus indicates that Pilate had used funds from "the sacred treasury known as the Corbonas." The Corban was a fund of *shekalim* contributed especially for purchase of sacrifical animals. The construction of an aqueduct must have been a major and costly project. Thus even if Pilate used primarily general Temple revenues, he apparently drew also on the special Corban fund. Thus the people's sensitivity about the expropriation of this special fund devoted to sacrifices may explain why they were moved to a massive outcry.[44]

This protest over the use of the sacred treasury, like that against the army standards, was basically a popular demonstration. Josephus uses the term *plēthos,* a "crowd" or "multitude" of the protesters, and makes no mention of paricipation by aristocracy, royalists, or scribe-teachers. Surely the priestly aristocracy would not have been involved since, however reluctantly, they must have cooperated in this use of the Temple treasury. However much Josephus tends to exaggerate, his "tens of thousands" (*Ant.* 18.60) nevertheless indicates that this was a large demonstration. The protest would not have been completely "spontaneous," for once the word spread that Pilate was traveling to Jerusalem there was time for large numbers of aroused protesters from the countryside as well as Jerusalemites to assemble in the city. This protest thus appears to be another deliberate and disciplined demonstration rather than simply the urban crowd's reacting spontaneously to a sudden provocation.

In contrast with his procedure on the demonstration over the Roman standards in Caesarea, this time Pilate did not give the protesters any chance to organize and sustain nonviolent resistance. He struck quickly as well as violently. The Jewish demonstrators, recoiling under the soldiers' blows, could not maintain group discipline, and panic set in, ending the demonstration.

THE MOTIVE OF OFFICIAL PROTESTS

To these two popular protests against Pilate's actions we should compare two other protests. The source for the first is the Alexandrian philosopher Philo's apologetic treatise the *Legatio ad Gaium.*

[Pilate] . . . not so much to honor Tiberias as to annoy the multitude, dedicated in Herod's palace in the holy city some shields coated with gold. They had no image work traced on them nor anything else forbidden by the law. But when the multitude understood the matter, . . . having put at their head the king's [Herod's] four sons . . . and his other descendants and the persons of authority in their own body, they appealed to Pilate to redress the infringement of their traditions caused by the shields and not to disturb the customs which throughout all the preceding ages had been safeguarded without disturbance by the kings and emperors. When he . . . stubbornly refused, they clamoured, "Do not arouse sedition, do not make war, do not destroy the peace. . . . The magnates sent letters of very earnest supplication to Tiberias. When he had read them through . . . he wrote to Pilate . . . with rebukes . . . and bade him at once take down the shields and have them transferred from the capital to Caesarea on the coast to be set up in the temple of Augustus, and so they were. (*Leg.* 299–305)

Despite any superficial similarities, this is clearly an event different from the popular protest over the introduction of the images of Caesar into Jerusalem. There is no common core to the event reported by Philo and that recounted by Josephus. Moreover, there are too many differences between the stories in particular aspects. The appeal to the emperor Tiberias indicates that this was a high-level protest. Such an appeal would hardly have been characteristic of the common multitude, but would have been the route followed by native ruling groups. In comparison with the massive six-day-long demonstration in Caesarea, the protest described by Philo appears as a minor event happening somewhat behind the scenes. Josephus the historian apparently does not deem it worthy of inclusion in either of his accounts; Philo the apologist uses it for rhetorical, almost philippic, purposes.[45] Chronologically, whereas the protest over the Roman standards with Caesar's images took place soon after Pilate's assumption of his duties (December, 26 C.E.), the appeal of the dedication of the imageless shields apparently happened after the death of Sejanus, the anti-Semitic adviser of Tiberias and one-time patron of Pilate. The fall of Sejanus, which brought about a dramatic change in Roman policy toward the Jews, would have provided the motive for Pilate's dedication of the shields in honor of Tiberias. As a friend and protégé of Sejanus, he needed to demonstrate his loyalty directly to Tiberias once Sejanus's policies had fallen into disfavor at the imperial court.[46]

Philo's apologetic point in recounting the incident is clearly to emphasize the extreme sensitivity of the Jews over infringement of their ancestral laws. Nevertheless, allowing for considerable rhetorical flourish and exaggeration by Philo, it remains that there was little or no reason for Jewish objection to the shields: "no image work . . . nor anything else forbidden by law." One cannot help but suspect that the ruling groups intervened with Pilate because of the actual or potential reaction by the common people with which they had become familiar from the earlier massive protests over the army standards and over the expropriation of the sacred treasury for construction of the aqueduct. That is, either the common people were restless over Pilate's dedication of the shields to the emperor, or else the Jewish ruling groups were apprehensive that they might become so.

The second protest by Jewish ruling groups took place soon after the removal of Pilate from office. Vitellius, the legate of Syria, proceeding to war against Aretas in Arabia, "had started to lead his army through the land of Judaea, [but] the Jews of the highest standing went to meet him and entreated him not to march through their land. For, they said, it was contrary to their tradition to allow images, of which there were many attached to military standards, to be brought upon their soil. Yielding to their entreaty, he abandoned his original plan and ordered his army to march through the Great Plain . . ." (*Ant.* 18.121–122). The issue is familiar. The principal officials of the Jews had learned from the massive popular outcry a decade earlier just how sensitive their people could be to the presence of imperial images in their territory. The prudent Vitellius, no doubt also aware of the importance of keeping his border provinces calm while campaigning on the Arabian frontier, cooperated fully with the Jewish ruling groups (including Antipas, whose palace decor violated the very laws he now seemed so concerned to protect!) in taking careful measures to pacify the Jewish people (*Ant.* 18.122–124).

The high priests and the Herodians apparently did not lead, let alone join, the initial protests over Roman abuses of their people's religious sensitivities. Only when they realized—in the wake of the massive popular demonstrations—the potential for disruption of the social order, with the resultant threat to their own position in the imperial system, did they begin to use their influence behind the scenes to ensure that potential new provocations did not touch off further popular unrest. Their very position in the imperial situation thus determined their mediating role between their people and the Roman officials.[47]

PROTEST OVER GAIUS'S STATUE

Gaius (Caligula) was the first Roman emperor actively to seek divine honors from his subjects. Most peoples of the empire readily responded. The Jews were the principal hold-outs, and this became an occasion for anti-Jewish attacks in some locations. In Alexandria in particular, the Jews' refusal to honor Gaius became the rallying point on which popular abuse and official persecution focused. In Philo's account of his "embassy to Gaius" he mentions also Jew-Gentile conflict in Jamnia. Collusion between the Gentile minority of the city and a Roman official named Capito brought an exaggerated accusation against the Jews for not according Gaius divine honors. This, according to Philo, became the immediate occasion for Gaius's order to erect a statue of Zeus with his own features in the Jewish Temple in Jerusalem. Both Philo's and Josephus's accounts, however, that the underlying

motive was Gaius's desire for divine honors and the celebrated case of
the Alexandrian Jews' refusal to so honor him had come not only to
the emperor's attention but directly to his hearing-chamber. It is most
useful to follow Josephus's account in the *Antiquities* (18.261–288,
adapted from Loeb ed.) of the major confrontation between Jews and
Roman imperial might prior to the great revolt of 66–70.[48]

Indignant at being so slighted by the Jews alone, Gaius dispatched
Petronius as his legate

> to Syria . . . with orders to lead a large force into Judea and, if the Jews
> consented to receive him, to set up an image of Gaius in the Temple of God.
> If, however, they were obstinate, he was to subdue them by force of arms and
> so set it up. . . . Gathering as many auxiliaries as possible, he marched at the
> head of two legions of the Roman army to Ptolemais, intending to spend the
> winter there and towards spring to engage in war without fail. . . . Meanwhile
> many tens of thousands of Jews came to Petronius at Ptolemais with petitions
> not to use force to make them transgress and violate their ancestral code. (*Ant.*
> 18.261–263) . . . Now Petronius saw from their words that their spirit was
> not easily to be put down and that it would be impossible for him without
> a battle to carry out Gaius's request and set up his image. Indeed, there would
> be great slaughter. Hence he gathered up his friends and attendants and
> hastened to Tiberias, for he wished to take note of the situation of the Jews
> there. As before many tens of thousands faced Petronius on his arrival at
> Tiberias. . . . "Will you then go to war with Caesar . . . ?" said Petronius.
> "On no account would we fight," they said, "but we will die sooner than
> violate our laws." And falling on their faces and baring their throats, they
> declared that they were ready to be slain. They continued to make these
> supplications for forty days. Furthermore, they neglected their fields, and that,
> though it was time to sow the seed. . . . (*Ant.* 18.269–272) At this juncture
> Aristobulus, the brother of King Agrippa, together with Helcias the Elder and
> other most powerful members of this house, together with the highest ranking
> men (*hoi protoi*), appeared before Petronius and appealed to him . . . not to
> incite the [people] to desperation but to write to Gaius telling how incurable
> was their opposition to receiving the statue and how they had left their fields
> to sit protesting, and that they did not choose war, since they could not fight
> a war, but would be glad to die sooner than transgress their customs. Let him
> point out that, since the land was unsown, there would be a harvest of
> banditry, because the requirements of tribute could not be met. . . .

(*Ant.* 18.273–274) [After agreeing to write to Gaius and not to proceed with the installation of Gaius's statues in the Temple, Petronius] requested those in authority to attend to agricultural matters and to conciliate the people with optimistic propaganda. (*Ant.* 18.284)

There are a number of differences between this account in the *Antiquities* and the earlier account in the *Jewish War,* and there are major discrepancies between Josephus's accounts and Philo's rhetorical embellishment of these crucial events.[49] Most of the serious discrepancies or variants, however, concern either the efforts toward diplomatic mediation in Rome by Agrippa I and in Tiberias by other members of Jewish ruling groups or the communications between Petronius and Gaius. However, there is basic agreement between our sources regarding the apparent motive of the Jewish protest against Gaius's highly provocative action, the massive scope of popular resistance and, in particular, the sustained peasant strike. Moreover, even the variant accounts of the ruling groups' lobbying efforts indicate how ineffectual their role was apart from the massive popular action and the serious economic threat it posed both to themselves and to the Roman officials.

Ultimately a more serious confrontation and widespread bloodshed were avoided because Gaius was assassinated in January of 41. Apart from that, Philo and Josephus agree that Agrippa successfully intervened with his friend Gaius to back away from his plan to install the statue in the Temple by military force. The two authors agree, moreover, that Petronius as well had reached the decision that he could not follow through in executing Gaius's original orders, whatever penalty he might suffer. How had he come to that decision?

On the assumptions frequently made that the high priests stood at the head of a united Jewish nation and that, as the custodians of the Temple as well as leaders of the people, they would have found Gaius's plan a matter of gravest concern, one would expect the high priests immediately to have led a protest to Petronius and the emperor. In fact Josephus mentions the role of particularly influential high-priestly leaders, such as the former high priest Jonathan, in other contexts (*War* 2.240,243; *Ant.* 19.313–316). Yet in this case, neither Jonathan nor the current high priest, Theophilus, "stands out as a leader of the successful

Jewish opposition to the sacrilege—which is surprising. . . ."[50] The fact that, even when faced with so formidable a threat to the religion of which they were the supposed guardians, the leading high-priestly figures did not head the protest, may be less surprising when we examine Philo's and Josephus's reports more carefully.

According to Philo's account, one of Petronius's first steps upon receiving Gaius's orders was to summon "the officers of the Jews, both [high] priests and magistrates, partly to explain Gaius's intentions and partly to advise them to accept the orders of their lord and master" (*Leg.* 222). These representatives of the ruling aristocracy, however, did not protest so much as simply lament the anticipated calamity (*Leg.* 223–224). Nor should Philo's report be surprising at this point, for the Jewish high priests and magistrates were in a compromised and somewhat helpless position, given their role in the imperial system. As Philo suggests, Petronius assumed that the ruling aristocracy could be depended upon to influence the rest of the population to acquiesce in Gaius's plan. The contrast with the Jewish aristocracy is striking when Philo relates the bold and dramatic popular reaction:

While they [the ruling aristocracy] were thus lamenting, the inhabitants of the holy city and the rest of the countryside hearing what was afoot marshalled themselves as if at a single signal . . . and issued forth in a body leaving cities, villages, and houses empty and in one onrush sped to Petronius in Phoenicia. (*Leg.* 225)

While officials lamented, the people organized; so writes even the sophisticated and aristocratic Alexandrian Jewish theologian.

Josephus records no prior consultation by Petronius with the Jewish officials, but only conferences with Herodians and other Jewish officials after the popular protest was well underway. When Josephus does have them speak to Petronius, they focus on the grave economic implications of the popular protest. Their role is that of mediators between the Roman rulers and their Jewish subjects. One gets the impression from Josephus's reports that the popular protest began before the Jewish aristocracy and Herodians became involved and that it was the popular protest (and not Gaius's order itself) that brought them into consultation with Petronius in the first place.

This protest against Gaius's plan to install a statue of himself in the Jewish Temple was clearly the largest, most widespread popular outcry during the whole period from the imposition of direct Roman rule until the outbreak of the great revolt in 66. The occasion for the massive protest was the most provocative action the Romans had yet taken in governing the Jews. The threat the Jews felt to their way of life was similar to that posed by the Romans' standards with the images of Caesar attached. This time the challenge was both more blatant and more direct and even threatened to invade the most sacred space of Jewish society, the Temple sanctuary itself. As in the case of the army standards, Josephus (like Philo) emphasizes the violation of the law. This repeated emphasis in our sources, particularly in the speeches placed in the mouths of the Jews, derives from Josephus's and Philo's concern to make the Jews appear politically loyal to Caesar and Rome (e.g., *War* 2.197; *Leg.* 230–232). Behind our sources' apologetic emphasis, however, lay a serious religious-political conflict rooted in the structural contradictions inherent in the imperial situation of Roman Palestine. By and large the Palestinian Jewish people had been realistic politically and had submitted to Roman rule. Yet there remained a potential resistance point, one that appears at the religious level but is not separable from the political dimension of the whole imperial situation. The plan to install a statue of Gaius in the Temple sanctuary brought Caesar's rule directly into confrontation with God's ultimate rule, indeed seemed totally to replace the rule of God with that of Caesar claiming to be a god.

According to all accounts, the popular protests over Gaius's bold plan were spontaneous and massive. Upon hearing of the expedition headed by Petronius to install the image of Caesar, the Jewish populace responded immediately. "Many tens of thousands" from the whole countryside flocked to confront Petronius and his legions at Ptolemais (*Leg.* 225–226; *Ant.* 18.263). Similarly, large crowds greeted him when he went inland to Tiberias (*Ant.* 18.271). Even allowing for exaggeration by our apologetic sources, the numbers were extensive, apparently including a sizeable proportion of the peasantry in the regions near Ptolemais and in Galilee closer to Tiberias. Whole families left their homes to join the demonstrations. Assuming that some had come even from Judea itself, the journey was much farther and more complicated than that involved in previous protests to the Roman governors Pilate and Cumanus in Caesarea.

According to some reconstructions of these events, an armed revolt by the Jews was imminent, some of the demonstrators having already taken up arms.[51] There is no solid evidence for this supposition. The only passage that mentions the possibility of a Jewish revolt (*Leg.* 215–217) consists of Philo's imaginative projection of what Petronius may have been thinking in debating with himself how to respond to Gaius's order. Josephus's references to "war" are to Gaius's policy (*War* 2.275) or to the war that the Roman forces might have to wage against a resistant Jewish people (*War* 2.287,295). Of course, the Romans may have believed that the Jews were about to take arms in resistance.[52] But the Jewish apologetic sources, Philo and especially Josephus, emphasize that the multitudes of Jews protesting were absolutely unarmed and nonviolent in their behavior throughout. "Slay us first. . . . We shall patiently endure . . . whatever the risks," say the Jews (*Ant.* 18.264,267,269). When Petronius asked, "Will you go to war with Caesar?" the Jewish protesters exclaim, "On no account would we fight, but we will die sooner than violate our laws" (*Ant.* 18.271). Josephus also has the Herodian Aristobulus emphasize that the Jewish protesters "had not chosen war, since they could not fight a war, but would be glad to die rather than transgress their customs" (*Ant.* 18.274). He also mentions that a "harvest of banditry" might result from the protest if prolonged much further. Banditry in this case refers not to some sort of "resistance movement" but to ordinary "social banditry," which often results from economic hardship and social dislocation. Even if we were tempted to explain away all these references to the Jewish protesters' nonviolence and readiness to die in pacifist resistance to Gaius's plan as simply Josephus's (and Philo's) apologetic rhetoric, nothing in our sources suggests that any Jewish revolt was imminent or that the demonstrations were in any way violent.

The protest over Gaius's statue in the Temple was not simply massive, involving tens of thousands of Jewish common people, but it was prolonged as well, not simply for days but for weeks. Even if the forty or fifty days mentioned by the sources are exaggerations, the people sustained their protest demonstrations for a remarkably long period of time. Had the protest not been during the agricultural cycle, it might have had little or no effect on the Jewish ruling groups and Petronius. According to both Josephus and Philo, however, the protest occurred during the agricultural cycle, and that is what made all the difference to both the Jewish and the Roman rulers of the society.

Thus, the prolonged protest demonstrations were also, in effect, a massive *peasant strike*. [53] Many of the protesters, including whole families, had abandoned their homes in order to resist the implementation of Gaius's plan to erect his statue in the Temple. In the course of demonstrating against the Roman advance far from their villages, of course, "they neglected their fields, though it was time to sow the seed" (*Ant.* 18.272). Moreover, their having "left their fields to sit protesting" (*Ant.* 18.272) must have been a deliberate and intentional "strike" by the Jewish peasants, for it involved a life-threatening economic risk on the part of the always-marginal peasantry.

Furthermore, both Josephus and Philo—and, according to them, both the Jewish ruling groups and the Romans—were fully aware of the effects of the Jewish peasant strike. "Since the land remained unsown, there would be a harvest of banditry, because the requirement of tribute could not be met" (*Ant.* 18.272). In Josephus's account, when Petronius finally discerns the economic "handwriting on the wall" etched by the prolonged Jewish peasant strike, he is at pains to get the agricultural cycle finally rolling again: "Go, therefore, each to your own occupation, and labor on the land," he says to the thousands of demonstrators. And he further "requested the officials and magistrates to attend to agricultural matters and to conciliate the people with optimistic propaganda" (*Ant.* 18.282–284). The extensive and prolonged popular demonstrations and strike proved a successful nonviolent means of persuading a high Roman official to desist from a deliberately provocative course of action that would have dramatically escalated the spiral of violence.

SUMMARY REFLECTIONS

It would seem clear that we can put behind us the picture of Jewish society at the time of Jesus as a hotbed of violent rebellion. If there had been any "Zealots" of the sort previously imagined, we would expect that they would have been highly visible in response to provocations such as Pilate's introduction of the army standards and Gaius's intention of placing his bust in the Temple. But far from there having been any "Zealots" around, there was apparently no indication of the propensity toward violence that has often been projected upon first-century Jewish society. Indeed, in the period between the widespread popular rebellions following the death of Herod in 4 B.C.E. and the great revolt in 66–70 C.E., the only occurrence of violent resistance was the terrorism of the Sicarii directed against their own high priests. Otherwise the Jewish resistance to Roman rule throughout the period, whether the two actions led by scholar-teachers in 4 B.C.E. and 6 C.E., the protests of the Jerusalem crowd or the wider popular demonstrations, was fundamentally nonviolent.

Moreover, aside from the two earlier actions led by intellectuals, Jewish protests against Roman provocations during the first century were largely spontaneous expressions of concern by the common people. Insofar as the high-priestly aristocracy and Herodian princes became involved at all, they played a mediating role. They appear to have stepped into that role, moreover, either only after numbers of their people had already generated a sizeable and serious demonstration, or in anticipation of the people's potential expression of concern. In cases of the images on the Roman standards and the expropriation of sacred Temple funds for the aqueduct, there is no indication of involvement by the ruling groups at all. In contrast with his earlier accounts of the toppling of the golden eagle and the "tax-resistance" led by the Fourth Philosophy—and also with his account of the outbreak of the revolt decades later—Josephus also makes no mention of the involvement of any intellectuals such as "sage-teachers" or "Pharisees." Far from being the organized expression of a nation united in its religious and/or political concerns, these Jewish anti-Roman protests were spontaneous demonstrations generated and, apparently, organized in remarkably self-disciplined fashion by the ordinary people.

In order to appreciate how the common people, largely peasants from the countryside, can mobilize such massive protests spontaneously and quickly, it may be useful to cite a comparative case. Although the social structure, economic system, and issue are rather different, one of the cases of *taxation populaire* from eighteenth-century France may provide an instructive parallel of rapid spontaneous mass mobilization by the common people. *Taxation populaire* is what the French called the imposition of an unofficial price control by collective popular action when grain and bread prices increased to unacceptable levels. Following a poor harvest the previous year, the price of bread had nearly doubled during April 1775. The government, meanwhile, did nothing to alleviate the problem. Appealing to precedent and to ancient custom, the common people finally invaded the market and compelled dealers to sell their wheat, and bakers to sell their bread, at a "just" or reasonable (the customary) price. To cite some of the aspects of the popular French protest of 1775 that appear parallel to the mass mobilization of the Jewish people against the Roman standards and/or Gaius's statue in the Temple: the French protesters were the common people from villages and towns acting, without official leadership or suggestion, as a spontaneous expression of popular alarm; the protest spread from village to village, town to town by force of example as well as by local initiative; and, starting from a town twenty miles north of Paris, the protests spread to other towns and villages as far as sixty to eighty miles away within a week's time.[54] This one striking comparative example is perhaps sufficient to illustrate how it is possible that the Jewish peasantry, along with some people from Jerusalem, could have come together in crowds and traveled the considerable distance to Caesarea to besiege Pilate over the Roman standards or could have flocked from Judea and Galilee together in massive demonstrations against Petronius at Ptolemais and Tiberias.

The popular Jewish nonviolent protests met with at least limited success in the context of the imperial situation and spiral of violence in Roman Palestine. Because of the Roman imperial system and governing practices, the popular nonviolent Jewish demonstrations evoked repressive violence, either actual or potential. In the cases of the sustained demonstrations against the Roman standards and the statue of Gaius, however, Pilate and Petronius, although they had deadly force ready to strike at their command, were persuaded not to carry out the inevitable massacres that would have ensued. It may be possible to analyze, albeit somewhat speculatively, the likely dynamics of the situation created for Pilate and Petronius by the large sustained popular demonstrations.

The massive and spontaneous character of the popular reaction over both the Roman standards and the emperor's statue dramatized vividly how much "authority" the emperor and/or his representatives had lost —or had never really possessed—among the Jewish populace. With every passing day of the sustained protests the authority of the Roman imperial rule eroded further in Palestinian society. In protest over the installation of Gaius's image in the Temple, moreover, the prolonged agricultural strike began seriously to threaten the Roman political power. It must have been increasingly distressing to Petronius and other Roman officials on the scene that they could no longer presume upon the habitual obedience and cooperation of this subject people to play their expected political-economic role as producers, which enabled the imperial system to operate and served to maintain the Romans and their client Jewish ruling groups in their dominant positions. Petronius was faced not only with problems of "enforcement" but with the potential disappearance of the usual economic support of Roman rule as well. As indicated in our sources—and as often happens in strikes and boy-cotts—it was the economic pressure exerted by the peasant strike that moved Petronius to seek some sort of accommodation with the multi-tudes of common people who had "left their fields to sit protesting."[55]

Reflection upon modern campaigns of nonviolent direct action have made us aware of ways in which nonviolent demonstrations such as these popular Jewish protests may have affected government officials such as Pilate or Petronius.[56] By no means are such nonviolent demonstrations always successful. Certainly, few such protests result in the "conversion" of the officials or rulers. However, disciplined nonviolent protesters, by controlling themselves, can also control the conflict in a certain way. Because the protesters maintain their own balance, the adversary can be thrown off balance by his own unretaliated thrust, and the protesters can even help him to regain his balance in a moral sense. Moreover, by their disciplined refusal either to flee or to fight, the demonstrators can communicate a gesture of trust and confidence to the adversary, who is thus invited to reciprocate. By their controlled and massive action the demonstrators show that they are secure in their strength, that they can themselves channel and set limits upon its use, and thus that they are in control of the situation. Through their massive but controlled action and limited demands the nonviolent demonstrators show the adversary that they are potentially cooperative persons seeking a change of policy or conditions to which the adversary can respond—but also that they are capable of action that would deepen and prolong the conflict.

In reconstructions of Jewish history of late second Temple times these protests are often characterized as religious or as protests over religious issues. This presents us with an ironic set of historical circumstances. If the threats to Jewish society posed by the Roman actions involved were basically "religious," then we would expect to find the Jewish "religious" leaders leading the protests. Yet the highest officials of the Temple cult, which was supposedly directly threatened in the cases of the Roman standards and the statue of Gaius, apparently did not protest prominently. Nor, in contrast to the golden eagle protest in 4 B.C.E. and the tax-resistance of 6 C.E., does Josephus mention involvement by any Pharisees or teachers of the Jewish Law. Perhaps this should lead us to loosen somewhat the attachment of our concept of religion to its institutional expression (Temple cult) and to reconnect it with other dimensions of the people's lives.

In any case, the religious dimension of life by no means should be isolated from other dimensions. Much attention has been devoted to the particular religious sensitivities of the Jews and their violation by the Romans. However, this focus on the particular prima facie religious issues involved may divert attention from deeper tensions, even structural conflicts, and the resultant concrete distress of which the religious protests were the expression. The popular Jewish protests were not artificial events. It was not the provocations by Pilate or by Gaius but rather extensive and prolonged resistance of Jewish common people that made the events and made them pivotal in the history of Palestinian Jewish society. The particular religious issues and the provocations that occasioned the popular protests and especially the massive protests themselves were expressions of the larger and deeper conflict between Roman imperial rule and the subject Jewish people who still remembered and celebrated their ancestors' liberation from Pharaoh's bondage.

5. Apocalyptic Orientation and Historical Action

A religious ideology of "zeal" for God and the Torah inspired the supposedly violent Jewish resistance to Roman rule in the first-century C.E., according to standard treatments in Jewish history and New Testament studies. The recent demise of the old "Zealots" concept, however, suggests that the ideal of zeal should also be critically reexamined. Apocalyptic vision of God's imminent redemptive action may provide a more credible explanation for the motivation of Jewish resistance. But the scholarly understanding of apocalypticism will itself require some critical review before the pertinence of apocalyptic visions to that resistance can be adequately assessed.

THE IDEAL OF ZEAL: MODERN RECONSTRUCTION VS. HISTORICAL REALITY

Consistent with their fundamentally idealist orientation, the fields of biblical studies and religious history understand ideas, especially religious ideas and divine inspiration, as the motive force of historical action. The history of first-century C.E. Jewish society leading up to the great Jewish revolt is thus logically explained in terms of the ideal of zeal leading to the formation of the Zealot party that eventually took zealous action. "Zeal," according to the standard conception, was a passion not simply for the internal purity of the Jewish people according to the Torah, but also for freedom from alien rule. The ideal of "zeal for the Law" was developed during the Maccabean revolt in conjunction with Old Testament models, Phinehas and Elijah. Then when Rome took over direct rule of Judea and conducted the census, "Judas the Galilean rekindled this ideal of 'zeal on behalf of the Law'. The liberation of Israel could not become a reality unless pious folks worked actively for its realization. This took place through 'zeal for the Law', i.e., through the armed battle against the pagans who were without the Law and the Jews who violated the Law."[1] Such a view has dominated treatments of Jewish history at least since the beginning of this century.[2] It is often simply accepted without question in textbooks, monographs, and articles in New Testament studies.[3]

This view persists even with those who recognize the lack of evidence for the Zealot movement as previously imagined. Writing now in terms of "the extremist movement" or "resistance movement," they find not only the motive of resistance but the connecting link between the different groups in religious ideals. It is supposedly possible to trace "the crystallization of the extremist ideology of freedom in Jewish Palestine from at least the time of the census of Quirinius, and its influence upon the course of events before, during, and after the Great Revolt."[4] Thus "wide circles with an extreme ideology . . . strove to realize their eschatological expectations through active and uncompromising deeds."[5] Even where the old Zealot movement is recognized as a historical fiction, the old ideal of "zeal" lives on. Indeed "zeal," under its new nomenclature, is now capable of performing the same function as the old "Zealots" for tenacious standard interpretation of first-century Jewish history: it binds the disparate resistance groups together once again under "the extremist ideology."[6]

This prominence and persistence of the ideal of zeal in connection with the lack of evidence for "the Zealots" calls for a critical reassessment of the relation of the "zeal" to Jewish resistance. Theoretically there is no reason why the ideal of zeal cannot have been a motive for resistance even though the Zealot movement never existed as imagined. Moreover, Jesus had a disciple nicknamed "the zealous one"; and the Zealots proper in 67–70 obviously picked up their name from somewhere. Critical reexamination, however, indicates that there is very little evidence for the supposed "ideal of zeal for the Law" as an important factor in first-century Jewish Palestine in any sense, let alone as a passion for freedom from alien rule. Indeed, what little evidence there is suggests that "zeal for the Law" was an individual, not a collective, feeling about the importance of other Jews' faithful observance of the precepts of the Torah, and had little or nothing directly to do with Roman domination. There is nothing to suggest that one who was zealous for the Torah was an "extreme nationalist."[7]

"Zeal" for the law was not among the most prominent themes in the Jewish literature and religion of the late second Temple period. This should be apparent simply from the paucity and fragmentary character of the evidence, which is acknowledged even by those who have constructed elaborate expositions of the "freedom ideology" or the "zeal for the Law."[8] Because of the scanty evidence from the first century itself, scholars have worked forward from the earlier biblical texts and backward from later rabbinic literature. In both the principal biblical texts adduced and in the later rabbinic literature, however, "zeal" pertains to the obedience or disobedience of the Jewish people internally and never is directed outward, as against some foreign enemy or oppressor.[9] Whether it be (a) the action against gross transgression and apostasy taken by the earlier biblical heroes Phinehas (Numbers 25.11–13), Elijah (1 Kings 19:10 and chap. 18) and Jehu (2 Kings 10:16) in their "zeal for Yahweh/God," or (b) the "zeal for the Temple" and the self-consuming zeal caused by the negligence of one's foes regarding God's word in postexilic Psalms (69:9;119;139:19–24), the zeal is oriented toward the internal relations of the people and their God. Somewhat the same situation prevails in the relevant rabbinic texts. Most passages dealing with *qanna'im* refer to private individuals who "take the law into their own hands," taking action on behalf of the community to enforce the Torah in the absence of a rabbinic court.[10]

Recent reconstructions of the ideal of zeal have focused on Phinehas as the great prototype who, filled with the spirit of God, took violent action to prevent further apostasy and to hold off more severe punishment by God. Based scripturally on Numbers 25:11–13 and Sirach 45:23–26, Phinehas was supposedly the great paradigm for "the Zealots" and his legacy the fundamental historical-theological justification for their own zealous action.[11] That Phinehas was associated closely with Elijah in certain rabbinic texts provides a further dimension of Phinehas as God's eschatological agent who would restore the people.

The principal textual basis of the modern concept of zeal, however, is 1 Maccabees 2:23–26,54. There the legendary patriarch of the Hasmonean family that led the Maccabean revolt is portrayed as "burning with zeal" against his fellow Jews who were submitting to the Seleucid emperor's program of forced Hellenization and suppression of the Mosaic Covenant. Mattathias killed the Jew about to offer pagan sacrifice upon the altar and simultaneously the imperial officer who was forcing the people to sacrifice. "Thus he burned with zeal for the law, as Phinehas did against Zimri the son of Salu" (1 Maccabees 2:26). On the basis of this passage, it is claimed that "zeal for God and his Law probably dominated the whole early period of the Maccabean revolt" and set the tone of Palestinian Jewish piety that persisted until Judas of Galilee formed the "Zealot" party in a time of supposedly intensified zeal against the Romans.[12]

The occurrence of "zeal" and Phinehas in 1 Maccabees 2, however, is a flimsy textual foundation for such an elaborate construction. "Zeal" does not occur as a theme at all in the rest of 1 Maccabees. This cannot be explained away as due to the change in the Maccabean revolt from resistance to explicitly "religious" persecution to assertion of political independence and territorial expansion. First Maccabees can hardly be read as a journalistic report or transcript of the long Maccabean revolt. It is rather a document of political propaganda designed to provide historical-theological legitimation for the Hasmonean regime founded by the sons and grandson of Mattathias, who had not previously been among the ruling high-priestly aristocracy. In this context the literary and ideological function of the portrayal of Mattathias as the new Phinehas burning with zeal becomes clear. In a subsequent paragraph (1 Maccabees 2:51–60), which calls to memory not only the great "deeds of the fathers" but their rewards with positions of authority and rulership as well, we read that "Phinehas our father, because he was deeply zealous, received the covenant of everlasting priesthood." In fact, when we look more closely at the other principal passages in which Phinehas is presented as the paradigm of zeal, it is apparent that they have a similar function: legitimation of the incumbents of the high priesthood. Numbers 25:11–13, written early in the Persian period when the high priesthood was becoming the vehicle of the ruling aristocracy, concludes with God's reward to Phinehas: "Behold I give to him my covenant of peace, . . . the covenant of a perpetual priesthood, because he was jealous for his God. . . ." And Sirach 45:23–26, part of a long poetic passage that climaxes in eulogy to the reigning Oniad high priest Simon, concludes with Phinehas rewarded with the leadership "of the sanctuary and of his people, . . . the dignity of the priesthood for ever." In 1 Maccabees 2, therefore, the Hasmonean family, which had no previous hereditary claim to the high priesthood, is being legitimated in its assumed role as rulers and high priests by appealing to the role of its patriarch, Mattathias, as the new Phinehas. Moreover, the close association of Phinehas with Elijah would appear to have had the same function of legitimating the Hasmonean regime. The dating of this identification in the first century C.E. assumes the existence of "the Zealots" as a party or movement from 6 C.E. on.[13] Partly because no such movement ever existed, an earlier dating is more convincing, since it places the identification of Phinehas and Elijah in the context of legitimation for the Hasmonean rulership.[14]

This is not to deny that Hasmonean propaganda may have been effective and successful in propagating a new ideal of zeal that may have persisted among certain circles. It would be difficult, however, to imagine which circles those might have been. Both the Qumran community and the Pharisees broke with the Hasmoneans even before the time of the composition of 1 Maccabees.

The principal difficulty for the modern concept of an ideal of zeal is the lack of textual evidence between the time of Maccabean revolt and of the New Testament literature. Jubilees 30:18 and the Testament of Levi 5:1–3;6:3 are both early enough documents. The pertinent phrase in Jubilees 30:18, however, is simply an explanatory subordinate clause explaining why Levi was given the priesthood. Test Levi 5–6 does provide (although not unambiguously) an example of vengeance on outsiders or non-Israelites (Shechem and the sons of Hamor, who had abused Dinah and the Israelites). Although the dating of the Testaments of the Twelve Patriarchs may be contemporary with the Hasmoneans or even pre-Hasmonean, it appears to have been written by a Hellenized Jew from outside Judea.[15] Hence is of uncertain relevance to the ideal of zeal within Judean society.

In the extensive literature found at Qumran, "zeal" occurs with striking infrequency and is surely not one of the more prominent themes. "Zeal for just laws" is one among several qualities that the sons of light manifest (1QS 4:3–4). That the conduct of the Master will include "zeal for the Precept whose time is for the Day of Revenge" has a more ominous and eschatological tone (1QS 9:21–23). In two places in the Hymns, the psalmist is zealous against the workers of inequity and against the "smooth interpreters" ("seekers of smooth things," i.e., Pharisees?); in both cases the zeal is oriented to internal matters of Jewish society (1QH 14:14 and 2:15). Besides not being especially prominent in the Qumran literature, these occurrences of zeal can be interpreted neither as a continuation of the zeal supposedly exhibited by the Hasmoneans nor as an obvious reaction against the Hasmoneans.

In any case, neither Qumran literature nor other texts of the late second Temple period (prior to the New Testament texts) exhibit any evidence of a prominent ideal of zeal that supposedly pervaded the society. There is certainly no evidence to link the supposed ideal of zeal to any particular group prior to the revolt of 66–70. That is, no available evidence suggests that the ideal of zeal was prominent among either the Pharisees, the Essenes (Qumran community), the Fourth Philosophy, or their apparent successor movement, the Sicarii. Indeed, the only explicit evidence that "zeal" may have characterized a particular group is Josephus's comment regarding the Zealots proper who originated in 67–68, that "they took their title from their professed zeal for virtue" (*War* 7.270).

Finally, the principal scholarly presentations of the ideal of zeal (perhaps partly because of the lack of solid evidence) argue quite inconsistently both that the ideal of zeal fired the anti-Roman insurrectionary activity of "the Zealot movement" and that zeal for the law and for God was "a typical characteristic of Palestinian Jewish piety."[16] If zeal for the law was "typical" of Jewish piety, however, and can be found behind any and every protest in first-century Palestine, then how can "zeal" be used to explain the Zealot movement and its armed insurrection in particular?[17] Not only "the Zealots" in particular but typical Palestinian Jews in general were supposedly imbued with "zeal for the Law." Or, once we recognize that there was no Zealot movement (at least not until the middle of the revolt, in 67–68), we must conclude that the historical situation would supposedly have been that no group in particular but typical Jews in general were filled with zeal.

Astonishingly, the principal evidence given for zeal as a typical characteristic of Jewish piety is from or about Paul, the apostle and former Pharisee. In these Pauline and the few other texts presented, "zeal" means something general and moderate such as "loyalty" or "devotion." In Acts 21:20 thousands of Palestinian Jewish Christians are characterized as devoted to the law ("staunch upholders of the Law" —Jerusalem Bible). In the Diaspora some Jews believed that one could still be "a devoted adherent of the traditions of the Jews" even without being circumcised (Josephus, *Ant.* 20.41; cf. the parallel phrase "a devotee of foreign practices," *Ant.* 20.47). Paul speaks of his fellow Jews as having "a zeal [devotion] for God" that is not yet enlightened with regard to God's new initiatives. Speaking in self-defense to a crowd of Jews, in Acts 22:3, Paul says that he is "zealous for God" ("full of duty towards God"—Jerusalem Bible) just as they themselves are.

In a fanatical person such as Paul, devotion could result in a more aggressive stance toward fellow Jews. In retrospect on his own earlier behavior, Paul says that he had been "so extremely zealous for the traditions of [his] fathers" that he had persecuted the church (Galatians 1:14). Paul's use of language in Philippians 3:6 probably indicates the way in which the term "zeal" should be understood even in description of such fanaticism as persecution. Paul says of himself that "with regard to the Law" he was a Phariseee and "with regard to devotion [religious loyalty]," he was "a persecutor of the church." That is, just as it was not the *Law*, but one's *interpretation* of the Law that made the Pharisees, so it was not *zeal* but one's degree or *intensity* of zeal that made the persecutor. A closer look at Galatians 1:14, in fact, reveals the same word usage. It is not his zeal as such but rather his far greater degree or intensity of zeal in comparison with others that motivated Saul to persecute.

This brief survey of the evidence (or the lack thereof) for the supposed "ideal of zeal" (for the Law and for God) in late second Temple Palestine leads us to conclusions very different from those prevailing in much secondary literature with regard to Jewish resistance to Roman rule. The ideal of zeal is not very prominent in Jewish literature of the period. The ideal of zeal had little or nothing directly to do with opposition to Rome or "recovery of the national autonomy through armed rebellion." Zeal for the Law does not appear to have been focused on any sort of "armed battle against the pagans," let alone on organizing insurrection specifically against the Romans.[18] In historical reconstruction and biblical interpretation, therefore, the question of opposition to Rome should be kept separate form the supposed ideal of zeal. Rather the terms "zeal" and "zealous one" throughout the late second Temple period texts, just as in earlier biblical references and later rabbinic passages, when it became intense ("burning"), focused primarily on fellow Jews who broke the Law in some significant way. Saul the Pharisee, intensely zealous like Phinehas "burning" with zeal, persecuted fellow Jews for breaking the Law. Such persecution, however, was far from armed revolt against the Romans. Paul's zeal focused on the internal affairs of the Jewish community. In short, those with an unusually intense sense of zeal were obsessed with sin and sinners. As we will see below, if there is any implication here for comparisons with the ministry of Jesus, the conflict between Jesus and the zealous ones would not have been over the issue of armed revolt against the Romans, but over ostracism of sinners vs. forgiveness of sinners.

Recognition of the lack of evidence for the ideal of zeal as the motivating force for resistance to the Romans, however, forces us to reexamine "pressure points" and motivational factors of that resistance. As was stressed earlier, our recognition of the "colonial situation" of Jewish society under Roman domination would appear to open up a more adequate alternative way of understanding the frustrations of Palestinian Jews. As participation in determining the shape of their own lives is denied to a colonized people, they may retreat further into their own cultural or religious traditions. Their religious traditions and rites take on increased importance as the only dimension of their life that remains under their own control. As a way of preserving some semblance of dignity, colonized people tend to focus all the more on their distinctive religious traditions, rules, and rituals as symbols of their former freedom and self-determination. This tends to make them all the more sensitive about violation of these symbols. As we have seen in the chapters on popular protests, it was often precisely when the Jews' heightened sensitivites to religious symbols were violated or threatened that the Palestinian Jews protested en masse. It is possible also to understand Paul's having been "so extremely zealous for the traditions of his fathers" in this same context of heightened sensitivity about religious symbols. One could thus find an indirect connection between "zeal" as devotion to Jewish traditions and some of the protests against the Romans. But there is simply no evidence for zeal as a passion for freedom from alien rule generally, much less as the primary motivating factor in some supposed fanatical Jewish drive toward violent rebellion against Roman domination.

APOCALYPTIC ORIENTATION AND MOTIVATION

In biblical scholarship the more credible explanation for Jewish resistance to Roman rule is "apocalypticism." There has been such confusion in the theologically determined discussions of apocalypticism, however, and more recently in some serious critical contextual analysis of apocalyptic literature, that we must dispense with previous reconstructions of apocalypticism itself before making any connections with Jewish resistance to Rome. Indeed, while questioning the traditional theologically determined views about apocalypticism, we should deal also with two hard questions that have repeatedly been raised by serious students: (1) Do people need a "religious" reason or divine inspiration to fight for their land, lives, and liberty? (2) How can we possibly know what motivated peasants or other common people, when they left no literature or other records of their thoughts and motives? That is, more precisely, what makes us think that we can use apocalyptic literature written by intellectuals with their own social roles, interests, and perspectives, as evidence for how the Jewish peasants or the Jerusalem crowd were oriented or motivated?

The answer to the first question, judging from various comparative material as well as biblical traditions, is yes; historically, in fact, people often did need "religious" or divine inspiration to fight for their life and liberty. When peoples have been overwhelmed by superior forces, it has helped motivate resistance to believe that they themselves have help from a transcendent almighty power. This religious factor may have been unusually important for the ancient Jewish people in particular. Their own historical tradition was full of stories of their ancestors' having been in despair, only to experience the divine assistance. The prototypical story of God's liberation of the Hebrews from Egyptian bondage, the many stories of God's inspiration of charismatic leaders such as Deborah and Gideon, and the stories of the inspiration of Elijah, Elisha, and the "sons of the prophets" provided a number of models that could have informed the people's understanding of their situation under the Romans. The distinctive forms taken by the prophetic and messianic movements among the Jewish peasantry suggest that the people indeed drew on such biblical traditions in responding to their circumstances.

But how can we know anything about the orientation of common people who left no sources? Or more precisely: Through earlier apocalyptic literature we know how the intellectuals understood the situation, but is there reason to believe that the common people shared the same or a similar perspective?

In many, perhaps most, traditional agrarian societies it would not be possible to assume or to hypothesize that the peasantry would have shared somewhat the same perspective as the intellectuals. As "retainers" the latter would ordinarily have been supported by and beholden to the governing class. But, as probed already briefly above, late second Temple Jewish society may have been different in this regard. By Roman times, Palestinian Jewish history already included a rich heritage of criticism of the ruling groups and institutions. Moreover, although the high priesthood was, in effect, integral to the imperial system and, particularly in the late second Temple period, the priestly aristocracy collaborated with the imperial rulers, at least some of the scribes and scholars had become semi-independent of their own rulers and hostile to the imperial regime.

This criticism of and opposition to the rulers is richly documented in biblical and post-biblical literature. The classical prophets had sharply condemned unrighteous rulers. Most pertinent to our immediate concerns, however, is the apocalyptic literature produced by scholar-visionaries in the second and first centuries B.C.E. As is indicated in the Dead Sea Scrolls, the scribal-priestly Qumran community absolutely condemned the ruling high priesthood and the current Temple as wicked and demonic. But other literature as well (e.g., Daniel 7–12; the early sections of 1 Enoch; Psalms of Solomon) indicates that the scholars or scribes who produced it sharply criticized their own high-priestly rulers and utterly condemned the alien empires. This literature, however, surely reflects more than the particular experience of the alienated scholars and scribes. That is, because the whole people, including the scribal-scholarly "retainers," were subject to overlords, the experience of the literate, at least since the Hellenizing crisis of the early second century, now paralleled or resembled the subjugation the peasants had experienced for centuries. Thus, what the scholar-scribes were writing in apocalyptic literature such as Daniel and 1 Enoch may well reflect a historical experience similar to that of the Jewish common people.

Furthermore, there is usually some regular interaction between the "great tradition" (including scripture and other literature) and the "little tradition" (the popular oral transmission of the people's traditions) in societies such as that of ancient Judea. Thus if those whose role it was to perpetuate and disseminate the "great tradition" were now undergoing experiences parallel to those of the ordinary people, we could reasonably surmise that the latter had a perspective or orientation similar to that expressed in the literature written by the scribes and scholars. Thus we may cautiously and critically use Jewish apocalyptic literature as about the only source available as evidence for the possible orientation and motivation of the Jewish people engaged in resistance to the imperial situation.

TOWARD A LESS DOCTRINAL AND MORE CONCRETE APPROACH

With regard to Jewish "apocalypticism" or the "apocalyptic" orientation, the first question is terminological. A number of different terms, none of them very satisfactory, have been used for the keen expectation of God's saving action that supposedly pervaded Jewish society in late second Temple times. "Messianism" has proven unsatisfactory because many of the highly varied expectations did not involve a human agent of any kind, much less an "anointed" king. More recently biblical scholars have reached instead for "millennarism" or "chiliasm," often used by social scientists for various comparative materials; yet the term "millennium," originally derived from the Book of Revelation, is itself infrequent in apocalyptic literature and not especially characteristic of Palestinian Jewish expectations. "Eschatology" was borrowed from Christian theology, but it is not clear that ancient Jewish expectations regarding the future were "eschatological"—i.e., that they referred to "last things" or "the End." "Apocalypticism" is derived from the Greek term for the mode of revelation by which some of the Palestinian Jewish expectations of future salvation were received; but recent scholarly investigations have broadened the understanding of the genre of apocalypse to include a wide variety of literature from other periods, places, and peoples. However, "apocalypticism" and "apocalyptic" may still be the best terms to use, since in the current discussion they still have the important connotations of yearning for revelation and eager anticipation of the attainment of what is revealed.

Previous discussions of apocalypticism in relation to Jewish resistance movements have been mired in mutual contradiction. On the one hand, apocalyptic visionaries are said to have been alienated from history and to have abdicated responsibility for historical life. On the other hand, apocalyptic fanaticism is viewed as the inspiration behind the Jews' attempts to defend their land and to assert their independence under the direct rule of God. Moreover, much of the discussion of apocalypticism generally has been carried on as if we were dealing primarily with a system of beliefs. In that connection apocalyptic symbolism has often been misunderstood, particularly in its relation to historical situations, persons, and events. One could say that scholarly study has often fundamentally misunderstood apocalyptic texts and motivations because (a) out of a certain literalism and doctrinalism, it has failed to appreciate the distinctive apocalyptic mode of revelation and symbolization; and (b) it has failed to investigate the social context comprehensively so as to appreciate the actual structure of concrete historical conflicts.

So far as we know, none of the Jewish resistance movements produced any literature; at least none is extant. We thus have no direct access to their particular understanding of their situations and actions. Instead, we must work by extrapolation from critical analysis of earlier Palestinian Jewish apocalyptic literature in order to reach some general sense of how Palestinian Jews may have been understanding their situation and symbolizing their hopes for deliverance.[19]

THE HISTORICAL ORIENTATION AND CHARACTERISTICS OF PALESTINIAN JEWISH APOCALYPTIC LITERATURE

Before analyzing the possible relevance of certain apocalyptic literature to some of the movements or incidents of resistance to Roman rule, it is necessary to counter some of the standard generalizations regarding "apocalypticism" that are rooted in earlier generations' theological agenda and that are the results of synthetic idealist treatments of the sources with little attention to concrete historical contexts. With illustrations from "proto-apocalyptic" and apocalyptic texts that were responses to either a newly imposed or a suddenly intensified imperial situation, the following discussion can focus on serious qualifications of three standard generalizations regarding apocalypticism.[20] (1) Palestinian Jewish apocalyptic texts did not manifest so much "a new symbolic universe" as an attempt to reaffirm and adjust the traditional "symbolic universe" in situations of crisis. (2) Palestinian Jewish apocalyptic texts do not manifest an alienation from history or a relinquishment of responsibility for history but rather an intensified concern for the survival of "Israel" and for the realization of God's purposes in history in situations that make that dream appear virtually impossible. (3) Palestinian Jewish apocalyptic literature and its authors and users did not stand "opposed to the dominant society" but rather to the dominant Jewish ruling group and the alien imperial regime. Appropriate correction in the areas of these important generalizations should help us appreciate the possible function of apocalyptic perspectives and motivations in the imperial situation of Palestinian Jewish society in the first century.

Renewal of the traditional "symbolic universe"

The central symbols and concerns of Israel's faith, as preserved in its "great tradition" (Torah, Prophets, Psalter, etc.) and remembered in the "little tradition," had always been generated from particular circumstances. Thus the earliest traditions emerged both from Israel's experience of liberation from oppressive structures and from the consequent responsibility of forming its own life of justice in its own land. Under the monarchy it was necessary to work out the conditions in which a centralized government would be acceptable and how its dominant political-economic-religious power could be held in check; hence the prominence of prophetic judgment against the oppressive practices of the monarchic state, including the Temple. Following the Babylonian destruction of the monarchy and Temple, concern shifted to the need for new divine acts of deliverance. Apocalyptic literature drew on, perpetuated, and renewed all of these concerns and their central symbolization as received in biblical traditions. Because it was written in response to historical crisis, however, it is not surprising that matters such as the means of divine deliverance and the mode of revelation were dominant. Moreover, because the severity of the new historical situations was unprecedented in biblical traditions, it is also not surprising that the traditional "symbolic universe" was adapted in certain respects. In comparison with other peoples whose cultural traditions were being called into question amidst a "colonial" situation, however, the ancient Jewish visionaries were remarkable for the extent to which they continued, rather than abandoned or changed, their received traditions. Unfortunately, much of the treatment of apocalyptic literature, predisposed to depreciate its value in comparison with the earlier prophets and subsequent early Christian literature, has distorted the differences rather than comprehended the continuities.[21]

(a) Apocalyptic literature continued the traditional biblical understanding and symbolization of God's redemptive or judgmental action. God's judgment or salvation was conceived as taking place simultaneously in heaven and on earth or as willed in heaven and then acted out or implemented on earth. Yet these were not separate levels of action, so that Yahweh and the heavenly hosts were portrayed as fighting directly against historical figures or forces. Thus, for example, prophets such as Micaiah ben Imlah, who were caught up (in visions or auditions) into the divine council, learned that Yahweh or other heavenly agents were taking actions that were understood as the ultimate causes of historical events such as the defeat of king Ahab resulting from his foolish trust in his court prophets who had been inspired by a "lying spirit" (1 Kings 22). In the early victory song of Judges 5 ("The Song of Deborah"), Yahweh and the heavenly hosts, indeed even the stars in their courses, fought against Israel's enemies led by the Canaanite general Sisera. In Isaiah 40–55, the return from exile was to be effected by the Persian emperor Cyrus (Isaiah 45:1) but was ultimately caused by Yahweh as announced in the heavenly council. Not only was the redemptive activity of God symbolized in traditional terms as the action of the divine warrior in "proto-apocalyptic" texts and the later Qumran War Scroll; but the redemption of the people and the defeat of Israel's oppressive enemies were portrayed as happening simultaneously on both heavenly and earthly levels as well. The broader or "higher" significance of the earthly events is expressed as a struggle happening also between God or his heavenly agents (e.g., Michael) and superhuman demonic forces or the people's imperial oppressors (Daniel 7,8,10–11). Apocalyptic texts such as Daniel 7 appear no more or less "mythic" than earlier biblical psalms or late prophetic texts, which had long since appropriated images from the surrounding Canaanite mythic culture. In Daniel 7, as in Isaiah 40–55 (see particularly Isaiah 51:9–11) images deriving originally from ancient Near Eastern myth (such as the portrayal of "the ancient of days" and the battle with Sea and Rahab, respectively) are used to embellish the significance of the historical deliverance anticipated in the vision or dream.

(b) Apocalyptic literature also continued the traditional symbolization of the modes of divine revelation concerning God's action in history. Thus the "heavenly journey" in 1 Enoch, etc., would appear to be developing the earlier tradition of visions or auditions in the heavenly court, such as those portrayed in 1 Kings 22 or Isaiah 40 (or Ezekiel 1–3). Similarly, the visions in Daniel 7 or 10–12 appear to be more elaborate developments of the prophetic tradition of dream-visions in Amos 7–8; Jeremiah 1 and 24; Zechariah 5:1–4, etc.[22]

(c) In two respects in particular apocalyptic literature would appear to have created new symbolic elements, which of course then became standard elements in the traditional apocalyptic "symbolic universe": the resurrection and the dualism of two forces, divine and demonic, light and dark. In both cases, however, the new elements arose in an attempt to comprehend and make manageable an otherwise-intolerable situation. Yet the new element became part of an overall symbolization of renewed faith that God was ultimately in control of history, despite external appearances, and would fulfill the biblical promises and vindicate those who remained faithful even when it meant martyrdom.

Because the idea of resurrection became so important in the rise of Christianity and because Christian scholarly study of first-century "Judaism" concentrated so heavily on the Pharisees, one of whose distinguishing beliefs supposedly was the resurrection, this topic has been blown up beyond its limited function in apocalyptic literature. The idea cropped up ever so briefly but in a highly important context in Daniel 12:1–3. The wise ones (*maskilim*) who saw themselves as leading the resistance to the Antiochene persecution expressed confidence that their fellow sages who had been martyred would be raised to glorious life at the time of deliverance. Insofar as the focus in Daniel was on these martyrs in particular, the idea was unprecedented in biblical tradition. Yet it probably built on earlier hopes that God would bring to life again the people as a whole (see Hosea 5:15–6:3; Isaiah 26:19; 66:7–9).

Most important for appreciating the significance of the hope for the resurrection of the scholarly martyrs, the broader context was the eventual deliverance and restoration of the people as a whole: "your people shall be delivered!" The parallel passages in Assumption of Moses 10 and Jubilees 23:27–31 appear to be part of an apocalyptic tradition building on the archaic Song of Moses (Deuteronomy 32), both portrayed God's vindication of the people against their enemies and the glorious revitalization of the society.[23] The historical situation to which Daniel's visions were responding was the most severe crisis imaginable: the imperial government's attempt to suppress the traditional faith, practices, and social organization of the people. The principal "revelation" articulated in Daniel's visions was that God was still in control of history and would vindicate and restore his people. Yet it was especially intolerable to faith that the very leaders who had been killed would not share in the restoration. Hence the resurrection, however vague and glorious its symbolization, became a supplementary part of the final reconstitution of the people as a whole.

Far more striking as a "new" component in Palestinian Jews' "symbolic universe" was the historical struggle being carried out between

God and Satan. It is found, for example, in these same texts with the resurrection (Assumption of Moses 10; Jubilees 23:27–31), then highly elaborated in the War Rule and the Community Rule from Qumran, and clearly presupposed in the gospel tradition as well. Because of its importance for understanding the actions and message of Jesus, this will require further treatment later. At this point, however, we should at least note how this seemingly new symbolic element functions in the apocalyptic attempt to maintain the traditional faith in the face of unprecedentedly severe circumstances. The standard "history of ideas" approach, of course, simply accounts for the biblically unprecedented appearance of the struggle between the Spirit of Light or Truth and the Spirit of Darkness or Falsehood, particularly in the Qumran scrolls, as due to Persian influence. That is a partial explanation at best. Whatever the original "source" of the idea or symbolism, the struggle by Satan or the demonic spirit(s) against God for control of history was used to explain the desperate situation of the people. It was of utmost importance to maintain the trust that God was ultimately in control of history and would eventually deliver the people from oppression, suppression, and persecution, just as God had liberated Israel in the past. The people who produced the apocalyptic literature, moreover, were faithfully adhering to the Torah as the will of God and the condition of their own salvation. Thus it was impossible to explain their situation either in terms of God's abandonment of his people or of their own transgression of the covenantal traditions. Indeed, in the concrete historical context, the people were in fact subjected to overwhelming and seemingly superhuman forces that were systematically destroying their traditional life. Given the fact that the biblical tradition had always thought in terms of a double level of historical action—i.e., action in the heavens determining or prefiguring that in the struggles of earthly life—it should not be surprising that apocalyptic visionaries would symbolize the historical situation in terms of superhuman demonic agents temporarily wreaking havoc in opposition to God. The symbols of Satan and the two Spirits may be new in comparison with older biblical traditions. Yet they serve to enable the apocalyptic visionaries to maintain the traditional faith so disastrously threatened in their hour of crisis.

Historical Orientation

A hostile modern scholarship has regularly accused Jewish apocalyptic literature of being alienated from history. In fact the fundamental orientation of apocalyptic literature remained concretely historical, in continuity with most earlier biblical traditions. This can be seen both in the contents of the typical hopes expressed in literature such as Daniel and 1 Enoch (and the Dead Sea Scrolls), which were vindication of the faithful and the restoration of the whole people, and in the situations with which the literature attempts to deal, i.e., oppression and persecution.

(a) Jewish apocalypticism is accused of reducing "the significance and power of mundane structures" to "nothingness" and of deriving "true identity" from what God is doing "on the cosmic level."[24] Now certainly neoplatonic philosophers of late antiquity, as they identified the true self with the transcendent rational soul, appear to have devalued the significance and power of the mundane and historical. And the character of Lucius in Apuleius's *The Golden Ass* appears to have derived his true identity from what the goddess Isis was doing on the cosmic level to effect his salvation by initiating him into her mysteries. But one would have to say almost the opposite about the Jews who wrote Daniel or 1 Enoch: they found what one might almost call world-historical significance in their own historical situation, which was so desperate that, as revealed in their visions, God was about to effect a decisive if not final historical deliverance that would be the restoration of societal structures according to the revealed divine will.

(b) Jewish apocalyptic visionaries are said to have sought deliverance out of history into a transformed or cosmically transcendent order, in contrast with "prophetic eschatology," in which divine actions were effected "within the structures of mundane reality and through the agency of human persons."[25] It is interesting to find that "proof-texts" for this generalization regarding the supposed apocalyptic search for cosmic redemption are often taken from late prophetic literature (e.g., Isaiah 65:17; Jeremiah 4:23–28). Whether based on late-prophetic texts or apocalyptic literature, such a generalization depends on a misunderstanding of how language was being used or of the relationship between prophetic-apocalyptic symbols or visionary imagery and the actual deliverance imagined.[26] What was meant by God's creation of "new heavens and a new earth" in Isaiah 65:17 becomes clearer in the ensuing parallel lines, particularly Isaiah 65:21–23: the people would finally be able to build houses and plant crops without others' seizing their homes and produce, and they would no longer bear children for calamity. Like the "new creation" symbol of redemption and restoration in Isaiah 65:17, the dream imagery of Jeremiah 4:23–26 was not meant literally; Jeremiah 4:27–28 makes it clear that a historical judgment was being imagined in visionary terms. It is the same in Daniel 7: dream imagery of vicious beasts followed by the dominion being given to the "human-like" figure ("one like a son of man") in the judgment turns out to be about the succession of foreign imperial regimes, the last of which was unusually brutal, followed by the final granting of rule to *the people* of "the saints of the most high."

In terms of God's acting through "the agency of human persons," the Enoch literature and Qumran scrolls appear to be no different from earlier biblical traditions. Just as God effected a judgmental end to Ahab and his oppressive rule through the "false consciousness" of the court prophets and a foreign enemy (1 Kings 22), so in the Animal Apocalypse, part of the Book of Dreams, 1 Enoch 83–91, an active role is envisaged for the righteous in the struggle against alien domination (Antiochus IV). Similarly in the Qumran texts, however much personal and historical conflicts were subordinate to the higher struggle between the Spirit of Light and the Spirit of Darkness, the Wicked Priest, the Righteous Teacher, the Romans (= the *Kittim*) and the Qumranites themselves were clearly actors in the historical drama. Far from an "abandonment of historical responsibility"[27] and "a retreat into a vision of the 'higher' reality," apocalyptic visions and literature attempt to make sense of and to respond to concrete historical situations of oppression and even persecution. Far from providing an escape, apocalyptic visions apparently helped people to remain steadfast in their traditions and to resist systematic attempts to suppress them.[28]

Resistance to Oppression

Jewish apocalypticism is also often conceived of as having been "a protest of the apocalyptic community against the dominant society."[29] Apocalyptic literature is often described as the product of "conventicles" within the society. It is clear, however, that the people who produced literature such as Daniel and 1 Enoch did not understand themselves as conventicles or sects standing in opposition to "the dominant society." Indeed, they saw themselves as the righteous ones faithful to the biblical traditions and the representatives of and spokespersons for and to the people generally. The enemies they opposed were the alien imperial regimes who oppress the people or even attack the Covenant (e.g., see Daniel 11:30) or the wicked, exploitative, and even apostate Jewish high-priestly rulers (and/or their cohorts, the wealthy, powerful "sinners," as in the "Epistle of Enoch," 1 Enoch 92–105) or a combination of the two (Daniel 11:31–32). In this same connection it is important to recognize that the problem that apocalyptic literature is attempting to deal with is not chaos or *anomie,* for which the solution would be order reinstituted by God. The problem is rather too much order, oppressive and repressive order, and a struggle to resist succumbing to that order; and the solution is liberation ("your people shall be delivered," Daniel 12:1). Finally it should be pointed out that we have little solid evidence on which to base hypotheses about any sort of "apocalyptic movement," whether only a conventicle or "a broad cross section" of the society.[30] Until more precise research is done on particular literature and situations we must be satisfied with the recognition that in apocalyptic literature such as Daniel and 1 Enoch the principal religious-political opposition is not between a conventicle and "the dominant society," but between the people generally and/or the faithful righteous on the one hand, and alien imperial regimes and/or the wicked and apostate Jewish rulers, on the other.

APOCALYPTIC PERSPECTIVE AND MOTIVATION IN JEWISH RESISTANCE

When we turn from this sketch of the fundamental symbolization, orientation, and situation of apocalyptic literature to the possible ways in which apocalypticism may have affected particular movements or incidents of resistance to Roman rule, we must recognize just how limited and fragmentary our evidence is. The only credible approach will be to carry out some informed and reasonable speculation regarding particular cases, keeping in mind that there could have been a number of variations (analytically speaking) along three interrelated spectra: (a) from general traditions, beliefs, and moods present but perhaps latent in the society to more active and explicit particular manifestations such as a vision, an action, or a text; (b) from particular expressions closer to the forms of classical prophetic phenomena to those that could be described as apocalyptic; and (c) from expressions among the common people to the distinctive expressions of the scholar-teachers. No projection or hypothesis should be made, moreover, without at least fragmentary evidence of a text or a movement. Considering this situation of evidence and historical context, finally, it is clear that "apocalyptic" can serve as a "necessary" but not as a "sufficient" or comprehensive term of historical explanation with regard to any of the known social movements, protests, or figures in first-century Palestine.

Thus, some phenomena do not appear to manifest distinctively apocalyptic features at all. The individual prophetic figures John the Baptist and Jesus son of Hananiah appear to have been closer to the classical oracular prophets than to apocalyptic literature in social form and in the style of their messages of divine judgment.[31] The hope for God's decisive action to restore the people to independence and justice was, of course, a long-standing tradition common to both classical prophecy and apocalypticism. It appears explicitly both in texts such as Psalms of Solomon 17 and Qumran texts (and the gospel tradition!) and, apparently, in a resistance movement as well. Behind Josephus's description of Judas of Galilee and Saddok the Pharisee urging the people to claim their freedom so that they "would pave the way for good fortune" (*to eudaimon, Ant.* 18.4–5) would seem to be just such an anticipation of the restoration of the people under the direct and sole rule of God.

Other phenomena would appear to be direct expressions of particular apocalyptic visions. The popular movements led by the prophets Theudas and "the Egyptian" are best explained if we think of the leaders and participants as convinced that God's acts of deliverance were taking place in their very processions to the Jordan River or to the Mount of Olives, respectively. If we can trust Josephus's account of the Roman siege of Jerusalem in 69–70, there must have been a number of vivid apocalyptic visions that helped inspire the desperate defenders of the city to continue resistance to their otherwise inevitable defeat (*War* 6.285–287). Some of these visions were apparently collective, as with the "star, resembling a sword, standing over the city" (*War* 6.289). Indeed, the one that was clearly the most important and prevalent, judging from Josephus's account, was virtually a mass vision:

There appeared a miraculous phenomenon, passing belief. Indeed, what I am about to relate would, I imagine, have been deemed a fable, were it not for the narratives of eyewitnesses. . . . For before sunset throughout all parts of the country chariots were seen in the air and armed battalions hurtling through the clouds and encompassing the cities. (*War* 6.297–299)

Almost certainly this was a collective apocalyptic vision in the long tradition of past experiences and future hopes that God and the heavenly hosts would fight on behalf of the beleaguered people. Jesus' comment in reproof of the disciples in the Matthean arrest scene (Matthew 26:51–55) is yet another piece of evidence that this particular apocalyptic expectation was not completely dormant.

From Daniel 12:1–3 it is clear that at least some intellectuals believed in resurrection as vindication of those who had died in martyrdom for the Torah. Such belief in resurrection had probably not achieved any sort of standardized form and was surely not ubiquitous in Palestinian Jewish society. Confidence in the future resurrection in some form, however, would appear to have been an important motivating factor both in the tearing down of the golden eagle over the Temple gate and in the Fourth Philosophy's tax-resistance, protests inspired or led by scholar-teachers (see the relevant analysis in chapter 3).

An "apocalyptic" feature shared in literate strata and common people alike was the belief that both individual and societal life were caught in the struggle between God and Satan. This is a far broader concern than individual demon-possession, a phenomenon common in the Hellenistic world at large, however conceived of in particular locales. The historical struggle between God and the demonic forces was shaped into systematic scholarly doctrine at Qumran; but the same or a similar sense of a fundamental superhuman struggle apparently also pervaded the society as a whole in the first-century C.E., for it is presupposed in both the Pharisees' accusation and in Jesus' refutation that he was "casting out demons by the prince of demons" (Mark 3:22–26; Luke 11:14–20).

For a final example, whether or not it is distinctively "apocalyptic," a particular pattern of expectation regarding future deliverance appears to have been operative both in the literate strata and the popular movements. According to this pattern the imminent future or present liberating action of God is conceived according to the model of a great historical deliverance, such as the exodus from Egypt or the wilderness journey or the conquest of the promised land, and the renewed society as a new covenantal community. The pattern can be discerned clearly in late-prophetic literature such as Isaiah 40–55. The new "exodus" to Qumran and the establishment there of the new covenantal Israel is extensively documented by the Dead Sea Scrolls. On a more popular level, the movements led by Theudas and "the Egyptian" were manifestations of the same pattern of expectation and action.

THE IMPORTANCE OF APOCALYPTICISM IN THE IMPERIAL SITUATION

Apocalypticism was the distinctive cultural form taken by imagination in late second Temple Jewish society. In that context apocalyptic traditions and literature carried the crucial liberative functions of the imagination or "fantasy" or "vision." It may be useful to reflect analytically on the particular interrelated functions of the imagination in order to discern more precisely just how important the apocalyptic orientation may have been in Jewish Palestine under Roman rule, especially under conditions of systematic injustice and forcible repression and, occasionally, of special provocation.

The function of *remembering* was foundational, for it maintained a historical orientation and perspective. Enforcement of the *pax Romana* (and before that, the consolidation and strengthening of the Seleucid empire) meant Jewish submission to payment of tribute to their conquerors and acquiescence to alien rule through the collaboration of their own priestly aristocracy. However, the memory of God's promises of blessings to the people, particularly of the great divine acts of deliverance from foreign bondage and domestic exploitation and of their earlier independence in their own land, informed the apocalyptic imagination.

But if life had not always been lived in subjection, then it need not remain in subjection for ever. Thus the apocalyptic imagination had a *creative envisioning* function as well.[32] Seemingly illusory fantasies of "new heavens and a new earth" in fact expressed the knowledge that life could again be human, that God, who willed human values such as justice and freedom from oppression, was still ultimately in control of history and faithful to the historic promises. It would again be possible to enjoy the fruits of one's labor free of conquest or exploitation.

In placing the then-current situation in historical perspective the apocalyptic imagination thus also involved a *critical demystifying* of the pretensions and practices of the established order. Emperors were not divine, and high priests were not sacrosanct. Indeed, far from being sacred or "ordained by God," the established order was permeated with demonic forces. The apocalyptic imagination thus had a strengthening effect on the people's ability to endure, and even a motivating effect toward resistance or revolt.

All the resistance movements or incidents analyzed in Part Two, and some of the other movements mentioned in Part One embodied some or all of these functions of the apocalyptic imagination. In contrast to the festivals of many peoples, which functioned mainly to integrate human life into the sacred annual natural cycle (which is often a legitimation of the political-economic order as well), the Jewish Passover celebrated the people's historical liberation. The memory evoked and celebrated in this festival became the occasion, as was noted above, for the Roman and Jewish aristocratic officials to increase their forces in Jerusalem precisely at Passover time. Thus the memory informing the people's fantasy of new liberation came face to face with the very imperial order from which they hoped for deliverance. Both under Archelaus in 4 B.C.E. and under Cumanus in the 50s, the vision of new liberation informed by the memory evoked and celebrated in the Passover appears to have been a central factor in the protests of the Jerusalem crowd. Memory of the exodus or the conquest also clearly informed the critical and creative imagination of Theudas and "the Egyptian" and their followers as well as the Righteous Teacher and other Qumranites; all these leaders and their movements rejected the established order (Temple and high priesthood included) and took direct action to realize their visions of the new exodus, conquest, or covenant.

The popular protests over the Roman army standards in Jerusalem, the statue of the "divine" Caesar to be placed in the Temple, the intellectual groups' attack on the golden (Roman) eagle over the Temple gate, and organization of resistance to the Roman tribute are all direct actions against the sacred pretensions or claims of the imperial establishment. In the cases of the eagle and the tribute, moreover, the actions were also in direct opposition to high priests and Herodians, who were cooperating with or even sponsoring the Roman practice. And in the cases of the attack on the golden eagle and the resistance to the tribute, the critical function is directly related to the creative vision of the restoration of the people's freedom and/or of the vindication of those who might be martyred in defense of the Torah.

In summary, it is clear that apocalyptic visions of God's imminent action evoked hope and motivation for resistance among Palestinian Jews living in the Roman imperial situation. In the general circumstances of oppression the people generally could hope for the renewal of their society because God was about to effect a decisive "revolution" (i.e., judging and removing the alien imperial regime and giving dominion to the people themselves). In the particular circumstances of persecution the faithful scholar-teachers in particular could endure and suffer martyrdom because God would vindicate them.

III. JESUS AND NONVIOLENT SOCIAL REVOLUTION

6. Abandoning the Unhistorical Quest for an Apolitical Jesus

TOWARD A MORE COMPREHENSIVE AND CONCRETE APPROACH

The standard picture of Jesus the advocate of nonviolence, as presented in books and articles in biblical studies and religious ethics is no longer historically credible. This situation calls not only for a new and more critical examination of the gospel evidence for Jesus' practice and preaching, but for an equally critical reassessment of our own assumptions and approaches to Jesus through that evidence.

OF FOILS AND FALSE STARTS

The portrait of Jesus as a sober prophet of nonviolence has been sketched with the Zealots movement as a foil. "The Zealots," one of the four principal parties or sects of "Judaism" and a prominent force in the society motivated by a fanatical zeal for the Law, were busy advocating violent revolt, indeed a "messianic holy war" against the Romans. Diametrically and directly opposed to "the Zealots," Jesus, understood as an apolitical religious teacher addressing the individual, taught "love your enemies," understood as nonviolence, and "turn the other cheek," understood as nonresistance vis-à-vis the Romans. He even purposely associated with tax collectors, who were despised by the Jews generally as hopeless sinners, and whom the fanatical "Zealots" would avoid absolutely as collaborators with the alien enemy. The fact that Jesus was executed as a political criminal is explained away by the claim that the charges brought against him in his trial were false. He was innocent, it is said. After all, when asked about paying the Roman tribute, which was sharply opposed by "the Zealots," he had declared "render unto Caesar." And what might have appeared as an attack on the Temple was really just a "cleansing," a purification, or a final call for repentance in anticipation of the coming of the kingdom he had been proclaiming. Virtually all the components of this picture are historically invalid or inaccurate as they stand in most of the scholarly and popular literature, and the foil on which the whole picture depends is now known to be without historical basis. Thus it is necessary to reexamine these, along with many other aspects of Jesus' ministry, in order to understand how Jesus dealt with the reality of violence. Before proceeding with such a reexamination, however, it would be well critically to review some of the approaches and assumptions typical of standard biblical studies.

At the outset we must abandon an approach that asks "What does Jesus (or the Gospel) say about violence or nonviolence?" An examination of the theme of "love" or of "peace" in the gospel tradition might seem to offer an appropriate approach to Jesus' "teaching" with regard to violence. But neither of these themes is all that important in the gospel tradition. Although "love" is a prominent theme in John's Gospel, 1 John, and Paul's letters, the term occurs relatively infrequently in the synoptic tradition. The group of sayings headed by "love your enemies" in the Sermon on the Mount (Matthew) and Sermon on the Plain (Luke), of course, have been extensively used in connection with the issue of violence/nonviolence, as well as in connection with the historical question of the Jews' response to Roman rule. But there is no indication in the Gospels that loving one's enemies had any reference to the Romans or that turning the other cheek pertained to nonresistance to foreign political domination.[1] Among other occurrences of "love" in the synoptic tradition, the principal passage that might have some relevance, albeit indirect, is the redactional phrase in Mark 10:21 that Jesus "loved" the rich man who asked how to inherit eternal life (but was unable to relinquish his great wealth): i.e., Jesus loved the rich man whom he and others had reason to resent. Exploration of the "love" theme simply does not generate much direct illumination on the issue of Jesus and violence.

Examination of the theme of "peace" might produce more of relevance to the issue of violence, but only indirectly. Only rarely in its relatively infrequent occurrences in the gospel tradition does the Greek term *eirene,* usually translated "peace," mean the absence of conflict, violence, or war. In the most significant of those occurrences, Matthew 10:34 and Luke 12:51, Jesus declares that he came "not to bring peace but a sword." Otherwise *eirene* occurs primarily in Luke, where it means something like "salvation" in a comprehensive sense. Like the Hebrew term *shalom,* for example, in the later sections of Isaiah (e.g., 48:18; 52:7; 54:10; 59:8; 60:17–18), where "peace" is parallel to "justice" or "righteousness" and has the sense of liberation from imperial oppression, *eirene* bears a sense of justice and liberation in Luke. A passage in Josephus provides a sense of the connotations of "peace" as the absence of conflict or war, in contrast with the liberation for the lowly that came with Jesus in Luke: Josephus says that in response to the sharply repressive violence unleashed by the Roman governor Florus, the chief priests and most powerful men, "being men of position and owners of property, were desirous of peace" (*War* 2.336–338). Unfortunately for the concern to find in Jesus a teacher of "love of enemies" in the sense of a nonviolent stance toward political enemies and a preacher of peace in the sense of an absence of conflict, thematic study of "love" or "peace" is not very fruitful. Besides being far broader and more concrete, our approach must move beyond the quest for what Jesus may have said about a particular issue.

MODERN ASSUMPTIONS VS. HISTORICAL REALITIES

In broadening and concretizing our approach it will be necessary to take into consideration and make critical allowances for some of our more determinative modern assumptions about reality. In post-Enlightenment Western culture generally there is a strong bias toward individualism. This bias is unusually determinative in philosophy, theology, and religious studies. It may well be legitimate to acquiesce in that individualism in our various apologetic hermeneutical attempts to make historical texts and events meaningful for modern "individuals." But the concern for contemporarily relevant interpretation seriously affects the selection of data and methods of historical investigation. The extensive influence and intensive resonance of Bultmann's "demythologizing" and his existentialist interpretation in New Testament studies well illustrates this problem.[2] What in the discourse of Jesus or in Jewish apocalyptic literature was an understanding of a whole life-world, of society and history as the context of people's own personal and community life, became reduced to "self-understanding." Jesus' message that the kingdom of God was at hand became reduced in its implication to the necessity of individuals to *decide* (!) about one's own "authentic existence." Correspondingly, the broader concerns of Jesus and his followers for community life, as well as the historical context of Jewish Palestine, were left relatively unexplored. The method of "form-criticism," which ostensibly promised a genuine sociological investigation of the historical context of gospel traditions, stopped short with contexts such as preaching and teaching—interestingly enough, contexts more appropriate to decision about individual existence. Far from existentialist interpretation's being a special problem, it is merely a symptom of an important underlying assumption that has strongly influenced our understanding of Jesus.

Integrally related to the modern individualistic focus is our assumption that religion is an area of life separable from the more material or social areas such as economics and politics. This is also part of modern Western culture, in which there has been a tacit agreement since the Enlightenment ("strangle the last king in the entrails of the last priest") that "religion" and "politics" should not interfere in each other's respective spheres. Indeed, in modern industrialized society we do in fact presuppose a considerable degree of institutionalized "structural differentiation" among the interrelated spheres of life. Of course this historical development has also tended to mean the reduction of "religion" to individual inner experience along with what takes place in churches or synagogues. Accordingly we have tended to read and interpret the Bible, particularly the New Testament, as if it dealt primarily or only with "religious" life. Of course, there was no such concept as "religion" when the materials in the Bible originated or were written.[3] More important, in traditional historical societies there was no separation of life into different areas such as "religion" and "politics" and "economics." Yet, in accordance with the modern assumption that "religion" is a separate area of life, New Testament scholars often interpret Jesus as utterly apolitical.[4]

The Bible, however, whether Old or New Testament, whether we refer to the priestly writers of the Torah or Jesus and the gospel tradition, exhibits no separation of "religious" and "political" or other areas of life. In historical biblical narratives about early Israel, for example, it is unavoidably clear that Yahweh was understood as the king of Israel, so that Israel should not have any human king "like all the nations" (Judges 8:22–23; 1 Samuel 8:4–7). In second Temple times, the income of the priestly aristocracy, and the basis of their wealth and power, was provided by the tithes and offerings given to "the god who is in Jerusalem" (Ezra 1:3; Nehemiah 10:32–39; 12:44–47; 13:10–14). The high priest was simultaneously the political head of the society, a Persian or Hellenistic imperial official, and the principal beneficiary of the tithes and sacrifices owed to God. As Josephus says, following the reign of the Herodian client kings the "constitution" of Judea again "became an aristocracy, and the high priests were entrusted with the leadership of the nation" (*Ant.* 20.251). There is no reason to believe, no evidence that Jesus and his followers or the gospel tradition were only or even primarily "religious" in their concerns. The evidence in the gospel tradition—e.g., the political symbol of "the kingdom of God" as his central message, the healing of bodies as well as souls as the activity for which he was most renowned—rather confirms the opposite: that Jesus was concerned with the whole of life, in all its dimensions.

Besides our modern individualism and our assumption that "religion" is somehow separate from the other dimensions of life such as "politics," we must take into account our own idealist orientation toward reality. It is understandable that people focused on religion and other cultural expressions should have idealist assumptions. In biblical studies and theology we have been working primarily with words, symbols, ideas, stories, and, through it all, texts. Our primary task is to glean new or renewed meaning from those texts, symbols, or ideas. It is a fundamental conviction in biblical literature and a basic commitment of faith for Jews and Christians, however, that meaning is incarnate, as it were, in historical life: in material, personal, social particulars. Thus, simply in order to be faithful to the material we are investigating and interpreting we must become far more concrete than is our habit. Serious commitment to becoming more concrete will have wide-ranging implications for historical inquiry into Jesus' practice, preaching, and effects.

For example, what if "Jesus of Nazareth" actually spent some of his formative years in Nazareth, which was a few miles from the small "city" of Sepphoris in Galilee. The Sepphoris area was the center of the popular movement that had acclaimed Judas, son of the brigand-chief Hezekiah, as its "king" in 4 B.C.E. When the Romans reconquered the area they devastated Sepphoris itself and sold the people into slavery (Josephus, *War* 2.56,68; *Ant.* 17.271–272,289). Sepphoris was then reconstructed as a Hellenistic city, with new, presumably Greek-speaking, inhabitants. If there was still sharp opposition between the people of Sepphoris and the Galileans in the surrounding area in 66–67 (*War* 2.511; 3.30–34,59–62; *Life* 373–395), then there must have been a good deal of conflict between Galilean villagers and the alien city in their midst earlier in the first-century as well. Thus memories of struggles to regain their autonomy and of renewed devastation and enslavement by the Romans, along with continuing conflict with an alien city to which they were subordinated, were probably important factors in the lives of Jewish villagers in the area.

In our idealist orientation and procedure we take seriously the importance of cultural factors such as the influence of foreign ideas, even when the influence is supposedly operating in a situation centuries removed from the original impulse. We "explain" images such as "one like a son of man" and "the ancient of days" as derived from "Canaanite myth." Or we "explain" apocalyptic dualism as "Iranian" influence. However, not only might those images no longer be expressions of a "mythic" view of reality; more importantly, they may be rooted in the concrete social-historical situation of the people responsible for the vision in Daniel 7. Or, not only might the dualism not be derived from Iran; but even if borrowed it may be, more importantly, an expression of Palestinian Jews' sense of being caught in the intensely conflictual situation of domination by foreign empires. Demon-possession may have more to do with the concrete political-economic-religious realities of the then-current imperial situation than with the transmission of particular cultural content, such as ideas of dualism.

Further examples: the crucifixion, central religious symbol for Christians, was a form of execution that the Romans used for those who disrupted the *pax Romana*. Compared with other issues, relatively little attention has been given to why, concretely, Jesus may have been crucified. Finally, eating and hunger are important themes in the gospel tradition. To be sure, people "do not live by bread alone." Considering the importance of the imagery of debt in Jesus' parables, however, it should be considered that sayings such as "blessed are you who hunger now, for you shall be satisfied" or "give us our bread for subsistence" had concrete as well as "spiritual" reference in Jesus' ministry. Or, to remind ourselves of the wider dimensions of concrete considerations, Jesus and his followers are significantly portrayed as eating together in memory and anticipation of God's historical activity of liberation and renewal.

Closely related to the concern for becoming more concrete is the recognition of social diversity and class conflict. In this connection the problematic assumption to be taken into account is less our belief that there is no such conflict in our own social experience than our habit of generalizing from the written sources, on which we are so dependent, to the society in general that we are dealing with. We thus constantly deal in abstractions such as "Judaism" or "apocalypticism," and we tend to proceed as if *everyone* in ancient society thought in the way manifested in our sources. The latter, of course, were produced by a literate elite who were more than likely being supported by the rulers. The vast majority of people in any premodern agrarian society could not write and left no records other than artifacts that can be unearthed by archaeologists, or stories that have been edited by the elite. Biblical narratives and prophecies and the gospel traditions, of course, are highly unusual as historical documents because they contain so much from popular culture and express the concerns of ordinary, illiterate people —concerns that may well conflict with views expressed in other literary sources.

THE CONTENT AND ORIENTATION OF THE GOSPEL TRADITION

NOT PEACE BUT CONFLICT

The gospel tradition is full of conflict. Often the conflict is violent. All three synoptic Gospels begin and end with conflict, the most prominent being the crucifixion of Jesus by the Romans, followed by his vindication in the resurrection. The enemies of God and of the people are the authors of the conflict and violence in some cases. At the beginning of the story in Matthew stands Herod's massacre of the innocents (Matthew 2:16). But God or Jesus himself also brings about or provokes conflict, sometimes violent. At the beginning of the story in Luke, Mary sings of God as "put[ting] down the mighty from their thrones and exalt[ing] those of low degree" (Luke 1:52). In Jesus' first action after calling some disciples in Mark, the unclean spirit cries out, "What have you to do with us, Jesus of Nazareth? Have you come to destroy us?" (Mark 1:24). Now it has become a standard generalization that our Gospels are, among other things, apologetic documents that have toned down the conflict, especially with the Romans. Yet the intensity and variety of conflict that runs through the gospel tradition is still overwhelming.

The situation in which Jesus heals and preaches is pervaded by conflict, some of it explicit, much of it implicit in stories and sayings. Most obvious, perhaps, is the conflict between rich and poor or between the rulers and the people. More particularly Herod Antipas arrests and then executes John the Baptist; the Pharisees keep Jesus under close surveillance; and finally the high priests and their governing council arrest him and hand him over to the Romans for execution.

Far from avoiding or transcending such conflicts, however, Jesus himself enters into them and even exacerbates or escalates them. He offers the kingdom of God to the poor and pronounces woes against the rich (Luke 6:20–24). Not only does he carry out actions that irritate the Pharisees, but he then criticizes them sharply and even pronounces judgmental woes against them as well (Luke 11:37–52). When certain villages do not respond to his message of the kingdom, he announces their condemnation. When told that Herod Antipas wants to kill him, he declares that he will continue his objectionable activities (Luke 13:31–33). Finally, following what appears to have been a highly provocative "messianic demonstration" at his entry into Jerusalem, he disrupts business in the Temple courtyard and not only challenges the authority of the chief priests but tells a parable clearly indicating their imminent judgment by God (Mark 12:1–12 and parallels). It is difficult to imagine more provocative behavior from a popular prophet. The only prophets from the biblical tradition to match or outdo Jesus were Elijah and Elisha, who were busily engaged in fomenting popular revolution against Ahab's oppressive regime. In terms of the spiral of violence, it is clear in the gospel tradition that Jesus directly and sharply opposed the oppression of the ruling groups and that he virtually invited their action in suppressing him.

Was Jesus, however, simply another popular prophet engaged in resisting injustice and oppression? Or are there aspects of the gospel tradition indicating that Jesus engaged more fundamentally in a revolt against the powers controlling the imperial situation in Palestine? Further, did Jesus simply move into the fourth stage of the spiral of violence, or did he in some way transcend or avoid violence while still catalyzing a revolution against the established order? These are the overarching questions that will be pursued in the next several chapters. Prior to more detailed exploration of gospel traditions leading toward a more precise and concrete understanding of Jesus' practice and preaching, we can first determine more generally that Jesus and perhaps some of his Jewish contemporaries as well were engaged in more than resistance to oppression.

JESUS AND THE REVOLUTIONARY PERSPECTIVE OF JEWISH APOCALYPTICISM

Jesus' overall perspective was that God was bringing an end to the demonic and political powers dominating his society so that a renewal of individual and social life would be possible. This is a perspective he shared with and probably acquired from the contemporary Jewish apocalyptic orientation. Until recently such a statement might have seemed utterly ridiculous in the field of biblical studies, which has viewed apocalypticism as alienated from history. Thus an explication of the statement should include an examination of how biblical studies have been decisively affected by the problematic modern assumptions mentioned above. If we can move beyond the previous understanding that has been limited by certain modern presuppositions, then it would be possible to discern that the "revelations" received by Jewish visionaries in late second Temple times were "revolutionary," at least in perspective.

Jesus preached that the kingdom of God was at hand. Since the turn of the century, beginning with the ground-breaking study of Johannes Weiss as popularized by Albert Schweitzer and especially through the pervasive influence of Rudolf Bultmann, Jesus' preaching of the kingdom of God has been understood against the background of Jewish apocalypticism.[5] "Jesus' message is connected with the hope . . . documented by the *apocalyptic* literature, a hope which awaits salvation not from a miraculous change in historical (i.e., political and social) conditions, but from a cosmic catastrophe which will do away with all conditions of the present world as it is."[6] "The Kingdom of God . . . is that *eschatological* deliverance which ends everything earthly. . . . It is wholly supernatural. . . . Whoever seeks it must realize that he cuts himself off from the world."[7] Now it is evident to anyone who sensitively or critically reads much of the synoptic Gospels and/or sections of the Book of Daniel or 1 Enoch that such bizarre descriptions constitute a gross distortion of both Jesus' preaching and Jewish apocalyptic literature. How can we explain that precisely the supposedly supercritical biblical scholarship can have been dominated by such a view for a half century or more? Here, in fact, is a prime example of how our rather nonhistorical view of Jesus as well as of Jewish apocalyptic literature is rooted in certain distinctive presuppositions of modern religious scholarship that we are now only beginning to recognize and take into account.

It would seem fairly clear what happened. Reading literature that portrays God as dramatically effecting the replacement of an old order with a new order, but assuming that this "revelatory" literature is only or primarily religious and not political-economic, we have emphasized the cosmic and supernatural imagery in which that dramatic replacement is portrayed. The effect is to divert attention from the social-political-economic dimensions in this literature and to find in Jesus' message not a hope for any "change in historical (i.e., political and social) conditions," but an end of the present world in "cosmic catastrophe." Correspondingly the discovery of the dramatic transformative aspects and implications of the kingdom of God in Jesus' preaching, far from challenging the individualism of ethical liberalism, in effect intensified it, particularly in Bultmann's demythologizing interpretation and nonethical existentialism. Since the kingdom of God was wholly superhistorical and supernatural, since it brought the End, people and their activities were no longer of any significance, but only God's power. Jesus' preaching of the kingdom brought people face to face with Eternity. The only appropriate response was decision about one's individual "authenticity." Ironic as it might seem, the understanding of Jesus' preaching of the kingdom in terms of cosmic catastrophe led to apolitical quietism.

What would appear as the overall thrust or perspective of apocalyptic literature and the preaching of Jesus, however, if we read them not only (a) less literally but with greater appreciation of the distinctive function of apocalyptic imagery, and (b) less doctrinally as a synthesis of theological ideas, but also (c) without imposing the modern separation between religion and social-political life? As was noted in the last chapter, recent studies of apocalyptic literature have provided us a sense of particular documents far more precise than that available a few decades ago.[8] Combining that more precise sense of particular documents with a more concrete sense of the referents of visionary imagery, we can take a more realistic look at the transformation portrayed in key apocalyptic texts. In Daniel 7, although some of the imagery had a background in Canaanite cosmogonic myth centuries earlier, it is used in a vision portraying a judgment scene in heaven, the point of which turns out to be that political dominion is about to be taken away from the oppressive Seleucid regime and the kingdom given to "the people of the saints of the Most High." In Daniel 10–12, the battles led by the heavenly prince Michael are clearly for the sake of the people caught in desperate historical circumstances. The language of the end refers not to the end of history or of creation but to the resolution of the historical crisis, and the main hope is for the deliverance of the people by the (divine) defeat of the Seleucid imperial forces.[9]

In each of these sections from apocalyptic literature prior to the time of Jesus the focus is on the judgment or defeat of oppressive historical enemies and the vindication and restoration of the people in independence and righteousness under God's rule. The enemies, moreover, are easily identifiable as the regime of Antiochus Epiphanes or the Roman empire and/or the Jewish ruling group collaborating with the imperial regime. What earlier biblical scholarship labeled as expectations of "cosmic catastrophe" typical of Jewish apocalypticism would be called, in ordinary contemporary language, eager hopes for anti-imperial revolution to be effected by God.

Jesus' proclamation and practice of the kingdom of God indeed belonged in the milieu of Jewish apocalypticism. But far from being an expectation of an imminent cosmic catastrophe, it was the conviction that God was now driving Satan from control over personal and historical life, making possible the renewal of the people Israel. The presence of the kingdom of God meant the termination of the old order.

THE CHARGES AGAINST JESUS NOT TOTALLY FALSE

Did Jesus' own activities match his revolutionary perspective? In being crucified, he was executed as a political agitator or criminal. The inscription on the cross, supposedly giving the reason for his execution, also indicates that the Roman and/or Jewish officials viewed him as an actual or potential revolutionary: "Jesus of Nazareth King of the Jews." Much standard interpretation of Jesus and the Gospels, however, understands the charges brought against Jesus as false, his crucifixion as resulting from the hostility of the Jewish rulers who manipulated both the crowds and the Roman governor Pilate, and Jesus himself as "innocent." Sometimes the latter claim is qualified to allow that Jesus' ministry was indeed a threat of some sort to the Jewish ruling groups, although by no means revolutionary, and that the Gospels, in attempting to have Jesus appear unthreatening to the Roman order (especially after the Jewish revolt of 66–70), wove apologetic themes and elements into their accounts, particularly the passion narratives.

Claims that the charges against Jesus were totally false and that Jesus was innocent, however, do not hold up to closer reading of the gospel texts. Moreover, even though the Gospels themselves have, as commonly agreed, overlaid the earlier traditions with a clearly apologetic layer, they still present Jesus as proclaiming and symbolically acting out the judgmental termination of the old order and the inauguration of the new. This can be discerned very clearly both in Mark, the earliest Gospel, and in Luke, supposedly the most politically apologetic.

The Gospel of Mark may not be sophisticated literature. But the story Mark tells may be more complex and subtle than has often been allowed. A clearly awkward insertion or addition may indicate more than simply the author's editorial clumsiness. In his account of Jesus' trial before the Sanhedrin, the Jewish aristocratic governing council dominated by the high priests, Mark explains that although sought, incriminating testimony against Jesus could not be found; he then says that many bore false witness but their witness could not agree; he then again says that some bore false witness about his claim to destroy and rebuild the Temple, yet their testimony did not agree (Mark 14:55–59). Moreover, in citing Jesus' claim to destroy and rebuild the Temple, Mark adds the phrases "made with hands" and "not made with hands," which are neither in Matthew's parallel nor in the mockery against Jesus on the cross about having made this same threat against the Temple (Mark 14:58; cf.15:29 and Matthew 26:61). We are left wondering if the falsity of the witnesses lay in their duplicitous intention or in their testimony. And why the explanatory phrases about the Temple that soften the severity of the charge? Awkward editing, to be sure, but likely intended to indicate something to the reader.

Mark is almost certainly presenting the events as having more than one level of significance. Yes, Jesus was convicted on the charge of threatening destruction of the Temple on testimony brought by "false witnesses." At a deeper level, however, the charge was true, as can be discerned by seeing the account of the trial in the context of the overall story.[10] Earlier in the narrative Jesus had dramatically disrupted activities in the Temple courtyard (Mark 11:15–19) and had predicted the destruction of the Temple (Mark 13:2). Then, following his condemnation and execution for threatening destruction of the Temple, the curtain of the Temple's inner court is rent in two, a clear sign of the impending destruction of the Temple. Mark intends the reader to understand the charge as true in terms of what is ultimately happening in these events, despite the apparently trumped-up character of the charge. Now, it would strain credibility to claim that Jesus originally was absolutely innocent of having said or done anything threatening to the Temple, and that Mark (or pre-Marcan tradition) invented the idea of the false charge as part of an apologetic strategy to place the blame for Jesus' crucifixion on the Jews. Moreover, the original motivation for the apology would virtually disappear on such a reconstruction. We must rather believe that it was firmly embedded historical tradition that Jesus had threatened the Temple in some way and that, although Mark provided an apologetic overlay of the "false witnesses" and ridiculous trial, he was also both transmitting and affirming that Jesus' actions and words (including his death at the hands of the ruling powers) meant the end of the old order.

Luke both elaborates on the charge brought against Jesus and adds apologetic touches to further soften the apparent Roman responsibility for Jesus' crucifixion. To Mark's brief account of the trial before Pilate, Luke adds the further accusations that Jesus had been "perverting our nation" and "stirring up the people," as well as "forbidding us to give tribute to Caesar" (Luke 23:2,5). Luke then seemingly counters the accusations by having Pilate declare three times that he finds no crime deserving death in Jesus (Luke 23:4,14,22). But this does not mean that in the Gospel as a whole Luke presents Jesus as innocent of the charges against him. The usual "proof-text" that Jesus was "innocent" (Luke 23:47) involves Luke's deliberate alteration of Mark and thus provides no historical evidence about Jesus' ministry. It is not clear, moreover, even at the Lucan level, how *dikaios* should be translated. Reading it as "innocent" would make a certain amount of sense, considering that it is a declaration by a Roman centurion. But the reading "surely this man was righteous" would fit well with Luke's overall interpretation of the historical-soteriological significance of Jesus as the prophet-messiah sent to Israel and then, although martyred, vindicated by God as "the righteous one." Might Luke have intended a double meaning?

In any case, even if "innocent" was the only sense intended, it would be Luke's own apologetic twist.

In the rest of the Gospel, however, Luke portrays Jesus in such a way that at least two of the three principal charges brought against him in the trial before Pilate ring true. Unclear, without further investigation, is whether Jesus was guilty of having forbidden the people to pay tribute. That Jesus was the annointed king, son of God, is clear at several points in Luke, including Jesus' baptism and "triumphal entry" (Luke 1:32; 3:21–22; 9:20; 19:37–38; cf.23:36–37). Most prominent are Luke's portrayals of Jesus' "stirring up the people." From the beginning of his ministry in Galilee, the crowd "presse[s] upon him to hear the word of God" or "to be healed" (Luke 5:1–3,15), while the scribes and Pharisees look on suspiciously. As Jesus moves toward Jerusalem, the crowds increase, as do the tensions between him and the Pharisees. Once in Jerusalem, he moves directly into the symbolic and material center of the society, the power base of the ruling aristocracy: "He was teaching daily in the Temple: The chief priests and the scribes and all the principal men of the society sought to destroy him; but they did not find anything they could do, for all the people hung upon his word" (Luke 19:47–48). The same opposition between Jesus and the people on the one side and the chief priests and other rulers on the other continues in a stand-off in the city until he is finally arrested (e.g., Luke 20:6,19; 21:37–38; 22:2). Jesus was indeed, especially from the rulers' point of view, "perverting our nation." Far from blaming "the Jews" generally for the crucifixion of Jesus, Luke's Gospel portrays a virtual class conflict between Jesus and the people on the one side and the Jewish rulers on the other. Nor did Luke invent this conflict, which is deeply rooted in the earliest gospel traditions. If Luke was attempting to soften the responsibility of the Roman officials for Jesus' death, he would hardly have created the element of class conflict, which was just as threatening to the Roman order as a popular provincial agitator.

It should thus be clear that the synoptic Gospels do not portray Jesus as "innocent" and innocuous. In fact they indicate rather clearly that Jesus had threatened the Temple, that he was understood as an annointed king, and that he had "stirred up" the people. Given their clear apologetic concerns vis-à-vis the Romans, it is difficult to imagine that the evangelists would have created such elements themselves. They must rather be presenting, with various adaptations and twists of their own, fundamental features of the ministry of Jesus. Indeed, the latter judgment is confirmed by the considerable amount of early or "authentic" material in the gospel tradition that has Jesus prophesying against the Temple, condemning the rulers, or lamenting over an imminently desolate Jerusalem. Such material will be examined more closely in the following chapters. At this point it is important simply to recognize that even our apologetic Gospels present a Jesus whose actions as well as perspective appear to have been revolutionary. Apparently he did not simply protest against or resist the oppressive features of the established order in Jewish Palestine; he articulated and acted upon his anticipation that God was now bringing an end to that order with the coming of the kingdom.

PROCEDURE

Attempting to understand Jesus in concrete social-historical context and without abstracting a separate "religious" dimension from the whole fabric of historical life may involve a serious departure from much previous biblical scholarship. Yet there are many scholarly treatments that can be followed and built upon as we move toward more comprehensive approaches. For example, we can follow Wilder in appreciating the special symbolic character of apocalyptic imagery, although not those who forget the realities of the earthly circumstance.[11] We can follow Weiss in appreciating that God reigns, but not those who forget that the kingdom of God is concerned with people in society.[12] We can follow Yoder in appreciating Jesus' nonviolence, but not those who forget about the politics of Jesus.[13]

Our fundamental mode of procedure will be critical probing of the synoptic tradition of Jesus' practice and preaching. We will be presupposing the standard solution to the "synoptic problem" (the relationship between our Gospels), according to which Mark was the first Gospel written, while Matthew and Luke both followed Mark and drew on a common "sayings source," "Q," besides each having his own special material. In our critical probing of the Jesus traditions we will be relying upon the method and results of form-criticism, as adapted by more recent reflection.[14] More particularly we will be attempting to explore the social context of both the origin and the transmission of Jesus' sayings and doings. It is virtually certain that Jesus did not speak and act in anticipation of his ministry's being "written up" into literature to be read. Rather, as the Gospels portray him, he moves from place to place speaking to people and acting in particular social contexts. Yet we must work through written texts to even begin to approach the origin and/or oral transmission of Jesus' sayings or reports of his actions. The analysis of such once-oral materials is hardly an exact science; criteria and techniques are hotly debated, and few are still under any illusions about reaching the precise words of Jesus. But in dealing with once-oral materials we are in a social situation, and this has certain implications that critics are only beginning to recognize.

We have been aware for some time that the words and deeds of Jesus (and other such figures) transmitted to us depend upon and involve the active role of people who heard and witnessed Jesus. More than that, however, what was remembered was remembered because it was significant for the people who remembered it. It is perhaps not too strong a statement to say that "what lives on in memory is what is necessary for present life."[15] Indeed, in contrast with the way in which we ordinarily experience the effect of the written word, "spoken words can produce the actuality of what they refer to in the midst of people."[16] Recognition of this possible effect or function of the spoken word in concrete situations will be important not only in working our way through the transmissions of gospel materials, but in our assessing the point and effects of Jesus' ministry in certain important connections.

The transmission as well as the origin of sayings and doings in an oral culture also involves concrete social context. Bultmann and other early form-critics held that the tradition of Jesus' words and deeds really began after the dramatic break and creative impulse constituted by the Easter experience of Jesus' closest followers. But much of the Jesus material has hardly been affected by the experience of Jesus resurrected and exalted. Indeed it has been argued that much of what is now in the synoptic tradition was transmitted by followers of Jesus who were not involved in, effected by, or interested in the resurrection.[17] We must take far more seriously than did Bultmann and early form-critics the concrete social context of oral transmission. Like the initial memory of sayings and doings, the continuing transmission of oral traditions depends upon social relevancy. This means, moreover, that the transmission of stories and sayings in the gospel tradition cannot be confined to a few leaders (disciples, teachers, or "itinerant charismatics"); the "common folk" cannot be ruled out.[18] In pursuit of the unfulfilled promise of "form-criticism"—assimilating much of the criticism of and adaptation of this method—we will be attempting throughout the explorations below to approach the context indicated in the content of reliable Jesus traditions.

7. The Kingdom of God and the Renewal of Israel

THE KINGDOM OF GOD: SOCIAL AND CERTAIN

Jesus' preaching and action centered around the presence of the kingdom of God: "the kingdom of God has come upon you" (Luke 11:20), "the kingdom of God is in the midst of you" (Luke 17:21), or (in Mark's summary of the Gospel, 1:15) "the time is fulfilled, the kingdom of God is at hand." Before examining particular sayings of Jesus, it may be expedient to question some of our own assumptions and interpretative categories in order to mitigate somewhat our projections onto the historical material. The painstaking investigations of form-critics and, in particular, the important and influential studies of Norman Perrin on "the kingdom of God" and the "teachings" of Jesus generally provide a solid and indispensable foundation for any further investigation and interpretation.[1] Yet such "mainline" scholarship, precisely because it has worked faithfully out of the established religious scholarly tradition, tends to perpetuate certain concepts and assumptions that may obscure rather than elucidate some aspects of the synoptic gospel materials.

THE KINGDOM OF GOD IS FOR PEOPLE

The kingdom of God in Jesus' preaching is surely not to be understood as a "realm" existing in some place such as "heaven" ("kingdom of heaven" being Matthew's typically Palestinian Jewish circumlocution for "kingdom of God"). Understanding the kingdom of God as God's rule or ruling has been an important corrective to that misunderstanding. Yet "rule" may be far too vague, general, and neutral a concept to convey the active, partial, and engaged character of the kingdom of God in biblical literature. Thus, more precisely, the kingdom of God means the use of power, in "mighty deeds," to liberate, establish, or protect the people in difficult historical circumstances such as the exodus from bondage in Egypt (as in the ancient "Song of the Sea" in Exodus 15:1–18). Remembering the great historical actions of liberation, the prophets and apocalyptic visionaries symbolized God's imminent future liberating actions in terms analogous to those past events.[2]

Under the continuing influence of the older synthetic doctrinal understanding of apocalyptic eschatology in terms of "cosmic catastrophe," however, we tend to perpetuate certain interpretative concepts that are inappropriate to Jesus' sayings and to the comparative Jewish materials. "The kingdom of God" and related symbols do not refer to "the last," "final," "eschatological," and "all-transforming" "act" of God. Especially misleading in this context is the reified concept of the End or the *eschaton*. The apostle Paul had a "word of the [resurrected and exalted] Lord" that pictured the resurrection and parousia in "final" terms, seemingly discontinuous with the historical process, of the faithful being caught up to meet the Lord in the air (1 Thessalonians 4:15–17). But it is difficult to find any prophecies or other sayings of Jesus suggesting that the new saving action of God is "final" or "eschatological" in the sense of "the last." For example, if the original kernel of any of the sayings about "the son of man coming with the clouds of heaven" (or simply seated or standing in heaven; e.g., Mark 13:26; 14:62) stem from Jesus, then, like the image in Daniel 7:13 to which they refer, they are symbolizations of the vindication of the persecuted or suffering righteous.[3] God's action in the coming of the kingdom would be "final," not in the sense of "last" or "the end," but only in the sense of "finally!" or "at last!"

Similarly, it is difficult to think of Jesus' sayings that envisage an "all-transforming" action in God's ruling. "Heaven and earth will pass away, but my words will not pass away" (Mark 13:31) is a statement about "my words," not about "heaven and earth." The darkening of the sun and moon (Mark 13:24–25) is hyperbole elaborating on how astounding the events of ingathering and restoration of the people will be—and in any case is part of the "synoptic apocalypse" not usually thought to stem from Jesus himself. Jesus' sayings portray not an

"all-transforming act" but a number of respects in which social relations (political-economic-religious) will be or are being transformed.
Thus also Jesus' preaching of the kingdom of God does not refer to an
"act" in the sense of one particular event. The kingdom of God clearly
entails continuing action by God as well as response and participation
by people. The liberating action or kingdom of God should also not
be thought of as God's "intervention in history (and human experience)".[4] Jesus, like most of his contemporary Palestinian Jews and most
of the biblical traditions, apparently, thought of God (and other divine
or demonic forces) as integrally involved in history and human life.
The cosmos and history were, generally speaking, under the rule of
God, although other forces were also involved in the historical process.
For Jesus the coming of God's kingdom brought special things, as we
will explore below. But it was not an "intervention" in a history that
God had otherwise left to its own devices.

Once we recognize that the kingdom of God in Jesus' preaching does
not refer to a particular action or event, much less to the final act or
the End, the whole convoluted debate about whether the kingdom as
preached by Jesus was already present and "realized," or was still future
but imminent, or somehow both present and future, appears to be a
subordinate issue.[5] No longer diverted to that debate, we are free to
explore the special liberating or saving activities involved in the "kingdom of God."

The divine activity of the kingdom of God is focused on the needs
and desires of people. Earlier generations, reacting against the old
liberal theological emphasis on building the kingdom of God on earth
or committed to kerygmatic theological emphasis on the glorification
of God, focused on the divine source of the kingdom. To continue to
insist that "at every point Jesus' announcement directs our attention to
God" would appear to be an unnecessary perpetuation of the misleading assumption that a religious dimension can be separated from the rest
of life.[6] In fact Jesus' preaching generally, and particularly his announcement of the kingdom of God, rarely calls attention explicitly
to God, but concentrates on the implication of the presence of the
kingdom for people's lives and on how people must respond.

That "the kingdom of God" also means certain qualities of life that people can experience is an important corrective to the previous emphasis, sometimes almost exclusively, on a particular "final" action or event. We should not think of this so much in terms of a "state secured for the redeemed," however, as in terms of active enjoyment of individual and social life. The "kingdom" involves not a blissful rest in static beatitude, but social interaction such as feasting. Similarly, the saving activity of God does indeed bring wholeness to indvidual persons; but this does not stand in contrast to restoration of society.[7] Personal wholeness is integrally involved with the renewal of social life, apparently even with certain transformations in the patterns of political-religious life.

It is important to keep in mind that "the kingdom of God" is a political metaphor and symbol. In Jesus' preaching and action the kingdom clearly includes the social-economic-political substance of human relations as willed by God. It is significant, as well as ironic, that we reach for the term "salvation" in order to express this substantive social aspect of the kingdom. Before it was spiritualized and etherealized in Christian discourse, "salvation" *(soteria)* meant the peace (especially law and order) and prosperity provided by the divine (Hellenistic or Roman) emperor for his subjects, particularly those in the Hellenistic cities, the political-cultural elite. For Jesus and many of his Palestinian Jewish contemporaries (such as the leaders of the Fourth Philosophy), however, the blessings of individual and social-political life would be provided by God as king, in contrast to the emperor. "Kingdom of God" is Jesus' "comprehensive term for the blessings of salvation."[8] The social-political dimensions are inseparable from the religious. Thus God's activity was political and Jesus' preaching of that activity was political—with obvious implications for the "imperial situation" then prevailing in Palestine.

It is appropriate that we attempt to adjust our approach to the preaching and actions of Jesus as we begin to recognize the differences between ancient realities and modern interpretative concepts and assumptions. In his investigation of "Jesus and the future," Perrin concludes that "almost all the elements in the tradition which give a definite *form* to the future expectation in the teaching of Jesus fail the test of authenticity. . . . The only elements which go back to Jesus here

are such general things as the expectation of vindication and judgment.
... The difference between this and the general expectation of the first
century, both Jewish and Christian, is spectacular."⁹ Perrin here was
merely working with the standard assumptions, concepts, and procedures that now appear to be an oversimplification of ancient sources
and events. His conclusions presupposed a synthetic view of Jewish and
Christian apocalyptic expectations composed of elements gathered
from here, there, and everywhere among the literary sources. This
understanding of the *"form* of future expectations," moreover, was
reached through a rather literal reading of the imagery used in that
literature. Against such a synthetically and literalistically constructed
view of "the general expectation of the first century," no wonder Jesus
appears so utterly unique. One suspects that if we took the same
approach to, say, one of the earliest sections of 1 Enoch or the Psalms
of Solomon we would conclude, similarly, that it was unique.

In fact Perrin shows in that same chapter that the "authentic" teaching of Jesus he arrives at through careful form-critical procedures does
"give a definite form to the future expectation." With regard to "the
son of man," for example, it happens to be closer to the original use
of that symbol of future vindication and restoration than were some
of the post-Easter followers of Jesus, who shaped the gospel tradition
in terms of Jesus himself identified with an imminently expected heavenly agent of judgment and vindication. The key procedural points are
to conduct our critical investigations with as much precision as possible
and to allow for distinctive imaginative use of language in relation to
particular historical circumstances. This means respecting the integrity,
distinctive imagery, style, and special circumstances of particular pieces
of literature or of historically attested movements. And it means searching for a figure's, movement's, or document's distinctive structure or
pattern of meaning and action in several overlapping sets of relations:
for example, between cultural symbolization and historical situation;
between heavenly-divine and earthly-human agency; between present
and future; between expectation and fulfillment; and between situation-
problem and response-solution. Comparisons then must be made between particular texts or movements, and not simply between Jesus and
some "general expectation."

With this somewhat looser but no less critical approach to the preaching and action of Jesus and·related materials, we must virtually reverse Perrin's conclusion: the general things such as the expectation of vindication and judgment are what Jesus shares with many Jewish (and Christian) apocalyptic texts and certain literate or popular movements. What is distinctive to Jesus' sayings and actions, the popular prophetic movements led by Theudas and the "Egyptian," and perhaps the Qumran community, to take some significant illustrations, is the conviction that God's new (expected) liberative action is at hand, is happening in and through the experience and actions of those very leaders and followers. The difference between Jesus and the popular prophetic movements is basically the amount of information available —so little on the latter as to make impossible a significant judgment about particular differences. The significant differences between Jesus and the Qumran community (from both of which there is now an abundance of sources) with regard to their respective symbolization and understanding of the divine liberative action in the present and future are integrally connected with the difference in social location of the participants: i.e., peasants in local village communities seeking renewal in and of the society generally, vs. a priestly-dominated and -oriented group alienated from the wicked high-priestly establishment seeking realization of the ideal covenantal life in the wilderness. Our keenest interest is surely in the distinctive aspects of Jesus' sense of renewal that came with the kingdom of God, although there may not be sufficient space for many particular comparisons below between Jesus and other movements, leaders, or texts. We should begin, however, with the more "general things" he apparently shared with many Jewish movements and texts.

THE CERTAINTY OF RENEWAL, VINDICATION, AND JUDGMENT

First of all, Jesus presupposed as his cultural context what is usually called the Jewish "apocalyptic" lore and worldview. Like the Jerusalem scribes or Pharisees who accused him of being "possessed by Beelzebul" and of casting out demons "by the prince of demons" (Mark 3:22; Matthew 12:24; Luke 11:15), Jesus viewed individual and social life as caught up in the struggle for control between God and Satan. According to Matthew 26:53, at least, Jesus shared the long-standing biblical and widespread contemporary belief in the heavenly hosts by which God would defeat the oppressive historical and demonic enemies of the people at the appropriate time. Similarly, as Perrin has shown to be likely, he knew and used the "son of man" (as in Daniel 7) as a symbol of the vindication or restoration of the people.[10]

More significantly, Jesus shared the apparently widespread popular Palestinian Jewish perspective, attested in a variety of apocalyptic texts (see Chapter 5 above), that God was expected to effect the restoration of the people, which would include vindication of the suffering righteous and judgment of the unrighteous oppressors, domestic rulers, and alien imperial regime. Jesus symbolized the deliverance and renewal of the people by means of the banquet of the kingdom or feast of fulfillment, among other images. Matthew 8:11 has preserved the more original form and wording of the key saying transmitted by Q (cf. Luke 13:28–29): "I tell you, many will come from east and west and sit at table with Abraham, Isaac, and Jacob in the kingdom of heaven." The same image of the future banquet of the kingdom occurs elsewhere in the gospel tradition, almost incidentally in a prophetic or apocalyptic saying perhaps originally from Jesus but placed on the lips of a fellow guest by Luke (14:15), and again in the account of the "last supper," where Jesus declares: "Truly, I shall not drink again of the fruit of the vine until that day when I drink it new in the kingdom of God" (Mark 14:25 and parallels; cf. Luke 22:15–18).[11] That some such saying about a feast in fulfillment was associated with the last supper and/or eucharist is confirmed by the "words of institution" in 1 Corinthians 11:23–26, where it has taken the form of the parousia of the Lord. The saying about the banquet in the kingdom (Matthew 8:11) is usually recognized as "a genuine saying of Jesus."[12]

Symbolization of deliverance or fulfillment in terms of a great feast was a long-standing tradition from the prophets Isaiah and Jeremiah. In Isaiah 55:1–5 the image of a good and delightful feast parallels that of a renewed and "everlasting covenant" in the anticipated restoration of Israel. In Jeremiah 31:10–14, the future feast is linked with mourning turning into joy, as previously scattered Israel is gathered and redeemed from those who have overpowered it; the more fantastic imagery of the later text Isaiah 25:6–8 provides similar associations. Later apocalyptic and rabbinic literature continued to draw on the image (e.g., 1 Enoch 62:14; Ex R 25:8). That a late second Temple Jewish community could focus on such a banquet as one of its central images of the eagerly awaited fulfillment is now clear from the scrolls left by the new convenantal community at Qumran (1QS 6:4–5; 1QSa 2:17–21). From its frequent occurrence in the gospel tradition and from the form of the saying in Matthew 8:11, which was apparently originally a prophetic warning, it is clear that Jesus presupposed the banquet as a standard symbol of deliverance and was confident of, indeed more or less assumed, such imminent future fulfillment. In its content, Matthew 8:11 says nothing about outcasts, and it may be only from the current literary context in Matthew that we receive any sense of inclusion of Gentiles, and hence an implication of universalism from the phrase "come from east and west. . . ."[13] The saying appears rather to speak of the gathering of the people of Israel, as in Jeremiah 31 (see also Psalm 107:3, from which Luke may get the expansion "and from north and south"). The saying in connection with the last supper indicates that this image of the kingdom was also closely linked with the restoration of the people as a new-covenant society.

Another form in which Jesus expressed confidence in God's deliverance is the "Lord's Prayer," which is clearly a prayer for the kingdom, as the comprehensive principal petition indicates. A possibly more original version than either Matthew's 6:9–13 or Luke's 11:2–4 has been reconstructed by Jeremias:

Father, hallowed be thy name. Thy kingdom come. Give us today the bread of tomorrow. Forgive us our debts as we herewith forgive our debtors. And lead us not into temptation.[14]

This is most likely a deliberate modification of the Kaddish, a prayer used regularly in Jewish synagogues in the time of Jesus.

Magnified and sanctified be his great name in the world that he has created according to his will. May he establish his kingdom in your lifetime and in your days and in the lifetime of all the house of Israel, even speedily and at a near time.[15]

It is surely significant to recognize that the Kaddish was a prayer spoken by whole communities for the establishment of the kingdom. The same was surely true of the prayer for the kingdom that Jesus taught his followers, despite any implications that it might be a private or conventicle prayer in the current literary contexts in Matthew 6:5–8 and Luke. Most significant is the confidence in God's action expressed in the prayer. Jesus taught his followers to petition God with personal familiarity in utter confidence that God will deliver. Jesus expressed this same confidence in God's deliverance or vindication in the parable immediately following in Luke about how any good friend would respond to one's needs even in the middle of the night (Luke 11:5–8) and in the parable of "the unjust judge" (Luke 18:1–8). Whether or not it is secondary, the brief saying in Luke 12:32 expressed the same surety of God's kingdom for the "little flock." Noteworthy especially in the Lord's Prayer and in the saying about the banquet of the kingdom is Jesus' overall confidence that God is bringing the kingdom. Jesus speaks and acts in that confidence.

As in Jewish apocalyptic texts, so also in Jesus' preaching the deliverance or renewal of the people involved both a vindication of the poor, suffering, or righteous and a corresponding judgment of those who opposed God's will. The heavily debated "future" or "apocalyptic" "son of man" sayings appear to have been originally expressions of confidence in divine vindication and judgment or even, more broadly, of full deliverance. In Daniel 7:13–14 "one like a son of man" was a dream image interpreted to mean that the people would finally be given the dominion as God judged the imperial regimes that had dominated and abused them. Subsequent apocalyptic texts then interpreted the imagery and the Daniel passage in various ways.[16] In one of these, for example, the Similitudes of Enoch (1 Enoch 37–71), Enoch, the archaic figure translated into heaven, is identified as the "son of man."[17] The visionary author of the Similitudes, understanding Daniel 7:14 to mean that God's role as heavenly judge had been given to "the son of man," still emphasized the functions of judgment of the alien kings and restoration of the people (especially chapters 46 and 62). Neither in 1 Enoch 37–71 nor in any other apocalyptic text, however, is there any evidence of a transcendent divine redeemer-figure called "The Son of

Man." The gospel writers and other early Christians may have understood the "son of man" to be Jesus, and the sayings about his "coming in the clouds of heaven" to refer to his parousia. But in the sayings themselves there is no indication that "the son of man" refers to Jesus. What we have in these "future" "son of man" sayings at the early stages of the gospel tradition, consistent with the occurrence of the imagery elsewhere in Jewish apocalyptic literature, is particular uses and interpretations of the imagery first visible in Daniel 7.

The saying in Luke 12:8–9 is a vivid indication of the vindication in the divine court that Jesus assumed: "And I tell you, everyone who acknowledges me before men, the Son of man also will acknowledge before the angels of God; but he who denies me before men will be denied before the angels of God." It is only because of Matthew's identification of the advocate at the judgment with Jesus (hence the "I" in Matthew 10:32–33) and Mark's expansion, with the Son of man "coming in the glory" (Mark 8:38) that the saying may have suggested Christ's parousia or the "last judgment." The more original form in Luke 12:8–9, featuring "Aramaisms" in both the unusual Greek of vs. 8 *(homologein en emoi/autō)* and the passive circumlocution for God's action in vs. 9, simply and clearly asserts the certain correspondence between the human confession (or denial) here and now and the vindication (or denial) in the divine court. The original form of the saying may have been only vs. 8, which was then expanded with the corresponding denial in vs. 9. But even if vs. 9 was not part of the original saying, it indicates that "the son of man" was understood simply as a symbol for the divine court or judgment in the earliest tradition, the divine court that would surely vindicate those who acknowledged Jesus and his message. One can easily imagine that the saying behind Jesus' response to the high priest's examination in Mark 14:62, "you will see the Son of man sitting at the right hand of Power, and coming with the clouds of heaven," whether or not it contained the last phrase about the "coming," was originally an expression of this same confidence in the expected vindication, again using the traditional image from Daniel 7.

Yet another "future" son of man saying, Luke 17:26–27, would appear to express the negative side of the divine judgment: "As it was in the days of Noah, so will it be in the days of the Son of man. They ate, they drank, they married, they were given in marriage, until the day when Noah entered the ark, and the flood came and destroyed them all." There is nothing in this or in the preceding saying, Luke 17:22–23 (cf. Matthew 24:26–27), that also refers to the "days of the Son of man," to suggest the parousia of a heavenly redeemer figure.[18] Luke 17:26–27 is rather another allusion to the divine-judgment connotations of the symbol in Daniel 7:13–14, this time emphasizing not the suddenness, but the certainty of divine punishment for those heedless of God's will.

In a number of other sayings Jesus expressed this same conviction of the certainty of divine judgment faced by his own generation. These sayings include one in which he used the same pattern of analogy between a great crisis of God's judgment in the past and that of the present. "The men of Nineveh will arise at the judgment with this generation and condemn it; for they repented at the preaching of Jonah, and behold, something greater than Jonah is here" (Luke 11:32). Even at the supposed "Jesus level" this saying has been understood in terms of the resurrection and "last judgment."[19] The verb *anistemi,* however, has a variety of meanings including resurrection but also, almost technically, to "arise" as a witness in court (cf. Mark 14:57). Although not referring to the "last judgment" in this saying, Jesus was using the historical example of Gentiles who responded to God's warning through Jonah's preaching to warn his own generation of the surety of divine judgment they must face.

Although in many sayings Jesus often used highly distinctive images, he shared with other Palestinian Jews of his time an orientation toward the deliverance and renewal of the people, including vindication of the righteous and judgment against unrighteous rulers that God was already or imminently effecting. This conviction that God was acting in deliverance and judgment helps explain the confidence with which Jesus proclaimed and mediated the presence of the kingdom of God in highly distinctive ways.

THE PRESENCE OF THE KINGDOM

The thrust of Jesus' ministry, his practice and preaching, was to realize and to make others realize the presence of the kingdom of God. Not only is Jesus confident that God is acting imminently to liberate and renew the people and to vindicate those who join in that renewal, but Jesus manifests and mediates God's activity in his own actions and teachings. He declares in no uncertain terms that the kingdom of God has come upon and is among the people, available to be recognized, received, and entered.

BANQUETING: JOYS OF THE KINGDOM PRESENT

A strikingly distinctive activity of Jesus and his followers was their regular celebration with festive meals, almost certainly a celebration of the presence of the kingdom. Since the discovery of the Dead Sea Scrolls the recognition that the Qumran community celebrated a similar "messianic banquet" has given us a greater appreciation of Jesus' anticipatory celebration of the kingdom of God. A surprising amount of the gospel tradition has to do with feeding, table fellowship, and related teachings, three or four kinds of material in particular leading to the conclusion that Jesus and his followers were indeed celebrating the presence of the kingdom.

Jesus had a reputation for "eating and drinking," one which led opponents to accuse him of associating with people who were indulgently enjoying life rather than observing the Torah. This behavior, moreover, was also a dramatic contrast to that of his supposed mentor, John the Baptist, who maintained an ascetic stance in the light of God's impending judgment. Thus the double criticism and accusation appearing in Q (Matthew 11:18–19 and Luke 7:33–34): "For John came neither eating nor drinking, and they say,'He has a demon'; the Son of man came eating and drinking, and they say, 'Behold, a glutton and a drunkard, a friend of tax collectors and sinners!' "[20]

Second, the central importance of festive table fellowship in the early church almost certainly was a continuation of Jesus' own "eating and drinking" with his followers. In Luke's idealizing phrases (Acts 2:46), "breaking bread in their homes, they partook of food with glad and generous hearts, praising God." These festive meals and what evolved as the "eucharist" celebration cannot be explained from the Jewish Passover meal (a once-a-year feast) or from other traditional Jewish customs and would appear almost certainly to have been simply a continuation of Jesus' own practice.

Third, the core saying (generally thought to be genuine) in one of the controversy stories, Mark 2:19a, is in effect a brief parable "explaining" that the celebration by Jesus and his followers is the only appropriate response, given the present situation, i.e., the presence of the kingdom: "Can the wedding guests fast while the bridegroom is with them?" The early church, of course, quickly allegorized and elaborated on the saying, understanding Jesus himself as the bridegroom and contrasting the period of his ministry with the subsequent situation of the church. But the original saying is a simple simile calling attention to a situation to which festivity was the only appropriate response. Also, although they are not reliable reports of particular events, the two great feeding stories (Mark 6:30–44 and 8:1–10) are nevertheless to be understood as portrayals of how God was finally feeding the people with miraculous abundance despite appearances of paucity.

The analogous "messianic banquet" celebrated at Qumran makes it clear that Jesus' festive "eating and drinking" was a present celebration of the banquet of the kingdom, the consummation of which he referred to in the saying about many coming from east and west to sit at table with Abraham, Isaac, and Jacob (Matthew 8:11 and parallels). Procedure for the banquet to be held by the Qumranites when the "messiahs" come is described at some length, 1QSa 2:17–21:

"[This shall be the ass]embly of the men of renown [called] to the meeting of the Council of the Community when [the Priest-] Messiah shall summon them . . . [when] they shall gather for the common [tab]le, to eat and [to drink] new wine, . . . let no man extend his hand over the first-fruits of bread and wine before the Priest; for [it is he] who shall bless the first-fruits of bread and wine, and shall be the first [to extend] his hand over the bread. Thereafter, the Messiah of Israel shall extend his hand over the bread, [and] all the Congregation of the Community [shall utter a] blessing. . . ."

However, after thus stating explicitly that this is the order of procedure for the banquet when the messiahs come, the text continues: "It is according to this statute that they shall proceed at every me[al at which] at least ten men are gathered together" (similarly, 1QS 6:4–5). The Qumranites were thus celebrating their regular community meals as if the messiahs were already there, i.e., were celebrating in anticipation of the future consummation. Jesus' table fellowship would surely have been far less rigid and hierarchical than that of the priestly-led Qumran community's. Yet judging from this vivid analogy from another community that understood its own life and actions as already "preparing the way of the Lord," Jesus' festive "eating and drinking" must have been a celebration of the presence of deliverance in active anticipation of banqueting in the fully consummated kingdom of God.

Corresponding to the deliverance or renewal side of the feasting in the kingdom now present, of course, was the presence of judgment, i.e., the possibility of exclusion from the present kingdom if one did not respond. This can be seen in the parable of "the great supper" (Luke 14:16–24; Gospel of Thomas no. 64; cf. Matthew 22:1–10). The story in the Gospel of Thomas is closer to the Lucan story than to the Matthean, and the Lucan story closer to the original of Jesus. The original was surely not an allegory of the "eschatological banquet," but a genuine parable calling for a judgment on the present situation portrayed as analogous to that of a great banquet to which invitations had been given.[21] The emphasis especially in the Gospel of Thomas no. 64 and in the story behind Luke 14:16–24 as well falls on the failure of those invited to come when summoned.[22] It is also relevant to note that two of the three groups in the Lucan version and perhaps all three in the Gospel of Thomas no. 64 are economically prosperous, in contrast surely to the vast majority of Galilean peasants. Thus the point of the parable must have been a warning about not responding to the presence of the kingdom, which the extended metaphor of a great banquet would surely have suggested for those familiar with one of the central prophetic symbols of God's future liberation and restoration of the people. Now that the summons to participate in the Kingdom had been given, those otherwise preoccupied (such as with expanding their own property holdings) would find themselves excluded.

HEALINGS AND FORGIVENESS

Jesus' healings and exorcisms were not signs that the kingdom of God was soon to come, but indications that the kingdom was already present. They were direct manifestations of God's liberating and restorative activity in people's personal lives. In approaching the healings and exorcisms, however, we are in a complex and awkward situation with regard to the gospel stories. As form-critics have long since recognized, these healing and exorcism stories have typical forms, some of them even bearing striking resemblances to stories told about near-contemporary Hellenistic healer-philosophers such as Apollonius of Tyana. Virtually none of these stories in our Gospels provides reliable historical information about a particular incident in Jesus' ministry.[23] On the other hand, both within the gospel tradition and in later Jewish tradition, Jesus has an unshakable reputation as a healer and exorcist. Thus we are confident that Jesus performed a number of healings and did "cast out demons." Yet we must use the gospel healing and exorcism stories not as direct evidence for any particular incidents but rather as general and typical information that must be examined critically for any distinctive features.

Healings and other "miracles" by prophets who had been charged by God with rallying the people to resistance against domestic oppression and foreign influence, of course, were well known from the biblical traditions of Elijah and Elisha. Comparative material from other times and societies also indicates that it is not unusual at all for charismatic preachers or prophets to perform healings as part of their mobilization of people in acute states of distress. Moreover, it is worth noting, lest we simply accept a medically defined model of "disease," that many of the typical problems dealt with by such prophet-healers can most adequately be explained as partly or largely due to the extremely stressful situation of their people. Thus it could be argued that Jesus' healings dealt with problems typical of just such a situation: besides possession, we find stories about fever, lameness or paralysis, consumption, hemorrhage, deafness and dumbness, blindness, epilepsy, deformity, and dropsy.[24] Thus, at the fundamental "psychosomatic" level, it seems highly likely that Jesus did function as the agent in a number of such cases of restoration to health.

It appears that God's forgiveness of sins announced or mediated by Jesus may have been connected with his healings. It comes as a surprise to many that the forgiveness of sins is not a more prominent element in the gospel tradition, particularly that there is very little by way of an interpretation of Jesus' death on the cross in terms of forgiveness of sins (Mark 10:45; Matthew 22:28; and Matthew's version of the Last Supper, 26:28 vs. Mark 1:4 and Luke 3:3, which understand John's baptism as having this function). Perhaps the relative scarcity of such an interpretation of Jesus' death in the Gospels helps explain the need in theologically oriented biblical studies to emphasize the connection of forgiveness of sins with Jesus' healings and with table fellowship. This connection, however, has been seriously overplayed by interpreters who are astounded that the forgiveness of sins is mentioned explicitly in gospel traditions only twice or that references to Jesus' associating with sinners are so few and so late.[25]

The forgiveness of sins, however, does appear to have been an important aspect of Jesus' practice. Besides the two passages in which Jesus explicitly pronounces God's forgiveness (Mark 2:1-12 and parallels; Luke 7:36-50, in which 7:48-50 is probably a Lucan composition on the basis of the other tradition in Mark), the petition in the Lord's Prayer (Luke 11:4 and Matthew 6:12) and the parable (Matthew 18:23-35) about passing on the forgiveness of debts are directly linked with, indeed presuppose, God's forgiveness of debts. The first half of the parable of the prodigal son and that about the Pharisee and the tax collector (Luke 18:9-14) also indicate that Jesus taught God's readiness to forgive, to "justify" a humble sinner. The connection of forgiveness of sins with healing is made primarily in the healing story behind Mark 2:1-12, which is compounded with a controversy in Mark 2:6-10. Some declaration such as Jesus' statement in Mark 2:5, with the passive indicating God as the agent of forgiveness, must be presupposed in the practice of Jesus as a basis for the conflict shaped into the typical "controversy story" of Mark 2:6-10, just as some practice of Jesus' healing on the Sabbath must lie behind this as another issue on which he came into conflict with representatives of the established order

(Mark 3:1–6). It thus seems highly likely that the link between forgiveness of sins and healing goes back to Jesus' practice.

Although this link may not have retained its importance in Matthew and Luke, which emphasize more the eucharistic celebration of Christ's death and Jesus' table fellowship with sinners, respectively, it is important for our examination of violence and injustice in an imperial situation because in Jewish society people's sickness and suffering was understood as caused by their sins. The Gospels themselves provide several indications that this understanding of sickness or misfortune and suffering were current assumptions in the context of Jesus' ministry (Mark 2:5 and parallels; John 9:2–3; Luke 13:2, where Jesus himself challenges the understanding only partially, in its extension to relative degrees of sin and suffering). Now the understanding of suffering perhaps implicit in the old Deuteronomistic or predeuteronomistic view of life, i.e., as the result of one's (or one's parents') sins may have been adequate for traditional independent village or tribal life. In an imperial situation, however, in which one's suffering may be the direct or indirect result of conquest or other forms of institutionalized injustice and violence, such an understanding of the cause of suffering or sickness becomes problematic. This is the understanding of suffering disputed in some of the dialogues in the Book of Job (e.g., 4:7; 8:4,20; 22:5), albeit without the benefit of a historical view of reality.[26] Despite efforts to counter such an understanding, such as the oracle concerning the new covenant by Jeremiah 31:27–34, especially 29–30, it persisted into the second Temple period, as is evidenced by a scribe such as Ben Sira (Sirach 38:9–11).

For the mass of ordinary people whom the system must keep in order, such an understanding of suffering or sickness can become "domesticating." In accordance with this understanding, they in effect blame themselves for their problems while they must simultaneously accept the necessity of an institutionalized system of atonement (sacrifices and offerings) in which God's forgiveness is conditional and is channeled through official mediators and regulators. Now if Jesus, when healing people's disorders, also dealt with the people's sense of sin in which (they and their officials believed) their sickness was rooted, then he would have been challenging one of the religious means by which the people were thus domesticated. By pointing to the forgiveness of God as directly available, Jesus was exposing the religious means by which the social restrictions on the people were maintained.[27] Thus, instead of the people continuing to blame themselves for their suffering, they were freed for a resumption of a productive, cooperative life in their communities.

EXORCISMS AND GOD'S DEFEAT OF DEMONIC FORCES

The kingdom of God is manifested as present in the people's experience more dramatically and more explicitly in the exorcisms than in any other aspect of Jesus' practice and preaching. As noted already in connection with the healing stories, the exorcism stories do not give us direct access to any particular incident of exorcism. Convinced by the strength of his reputation that Jesus in fact did perform exorcisms, we must work more generally and critically with the synoptic gospel materials against the background of the concrete situation in Palestine. And in any case, while the fact that Jesus did "cast out demons" is essential, the significance seen in the exorcisms is even more important for our present considerations.

Judging from how prominent a feature exorcism is in the gospel tradition generally, Jesus must have encountered a number of people who were possessed by alien forces thought of as "demons" or "unclean spirits." Viewed phenomenologically, the hostile alien force(s) would enter or seize control of a person so that s/he was no longer "her/himself." The stories speak, for example, of "a man with an unclean spirit" who was acting uncontrollably, but then it was the "spirit" who spoke when "the man" opened his mouth (Mark 1:23–24; 5:2–9) or a man was dumb because possessed by a dumb demon (Luke 11:14). The effects of possession were violent antisocial and self-destructive behavior (Mark 5:2–5; 9:18). The exorcism itself involved a struggle by the alien forces to maintain their control of the person, and the actual "driving out" involved violent convulsions of the possessed (Mark 1:24–26; 5:7–10; 9:20–26). The successful exorcism, however, left the persons restored to "their right mind" and normal behavior (Mark 5:15; Luke 11:14).

The significance of Jesus' exorcisms is articulated in two related passages, Mark 3:22–27 and the addition to that passage from Q in Luke 11:19–20 and Matthew 12:27–28.

And the scribes who came down from Jerusalem said, "He is possessed by Beelzebul, and by the prince of demons he casts out the demons." And he called them to him, and said to them in parables, "How can Satan cast out Satan? If a kingdom is divided against itself, that kingdom cannot stand. And if a house is divided against itself, that house will not be able to stand. And if Satan has risen up against himself and is divided, he cannot stand, but is coming to an end. But no one can enter a strong man's house and plunder his goods, unless he first binds the strong man; then indeed, he may plunder his house." (Mark 3:22–27)

"And if I cast out demons by Beelzebul, by whom do your sons cast them out? Therefore they shall be your judges. But if it is by the finger[28] of God that I cast out demons, then the kingdom of God has come upon you." (Luke 11:19–20)

However this material may have been shaped or edited in the gospel tradition, the sayings in Mark 3:24–26 and 27, individually and collectively, presuppose the charge made against Jesus in Mark 2:22 or something very similar. Thus these sayings and the issue they address require, and must have originated in, a very particular setting in the ministry of Jesus, his practice of casting out demons. The saying in Luke 11:20 presupposes both the same setting in the ministry of Jesus and, at least in its present form ("but if it is by the finger of God . . ."), the point or judgment based on the analogies in the preceding sayings (Mark 3:23–26; Matthew 12:25–26; Luke 11:17–18), i.e., "Since it is thus absurd that I would cast out demons by Satan, then it must be by the only other alternative." Although modern readers and interpreters have been uncomfortable dealing with demons, exorcisms, and the ancient apocalyptic dualism between God and Satan, these phenomena and these particular passages contain a number of implications that are extremely important for an adequate understanding of Jesus' practice and preaching.

The view of reality as involving a struggle between God and demonic forces must have prevailed among the ordinary people in Jewish society. It was certainly shared by Jesus and his opponents in the texts just cited. Moreover, besides the "scribes" of Mark 3:22 ("Pharisees" in Matthew 12:24), other literate strata in the late second Temple period shared this view, and the authors of the scrolls from Qumran articulated it in more systematic form, thus providing us with important comparative material.

In this view of reality, the struggle between God and demonic forces is taking place at three distinguishable but closely interrelated levels. Ostensibly, the struggle was one in the superhuman, divine-demonic world between God and Satan or, in Qumran literature, between the Prince of Light (or Angel of Truth) and the Angel of Darkness (or Belial or Satan; see especially 1QS 3:18—4:24; 1QM 1–2, 15–19). It is perhaps misleading when this is labeled as a "cosmic" or a "mythic" struggle. Whatever the derivation of some of the imagery employed, this is not at all the same as the struggle between the divine natural (and civilizational) forces of cosmos such as Lord Storm (Baal) against the divine natural (and anticivilizational) forces of chaos such as Sea or Death recited and acted out in an annual cycle of myth and ritual in the royal temples of the ancient Near East to ensure the productivity (i.e., fertility) and stability of the established order. The apocalyptic dualism portrays rather a struggle between divine creative forces and demonic destructive forces for control of the historical process. The struggle between God and Satan, between the Prince of Light and Belial, explains, determines, and is thus concerned with what is happening on the second level, of the people and their historical situation. The Qumranites thought that the same decisive battle would involve the Kittim (i.e., the Romans, by the time of Jesus) as well as Belial/Satan and the priests and people along with the heavenly hosts. At yet another, though obviously closely related level, the struggle between the two spiritual forces was taking place in the hearts of individual persons such that their personal behavior as well as their social-political group was determined by their relative portion of the two spirits, of truth and falsehood (1QS 4:2–12,22–24). The views of Jesus and probably of the vast majority of Jewish society were not nearly as rigidly dualistic at the social-political and individual levels, yet they apparently thought of Satan as having a certain dominion socially-politically, and of the demons as controlling possessed persons.

This view of reality was both a revelation about and a mystification of the situation in which these people lived.[29] Modern biblical interpreters thought of such apocalypticism as alienated from history. When we attend to the concrete imperial situation, however, it is clear that the violent struggle between God and demonic forces was simply a symbolization or reflection of the violent social-political-religious conflict in which the people were caught individually and collectively. Seeing their own conquest and subordination in the context of Satan's struggle against the divine purposes provided both reason for and significance to their otherwise inexplicable misfortune or fate. It would have been difficult to "explain" the degree and persistence of their subjugation and suffering without conceiving of superhuman forces involved. Belief that Satanic forces were the causes of their miserable situation enabled them not simply to further blame themselves. Believing that God was still ultimately in control of history and was locked in struggle against the superhuman oppressive forces enabled the people to live in their traditional way rather than to die, either by giving up or by assimilating to the dominant culture. Trust that God "had ordained an end for falsehood" and would finally win the struggle and liberate the people symbolized their own will to resist. It enabled them not simply to strike out blindly and go down fighting but to persist patiently and stubbornly in their traditional ways and commitments while probing patiently for appropriate forms of resistance.

The view of life as caught in the struggle between God and Satan, however, was also a mystification of the imperial situation. Believing that Satan and demonic forces were at work behind one's subjugation and suffering may have enabled the Jews individually and collectively not to strike out in frustration directly against the Romans, which would have been suicidal. But this belief may have also diverted attention from the concrete realities. Even possession by a demon (or a psychosomatic paralysis) may have been a self-preservative phenomenon insofar as it prevented (or replaced) an act of direct counterattack against Roman domination. But the cost was a partial self-destruction or self-diminution. Focusing on the struggle against demonic forces may have enabled the people to carry on a symbolic resistance, as was maintained collectively at Qumran (see the War Scroll) and individually by possessed persons, but this meant that resistance occurred in a way that proved very "functional" for the system. That is, aggressiveness stimulated among those subjugated by the violence of conquest and injustice was worked out in a way that did not disrupt the repressive *pax Romana*.

Besides having been functional simply by itself in channeling counteraggression into nondisruptive symbolic outlets, belief in Satan and demonic forces was useful to representatives of the established order in maintaining social control. A disruptive person could be accused of "having a demon." Or, more seriously, just as many a "wise woman" or folk healer was charged with effecting her cures by witchcraft in league with Satan in the great European witch hunts, so Jesus was accused of "casting out demons by the prince of demons."[30] Thus, besides the important ways in which the apocalyptic dualism was truly "revelatory" and preserved Jewish life and traditions, it was also undoubtedly mystified and helped maintain the very imperial situation it helped the people explain and deal with.

Jesus' interpretation of his exorcisms is revelatory and liberative at every level. He starts from the concrete experiences of people having been liberated from the hostile alien forces that had possessed them and from the accusations that he had effected them by the power of Satan. His analogies of the kingdom and house divided presuppose and refer to the struggle between God and Satan on the transhistorical spiritual level. Presupposing the integral relation or continuity of action between the two levels, he juxtaposes the concrete experiences of demons being driven out and the reality of God and Satan warring against each other for control. The analogies of Mark 3:24–26 call for the judgment that it would be absurd for Satan to be at war against himself (necessary if the accusation against Jesus were true). But the analogies also make the point that if Satan were divided against himself, then in any case his dominion "is coming to an end." The further analogy in Mark 3:26 makes the same point somewhat differently, juxtaposing the experience of exorcisms with the notion that a strong man must first be bound before his goods can be plundered. That is, if the demons are already being driven out, then Satan must already have been bound. It would be appropriate to consider in this connection also the brief saying of the "visionary" Jesus in Luke 10:18. The current setting is not only secondary but clearly editorial, but an exorcism context in the ministry of Jesus or the mission of his disciples could well have evoked or have been evoked by the saying "I saw Satan fall like lightning from heaven." If the visionary, in ecstasy, has seen Satan fall, then surely his power over people is coming to an end, and vice versa.

The saying in Luke 11:20 shifts the focus from the defeat of Satan to the victory of God, again starting from the concrete experiences of people being freed from the hostile forces. "The finger of God" is an allusion to Exodus 8:19, in which God accomplishes a feat of magic (plague of lice) completely beyond the power of Pharaoh's magicians in effecting the liberation of the people from bondage. A rabbinic midrash (Ex R 10.7) says that the magicians recognized that the plagues "were the work of God and not the work of demons."[31] In the world of apocalyptic dualism there are only two alternatives, and Satan has been excluded. Thus, in a saying suggesting a new exodus is underway, "if it is by the finger of God that I cast out demons, then the kingdom of God has come upon you."

This saying also clearly focuses on the people, the societal-historical level, not the heavenly one. The "argument" of the saying goes from the experience of individuals having been freed of the demonic forces to the implications for the people and for the historical situation.[32] It has been suggested that another of the most important "kingdom" sayings, the one almost impossible to reconstruct in fully satisfactory form, "from the days of John the Baptist until now the kingdom of heaven has suffered violence, and men of violence take it by force" (Matthew 11:12 and Luke 16:16), should also be understood in terms of God's struggle against the powers of evil.[33] Although it is not explicit in the saying, the current social-political struggles of the people would probably have been understood in the context of the broader spiritual struggle between God and Satan. In any case, this is another key saying of Jesus indicating that the kingdom of God is present here and now in the experience of the people. Similarly, a third principal "kingdom" saying confirms this reading of "the kingdom of God has come upon you": "The kingdom of God is not coming with signs to be observed, nor will they say, 'Lo, here it is!' or 'There! for behold, the kingdom of God is in the midst of you' " (*entos hymon* = "among you"; Luke 17:20–21). In all of these key sayings the kingdom is already present and active among the people.

Thus, strange as it may seem, Jesus' statements concerning the significance of his exorcisms have clear political implications. As was manifested precisely in the liberation of "possessed" individuals, Satan and the demonic forces were being defeated. Insofar as all historical conflict would be comprehended in the perspective of the struggle against Satan, since Satan was now being defeated, the days of Roman domination were numbered, and broader societal liberation and renewal were now possible.

A last noteworthy point regarding Jesus' exorcisms—and one not made necessarily as evidence for the previous point, because Jewish scribes and rulers would not have known Jesus' interpretion of the significance of the exorcisms—pertains to the scribes' and Pharisees' and even Herod Antipas' reported concern about Jesus' healings and exorcisms. According to gospel traditions, it was the scribes and Pharisees who attempted to counter his activity with accusations of demon-possession and collusion with Satan. Then, in a most revealing bit of biographical tradition usually judged as early and "authentic," Antipas' concern to suppress Jesus appears to focus precisely on this healing and exorcising activity: "Get away from here, for Herod wants to kill you." To which he replies, "Go tell that fox, 'Behold, I cast out demons and perform cures today and tomorrow, and the third day I finish my course' " (Luke 13:31–32). Thus there are fairly solid traditions that the rulers and/or official representatives viewed Jesus' healing and exorcising activity as a threat to the established order. The liberation of persons from demonic alien forces, God's defeat of Satan, and the ending of the oppressive established social order were all happening simultaneously.

THE RULE OF GOD AND THE SOCIETY OF GOD

In the gospel materials examined thus far, the distinctive ways in which Jesus portrayed and manifested the presence of the kingdom of God were all concerned with the welfare of people. Biblical scholarship, on the other hand, surely because of its own theological origins, orientation, and task, tends to emphasize that the kingdom of God in the teaching of Jesus is "God's ruling activity" or "God's self-revelation."[34] Jesus, of course, apparently shared some of modern theologians' concern for the glorification of God. Besides the extensively cited story about the "good Samaritan" there is a lesser-known story about a "grateful Samaritan," the only one of ten lepers he cleansed who thought to "give praise to God" (Luke 17:11–19). The story is obviously told to admonish people concerning the appropriate gratitude due God for their salvation. In the earliest gospel traditions of the preaching of Jesus, however, there is little or no concern directly with God. This may seem strange, perhaps because influential gospel passages such as the doxology added to the Lord's Prayer in Matthew loom so large in our consciousness. Yet it is striking, for example in connection with the central proclamation of the kingdom of God, that Jesus rarely refers to God as king (e.g., only in passing, as it were, in Matthew 5:34). Instead, Jesus refers to God primarily as "Father." And although some sayings (relatively late ones? e.g., Mark 8:38) portray the "Father" in heavenly glory surrounded by the angels in royal splendor, the dominant tone is more the accessible (and very anthropomorphic!) figure who feeds the birds, clothes the flowers, and cares for his people, and whose mercy is to be imitated (Luke 12:22–31; 6:36). In the preaching and action of Jesus, including the "kingdom of God" sayings and references to God as Father, the focus is almost always on the people, and the concern is not abstract or even primarily religious, but is with the people's concrete circumstances, both somatic and psychic, both material and spiritual.

The shape of this concern for people can be further discerned and delineated through examining other kingdom sayings, particularly those speaking of being "in" or of "entering" the kingdom of God. In addition to the sayings already examined concerning "sitting at table" or "drinking the fruit of the vine in the kingdom of God" (Matthew 8:11; Mark 14:25; cf. Luke 14:15), the Q saying of Luke 7:28 and Matthew 11:11 and the saying in Matthew 5:19 speak of being located in, a member of, and participating in the activities of a community or society. Similarly, a number of sayings about "entering the kingdom of God" (Mark 9:47 and parallels; Mark 10:15 and parallels; Mark 10:23–25 and parallels; Matthew 5:20; 7:21; 23:13) and related sayings such as those about entering a gate (Matthew 7:13–14 and parallels), and "seeking" or "being fit for" the kingdom of God (Luke 9:62; 12:31) refer to a society or community of some sort.

Indeed, closer examination of these sayings indicates that Jesus had in mind some fairly definite and distinctive patterns of social relationship for the kingdom-society that is to be entered or as the requirements for entry. The disposition necessary for entry and continuing participation was childlike trust and humility: "whoever does not receive the kingdom of God like a child shall not enter it" (Mark 10:15 and parallels). Entry and enjoyment of the kingdom required rigorous observance of the will of God and/or of the teachings of Jesus: "Not everyone who says to me 'Lord, Lord,' shall enter the kingdom of heaven, but he who does the will of my Father" (Matthew 7:21); and "enter by the narrow gate, . . . for the gate is narrow and the way hard, that leads to life" (Matthew 7:13–14; cf. further, Matthew 5:20; Mark 9:47 and parallels). The kingdom would also require egalitarian, nonexploitative, and nonauthoritarian social relations: "How hard it will be for those who have riches to enter the kingdom of God. . . . It is easier for a camel to go through the eye of a needle than for a rich man to enter the kingdom of God" (Mark 10:23b,25 and parallels); "Woe to you, scribes and Pharisees, hypocrites! because you shut the kingdom of heaven against men; for you neither enter yourselves, nor allow those who would enter to go in" (Matthew 23:13; cf. the parallel, Luke 11:52, without the "kingdom," 52a, but including the "entering," 52b). It is even evident that the kingdom as society has a historical location. Even though most of the "entering" passages speak in terms of an entry yet to be made, two sayings suggest that the kingdom began since (or with) John the Baptist: "I tell you, among those born of women none is greater than John; yet he who is least in the kingdom of God is greater than he" (Luke 7:28; Matthew 11:11); "the law and the prophets were until John; since then the good news of the kingdom of God is preached, and everyone enters it violently" (Luke 16:16; Matthew 11:12 has serious variations).[35] These sayings, whatever their original form was precisely, suggest that the kingdom as society replaces that governed by the "law and the prophets," and yet is somehow the proper fulfillment of the law and prophets as well (Matthew's composition in 5:17–20 would appear to have a solid "dominical" basis).

THE RENEWAL OF ISRAEL

If God was thus bringing the old order to an end and effecting a renewal in the individual and social life of the people in distinctive ways, then the social form of that renewal must have been a restoration of Israel. As dissatisfaction mounts not only with the old liberal or more recent existentialist individualism projected onto Jesus but also with the doctrinal scheme of otherworldly apocalypticism projected onto "Judaism," there has been increasing willingness to entertain the notion that Jesus may have been concerned with his own people, Israel.[36] Without suggesting that Jesus had some schematic program in mind, we can explore the ways in which he may have been striving for a restoration or renewal of Israel. Assuming that it is highly unlikely that Jesus was a man completely out of time and place, we should begin with the expectations his contemporary Jews held regarding the future renewal of the people.

Recent treatments of Jesus and of the restoration of Israel have been less than satisfactory, because they either treat Jesus as if he were a reflective systematic theologian, or project a modern sociological scheme onto the historical material, or are still working with some of the old synthetic conceptual schemes.[37] The cornerstone of one interpretation, for example, is that Jesus expected not only the destruction of the existing Temple but also the imminent rebuilding of a new Temple in Jerusalem. As we will see in chapter 10, however, the notion that Jesus conceived of a restoration of Israel focused on a rebuilt Temple in Jerusalem can thus be excluded for simple lack of evidence.

The fundamental hope was for the restoration of the people. This sometimes included the imagery of the restored twelve tribes of Israel and the gathering of exiles from afar. Expectations also included the Gentiles. Occasionally, as in Isaiah 60 and the War Scroll from Qumran (1QM 12 and 19), this was symbolized in more imperial form, with the finally subdued foreign kings pictured as doing obeisance and bringing tribute to Israel and God. Isaiah 40–55, which was so influential in shaping the fundamental symbolism and pattern of subsequent Jewish hopes, however, has a far more benign, even universalistic, expectation regarding the Gentiles. Informed by the tradition of the promises to Abraham, Isaac, and Jacob, that besides Israel's becoming a great people with land, all peoples would be blessed, the prophet imagines that a restored Israel would become the basis for justice eventually reaching to all peoples (see especially Isaiah 42:1–7; 49:1–6). It is important to note, however, that the fundamental concern is with the restoration of Israel, and that restoration means the establishment of justice. The apostle Paul's reflections on his own mission in Romans 9–11 provide a dramatic confirmation that at the time of Jesus the restoration of Israel was expected as the first step in the fulfillment of the historical promises, virtually the presupposition for the next step of the inclusion of the Gentiles. That is, Paul's own struggle to figure out how the original plan of salvation did not work and had to be revised—such that the Gentiles would respond first so that a jealous Israel would finally respond to the fulfillment—proves the existence of the original expectation regarding the restoration of Israel.

Three themes or sets of material in the gospel tradition in particular indicate that Jesus was almost certainly working for the renewal of Israel: the location of his ministry in the villages and towns of Galilee (vs. the cities) and its restriction to "the house of Israel"; Jesus' continuity with John's call for repentance and the threats of judgment Jesus pronounced on whole villages or on "this generation"; and Jesus' constitution of the twelve disciples as symbolic of the renewal of the people of Israel.

TO THE LOST SHEEP OF THE HOUSE OF ISRAEL

Jesus apparently focused his ministry on the ordinary people in the villages and small towns of Galilee, judging from the place names in the gospel traditions. Before his journey to Jerusalem there is no mention of his having visited—indeed one gets the impression he must have avoided—the small cities in or around Galilee, such as Tiberias, Antipas' capital, and Sepphoris, rebuilt in Hellenistic style after being destroyed by the Romans in 4 B.C.E. If he had been following some grander design for his own ministry, one would expect him to have taken the opportunity to preach in nearby Gentile territories.

According to gospel traditions, moreover, he understood his mission and that of his disciples as directed to "the lost sheep of the house of

Israel" (Matthew 15:24 and 10:6). Even though these traditions are preserved only in Matthew, they must be judged to be extremely early or originally from Jesus himself. The early churches already actively engaged in, or resulting from, the mission to the Gentiles would not have made them up (one need think only of Paul's own mission, the ending of Matthew, and the perspective of Luke's Gospel and Acts). If they originated with the earliest church in Jerusalem, then they represent Jesus' earliest followers' own lack of concern about any mission to the Gentiles (e.g., Acts 11:19) by appeal to Jesus' own practice. But then it makes more sense to view these traditions as stemming originally from Jesus.[38]

Jesus' statement that he "was sent only to the lost sheep of the house of Israel" is paralleled by two stories in the gospel tradition in which Jesus encounters Gentiles and does healings, reluctantly and at a distance. In both Mark 7:24–30 (into which Matthew placed 15:24) and Matthew 8:5–13 Jesus finally responded to their persistent faith. But especially in the story of the Syrophoenician woman Jesus' initial stance was harsh and forbidding: "Let the children first be fed, for it is not right to take the children's bread and throw it to the dogs" (Mark 7:27), not a comment likely to have originated with the Gentile church. By contrast, in two other stories (both in Luke 13:10–17; 19:1–10) Jesus is portrayed as healing a woman or accepting hospitality from Zaccheus precisely because they were "a daughter" and "a son of Abraham" (Luke 13:16; 19:9). Jesus apparently understood his mission as being "to the lost sheep of the house of Israel," i.e., to God's special flock who were in a condition of being "lost."

REPENTANCE AND JUDGMENT

An essential and central aspect of the hopes for restoration of Israel was that the people would return to the Lord in a renewal of justice (e.g., Isaiah 44:21–22; 55:6–7). Jesus would appear to have been advocating just such a renewal in his preaching. Under the rubric of "repentance" (a term that actually occurs infrequently in the gospel tradition), this renewal is often reduced to a religious dimension, and hence misunderstood. The misreading of much apocalyptic imagery of judgment, including some of that used by Jesus, as referring to the last judgment, the End, has contributed to this misunderstanding. Recently the repentance issue has been distorted once again by setting up a concept of "national repentance" from biblical and apocryphal passages, and then discovering that Jesus' preaching is only individualistic.[39] But this is a reversion to the old idealist approach whereby scholarship set up a synthetic concept, for example, of the expectation of "the Messiah" or "the eschatological prophet," and then searched for texts to show that Jesus did (or did not) fulfill the expectation. It should be obvious, however, that a synthetic concept of national repentance constructed from passages about future hopes and the concrete efforts of a prophet to induce people to "change their ways" are not comparable entities. It is difficult to imagine how a preacher of repentance would proceed concretely in a traditional agrarian society except by addressing relatively small groups and, by means of parables, promises, and threats, inducing individuals to change their patterns of social behavior. The abstract concept of "national" vs. individual repentance distorts the issue of renewal of justice, which can be effected only by a number of individuals deciding to change their social relations.

The starting point on the issue of repentance must be Jesus' relation with John. There is widespread agreement that John practiced and preached "baptism" as a rite of returning to God in rededication to maintaining just social relations. Preaching his conviction that God's judgment was imminent—"Even now the axe is laid to the root of the trees"—John called for righteous social behavior: "Every tree, therefore, that does not bear good fruit is cut down and thrown into the fire" (Luke 3:9; Matthew 3:10). Rigorous reorientation of individual and collective life was urgent because after John there was coming "a mightier one" whose "winnowing fork is in his hand, to clear his threshing floor, and to gather the wheat into his granary; but the chaff he will burn with unquenchable fire" (Luke 3:16–17; Matthew 3:11–12). In an action that many believe indicates that Jesus started as a follower of John, Jesus himself came to be baptized (Mark 1:9). Moreover, as noted already, Jesus viewed John's ministry as the turning point in history between the old era governed by "the law and the prophets" and the new situation of the presence of the kingdom (Matthew 11:11–12 and parallels). Thus the crisis created by the coming of the kingdom was virtually the same as or continuous with the crisis of judgment and repentance already announced by John.

Indeed, much of Jesus' own preaching of the kingdom is very reminiscent of John's urgency about the renewal of righteousness in the face of judgment, including the common use of the harvest imagery traditional among biblical prophets. Jesus compared the kingdom of God to harvesting a field in which both wheat and tares had been growing simultaneously, where the reapers were told, "Gather the weeds first and bind them in bundles to be burned, but gather the wheat into my barn." He also compared the kingdom to "a net which was thrown into the sea and gathered fish of every kind; when it was full, men drew it ashore and sat down and sorted the good into vessels but threw away the bad" (Matthew 13:24–30,47–48). The parable of "the great supper," similarly, portrays a situation in which those who knew all along they were "invited" were suddenly called to respond because the "banquet" was now ready, and were excluded when they failed to come (Luke 14:16–24; Gospel of Thomas no. 64, which provides the most original version, as noted above). In contrast with the preaching of John (at least the fragments available in Matthew 3 and Luke 3), however, Jesus used positive inducement as well as the threat of judgment. Some of the parables portray how ready God is to forgive and accept, indeed is persistent in pursuit of the "lost": e.g., the first half of "the prodigal son," "the lost sheep," and "the lost coin" (Luke 15:11–24,3–6,8–9).

That Jesus was concerned not simply with individuals but with the people generally is indicated especially in the woes he pronounced over unresponsive Galilean towns and the threats he uttered against his own "generation."

"Woe to you, Chorazin! woe to you, Bethsaida! for if the mighty works done in you had been done in Tyre and Sidon, they would have repented long ago, sitting in sackcloth and ashes. But it shall be more tolerable in the judgment for Tyre and Sidon than for you. And you, Capernaum, will you be exalted to heaven? You shall be brought down to Hades." (Luke 10:13–15; Matthew 11:21–23)

Besides employing a traditional prophetic form (e.g., Amos 6:4–7; Micah 2:1; Zephaniah 2:5) in invoking judgment on the towns in which he had worked but which had not "repented," Jesus also apparently evoked an old prophetic tradition of woes against the old enemy maritime cities (e.g., Jeremiah 47:4; Ezekiel 28:2–23; Zechariah 9:1–4), only now in curses upon the intransigent in Israel.[40] These woes indicate that Jesus, like the classical biblical prophets, expected more than an individual response to his practice and preaching, and that he presupposed collective accountability as well. A similar presupposition of collective accountability is expressed in the related sayings transmitted in the "mission discourse" in both Mark and Q:

"But whenever you enter a town and they do not receive you, go into the streets and say, 'Even the dust of your town that clings to our feet, we wipe off against you; nevertheless know this, that the kingdom of God has come near.' I tell you, it shall be more tolerable on that day for Sodom than for that town." (Luke 10:10–12; cf. Mark 6:10–11)

Individuals had to decide to change; but they were still members of local villages and towns, the concrete social form in which "Israel" was socially embodied. Jesus was clearly concerned that the people generally, village by village, town by town, respond to the new possibility, the presence of the kingdom.

Two originally separate traditions were apparently combined in Q because of the occurrence of the name Jonah in both of them: Luke 11:29–30,31–32 and Matthew 12:38–42. The first, Luke 11:29b, expanded and explained in 11:30, is thought to be more original in form than its parallel in Mark 8:12: "This generation is an evil generation; it seeks a sign, but no sign shall be given to it except the sign of Jonah. For as Jonah became a sign to the men of Nineveh, so will the son of man be to this generation." Matthew's different version of the second or "explanation" half of the saying, draws the analogy between Jonah in the whale and Jesus in the tomb before resurrection. The more original form of the "explanation" in Luke clearly suggests a prophet's preaching, possibly John's, probably Jesus', as "the sign to this generation," by analogy with Jonah and his preaching as the sign to the people of Nineveh to repent. But even if the explanatory statement is secondary, it indicates how the stark original saying was understood early in the tradition: no sign would be given to that generation; no sign, that is, but the preaching of repentance, by analogy with the sign that Jonah was to the Ninevites with his preaching.

The second tradition in this Q passage is a dual saying:

"The Queen of the South will arise at the judgment with the men of this generation and condemn them; for she came from the ends of the earth to hear the wisdom of Solomon, and behold something greater than Solomon is here. The men of Nineveh will arise at the judgment with this generation and condemn it; for they repented at the preaching of Jonah, and behold, something greater than Jonah is here." (Luke 11:31–32; Matthew 12:42,41)

As mentioned above, there is no reason to think of the "resurrection" and "last judgment" here; the Queen of the South and the Ninevites are simply portrayed as arising in the divine court as witnesses against "this generation." And again, there is no reason to think of these sayings as anti-Jewish "Christian polemic." Jesus uses these famous Gentile responses to the world-renowned wisdom coming from an Israelite king and to the preaching of repentance from an Israelite prophet to shame his contemporary "Israelites" for not responding to the current crisis, the presence of the kingdom (cf. Amos 9:7). He is concerned to reach his people generally through his preaching of the kingdom; but as is indicated by the pejorative phrase "this generation" in context, he is finding his contemporaries intransigent. Ironic as it might seem, it is in these woes and threats of judgment that we can discern Jesus' concern for the renewal of the whole society.

THE TWELVE DISCIPLES AND THE TWELVE TRIBES OF ISRAEL

One of the principal indications that Jesus intended the restoration of Israel was his appointment of the Twelve. Although some important critics have claimed that the twelve disciples were the creation of the early church as "eschatological regents," scholars more generally view them as appointed by Jesus during his ministry, at least as a symbolic number.[41] First Corinthians 15:3–5 provides early evidence that the Twelve were a solid and standard pre-Pauline tradition. Moreover, the disciples and particularly the Twelve play a very important role in gospel traditions (even if they are not prominent in Q). Two lines of reasoning about some of these traditions lead to the conclusion that the twelve disciples go back to Jesus' ministry rather than only to the early church. The first is the embarrassment that one of the Twelve betrayed Jesus: the church would hardly have created the idea of the Twelve, including Judas, judging the twelve tribes (Matthew 19:28) after the fixing of the tradition of Judas' betrayal. The second is the minor disagreements among the lists of the names of the Twelve: these slight discrepancies are explicable if the number twelve was already fixed but the memory of a few particulars somewhat dim or variant, but it is hardly credible that the church would have created the Twelve as a group of regents and then make lists that disagreed. We know little or nothing in particular about any of the Twelve—least of all that some of them may have been representatives of various factions within Jewish society at the time; e.g., that one was a "Zealot" or that one was a tax collector (a tradition stemming from the early church). But the basic existence of the Twelve during Jesus' ministry, at least as a traditional symbolic number of disciples, appears to be a secure datum.[42]

Even apart from the key text of Matthew 19:28 and parallels, there appears to be solid evidence that the twelve disciples were symbolic of the restoration of the twelve tribes of Israel. The twelve tribes had become one of the principal images of the future restoration of the people. In one of the "servant songs" in Second Isaiah the restoration of the tribes is linked with the fulfillment of the promise to the ancestors; the servant is called "to raise up the tribes of Jacob" prefatory to becoming a light to the nations (Isaiah 49:6). Ben Sira (Sirach 26:11) appeals to God to gather the tribes of Jacob and give them their inheritance, and anticipates that one of the appointed tasks of the returning Elijah will be "to restore the tribes of Jacob" (Sirach 48:10). Psalms of Solomon 17:28–31,50 appeals for the reestablishment of the tribes on the land as well as their gathering together. Revelation 21:10–14 and Acts 26:7 indicate that the early Christian tradition had simply continued this standard symbolization of the fulfillment of the promises to the ancestors, the restoration of Israel according to the twelve tribes.

Most striking is the evidence from Qumran: that a contemporary community, acting in anticipation of the imminent fulfillment, structured its leadership in terms of twelve (symbolic) representatives of the twelve tribes: the Council of the Community consisting of twelve laymen along with the three priests (1QS 8:1–2); the twelve chief priests and twelve representative Levites, "one for each tribe" (1QM 2:2–3); the twelve chiefs of the twelve tribes, along with the "prince" and priestly leaders (1QM 5:1–3); and twelve loaves of bread offered by the heads of the tribes (11QTemple 18:14–16). Revelation 21:10–14 reveals the same symbolization of the twelve apostles as representative of the twelve tribes already well established in the communities of Jesus' followers. It seems highly credible, therefore, when New Testament scholarship claims (or simply assumes) that the twelve disciples, almost certainly appointed during Jesus' ministry, symbolized the imminent restoration of Israel in its twelve tribes.

Matthew 19:28 and Luke 22:28–30 then provide explicit evidence that Jesus was symbolizing the restoration of Israel in constituting the Twelve. Keeping in mind possible variations in the sequence of words and phrases, and anticipating justification given below for the translation of certain terms, we can use a critically justified reconstruction of the saying as it may have stood in Q:

You who have followed me, (in the restoration) when the son of man shall sit on his glorious throne you yourselves will also sit on twelve thrones saving (effecting justice for) the twelve tribes of Israel.

Bultmann, followed by others whose radical scepticism, theological inclinations, and refusal to pursue form-criticism into genuine social contexts led him to posit a radical break between Jesus the teacher and the early church, concluded that we hear in this passage only "the risen Lord," since it was only in the early church that "the Twelve were first held to be the judges of Israel in the time of the end."[43] Such a declaration, of course, does not satisfy form-criticism's own criterion of "dissimilarity"; for the the function of the twelve disciples here is surely different from their other functions, which are most definitely those discerned as important in the post-Easter church, such as witnesses to the resurrection and guarantors of the gospel traditions.

Indeed, much of the previous interpretation of this passage illustrates how the (in)authenticity of a saying and its supposed meaning have been determined by the presuppositions of the modern interpreters and by their assumptions concerning the meaning of certain terms in the passage. Much modern New Testament interpretation, whether by liberals, existentialists, and/or form-critics, presupposes that Jesus was primarily a teacher, that he addressed individuals, and that it is not necessary to bring concrete social (i.e., political-economic) context into consideration. Moreover, much of the interpretation of this passage has assumed that *krinein* meant "judging" *(richten)*, or at most "ruling," that the passage referred to some sort of "last judgment," that "the Son of man" either referred to Jesus' return in judgment at the "end-time" or was an indication of the inauthenticity of the whole passage, and/or that *palingenesis* in Matthew 19:28 meant "the new world" (RSV) somewhat in the Stoic sense of the regeneration of the world. None of these assumptions is valid. A change or shift in any one or more makes a considerable difference in how the passage is understood and in what context it would have made sense.

One of the principal points of our agenda is to take seriously the concrete social (i.e., political-economic as well as religious) context of Jesus' ministry and the movement he catalyzed. Instead of assuming that there was no social context and orientation to his ministry (and correspondingly dismissing as inauthentic any material referring to a community or other social-historical dimension), we should explore what the character of that context and orientation may have been. Reexamination of the previous assumptions about the meaning of certain terms in Matthew 19:28 and Luke 22:30, assumptions that corresponded to the attribution of the passage to the early church, may help us discern more precisely what the social orientation of this saying may have been in the context of Jesus' ministry.

First of all, *palingenesis* need not be read in the Stoic sense of regeneration of the cosmos, as is usually assumed.[44] That was precisely the term used by Josephus when describing a historical renewal or restoration of the people in their land, and one, moreover, that he portrays also in terms of the twelve tribes (*Ant.* 11.66,107). Even if the Aramaic equivalent of the term was not part of the original saying, but was added in Q or by Matthew, it provides a clear indication of how the passage as a whole was understood in the tradition: in terms of the future restoration or reconstitution of Israel in the land, i.e., as had happened previously in the return from the Babylonian exile.

Second, it is clear that the early church had indeed identified the exalted Jesus Christ, with the "son of man" conceived as a figure coming in judgment, and hence that some of the "son of man" sayings should be viewed as stemming originally from that early church. Nevertheless, even as it is clear that in some sayings Jesus thinks of the "son of man" as a symbol or a figure different from himself, so it is highly likely that, especially Jesus himself, prior to exaltation as the risen Lord, could have used the symbol "son of man" in the original Danielic sense, perhaps even in direct allusion to the vision of Daniel 7. The saying of Jesus reported in his trial before the Sanhedrin in Mark 14:62 is clearly an allusion to the scene portrayed in Daniel 7. It is thus at least conceivable that the phrase "when the son of man shall sit on his glorious throne" in Jesus' saying in Matthew 19:28 should be read somewhat in the original Danielic sense as a symbol for "the people of the saints of the Most High" being granted rule and dominion themselves (Daniel 7:13–14,27). That is, the meaning of "the son of man sitting on his glorious throne" would thus parallel, indeed be almost synonymous with, the *palingenesis,* the restoration of the people in their land.

The most determinative assumption has been that *krinein* means "judging" or "ruling." It is then supposed that the reference is to the Twelve judging Israel (e.g., for having rejected Jesus and his message), and that such judicial activity would contradict Jesus' concern for Israel in the light of the inbreaking of the kingdom.[45] The activity of the Twelve has also been interpreted as "ruling"; but that meaning is dismissed because it would seem to contradict other teachings of Jesus that the greatest among the disciples must be servants or childlike.[46] Even though *krinein* means simply "judging" elsewhere in the gospel tradition (e.g., Matthew 7:1; Luke 7:43; 12:57), "judging" and "ruling" are by no means the only possibilities for our understanding of the term in Matthew 19:28 and parallels.

It is curious that so little attention has been paid to the "biblical" Greek *krinein* and related terms in the Septuagint, and to the Hebrew s ˘apat and related terms behind them. In most English traditions of Bible translation, *krinein, šapat,* and related terms have usually been translated with the terminology of "judging, judge, judicial," etc. (similarly in German translations). However, the article on *krinein* and related terms in the *Theological Dictionary of the New Testament*, inadequate as it is, should have been a tip-off with regard to this passage, along with most of the passages concerning "judges" and "judging" (especially God's) in the Old Testament. That article makes repeated comments to the effect that, despite their usual judicial meaning of "judging" or "deciding," *krinein*, etc., and *šapat*, etc., in biblical usage go beyond the usual Greek meaning of *krinein* and "have to be differentiated from the Roman concept of law" or from the idea of distributive justice; indeed, that the terms have connotations of deliverance, grace, and salvation, and that God's judging or justice "regulates the social relationships of the people" and asserts the rights of the oppressed against the oppressors.[47]

If we go so far as to examine texts in which the "judging" terminology is used, it is clear that those who, filled with the Spirit of God, lead the people of Israel in reasserting their independence from conquerors or exploiters are "liberators" or "saviors," not "judges" (Judges 2:16; 3:10; 4:4, in context; even 11:27). Similarly, Yahweh does not "judge," but rather "liberates," "delivers," "saves," or "effects justice for" the orphan, widow, poor, or oppressed in passage after passage (see especially Psalms 9; 10:18; 35; 58; 72:4; 76:9; 82:1–4; 94; 103:6; 140:12; 146:7; note that the numbering of psalms is one lower in the Septuagint). Appealing to God's characteristic concern for and previous liberation of the poor and oppressed (e.g., Deuteronomy 10:18), the prophets castigate predatory rulers for their exploiting the "righteous" poor, etc. (e.g., Isaiah 1:17; 10:1–2). Expectations of God's future "judgment," or more properly "liberation" or "salvation," were almost certainly influenced by the portrayal of Yahweh's coming to deliver "the world with righteousness, and the peoples with his equity/truth" (Psalms 96:13; 98:9). For example, the "servant of Yahweh" who is to restore the twelve tribes of Israel in Isaiah 49:6 is expected to bring "justice" (not "judgment") to the peoples in Isaiah 42:1 (parallel surely to the "salvation" in 49:6). Now, there is every reason to believe that this meaning would have carried over among people who continued to speak Hebrew, or Aramaic informed by biblical Hebrew, even though that meaning did not carry over once the terms were translated into Greek, Latin, and finally into English and German. Indeed, the only sound method would be to assume the meaning (behind the *krinein* in this passage) closer to *šapat* in biblical Hebrew, rather than the meaning assumed by modern English- or German-speaking scholars. Thus the sense of the saying would have been that the Twelve would be sitting on the thrones "liberating/redeeming/establishing justice for" the twelve tribes of Israel.

This interpretation of Matthew 19:28 and parallels can be confirmed by comparison with two contemporaneous examples that also combine both the symbolic twelve tribes and a sense of fulfillment with the idea of the establishment of justice/salvation (i.e., more positively active and liberating than is connoted by "judgment"). Psalms of Solomon 17:28–32 expects that the anointed son of David will "gather together a holy people, whom he shall lead in righteousness, and . . . will "effect justice for" (or "deliver") the tribes of the people that have been sanctified by the Lord his God." This means, according to the following lines, that he will no longer allow any injustice in their midst, and that he will establish them according to their tribes in the land. What has been translated as "judging" was really a concrete liberating or justice-establishing aspect of the restoration of the people, the tribes of Israel, in their land. Secondly (and more striking in terms of the parallel to the twelve disciples), although the same term (*šapat* or equivalent) may not be used, the representative "twelve men and three priests" who comprise "the Council of the Community" at Qumran are described as having a similar function (1QS 8:1–4), as they effect "righteousness, justice, lovingkindness, and humility, . . . preserve faith in the land, . . . and atone for sin by the practice of justice."[48]

Finally, according to this biblical way of understanding *krinein*, the liberating or justice-establishing activity of the Twelve in Matthew 19:28 and parallels stands in continuity with the "mission" they were given during Jesus' ministry, whereas it appeared as puzzlingly different when the Twelve were understood to be "judging" Israel (which was the principal grounds for denying the "authenticity" of Matthew 19:28!). According to the "mission discourses" in Mark and Q, the disciples are charged with healing, exorcism, preaching the presence of the kingdom, and spreading "peace" (i.e., *shalom* = salvation/liberation) to those they visit and, in Q and Luke 10:10–11, pronouncing judgment against those towns that do not respond positively. The disciples are thus sent out to continue and expand Jesus' own mission of the liberation and renewal of the people. Some of the earliest gospel traditions (e.g., Matthew 11:5 and Luke 7:22) understand Jesus' activities as the fulfillment of the eagerly awaited deliverance prophesied by "Isaiah" (Isaiah 35:5; 61:1–2). Now, this is exactly what the future deliverance or *mišpat* was expected to be: seeking the lost sheep of the house of Israel, binding up the crippled, and strengthening the weak; in sum, "feeding them in justice" (Ezekiel 34:16). The role of the Twelve thus continues and extends that of Jesus even as it fits within and acts out the very (temporal) structure of the historical fulfillment and renewal of Israel. Parallel to the way in which the kingdom of God is already present in the midst of the people, is available to be entered and yet is still to come "with power," the twelve disciples are already engaged with Jesus in saving activities (healings, exorcisms, preaching the kingdom's presence), and the same representative Twelve will continue their saving and justice-establishing activities in completing the renewal of the twelve tribes of Israel.[49]

The principal point to be derived from Matthew 19:28 and Luke 22:30, of course, is that, whether in the already-present reality of the kingdom or in the imminent completion of the kingdom's realization, Jesus is concerned with the restoration or renewal of the people of Israel, as symbolized during his ministry in the constitution of the twelve disciples. Just as they were sent out to heal and preach to the lost sheep of the house of Israel, so in the final restoration of the people in the land, they would still carry out functions of redemption and the establishment of justice for the twelve tribes of Israel. Not even Matthew or Luke views the saying (Matthew 19:28 and Luke 22:30) as an institution of some office or function of the twelve apostles in the church or early Christianity. In Q, as reconstructed above, and, originally, as a statement of Jesus, this saying provides clear indication of Jesus' understanding of his ministry as directed toward the renewal of the people of Israel. The twelve disciples were symbolic of the twelve tribes of Israel who, in turn, were a standing symbol for the restoration of Israel.

When Jesus preached that the kingdom of God was at hand, he was not referring to a place or to some particular cataclysmic final eschatological act of God that would bring an end to history. The "kingdom of God" in Jesus' preaching refers to God's saving action, and the people who receive benefit from God's gracious action are expected to glorify God in gratitude. The focal concern of the kingdom of God in Jesus' preaching and practice, however, is the liberation and welfare of the people. Jesus' understanding of the "kingdom of God" is similar in its broader perspective to the confident hopes expressed in then-contemporary Jewish apocalyptic literature. That is, he had utter confidence that God was restoring the life of the society, and that this would mean judgment for those who oppressed the people and vindication for those who faithfully adhered to God's will and responded to the kingdom. That is, God was imminently and presently effecting a historical transformation. In modern parlance that would be labeled a "revolution."

The principal thrust of Jesus' practice and preaching, however, was to manifest and mediate the presence of the kingdom of God. In the gospel traditions of Jesus' words and deeds, we can observe the kingdom present in the experience of the people in distinctive ways. Jesus and his followers celebrated the joys of the kingdom present in festive banqueting. In the healings and forgiveness of sins and in the exorcisms, individual persons experienced the liberation from disease and oppressive forces and the new life effected by God's action. Jesus' interpretation of the exorcisms, moreover, points to the broader implications of God's present action among the people. That is, since the exorcisms are obviously being effected by God, it is clear that the rule of Satan has been broken. But that meant also that the oppressive established order maintained by the power of Satan (according to the apocalyptic dualistic view of reality that was shared by Jesus and his contemporaries) was also under judgment. The old order was in fact being replaced by a new social-political order, that is, the "kingdom of God," which Jesus was inviting the people to "enter."

Indeed, Jesus was engaged in catalyzing the renewal of the people, Israel. Far from being primarily a "teacher" of timeless truths or a preacher of cosmic catastrophe calling for authentic "decision," Jesus ministered "to the lost sheep of the house of Israel." He summoned the people to recognize the presence of the kingdom and to enter the kingdom, but if they did not respond to the historical crisis, he did not hesitate to pronounce judgment. It is precisely in the pronounced woes against whole villages or against the whole (sinful) "generation" that we can discern that Jesus was not simply addressing individuals but was calling for collective, social response.

The renewal of a people, however, can happen only in concrete terms; it must take some concrete social forms. Hence the next step is to examine the gospel traditions for evidence about who responded to the presence of the kingdom and in what particular ways the renewed Israel was to take shape.

8. The Renewal of Local Community, I: Egalitarian Social Relations

JESUS' FOLLOWING: NOT PARTICULAR GROUPS BUT LOCAL COMMUNITIES

Some treatments of Jesus, even very important and influential ones, have barely mentioned any community with which Jesus may have interacted. More generally, interpretations of Jesus and of the earliest "church" refer to such a community in vague terms, such as "the eschatological community," "the community around Jesus," "those gathered round Jesus," or "the band of disciples."[1] The old theologically determined picture of "Christianity" as having been started by a handful of disciples who, fired by the experience of Jesus' resurrection and ascension, spread the Gospel outward from Jerusalem and gathered churches together, largely among the Gentiles, probably still influences us more than we think. Strongly influenced by the passion narratives, the earliest chapters of Acts, and some Pauline passages, this picture conceives of the very earliest church as a small group gathered in Jerusalem eagerly awaiting the return of Jesus. It was the resurrection experience that first galvanized the formation of the community and the disciples, now become "apostles," who organized it as missionaries. Behind the resurrection and the formation of a "church" lay only the ministry of Jesus himself and a vaguely conceived band of literal and figurative "followers" who, far from having any group identity, simply scattered when Jesus was arrested. This traditional picture makes the people to whom Jesus ministered virtually superfluous to salvation-history (after all, "the Jews" rejected Jesus, the Messiah, so the disciples-become-apostles made a church out of Gentiles).

We should be well aware by now that this picture, including such idealized features as the people selling their possessions and holding all things in common (Acts 2:44–45; 4:32–35), is a schematic projection by Luke—and by others less ancient. To think more concretely regarding such a picture and its features, for the long-range sustenance of such a community it is insufficient to organize only consumption, however communally; production also must be organized in some way. We may doubt whether the Jerusalem community, cut off from any productive economic base, could have survived very long, even if the "collections" engineered by Paul had been frequent and generous (cf. 1 Corinthians 16:1–4; 2 Corinthians 8–9). The "Jesus movement" must have had some economic base in Palestine other than a few dozen propertyless missionaries and converts in the "Jerusalem community," and that base must have put down roots prior to the crucifixion and resurrection–exaltation of Jesus. That is, there must already have been a more concrete "community" than a vaguely conceived group of "followers" during the ministry of Jesus.

A somewhat more "social" but still vague variation on this traditional picture is that the disciples themselves formed a "community" around Jesus.[2] Yet there is little or no evidence for this, either in the gospel tradition or in Acts. In the early chapters of Acts the Eleven reconstituted to Twelve serve a symbolic transitional function, after which some of them work as missionaries outside Jerusalem, while Peter and eventually James the brother of Jesus take over leadership of the Jerusalem "church." There is no indication that the Twelve or some larger group of "disciples" formed any sort of community prior to or after the resurrection. In the synoptic gospel tradition the Twelve are a symbolic number representing the restoration of Israel, as we have seen. The term "disciples" occurs frequently, but usually in editorial contexts. Moreover, its usage fluctuates widely between a small number of special disciples and a very large number of people. Neither the inner circle nor the large group is portrayed as forming a community in some way. The same fluctuation between small and very large numbers is true of the usage of the verb for "following" Jesus. Further, whether it be "the twelve" (Mark 6:7; Luke 9:1), the "twelve disciples" (Matthew 10:1), or the "seventy others" (Luke 10:1), they are all preachers and healers sent out on mission to the villages of Galilee, with no indication of any sort of base. Community must be located and structured in some concrete way, but the disciples or followers of Jesus appear to be amorphous and mobile.

With regard to both the "post-resurrection Jerusalem community" and "disciples" as a picture of the "Jesus" community, we have similar cases of vague social images with little or no historical evidence. Both have been determined by the theologization of history; i.e., when no distinction is made between them, then theological ideas can be mistaken for or simply become social-historical assumptions.

A very important development has been the increasing recognition that, at least in the early strata of the gospel tradition, there was no sense of a "church" or "Jesus community" separate from Israel.[3] There were no special name, rites (other than table fellowship; baptism was initiated by John and not distinctive to Jesus' followers), and organization separate from the rest of Jewish society. The Twelve, like the "seventy," were messengers to the villages and towns in Israel, not the teachers or officers of a separate community in the process of formation. Jesus preached the presence and availability of the kingdom of God for the people generally, seeking the renewal of Israel as a whole people, not the establishment of a separate community or the separation of a "remnant." After the crucifixion and resurrection Jesus' followers apparently went on living within the already-existing Jewish societal forms.

It is clear that the social context of Jesus' ministry is now being taken more seriously. Yet, although no systematic study has been made of the concrete social context of Jesus' ministry, a number of recent treatments of Jesus have claimed that the majority of his followers were of some particular groups within Palestinian Jewish society. A critical review of evidence adduced from the gospel tradition indicates that these claims do not hold up. More important, this review suggests that looking for distinctive people or groups as Jesus' followers is an inappropriate approach to the issue of the concrete social context of his ministry. Our approach must be broader in focus because of the character of our evidence. Examination of the usually somewhat indirect evidence available will suggest that we look for those to whom Jesus ministered and who may have responded to his teachings and actions in the village communities of Galilee, not in some separated community or particular groups.

TAX COLLECTORS

At three points in the synoptic Gospels it is either reported or charged that Jesus associated with "tax collectors and sinners" (Mark 2:15; Matthew 11:18–19; Luke 7:33–34; Luke 15:1–2). These reports have taken on a crucial importance in recent scholarly interpretations of Jesus in two regards. First, on the assumption that "tax collectors" were collaborators with the Romans, Jesus' reported fellowship with such "quislings" has become one of the few principal points in the argument that Jesus opposed the Zealots.[4] Second, on the assumption that the tax collectors had "made themselves as Gentiles," i.e., excluded from the Jewish community, Jesus' supposed fellowship with these despicable "outlaws" became the principal factor that drove the Jewish authorities to the desperate measure of turning a fellow Jew over to the Romans for execution.[5] Unfortunately for these interpretations (almost a consensus), the assumptions on which they are based are simply unwarranted; and there is little or no evidence that Jesus held table fellowship with tax collectors in the first place, let alone that they constituted a significant element among his following.[6]

The *telonai* in the gospel reports were surely not the wealthy large-scale "tax farmers" called *publicani,* infamous for their fortunes and fraud in the late Republican period of Roman imperialism. They were rather the "toll collectors" who handled tariffs and custom duties in Roman provinces. They were largely small-scale toll collectors under the authority of a more powerful officer, an *architelones* (such as Zaccheus, in Luke 19:2–9 ?). More important, there is no clear evidence that they would have been viewed as "quisling" collaborators with the Romans in the context of Jesus' ministry. Toll collectors in Galilee at the time would have been part of the administration of Herod Antipas, not of the Roman governors who took over administration of Galilee as well as Judea after the death of Agrippa I in 44. Neither were they in the employ of the Romans, nor were they involved in direct taxation of the produce of the land. They may well have been disliked or even hated and resented because of their dishonesty and extortion, but they were likely not viewed as collaborators during the time of Jesus' ministry in Galilee. The passage about John's preaching in Luke 3:12–13 confirms this.

Nor is there much evidence that these "toll collectors" were such heinous sinners that they had made themselves "as Gentiles," i.e., completely outside "Judaism" and its Law. In later Mishnaic and other texts discussing persons thought to be dishonest because of their professions, such as herdsmen, tax collectors, and toll collectors, the latter are not necessarily excluded as witnesses. There is simply no conclusive evidence that either tax or toll collectors were regarded as Gentiles.[7] Thus even if Jesus did associate with "toll collectors," this provides no evidential basis for supposing that he took a nonresistant stance toward Roman rule or that it was his inclusion of toll collectors that led to his execution.

It has become a virtual consensus in recent books, however, that Jesus did in fact consort with "tax collectors and sinners," even that this fellowship was the most distinctive aspect of his ministry.[8] Ironically, the very scholars who make such claims also carefully point out that "we have only scant traditions" for the information that Jesus associated with toll collectors and sinners or that Jesus supposed table fellowship with such people "has all but disappeared from the gospel tradition."[9] It is important therefore to take a more careful look at how thin and problematic the evidence is for Jesus' supposed association with "toll collectors."[10]

The fragment most likely from Jesus himself, or at least from very early tradition, is a saying in connection with a parable: "Truly I say to you, the [toll] collectors and the harlots go into the kingdom before you" (Matthew 21:31b). The saying is evidently addressed to those who assume themselves to be righteous or already to have a claim on salvation, and hence are unresponsive to Jesus' preaching of the kingdom. This saying, moreover, assumes and expresses the same disparaging evaluation of toll collectors and harlots as that held by the addressees. Reference to the toll collectors and harlots going into the kingdom in this saying is used as a rhetorical device against the obstinacy of the righteous or the religious establishment. We cannot even determine from the saying itself whether "the toll collectors and harlots" actually did respond to the offer of the kingdom. And it is difficult to know if there is any historical reliability in the supplement to the saying supplied by Matthew in vs. 32, that the toll collectors and harlots responded to John's preaching of the way of righteousness.

The same disparaging view of toll collectors—even setting them parallel with "Gentiles"—occurs in a similar rhetorical admonition in Matthew 5:46–47: "For if you love those who love you, what reward have you? Do not even the [toll] collectors (Luke 6:32: "sinners") do the same?" Although the current form of the saying is less certainly solid Jesus tradition than Matthew 21:31b, the juxtaposition of toll collectors and "Gentiles" suggests a Palestinian Jewish context. Of course, the parallel of "toll collectors" and "Gentiles" here may be due to Matthew himself, since it occurs elsewhere only in Matthew 18:17. At whatever stage the juxtaposition of the two in these sayings originated, however, the saying in Matthew 18:17 indicates that at least some communities among the early churches viewed both negatively and definitely as outsiders people who were, in no uncertain terms, *not* members of the community. Certainly the Matthean church, or the community that had carried the tradition in Matthew 18:17, did not see itself as perpetuating any distinctive tradition of Jesus' table fellowship with toll collectors! More to the point for determining the character of Jesus' following, nothing in the Jesus sayings examined so far would indicate even a receptive attitude toward toll collectors, let alone a close association with them.

Two of the passages referring to Jesus' fellowship with "tax collectors and sinners" take the form of accusations by his critics, in Matthew 11:18–19 and Luke 7:33–34 and Luke 15:1–2. The latter passage is a curious nonsequitur, probably due to Lucan editorial arrangement of a setting for the stories of the lost sheep and the lost coin. Matthew 11:18–19 and Luke 7:33–34, surely an early tradition, located in the Q discourse concerning the relative significance of Jesus and John, is far more important and revealing:

"For John came neither eating or drinking, and they say, 'He has a demon'; the Son of man came eating and drinking, and they say, 'Behold, a glutton and a drunkard, a friend of tax collectors and sinners!' "

Even if the saying in its present form is a product of the early church, the tradition is very early. Moreover, the early church would not itself have originated the notion that Jesus ate with toll collectors and sinners. Indeed, most scholars would agree that "the deep contempt expressed" in sayings such as Matthew 11:18–19 indicates that "these phrases were coined by *Jesus' opponents.*"[11] Such a charge about Jesus' association "has the same probability of authenticity as has the accusation that Jesus exorcised by a demon."[12] The authenticity of the accusation, however, does not make it true. In this case there are two decisive arguments against the truth of the accusation. Jesus was charged with casting out demons by Beelzebul, the prince of demons, and of being in league with Satan. But he sharply refutes the charge, and few of us would be inclined to accept the truth of the accusation. Moreover, in Matthew 11:18–19 and Luke 7:33–34 the parallelism in the passage itself indicates clearly that the accusation was untrue. Surely the charge that John "had a demon" (because he came neither eating nor drinking) was not viewed as true in the saying itself. No more was the accusation accepted as true that "the Son of man" was "a glutton and drunkard, a friend of toll collectors and sinners" (because he came eating and drinking).

Besides the passages in which Jesus is accused of associating with toll collectors, however, there are two passages in which he is described as actually eating with them. As has long been recognized, however, both of these passages are almost certainly constructions of either the gospel writers or their sources.

The story of Zaccheus (Luke 19:10), besides being peculiar to Luke, has been recognized as a story based on, indeed perhaps an extended version of, the combination of the call of Levi and the "controversy story" reporting Jesus eating with toll collectors in Mark 2:13–17. Hence, if it is based on Mark 2:13–17, it provides no independent evidence regarding Jesus' actual behavior. Mark 2:15–17, in fact, is the only reference to toll collectors in the Gospel of Mark. Not only was the call of Levi story originally independent of Mark 2:15–17, but the description of Jesus at table "with toll collectors and sinners" was created in the early church as an occasion for the saying attributed to Jesus, that "those who are well have no need of a physician, but those who are sick" (Mark 2:17). The situation in the story is quite incredible, with the sudden appearance of the scribes and the Pharisees (were they spying through the window?) and the awkward address of the question to the disciples, immediately followed by Jesus' answer.[13] It has been suggested that in the redactional process, attempts would have been made to make Jesus' table fellowship with toll collectors and sinners more understandable. Available synoptic evidence, however, indicates that it was the early church that constructed the principal passage in which Jesus is portrayed as engaged in such fellowship, as a setting in which a saying of Jesus could be made understandable. Perhaps the early church was somewhat defensive about the accusation that Jesus had associated with the toll collectors and sinners (and/or defensive about some of its own membership, some toll collectors and sinners having joined the communities of Jesus' followers). But its anxiety about them does not give the accusations of Jesus' opponents or its own controversy stories any greater historical veracity.

The last line of defense for those who still want to claim that Jesus associated with "tax collectors" appears to be the gospel tradition of a toll collector among Jesus' followers. In a passage that serves more to acknowledge the lack of evidence than to establish the credibility of his speculative contention, Sanders contends weakly:

Jesus probably did have a tax collector among his followers—even though his name was not securely remembered—and it is probably this fact which gave immediate substance to the charge that he ate with tax collectors. The Gospel tradition subsequently expanded this point ("many tax collectors and sinners," Mark 2:15 and parallels), but we can safely assume that there was at least one.[14]

In the following note, however, even Sanders admits that the passages depicting the call of disciples, such as Mark 2:14, are "ideal scenes."[15] In this case, moreover, the problematic character of the history of the tradition of the call and even the identity of "Matthew/Levi" is compounded by the textual variants in the manuscript transmission. "The tradition is ambiguous regarding the exact identity of the man being called . . . whether he was one of the Twelve, and indeed, whether he was even a tax collector."[16] There is simply little or no evidence that Jesus associated with toll collectors, let alone that he regularly banqueted with them. A few toll collectors may well have responded to

Jesus' preaching of the kingdom. But there is no solid evidence that they constituted a significant element in his following.

SINNERS

The importance attributed to Jesus' association with "sinners" is matched only by the confusion about to whom the term referred—and the inconsistency of scholars in dealing with this issue. A recent book on Jesus concludes that one of the only "certain or virtually certain" things we know about Jesus is that "he promised the kingdom to the wicked" (= sinners).[17] Perhaps. However, theological concerns have led scholars aware of the lack of evidence to overestimate the importance of Jesus' association with sinners in gospel traditions and in the historical reality behind those traditions.[18]

There is simply little or no direct evidence in the gospel tradition that Jesus held table fellowship or otherwise associated with "sinners." As noted above, the phrase "toll collectors and sinners" occurs only three times in the gospel traditions, and none of those texts provides evidence for Jesus' association with sinners. Luke 15:1 is widely recognized as Luke's own composition. Mark 2:15–16 and parallels—the only mention of either toll collectors or sinners in Mark—is part of the "controversy story" constructed as a setting for the saying(s) in Mark 2:17 and is usually recognized as a construction of the early church. Matthew 11:19 and Luke 7:34 are more solid as Jesus tradition, but the statement about Jesus as a "friend of toll collectors and sinners" is an accusation made by others, parallel to that against John the Baptist of having a demon. Yet, as was noted already, just as the accusation against John is regarded as untrue in this passage, and just as the accusation against Jesus (in Luke 11:15 and parallels) that he exorcised demons by the prince of demons is understood as untrue, so the accusation of being "a friend of toll collectors and sinners" is regarded as untrue.

There is also no direct or solid evidence that Jesus offered the kingdom specifically, let alone primarily, to "sinners." The application of the parables of the lost sheep and the lost coin are Lucan, and the theme of joy in heaven over the "one sinner who repents" is a Lucan theme (Luke 15:7,10; cf. 15:18–24), as can be seen from its absence in the Matthean parallel to the parable of the lost sheep (Matthew 18:10–14). Accordingly, one might also suspect that the story of the Pharisee and the toll collector (Luke 18:9–14), with its emphasis on self-humbling breast-beating, is Lucan (or pre-Lucan) more than "authentic" Jesus tradition.[19] The Zacchaeus story is clearly secondary, if not Lucan (19:1–10). We are thus left with only the saying in Mark 2:17b and parallels: "I came not to call the righteous, but sinners." But form-critics have always been suspicious about the authenticity of the "declarations of purpose" couched in the form of "I came. . . ." Indeed, this saying, coupled with Mark 17a, "those who are well have no need of a physician, but those who are sick," in its current setting, Mark 2:15–17, has an apologetic sound, explaining and justifying Jesus as charged with associating with toll collectors and sinners. Ironically, then, the saying that Jesus came to call sinners may have originated as a defense against the accusation that he was associating with sinners. But there is no substantiating evidence that such an accusation was true. Hence neither the accusation nor the declaration of purpose can be used to support the other; and we are left with no evidence, either that Jesus actually had table fellowship with or opened the kingdom specifically to toll collectors and sinners.

A different approach to the question of Jesus' relation with "sinners" is in order. It would seem appropriate to analyze not simply the three "tax collectors and sinners" texts and other passages in which the term "sinners" appears to mean "wicked,"[20] but to analyze all the references to "sinners" in the gospel tradition, and to do this against the background of typical usage of "sinners" and related terms in then-contemporary Jewish literature.[21]

There appear to be three different meanings or uses of "sinners" in the gospel tradition.

(1) In Mark 14:41 (and Matthew 26:45; cf. Luke 24:7), "sinners" refers obviously to Jesus' hostile enemies, the priestly aristocracy who ruled Jewish society for the Romans. In Sirach the "sinners" are the wealthy and powerful, viewed almost as apostates, who exploit the righteous (Sirach 41:5–10; 21:8; 34:20–22). They may not be simply identical with the priestly elite, but they have close identification with the Temple cult, apparently trusting that they can buy God off with

their sacrifices and offerings (Sirach 7:9; 35:12). Similarly, in 1 Enoch 91–104 the "sinners" are the wealthy and powerful who exploit and do violence to the righteous (1 Enoch 94:7–8; 96:4; 96:7–8). If they are not identical with the rulers, they have the latter's support, are apparently also collaborators with foreign rulers (1 Enoch 104:3; 103:14–15), and are seen as compromising or tampering with the Torah (1 Enoch 99:2; 104:10). The Psalms of Solomon, finally, display the same understanding of who the "sinners" are, but the violent and exploitative wealthy and powerful are now identical with the high-priestly rulers (the Hasmoneans) in 17:6–8.

(2) Insofar as all Jews could and would in some way transgress the provisions of the Torah, i.e., would "sin" to a greater or lesser degree, anyone in particular or everyone in general could be called a sinner or sinful. Thus in the same text in which particular "sinners," who are the oppressive rulers, are mentioned, the whole people can be portrayed as sinful, none among them having wrought righteousness and justice (Psalms of Solomon 17:21–42). In accordance with this more general meaning, the fate of the Galileans whose blood Pilate mingled with their sacrifices becomes an occasion for the exhortation that all are in effect "sinners" in need of repentance in the face of the presence of the kingdom (Luke 13:1–3).

(3) The current consensus among New Testament scholars appears to be that "sinners" meant deliberate and unrepentant transgressors of the Torah, such as toll collectors, prostitutes, usurers, and suchlike— i.e., the "wicked" who thus became despised outcasts. This meaning of "sinners" has been established on the basis of later rabbinic literature and projected back as *the* meaning in the context of Jesus' ministry.[22] This might well appear to be an appropriate approach, since the texts these scholars are trying to elucidate are those in which "sinners" appears primarily in accusations on the lips of Pharisees and scribes (with whom the rabbis supposedly stood in continuity), who are portrayed as watching and censuring Jesus' conduct, or in editorial settings and responses to their charges.

There are some serious problems, however, with both the evidence on which this consensus is based and the arguments from that evidence. The evidence presented consists of several rabbinic lists of despised trades.[23] However, not only are the lists "late Rabbinical homiletical exaggeration . . . making all sorts of trades the equivalent of usury . . . with an observable tendency to lengthen," but "tax collector" and "publican" appear only in an extremely late addition to only one among the several lists, and "prostitute" does not appear in any of the lists.[24] Moreover, Luke 18:11 does not belong with such a list of despised *trades,* since "robbers, evil doers, and adulterers" are rather categories of those who violate certain commandments. Thus these lists do not even provide good evidence for a list of despised trades at the time of Jesus, let alone evidence that toll collectors or prostitutes were among them. Most important, these lists provide no evidence that those occupied in such despised trades were what was meant by "sinners." Finally, no evidence is even provided, in this consensus viewpoint, that "sinners" may have meant something like "those who notoriously failed to observe the commandments of God and at whom, therefore, everyone pointed a finger."[25] That sounds like a highly attractive educated guess for what the term may have meant (e.g., in the story about the woman who anointed Jesus' feet, Luke 7:37,39,47), but there is no obvious comparative material for establishing the meaning of "sinners" in those few passages where it occurs in the phrase "toll collectors and sinners."

Hence we are left with the passages themselves; moreover, since Mark 2:15–16 and parallels and Luke 15:1–2 are thought to be secondary, we should focus on Matthew 11:19 and Luke 7:34, which, besides being a solid Jesus tradition, offer a context that may be some guide to the meaning of the term. Upon closer critical examination it is immediately evident that—unless it was part of an idiom in Aramaic or Greek no longer accessible to us—"toll collector" (*telones* in Greek) does not make any sense in the context. The phrase "toll collectors and sinners" stands parallel, supposedly synonymously, with "glutton and drunkard" in a context where Jesus is portrayed as having come "eating and drinking," i.e., celebrating and banqueting instead of fasting like John. One can imagine that disreputable revelers could be labeled as "sinners." But were "toll collectors" known for their partying? Now, it was pointed out some time ago that the Aramaic word *telane,* from the root "to play or sport," likely sounded very much like the Greek *telones* (toll collectors).[26] Thus there may have been an Aramaic term that sounded like and could easily have been confused with "toll collectors," which would fit the context of the gospel tradition in Matthew 11:16–19 and parallels nicely, with a meaning similar to but more precise than "sinners."[27]

Thus perhaps New Testament theologians should not make so much of the "sinners" or the "tax collectors and sinners" as if this were a major category of stigmatized people, even "outcasts," in Palestinian Jewish society at the time. Two of the three relevant texts are based on Matthew 11:19 and parallel and the latter may involve a traditional mistranslation and misunderstanding of a phrase used to accuse Jesus of reveling with "playboys and sinners" (the phrase having been used to reject or dismiss Jesus, and not to label him as guilty of some sort of "capital" offense).

The gospel materials regarding "sinners" can be evaluated in the light of these three different usages, taking into full consideration their typical concrete context. In the three "toll collectors and sinners" passages, Luke 15:1–2; Mark 2:15–16 and parallels; Matthew 11:19 and Luke 7:34 (once the phrase was fixed in Greek), the "official" under-standing articulated by scribes and Pharisees defines the issue. Moreover, as has been explained, that Jesus is accused of associating with toll collectors and sinners is not evidence that he actually did so. Indeed, readers or hearers of the gospel traditions would have assumed the accusation against Jesus to be false.

Two things can have come together, however, to explain why Mark 2:15–17 appears in the gospel tradition. Matthew 11:19 and parallel is solid evidence that Jesus was *accused* of eating with sinners. And it is likely, based on memories in the gospel tradition and on comparative study of movements of social renewal, that disreputable and marginal people were attracted to Jesus' movement. Mark 2:15–17, picking up on the original accusation against Jesus, attempts to explain what has turned out to be true in a sense. But, far from being evidence for Jesus' actual behavior, it is apologetic, similar to other controversy stories defending Jesus' behavior against official (Pharisaic) criticism that accompanies it in Mark 2:1–3:6. Thus Mark 2:15–17 was probably formu-lated not as a programmatic statement about Jesus' overall mission but in a rather more focused manner over against Pharisees and others who responded negatively to Jesus' teachings and actions. No matter how many (repentant) "sinners" may have been attracted to Jesus' movement, however, Jesus' followers at least on occasion thought of outsiders to their new covenantal community as "sinners" (Luke 6:32–34; an expansion of Luke 6:27–31,35–36 in Q?) or as the equivalent, "toll collectors" and "Gentiles" (Matthew 5:46–47; typical Matthean terms, as also in 18:17).

Mark 14:41 and parallels indicates that Jesus' followers, at least, if not Jesus himself, thought of the high-priestly ruling group as "sinners" in the same way as had earlier generations of Jews who viewed themselves as oppressed and exploited by the wealthy and powerful rulers who controlled Jewish society in collaboration with an alien imperial power. That this usage is not more frequent in the gospel tradition may or may not be an indication that communities of Jesus' followers felt themselves to be less defensively self-righteous over against the hated ruling groups. If so, this could be explained by the second sense (above) in which "sinners" is used in the gospel tradition: that all Jews were sinners and in need of repentance in the face of the presence of God and his kingdom as announced by Jesus (as in Luke 13:1–3; cf. Mark 8:38). The woman who anointed Jesus' feet could also be understood as a "sinner" in this same sense, although her sins were many (Luke 7:37,39,47).

Jesus' followers thus understood themselves as repentant and forgiven sinners now participating in and responsible for the new life made possible by God's initiative in offering the kingdom. Although it is not widely attested in the gospel tradition, one would surmise that this is the usual way in which Jesus and his followers would have thought of "sin" and "sinner." It is interesting to note that, if taken out of its current literary context, the saying in Mark 2:17b, whether original to Jesus or simply early tradition, and especially if it had been formulated over against the Pharisees' rejection of his ministry, could easily be understood in somewhat this way. That is, the people of Israel generally were "lost sheep" and "sinners"; the Pharisees and other "righteous" people, whatever their criticism of Jesus, could take care of themselves and were not his particular concern, which was broader and more comprehensive than they were capable of recognizing.

There is thus no evidence that "sinners," in the sense of "despised outcasts" or simply of "the wicked," constituted an important element among Jesus' following. If anything, Jesus and his followers understood themselves and the people generally as sinners in need of repentance (again, see Luke 13:1–3). Not surprisingly, of course, those who responded to God's offer of the kingdom and forgiveness surely included some whose "sins were many" or serious (Luke 7:47; 18:13).

PROSTITUTES

It has also been claimed that, along with "tax collectors and sinners" there were prostitutes among Jesus' followers. This has been based on Matthew 21:31, which is very early Jesus tradition. (The supplementary vs. 32 has long been recognized as a Matthean addition.) It is a misunderstanding of the style of a saying such as Matthew 21:31b, however, to rely upon it as a source for historical information. A similar saying would be "It is easier for a camel to go through the eye of the needle than for a rich man to enter the kingdom of God" (Mark 10:25). The saying clearly is a rhetorical statement directed against those who think they have already been doing the will of God but in fact have not, so that even the most notorious violators of the Torah will precede them into the kingdom. If anything, the implication of the saying is that neither the tax collectors and prostitutes nor the addressees of the saying will enter the kingdom. Luke 7:35–50, behind which supposedly lies an early story about a sinful woman who anointed Jesus' feet, has also been used as evidence that prostitutes joined Jesus' following. But there is no indication anywhere in the story that the woman was a prostitute; she is called simply a "sinner." It is even possible that behind the Greek term "sinner" is the Aramaic term that really means "debtor" (see the Matthean version of the Lord's Prayer, 6:12), thus providing a link with the parable about the two debtors (Luke 7:41–43), which is combined with the story about the woman in this Lucan passage. The only other occurrence of the term "prostitute" in the synoptic tradition is in reference to the behavior of the Prodigal Son (Luke 15:30), hardly meant as an analogy for Jesus' associations. Thus there is no evidence for the claim that Jesus' followers included prostitutes.

BEGGARS, CRIPPLES, AND THE POOR

It has been claimed also that, along with tax collectors, sinners, and prostitutes, beggars, cripples, and the destitute—in short, the "scum" of Palestinian Jewish society—were a significant part of Jesus' following or movement.[28] As with the tax collectors, sinners and prostitutes, solid direct evidence for these other people as followers of Jesus is difficult to find in the gospel traditions. The one report of a beggar or a cripple actually "following" Jesus is probably attributable to Mark. The passage, Mark 10:46–52, does say that once the blind beggar Bartimaeus received his sight he "followed" Jesus on the way. The immediate meaning of "followed on the way" here is physical; i.e., Jesus was walking along the way from Jericho to Jerusalem. A symbolic or figurative meaning is surely present as well (Jesus' being on his way to suffering and death in Jerusalem), but is due to this particular placing of the story by Mark. Otherwise it is not clear that Bartimaeus became a "follower" of Jesus in any special sense different from that in which all the crowds are said to "follow" him.

In contrast with the cases of tax collectors, sinners (as "outcasts" or "wicked"), and prostitutes, however, it seems clear that Jesus did minister to beggars, cripples, and the poor. It is just that most of the evidence is indirect, much of it contained in healing stories that are not direct evidence for situations in the ministry of Jesus. Moreover, even if we are able to conclude that Jesus ministered to beggars, cripples, and the poor, we are still left without any indication of whether and in what way such people became part of Jesus' following or movement. It is clear that little can be gained by combing the synoptic gospel tradition for occurrences of the "cripples," "beggars," and "the poor." Our approach must be broadened and loosened in accordance with the character of the material available to us without lessening the orientation to the concrete social realities (as opposed to the theologically shaped questions that have shaped many previous investigations).

Matthew 11:5 (2–6)—see parallel, Luke 7:22 (18–23)—usually recognized as early Jesus tradition, has been adduced as evidence for beggars, cripples, and the poor among Jesus' "followers." Such a passage, however, hardly provides direct "sociological" evidence. It expresses primarily the sense of fulfillment of expectations happening in Jesus' ministry; the particular kinds of people it mentions are derived from biblical prophecies and are surely meant in a symbolic programmatic sense. It would be foreign to the spirit and style of the passage to argue that there was a one-to-one correspondence between every kind of people mentioned and some particular actions by or followers of Jesus. Nevertheless, Matthew 11:5 and Luke 7:22 does give us information indirectly on those to whom Jesus ministered and who may have responded to that ministry. The passage is recognized as probably an authentic Jesus tradition precisely because it expresses the sense of fulfillment of expectations.[29] Those expectations stood in familiar prophecies such as Isaiah 61:1 and 35:5–6. Hence, as the current setting of the saying (which may well be secondary) indicates, it must have been the actual healing and preaching activities of Jesus that suggested the conclusion that just those expectations were being fulfilled. That is, Jesus must have healed just such cases as the blind, deaf, crippled, and lepers. And he must have addressed his message of the kingdom to the poor. "The poor" in this case does not refer merely to the spiritual poverty of those who stand as humble supplicants before God. Rather it means either the destitute as a type of people somewhat parallel to the blind, cripples, and such; or more likely it is a general term including the blind, cripples, and all others who are oppressed, desperate, hopeless, and unable to defend and perhaps to support themselves.[30]

The beatitudes in Luke 6:20–21, although principally an announcement of blessings, also indicate those to whom Jesus directed his ministry. The term "the poor" here, somewhat spiritualized in the Matthean version, appears to be a general reference to those actually struggling for an existence, and including, or at least overlapping with (as opposed to a special group separate from), "the hungry" and "the mournful." Even if one views these beatitudes as secondary, and regardless of whether they were linked with the corresponding "woes" in Luke 6:24–25, they still indicate either directly or by memory that Jesus offered the kingdom to the poor as opposed to the wealthy.

The term "the poor" in Luke 6:20 and 7:22 may refer to the oppressed and suffering Jewish peasantry generally. Or it may refer more narrowly to the absolutely destitute who have lost all means of support, in which case they would likely be seen by people still in possession of their land as examples of how they themselves might end up. In either case Jesus appears to have addressed his message of the kingdom to the common people generally, in the context of which the healing powers affected individuals suffering under particular ailments and distress. Thus such passages provide at least some indirect evidence for the identity of the followers of Jesus, as well as an indication of the social context in which Jesus' ministry and nascent movement took shape: that is, among the common people or peasantry.

Because the reports of Jesus' having performed healings and exorcisms are so solidly rooted in the gospel tradition, we are virtually certain that he indeed performed such healings and exorcisms. On the other hand, it has long been recognized that the healing and exorcism stories, because they have taken a form so similar to standard Hellenistic miracle stories, do not provide much by way of direct access to the situation of Jesus' ministry. Thus we have only indirect evidence that certain cripples, beggars, and suchlike, were healed by Jesus. But did they also become his followers? Because of the character of the only source material available, the approach to that question must be indirect. Moreover, once we broaden our approach adequately, the answer to that question may be that it is the wrong question, not appropriate to the situation manifested behind our source material. Besides confining our investigations to discrete sayings or healing stories that mention a cripple or a beggar, we have tended to focus on individuals abstracted from concrete social context, in accordance with our modern individualistic presuppositions. Even more than Jesus' "teachings," interpreted by most modern interpreters as addressed to the individual, the "miracle stories" lend themselves to such a narrowing focus. Unlikely as it might seem initially, a close examination of the healing stories can lead to a more precise sense of the response made by those to whom Jesus ministered.

Faith is linked with healing miracles in both the gospel traditions and Hellenistic sources. But in the latter, faith is individualistic and cognitive, whereas in the gospel traditions it is relational and integral to the healing events themselves. In Hellenistic literature and inscriptions, faith is basically an attitude of the listener or onlooker as a consequence of the story or incident. In the gospel stories, faith is a basic trust or even persistent seeking by the principal actors in the story and is a condition, sometimes almost a cause, of the healing itself. Both Matthew and Luke have altered the meaning of faith, somewhat in the Hellenistic direction. As can be seen in their changes to stories such as that of the woman with the flow of blood in Mark 5:25–34, Matthew 9:20–22 thinks of faith more as a petitionary prayer, while Luke 8:43–48 emphasizes gratitude in response to the healing.[31] Yet this only makes all the more striking that in Mark and apparently in the pre-Markan traditions, faith is the trust of those involved as the enabling or effecting condition of the healing. The distinctive character of faith in the Markan and pre-Markan stage of the gospel healing stories suggests that the latter are telling of concrete relational phenomena, not proofs leading to cognitive recognition. The powers at work behind the gospel stories are a relational matter between the Divine (the ultimate source), Jesus (the vehicle or agent), and the persons (to be) healed, for whom the healing powers are unblocked, released, or made effective through their trusting response to Jesus' message and actions.

Yet all of this involves still another dimension (usually not noted because of our reductionist focus on individuals): the social relations manifested in certain particulars in a number of the healing stories. For example, the persons to be healed have obviously heard about Jesus and the special powers working through him in a social context. In several stories (e.g., Mark 2:1–5; 7:31–37; 8:22–26), friends and relatives of the persons to be healed are involved in enabling a paralytic or a blind person, for instance, to come to Jesus for healing and thus clearly have been involved in the faith that is the condition of the healing. And, although the stories themselves typically dwell on the excitement and astonishment over the healing, the healed are restored to regular social interaction, even to a renewed Israel (Luke 13:16). Thus, even though the gospel healing traditions must be read as typical stories and not as direct historical accounts, they nevertheless indicate that Jesus was not healing individuals in order to lead them off into some vaguely conceived "discipleship" or into some utopian community in a new location, like Qumran, but was in effect sending them back to their own homes, which already, to a degree, involved a certain "community" of faith in response to Jesus' preaching and healing.

This survey of the suggestion that beggars, cripples, and the poor formed a significant part of, or played an important role in, Jesus' following or movement leads to the conclusion that the question should be reformulated in accordance with the kind of source material available and the historical situation indicated, albeit indirectly, by those sources. Little can be gleaned from the gospel traditions by searching for explicit occurrences of beggars, cripples, and/or the poor. There is no indication whatever that Jesus in any way recruited or even specially welcomed particular groups of people, such as beggars or cripples, to form a significant part of some following or movement distinct from the rest of Galilean society. Rather, he seems to have directed his announcement of the presence of the kingdom of God to the common people in general, with special emphasis on its availability to the sick and suffering, the hungry and the mournful, for which "the poor" may well be a general inclusive term. The healing stories, however indirectly, indicate in fact that Jesus, far from forming any special following or movement out of the cripples or beggars responding to him in faith, restored them to regular social interaction in their own communities. Preaching the kingdom of God to the poor and healing the sick clearly had something to do with the renewal of people's lives in their own communities.

WANDERING CHARISMATICS

Theissen has claimed recently that Jesus "did not primarily found local communities, but called into being a movement of wandering charismatics." These "travelling apostles, prophets, and disciples who moved from place to place" were characterized primarily by "homelessness" and "lack of family, . . . possessions, . . . and protection."[32] This rather abstract "sociological" analysis of Jesus' sayings, however, is based in an often-superficial reading of gospel texts and lacks a sense of concrete social context.

Theissen apparently derived the basic concept of "wandering charismatics" in Palestine by analogy with itinerant apostles outside of Palestine, such as Paul and Barnabas. Most of the texts cited do not attest or presuppose even the existence of such "itinerant charismatics," let alone provide evidence that Jesus inaugurated a movement of them. For example, in support of the "homelessness" feature, Didache 11:5 and 8 are either misread or twisted to fit the argument. Flight into the next town to avoid persecution (Matthew 10:23, taken from the synoptic apocalypse in Mark 13) is hardly evidence for an *intentional* homelessness of the wandering charismatics. Many of the gospel passages cited on lack of possessions or lack of protection have an application far broader than simply to a few dozen itinerant prophets and disciples: see, for example, the blessings and woes in Luke 6:20–26 (and parallels), sayings such as not being able to serve both God and mammon (Luke 16:18); the lengthy passage that climaxes in "seek first the kingdom . . ." (Matthew 6:25–33 and parallels); turning the other cheek and going the second mile (Matthew 5:38–43 and parallels). Similarly, texts adduced for "lack of family" (even "anti-family"), many of them pulled out of context in the gospel tradition or taken in a literal sense, without sensitivity to figurative or analogical meaning, would also appear to be addressed not simply to a few itinerants but to a more general audience. "Hating" one's family (Luke 14:26), for example, should probably be read as a very severe illustration of "counting the cost" and is parallel to other examples given in Luke 14:27–32. Furthermore, Luke 14:26 should probably be understood in the context of the broader social conflict to be expected with the coming of the kingdom and the decisions it will require, as in Luke 12:52–53; Matthew 10:35. Some passages are simply misconstrued: Mark 6:4, far from indicating that a family was forsaken by a son, says rather that a vociferous local agitator was rejected by his hometown. Some of the texts cited even tend to suggest something very different from what Theissen claims: Mark 10:28–29, Peter's plea for those who had indeed "left everything and followed" Jesus, when read in its full context, 10:28–30, promises full restoration to a new "home" and the broader "family" of a renewed community, and with lands!—hardly the homeless wandering of the supposedly itinerant charismatics.

Indeed, the only synoptic gospel texts that can be read to support the existence of "wandering charismatics" are the "mission discourses" in Mark 3:13–15; 6:7–11 and parallels; and Luke 10:1–12 (Q), and the brief "calls" of Peter, James and John in Mark 1:16,20. Itinerancy and charismatic action (healing and exorcism) can be found here, along with the characteristics of at least temporary homelessness and lack of possessions and protection. But the mission discourses also provide more information about the concrete social context of the disciples' mission, which the thesis of the wandering charismatics tends to ignore, as we will see. Perhaps not surprisingly, given the lack of evidence in the synoptic sayings material, but completely contrary to his own stated fundamental procedural principle, Theissen has reached for Hellenistic sources for his comparative model in positing the movement of itinerant charismatics as the essence of the Jesus movement. He argues that "the ethos of the the early Christian sayings tradition" is comparable to "the ethos of Cynic philosophy" in the three crucial characteristics of renunciation of home, family, and ownership. Accordingly, he claims that the wandering charismatics constituted a comparable social group.

Closer reading of the "mission discourses," however, indicates that there were decisive differences between the vagabond Cynic philosophers and the itinerant preachers and healers commissioned by Jesus. One of the principal texts on which the very existence of the wandering charismatics is projected (Mark 6:8; see Luke 9:3 and 10:4) makes a pointed distinction between the instructions to the disciples and the typical behavior of the Cynics (Jesus prohibiting even a staff, bag, money or food, the typical minimal equipment of the itinerant Cynic). Further, whereas the Cynic philosophers appeared primarily in cities throughout the Hellenistic-Roman world, Jesus' disciples confined their mission exclusively to the villages of Jewish Palestine. Moreover, although both may have understood themselves as "called," the respective implications were very different. The Cynic philosophers were called to become individual virtuosi and paradigms of virtue for other individuals who might emulate their example. Jesus' disciples, by contrast, were commissioned as catalysts of a broad popular movement apparently conceived of as the eschatological restoration of Israel. Finally, whereas the Cynics not only were not a social group but had no community base, the preachers and healers, as instructed in the mission discourse(s), while not a social group themselves, nevertheless worked in community bases. Cynic philosophers were indeed apparently vagabond beggars. Jesus' disciples, however, were instructed to preach and heal in villages and towns, blessing those places that responded positively and cursing those that rejected them, as well as to stay in local houses, eating what those households provided (Luke 10:5–12). Indeed, Jesus' disciples were not simply supported by local households but, as catalysts of a larger movement, focused their activities on the revitalization of local community life as well.

There is thus little or no evidence in gospel sayings material that Jesus "called into being a movement of wandering charismatics." It is difficult if not impossible to imagine what the concrete social reality of such a "movement" might have been. The individualistic Cynic virtuosi hardly provide an adequate analogue. In fact the only gospel texts that attest the features Theissen claims characterized the itinerant charismatics indicate that the purpose of commissioning disciples was that they would announce and manifest the presence of the kingdom of God in Palestinian Jewish villages. That is, the focus or concern of Jesus' ministry, thus extended through the mission of the disciples, was apparently on local community life. The result of this critical review of the "mission discourse(s)" (and of the "wandering charismatics" hypothesis) parallels that of our probe into the suggestions that beggars, cripples, and the poor were significant groups among Jesus' followers. That is, the texts that have been used as evidence for the prominence of cripples and the poor or for the itinerant charismatics indicate rather that Jesus' ministry concentrated on village communities. Of course, that should not be surprising if the restoration of Israel was integral to the coming of the kingdom of God, for the fundamental form of societal life in Israel was the village community.

EGALITARIAN FAMILIAL COMMUNITY

Many important teachings of Jesus clearly concern local community relations, yet there is no reason to believe that these pertained only or primarily to the inner group of the disciples or to the earliest post-resurrection community in Jerusalem. The only realistic concrete alternative would appear to be local (town or village) communities, where the ministry of Jesus and his disciples was focused.

NONPATRIARCHAL SOCIAL RELATIONS

In a traditional agrarian society, the local village community constituted the context of nearly all dimensions of life, including production, consumption, and celebration, and this through multiple generations of the same family or "house" (of the father) living and working on its ancestral land. Each family and each village, of course, was an almost organic component of the larger "community" of the people, in this case the "house" of Israel. But nearly all social interaction occurred in the local village community, however much the actions of the wealthy and powerful who dominated the society as a whole might affect it.

Both locally and society-wide, in such a culture, where the principal symbolization of social relations was in terms of kinship, the social structure was patriarchal. The father was the head of the family, in no uncertain terms; this is why it often appears to us that wives and children in such traditional patriarchal societies are treated in legal and other material as almost the property of the male head of household. Similarly, and almost certainly by "organic" analogy, the head of the society as a whole was its "father." Intermediate social structures were also patriarchal. Locally, although the village community may have been relatively more egalitarian, the elders of the community were usually the heads of the most important families or houses. The monarchy or high priesthood, of course, had its "retainers" (scribes, Pharisees, and others, at the time of Jesus) who represented the power and authority of the patriarchal head(s) of the whole to the local communities and families. One indication of how persistent and pervasive the "patriarchal" patterns were is the fact that once the high priesthood had been replaced by the somewhat collegial rule of the rabbis in second-century C.E. Palestine, individual rabbis were referred to as "father."[33]

One of the effects of Roman domination of Palestinian Jewish society would have been a breakdown in the traditional patriarchal authority, both in village communities and in the society as a whole. As peasant familes fell ever more heavily into debt under the steady economic pressures of double taxation, or because of special emergencies of war or drought, it became increasingly difficult for the fathers of families to avoid having a family member taken into debt-slavery or to avoid forfeiting the ancestral land that had been in the family for generations. The prominence of the theme of indebtedness in Jesus' parables, the evidence for the growth of large estates, and the evidence for large numbers of day laborers available locally and for the thousands of workers at the reconstruction of the Temple in Jerusalem suggest that many "fathers' houses" had lost their ancestral land, and that this was construed as failure of the "fathers." Such evidence suggests that the traditional patriarchal family was in crisis.

The traditional governmental representatives or authorities were surely experiencing a similar crisis. As was noted in chapter 3, Herod had "demoted" and diminished the influence of the Pharisees and other scribes and teachers. In Galilee at the time of Jesus, the scribes and Pharisees (presumably representatives primarily of the high-priestly government) had to share influence or perhaps compete with the "Herodians" of Antipas' regime; and the Judean Pharisees and other representatives of the high-priestly government were subordinated to, and felt their authority relativized by, the "higher" authority of the Roman governor. There was thus a genuine crisis in the concrete social situation that Jesus addressed, a decay in the traditional patriarchal social-economic-religious infrastructure of Jewish Palestine.

Several passages in the gospel tradition suggest that Jesus broke rather sharply with such traditional patriarchal structures. Some of these passages are the sayings that have been used recently to claim that Jesus was antifamilial. Placed in a broader context of Jesus' teachings and ministry as a whole, however, these passages indicate rather that while Jesus did indeed challenge the patriarchal family pattern, he nonetheless replaced it with an egalitarian nonpatriarchal pattern of relationships that still conceived of community in familial (kinship) terms. This can be illustrated from four particular sets of passages.

(a) Matthew 10:34–36 and Luke 12:51–53: Form-critics would deny that this is original to Jesus because of its form as an "I-saying."[34] Yet its presence in Q indicates that it is an early tradition. Whether original to Jesus or not, it reflects the experience of the effects of Jesus' ministry, however much it also still fit the experience of later generations of people whose "conversion" to Christianity caused divisions in their families.

The Matthean version is the more original. It is clearly an allusion to, even a paraphrase of Micah 7:6. Along with Mark 13:12 and parallels, Matthew 10:34–36 is often described as a standardized apocalyptic image for the conflicts expected to occur in the cataclysmic "last days" at the "end of the world." Besides being a literalistic misunderstanding of apocalyptic imagery, such an interpretation perpetuates the old synthetic approach, in contrast to more precise textual and contextual analysis. The "proof-texts" usually cited have so little in common that they cannot represent a standardized apocalyptic image (cf. 1 Enoch 56 and 99:5), some of them portray not the end time but historical events (Jubilees 23:16–17; 1 Enoch 100:2—rise of the Hasidim and conflict with the Hellenistic reformers?), and all these Jewish apocalyptic texts display more generalized social conflict than does Matthew 10:34–36 and parallels.

As in Micah 7:6 the situation portrayed in Matthew 10:34–36 is a crisis of the breakdown of fundamental social relations. In contrast to the broader literary context in Micah 7:1–7, however, Matthew 10:34–36 focuses on the core of all social relations, those of the patriarchal family. Surely the allusion is not to the broader context in Micah 7, as if Jesus were the cause of the complete breakdown of society. Rather the reference is more precisely to the disruption of local family or perhaps other kinship relations, especially the younger generation's break with the authority of the older generation. In contrast to the expected role of Elijah in reconciling the fathers to the children and the children to the fathers in anticipation of the terrible "day of the Lord," Jesus' ministry was causing people to break with the authority of the elders.

Matthew 10:37 (and Luke 14:26), which form-critics are more inclined to accept as an authentic saying of Jesus, provides a similar picture of the disruptive effect of Jesus on patriarchal families in the local community context.[35] A comparison of the more original Matthean version of the saying with Luke 14:26 indicates how radical Jesus' demands on people may have been. The addition of "wife . . . and brothers and sisters" makes it appear that only men are involved and that only one person is leaving a local family situation. The more original saying indicates that the fundamental division was generational (as in Matthew 10:34–36 and Micah 7:6), that the chain of generational authority and concern for preservation of the patriarchal family is being challenged.

In Matthew 10:34–36 and 10:37, whether the conflict is understood strictly within the confines of the nuclear family or more generally within a somewhat wider kinship or residential unit, Jesus' ministry was disrupting local communities. But these sayings do not mean that Jesus was "antifamily." They do indicate that the response called for by Jesus' announcement of the presence of the kingdom of God might well mean a break with one's family and, apparently, that this would entail a, challenge to the traditional authority of the patriarchal family.

(b) One clear indication that Jesus and his following were not antifamily is his declaration about marriage and his prohibition of men unilaterally putting away their wives. The three passages concerning marriage and/or divorce in the gospel tradition all reject the patriarchal form of marriage, and two of them solidly undergird marriage, the basis of the family.

The legal saying of Jesus that "every one who divorces his wife and marries another commits adultery [against her] . . ." is transmitted in both Q and Mark (Luke 16:18 and Matthew 5:32; Mark 10:11–12 and Matthew 19:9). The Torah (Deuteronomy 24:1–4) allows divorce by the husband, and contemporary Jewish legal debates revolved primarily around the permissible grounds. Jesus' saying both prohibits divorce and does it directly against the patriarchal formulation in the Jewish tradition. The prohibition of divorce also, in effect, reinforces the nucleus of the family (supposedly now no longer so patriarchal in its presuppositions and sanctions) insofar as the man is no longer allowed to take unilateral action in terminating one marriage and initiating another.

The grounds for the prohibition of traditional patriarchal divorce may become clear through examining the second text, the controversy story in Mark 10:2–9 (and Matthew 19:2–8), which was originally separate from the legal saying in Mark 10:11–12. Although the story as a whole is a secondary composition in the gospel tradition (with Mark 10:9, for example, having originally been a separate saying with a Hellenistic concept of marriage as a "yoking"), the quotation of one Torah text against another likely goes back to Jesus himself.[36] Thus the developed controversy story in Mark 10:2–5 has made explicit what must have been at least implicit in some form in an original Jesus saying, i.e., that the traditional conception of marriage as dissolvable at the initiative of the husband (see Deuteronomy 24:1) was being rejected. The reference in Mark 10:6–8 to both creation stories, in particular both Genesis 1:27 and 2:24, is then a highly positive affirmation of the marriage bond as a unity grounded in God's very act of creation. The implication, moreover, is that the era and the conditions that allowed for human transgression and patriarchal domination are now transcended, since they were not present in God's original creation. It is tempting to see a link here with the thought in Mark 3:35, that true "family" members are those who do the will of God. Correspondingly, true marriage would be according to the will of God "from the beginning of creation" when "God made them male and female. For this reason a man shall leave his father and mother and be joined to his wife, and the two shall become one." Mark 10:6–8 is thus a sharp rejection of the traditional patriarchal form of marriage. It is simultaneously a highly positive affirmation of marriage and indirectly of the family as well.

Another controversy story, that in Mark 12:18–27 and parallels, might at first glance appear somewhat to contradict this affirmation of marriage as if conditions of a new creation were now present. This is not the case at all so long as we allow Jesus the possibility of distinguishing between the present time of renewal, including the fulfillment of historical promises and expectations, and the future (eschatological) conditions of the resurrection. Once this distinction is clearly discerned, Mark 12:18–27 can be seen as yet another text that critically challenges patriarchal structures and assumptions. For the issue of marriage and the family, the core of the controversy story is Jesus' declaration in Mark 12:25: "When they rise from the dead, they neither marry nor are given in marriage, but are like angels in heaven." This "legal saying" reflects the contemporary Jewish apocalyptic milieu (cf. 1 Enoch 104:4–6; 2 Baruch 51:10) and is possibly from Jesus.[37] By itself it would appear simply to declare that patriarchal marriage was a social institution for historical conditions (for perpetuation of the race) but would be transcended in the resurrection life when people would be like the angels.

In the context of this controversy story, which may well reflect the original issue or context of the saying, it is a response to the question of how levirate marriage (Deuteronomy 25:5–10), in which the brother(s) of a deceased husband would marry and have children by the widow, could possibly be reconciled with belief in the resurrection of the dead, at which point the woman would be married to two or more brothers simultaneously. The purpose and effect of the levirate marriage, while providing a social role and economic security for the potential widow, was mainly to secure the continuation of the patriarchal family line and the family inheritance ("house," lands, etc.) from generation to generation. In the context of this issue, the saying in Mark 12:25 is directed against the idea that the institution of levirate marriage and the perpetuation of the patriarchal family inheritance that it secured would stand forever.[38] According to the orientation of Jesus and others, the conviction that historical conditions would eventually have a terminus (as well as a renewal or fulfillment) meant that institutions such as the patriarchal family were relative and conditioned.

Moreover, the implication is clear: that such a challenge to the levirate marriage and patriarchal family inheritance would have been directed at those who, under the current economic conditions, were benefiting from such traditions. The latter were hardly of much benefit to the heavily indebted peasants who were losing their family inheritances or to the destitute widows and children who had already fallen victims to the tightening noose of institutionalized injustices such as double taxation, heavy indebtedness, and loss of land. Thus, far from contradicting Jesus' highly positive declaration about nonpatriarchal marriage being grounded in renewed conditions of divine creation in Mark 10:6–8, the controversy story and saying in Mark 12:18–25(–27) further challenge the sanctity and supposed perpetuation of local patriarchal structures that maintained the system of domination at the village level.

(c) Jesus had a highly positive sense of the family, but he transformed the criterion for membership from physical kinship and adherence to patriarchal authority to doing the will of God, as in Mark 3:35 and parallels: "Whoever does the will of God is my brother and sister and mother." Although the "pronouncement story" in Mark 3:31–35 (or

3:20–21,31–35) as a whole is surely secondary, there is no reason why the saying in 3:35 itself cannot be early and perhaps original Jesus tradition.[39] The occurrence of the similar saying in Luke's special material (Luke 11:27–28) suggests that doing the will of God was a special concern of the Jesus tradition (see the more developed form of the Lord's Prayer in Matthew 6:10, compared with Luke 11:2), and it may be significant that doing the will of God is contrasted with literal kinship in this other pronouncement story as well.

At first glance the saying in Mark 3:35 might not appear very striking in the context of a society that symbolized social relationships generally in kinship terms. "Brother," for example, was regularly used with reference to one's neighbors or fellow society members (e.g., Matthew 5:22–24; 7:3–5). A comparison of the saying itself with its secondary pronouncement-story context, however, indicates both that the saying is using explicitly familial terms, however figuratively, and that it signals a break with the patriarchal family. The context has only "mother and brothers," while the saying itself mentions "sisters" as well. "Father," however, is missing—a fact that cannot simply be attributed to the later traditions in Luke 1:26–38 and Matthew 1:18–25.

That is, Jesus apparently did not think in terms of human fathers, and that is evident in precisely the context in which he symbolized those who faithfully did the will of God as family members. There is no reason to think that Jesus meant this symbolization to be confined narrowly to the inner circle of disciples. It is conceivable that the familial terms had society-wide reference. The primary context, however, must have been the local residential community. As with the original covenantal principles of social policy, such as "thou shalt not steal" or "thou shalt not covet," the principal locus of practice or realization would have been the primary context of social life, the local village community. But that was also precisely where conceiving of the whole community in terms of family members who did the will of God would have helped provide a sense of solidarity and mutual caring.

(d) Just how concretely and locally the new familial community was envisaged can be seen in the Jesus tradition behind Mark 10:29–30 and parallels, which speaks of "houses . . . and lands, now," being restored to those who left homes for the sake of the kingdom. Whatever original Jesus saying may lie behind this text has undergone considerable expansion, development, and redaction in the history of the tradition. The introduction in Mark 10:28 makes the saying about restoration apply to the disciples; earlier forms of the core saying likely had broader or even general application.[40] The content of the promised reward has undergone expansion: the eternal life "in the age to come" is surely a late development, the distinction between the "ages" occurring primarily in later rabbinic literature.[41] The phrase "for the sake of the kingdom of God" in Luke 18:29b would fit the rest of the saying better than "for my sake and for the gospel," a typical Markan phrase (cf. 8:35). One would think that the form-critical conclusion that this saying is "not sufficiently characteristic to support a judgment" regarding how Jewish material may "have been taken over by the Christian tradition and ascribed to Jesus" might have suggested a saying distinctive to Jesus according to the criterion of disimilarity.[42] The "house" and "land" in particular would appear to fit the more recently popular criterion of "vividness of imagery."[43]

Thus even if we regard their repetition in v. 30 as secondary, the particulars in Mark 10:29–30, along with the striking "now (in this time)," indicate that early in the transmission of the saying the restoration or reward was understood in most concrete and local terms. The new nonpatriarchal familial community was to be solidly rooted in lands, the prerequisite for any traditional agrarian or peasant society and the fundamental basis for traditional peasant utopian images: everyone under his vine and fig tree (Micah 4:4) as well as Israel's covenantal life under God's kingship (Exodus 20:17; Leviticus 25). Matthew's insertion of 19:28, concerning the restoration in which the disciples would sit on twelve thrones bringing justice to the twelve tribes of Israel, shows precisely in this context that he also understood the reward in highly concrete terms and as being in imminent. Finally, the likely general application of the saying, combined with the vivid verbal element of one "leaving" home, etc., should not mislead us into imagining that all or most of those who responded to Jesus' message of the kingdom literally left their village homes and settled in some utopian community elsewhere. This, apparently, is precisely what the "followers" of Jesus did not do. Rather, as is suggested in this and related sayings, they were guided by Jesus to anticipate, and indeed to form, renewed local covenantal communities conceived of in nonpatriarchal familial terms.

COMMUNITY WITHOUT HIERARCHY

Besides leading his followers to constitute their new communities in nonpatriarchal familial terms, Jesus exhorted them to maintain egalitarian social relations by not reverting to the traditional hierarchies by which the chain of domination had been maintained. It seems likely that the "secular, prudential" wisdom saying that occurs at four different points in the gospel tradition—"whoever exalts himself will be humbled, and whoever humbles himself will be exalted" (Matthew 23:12; cf. 18:4; Luke 14:11; 18:14)—may have been a sanction for this concern. The passive verbs in such sayings probably refer to God's eschatological judgment (and this provides one of the principal reasons for viewing the saying as original Jesus tradition).[44] Although the saying does not fit fluently or logically with its context in Matthew 18:1–5 and Luke 18:1–14, its linkage with other material about maintaining humility or avoiding hierarchy in the community (Luke 14:7–10; Matthew 23:8–11) tends to confirm this understanding of the saying as sanctioning egalitarian social relations.

In one of the sayings with which the exhortation to maintain humility is linked, Matthew 23:8–9, Jesus insists that his followers avoid reverting to both local family and village patriarchal authorities and regional governmental officials. Even the most sceptical and cautious of form-critics thought that Matthew 23:8–9 could be "dominical."[45] According to an insightful recent reconstruction that cuts carefully and comprehensively through the accretions and changes to the saying in the course of its transmission and redaction, the original form of the prohibitions would likely have been: "But you are not to be called rabbi, for you have one teacher and you are all disciples (brothers). Call no one father, for you have one father (and you are all siblings)."[46] "Rabbi" was apparently already at this time a deferential term or honorific title used in reference to a teacher such as a Pharisee or other representative of the high-priestly government whose role was to maintain social order in towns and villages. Jewish society had a long heritage, legitimated by the Torah, of the Aaronide and/or Levitical priests and later of the scribes and scholars (Pharisees and others) as the "teachers" of the people (Exodus 24:12; Deuteronomy 4:5,14; Leviticus 10:11; Deuteronomy 33:10; Josephus, *Ant.* 13.296–298).[47] Thus it may not be so surprising that, following the Roman reconquest of Jewish Palestine in 67–70 C.E., the "Pharisees" (and other scholars), "the rabbis," eventually became the administrators of the society, directly under Roman authority. "Father" would have been used with reference to respected local or regional authority figures as well as heads of households. For example, from somewhat later inscriptional evidence we know that wealthy, powerful, and official persons who became patrons of local synagogues were called "father of the synagogue" or "father of the people."[48] Although there is no question of the actual title "father of the synagogue," Luke 7:1–10 provides an illustration of how a local military or customs official could be a patron of the synagogue, in this case a Gentile in the administration of Antipas (cf. John 4:46) who had apparently cultivated close relations with the elders of the town (vv. 4–5). More pertinent to Matthew 23:8–9, probably, it is highly likely that "father" (ábba) was already being used in reference to scholar-teachers (Pharisees and others) and other distinguished people, just as it was used for the later rabbis.[49]

Highly noteworthy in Jesus' prohibition of local authority figures is the parallel to the way the original Mosaic Covenant displaced and avoided centralized power of human kings. In the original covenantal constitution of premonarchic Israel, Yahweh was the actual "king," so that there could be no legitimate human monarch (see, e.g., Judges 8:23; 1 Samuel 8:7). God, of course, was still the only proper king of Israel in Jesus' day. In the sayings behind Matthew 23:8–9, however, Jesus made God into the true father (Luke 11:2–4; 12:30; Mark 11:25) and teacher as well. Thus it was inappropriate and prohibited to defer to any human as "rabbi" or "father."

Jesus had a solid basis in biblical prophecy for understanding God as the one teacher. The new covenant announced by Jeremiah 31:31–34 was to mean the internalization of the Torah and spontaneity of covenant-keeping, with no apparent need for intermediaries, indeed no need for any teaching, since "they shall all know me [God]." Even more striking in connection with Matthew 23:8–9 is Isaiah 54:13–14:

"All your [Israel's/Jerusalem's] sons shall be taught by Yahweh and great [*rav*] shall be the prosperity [*shalom*] of your sons. In righteousness you shall be established; you shall be far from oppression."

Besides the parallel themes readily evident to the English reader's eye —the liberation from oppression, rebuilding of the society in social relations, and God's direct teaching of the Israelites—there is another, highly suggestive potential allusion in the Hebrew word *rav*, which, by Mishnaic times at least, is the ordinary term for "teacher." In synonymous parallelism with "sons taught by Yahweh" the second line could easily have been understood to refer to God as the "teacher" bringing *shalom* (= wholeness/welfare/salvation in the broadest, most concrete sense) to the people who, as "sons" (children) are thus all brothers (siblings) under the direct divine instruction. It has even been suggested that the saying behind Matthew 23:8–9 must have been a midrash on Isaiah 54:13 because of such suggestive similarities between them.

The conception and address of God as "father" (*ábba*) was apparently emphasized by Jesus and his followers. Although not all the passages in which "my [or "our"] father" or "your father" occurs are early traditions, that Jesus addressed God as *ábba* is solidly rooted in the gospel tradition generally, most significantly perhaps in his prayers (e.g., Mark 14:36; Matthew 6:9 and parallel Luke 11:2; Matthew 11:25 and parallel Luke 10:21; Mark 11:25; Luke 12:30,32).[50]

The two most significant implications for the issue at hand are both explicit at several points in the gospel tradition. Addressing God as "father" meant a certain directness and intimacy between "the children" and God, and if the members of the community or kingdom were all "children" of the "father," then they were all "brothers" (Matthew 23:8, and sisters(!), as explicitly in Mark 3:35). That God was both the one teacher and father was the basis of the egalitarian relations within the local community. The direct relation now possible with God meant that there would be no "fathers" in the local community, especially no "teachers" as representatives of the traditional established order.[51]

Corresponding to his urging the avoidance of patriarchal hierarchy in local communities, Jesus apparently also insisted on nonhierarchical egalitarian relations for the society as a whole. Mark 9:33–37 and parallels and Mark 10:(35–)42–45 and parallels are often read as pertaining only to the church or, at the earliest, to the disciples, perhaps because of the literary context provided for the core sayings (Mark 9:35; 10:43–44) in the gospel tradition. In particular, the attention lavished upon Mark 10:45, which is so unusual in the synoptic Gospels yet so important for Christian theology and ritual, has distracted attention from the possible meaning of the terms and the overall contrast presented in Mark 10:42–44. Not counting the close Matthean parallels to Mark, the core saying, which is thought to go back to Jesus in some form, has four variants.[52] Mark 10:43–44 is a double-membered saying with the pairs "great . . . servant" and "first . . . slave." Matthew 23:11 has only the first pair; Luke 22:26, parallel to Mark 10:43–44, varies the terms to "greatest . . . youngest, leader . . . servant." Mark 9:35b collapses the double pair into one, "first . . . servant" and by adding "last" merges the originally separate contrasts of "first and last" with "first and slave." Mark 10:43–44 or Matthew 23:11 would appear to be the most original form of the saying.

Modern interpretation of these texts is usually couched in rather vague terms of relative prominence or precedence or privilege.[53] The principal terms used in the pairs of contrasts, however, had far more precise reference to roles of power and domination vs. subservience. A "great one" could be simply a highly powerful leader in a city-state (cf. Plato, Laws 5.730d), but in biblical history the reference was more likely to great kings and emperors, as in the famous promise to David that he would have "a great name, like the name of the great ones of the earth" (2 Samuel 7:9; 1 Chronicles 17:8). "Great" was also used of priest-princes of temple states.[54] "The first" or "the first ones" could refer to the heads of a city or an area or people (Mark 6:21; Luke 19:47 and frequently in Josephus), but it could also be used for the chief priest (1 Kings 2:35; 2 Kings 25:18) and especially for the highest royal or imperial officials charged with dominion in a given area (1 Chronicles 27:33; 2 Maccabees 8:9; and see 1 Maccabees 10:59–65; 11:27 with reference to the Hasmonean high priest Jonathan as "first friend" of the Seleucid emperor). "Servant" *(diakonos),* on the other hand, indicated personal service rendered to another, possibly menial, but including the taking of orders. Thus the term was used for "the servants" of a king (Matthew 22:13), who could of course be "great ones." "Slave" *(doulos)* referred not to a chattel slave but to any and all who were under the dominion of some ruler or god. All subjects of a ruler were "servants" who were expected and required to take orders or to render tribute and deference.

Thus it should be clear simply from the fundamental terms used that the saying in Mark 10:43–44 and Matthew 23:11 is dealing not merely or vaguely with rank within a community of disciples but with relations of political domination and subservience. The link with Mark 10:42 makes this unmistakeable. Earlier form-critics saw Mark 10:43–44 as a saying of Jewish origin for which the early Jesus tradition provided 10:42 as a foil. But why could not Jesus have provided the foil and, for that matter, have articulated the combination of Mark 10:42–44 as a whole? (It would surely satisfy the criterion of double dissimilarity if measured against the Jewish and early Christian literature ordinarily used for comparisons.) Indeed, v. 42 has more recently been viewed as part of the original saying that in some form goes back to Jesus.[55] Thus v. 42 makes it explicit that, by analogy with "the nations," the subject under discussion is the governance of the society generally, the whole people of Israel, and not the smaller circle of the disciples, as is often supposed. Moreover, the strong verbs used (with genitive of those subjected) in drawing out sharply the point of the analogy, "exercise complete domination over" (cf. Psalm 72(71):8; 1 Peter 5:3) and "exercise absolute authority over," portray the unacceptable authoritarian and oppressive mode of domination characteristic of the supposed "governors" and "great ones" at the head of the nations and empires.

In his "secular, prudential wisdom" Jesus thus insisted that the renewed covenantal community avoid the patriarchal social-economic-political hierarchy that constituted the chain of domination maintaining institutionalized injustice. In different sayings he both spoke against reversion to patriarchal forms of domination in the local community and he called for the virtual transformation of the age-old royal-imperial forms of authoritarian domination only too familiar to Jews and others in the ancient Near East. One who would be "great" or "first" would have to be a "servant"—which meant in effect there could be no great kings and high officials at all in the renewed Israel (note the contrast to 2 Samuel 7 or Psalm 2). The renewed covenantal people of Israel were to have egalitarian social relations both in its "familial" local communities and among the people as a whole.

We should note, finally, that the Lucan juxtaposition of the Twelve sitting on twelve thrones with the saying about the "great" and the "first being servants" (although perhaps not the Matthean positioning of the Twelve on thrones as a reward for relinquishing families) is not contradictory, especially once we have recognized that the Twelve are not to be "judging" but rather "effecting justice for" the people of Israel. The thrust of Mark 10:42–44 and parallels was precisely to maintain the renewed justice that would be threatened if there were a reversion to the traditional patriarchal forms of dominion.

9. The Renewal of Local Community, II: Social-Economic Cooperation and Autonomy

FORGIVE US OUR DEBTS

There were very practical reasons why earthly as well as heavenly monarchs were concerned about the economic welfare of their people. In a traditional agrarian society the peasantry were the economic base for the rulers, who supported themselves by expropriating a portion of the peasants' products. They then used that tax or tithe to maintain their military and bureaucratic apparatus and to fund service industries of which they were the principal consumers. With the products of such industries and the peasantry they also supported building projects of which they were the sponsors and beneficiaries, and traded for the luxury goods they desired.

In a traditional agrarian society, however, productive forces were not highly developed. The vast majority of peasant producers enjoyed little more than a subsistence living, and the margin for increase of output was very limited. Thus, whether the cause was exploitative governmental officials, drought, or conquest, the productive base of the rulers was subject to serious damage, and the rulers' power to exploit the peasants could easily be weakened. The principal mechanism through which the peasantry could be destroyed was indebtedness. Because of bad harvests or unusual demands for tribute, taxes, or tithes, already-marginal peasant families would fall into debt. Then failure to pay the debt would lead to one or more family members' becoming debt-slaves, and finally to loss of land. The greatest threat to peasants, and probably their greatest fear, was falling heavily and hopelessly into debt.

Not surprisingly there developed a prudential ideology of kingship according to which the king would protect not only the nonproductive victims of social misfortune, such as orphans and widows, but the downtrodden peasantry generally (against the depredations of his own royal "servants," among others). Looking to the protection of their divine king as ultimately responsible for the welfare of the people, Israel attributed this ideal to Yahweh (as in Psalm 146:5–9). Ancient Israel and the biblical tradition, of course, had gone even a major step further. Out of its early historical experience Israel had developed a distinctive loyalty to its divine king as one who liberated oppressed people and maintained their independence from bondage and exploitative service to human overlords (e.g., Exodus 15; Judges 5; Psalm 78). Moreover, Israel's divine king did not demand much by way of material tribute, and what little was demanded was for feeding the victims of misfortune, for whom God was especially concerned (e.g., Deuteronomy 26:1–15).

Out of its own bitter experience Israel had also learned that a monarchy like that in other societies was, virtually by definition, exploitative (e.g., 1 Samuel 8:4–18). The great biblical prophets had invoked divine judgment against kings as well as against royal officials for exploiting the peasantry and especially for bringing them into debt and forcing them off the land (e.g., Isaiah 3:13–15; Hoseah 5:10; 8:4; Amos 5:10–12; 6:1; Micah 3:1–4, 9–12; Jeremiah 22). Accordingly, Israel had developed its own egalitarian covenantal ideals and mechanisms to protect a free and independent peasantry. The most important provisions for maintaining the family inheritance and avoiding permanent servitude and loss of land were leaving the land fallow every seventh year (Exodus 23:10–11; Leviticus 25:11–12), the cancelation of debts and the release of debt-slaves every seventh year (Exodus 21:2–6; Deuteronomy 15:1–18), the redemption of land for relatives by the nearest kin (Leviticus 25:25–28), and the "jubilee" every fiftieth year, according to which ideally everyone returned to the family inheritance (Leviticus 25:8–10,13). It is in the context of the continuing cultivation of such biblical ideals and covenantal-legal traditions that we should consider a number of gospel passages that deal with social-economic matters.

CONCERN FOR THE ALLEVIATION OF POVERTY

Fundamentally and generally, the gospel tradition is oriented toward the poor and condemns the wealthy. Whether it be in the blessings of the kingdom now at hand or in a number of summarizing statements of Jesus' preaching and practice, the kingdom was offered especially to the poor (e.g., Luke 6:20; Matthew 11:4–5). Correspondingly, whether we deem them original to Jesus or secondary, prophetic woes were pronounced against the wealthy. One effect of the statements against the rich may have been to reinforce a newly instilled sense of self-worth and solidarity among the ordinarily self-devaluing and divided peasantry. This effect, however, does not diminish the substantive thrust of Jesus' statements against the wealthy: "Woe to you that are rich, for you have received your consolation. Woe to you that are full now, for you shall hunger" (Luke 6:24–25a). Less sharp but no less firm was the exclusion of the wealthy from the kingdom: "How hard it will be for those who have riches to enter the kingdom of God. . . . It is easier for a camel to go through the eye of a needle than for a rich man to enter the kingdom of God" (Mark 10:23b,25 and parallels).

For the wealthy, exclusion from the kingdom was really self-exclusion, as is indicated in the (secondary) pronouncement story preceding these sayings in the Gospels and in Jesus' saying about the impossibility of serving two masters. The rich man who came to Jesus—and who supposedly has kept all the fundamental commandments (Mark 10:19–20)—is told he must sell his possessions and give to the poor.[1] Why? And what might it mean, when Jesus declares (in a saying transmitted through Q, to Matthew 6:24 and parallel Luke 16:13): "No one can serve two masters; for either he will hate the one and love the other, or he will be devoted to the one and despise the other. You cannot serve God and mammon"? Recognizing that "mammon" did not mean simply "money," we may find some indication of its meaning in the preceding sayings in Luke 16:10–12. "Mammon" apparently meant that in which one placed trust or commitment; hence "unrighteous mammon" would have meant, in effect, trust in unrighteous dealings.[2] In biblical terms this was exactly the way one would acquire wealth. That is, in the context of the discussion above, the principal ways one could gain wealth would have been at the expense of the peasant producers, either through fraud in collecting taxes and tithes, or through lending to peasants having trouble meeting their obligations and then foreclosing or calling in the loans (see, e.g., Matthew 18:23–30). What God required in the covenantal commandments was just, nonexploitative social relations. The rich man's wealth was, almost by definition, gained by "unrighteous mammon." To further combine these two passages, the only way the rich man could inherit eternal life or enter the kingdom would be to change masters, i.e., to follow the will of God by giving back what he had gained by "mammon." The rich excluded themselves from the kingdom of God, in effect, because their wealth (whether inherited or not) had been gained by impoverishing peasant producers and in fact really belonged to those who had thus become destitute.

Jesus directed his practice and preaching primarily to the poor: "Blessed are you poor, for yours is the kingdom of God." Before focusing directly on such sayings, it would be well to affirm once again an interpretative principle that may be virtually the opposite of that traditionally followed in New Testament studies. We should assume that Jesus' preaching and practice referred to the several inseparable dimensions of life unless a particular passage gives a clear indication that primarily or only a "religious" dimension is intended. Reaffirming this principle is particularly important in application to passages such as the beatitudes, which may already have been somewhat spiritualized in the Gospels. However, even though Matthew (5:3,6) has added "in spirit" to "blessed are the poor" and "and thirst for righteousness" to "blessed are those who hunger," the meaning may not be appreciably different from that of the more original form in Luke 6:20–21 and Q. The blessings of the kingdom, including the provision of enough to eat, are here promised to those who are concretely, economically poor and hungry. The spiritual or psychological effects of being poor and hungry are also included: "blessed are you that weep." "Those who hunger and thirst for righteousness" is surely potentially more inclusive than "the hungry," but underlying the hunger for justice (in a peasant ethos in which most peasant families have a subsistence living at best) would have been, directly or indirectly, the experience of or anxiety about physical hunger. Even if what underlies Matthew's phrase "poor in spirit" was the Jewish ideology of the *ànawim*, (literate groups who, viewing themselves as oppressed, applied the traditional biblical imagery of God's concern for the poor to themselves), it still refers to a community that is relatively poor, and it would highlight the reality of the *poor* to whom Jesus promised the kingdom.

Although many of the summaries of Jesus' message or ministry are secondary or simply the formulations of the gospel writers themselves, two of the summaries that have a claim to be early traditions emphasize the good news preached to the poor, and one of these may be far more specific than it might seem at first. The story in Q (Matthew 11:2–6 and parallel Luke 7:18–22) about Jesus' response to the disciples of John sent to ask if he were "the one who is to come" is generally thought to contain a reliable early tradition: "Go and tell John what you have seen and heard: the blind receive their sight, the lame walk, lepers are cleansed, and the deaf hear, the dead are raised up, the poor have good news preached to them." The tradition contains allusions to several phrases from the book of Isaiah (in 29:18–19; 35:5–6; 61:1) understood as prophecies now being fulfilled in Jesus' actions and preaching.

The other passage of interest, Luke 4:16–21, is special to Luke, and had until recently been thought to be part of a Lucan rewriting of the story of Jesus' rejection in Nazareth in Mark 6:1–6. Recent criticism has traced this passage back to Q and even back as close as possible to Jesus.[3] Because this passage also quotes from Isaiah 61:1 it is often understood in terms similar to Matthew 11:4–5 and parallel Luke 7:22. Closer scrutiny, however, shows that it is more precisely and concretely focused on social-economic liberation. A comparison of the text of Luke 4:18–19 with that of Isaiah 61:1–2 indicates that a clear principle of inclusion and exclusion, or even of substitution, was involved well before Luke's use of the tradition. Included from Isaiah 61:1–2 were the clauses "The Spirit of the Lord is upon me, because he has anointed me to preach good news to the poor; he has sent me to proclaim release to the captives and recovering of sight to the blind . . ." and "to proclaim the acceptable year of the Lord." Although the clause about the blind's recovering their sight has been conformed to the Septuagint, which would appear to have been influenced by Psalm 146:7–8, the meaning of the somewhat imprecise Hebrew would likely have been retained in the pre-Greek tradition in any case, since "opening the eyes" was a standing metaphor for liberation from prison, as can be seen from Isaiah 42:7. Excluded from Isaiah 61:1–2 were the clauses about "binding up the brokenhearted" and "comforting all who mourn," along with that about God's "day of vengeance." Substituted from Isaiah 58:6d was the clause "to set at liberty those who are oppressed."

That is, the clauses referring to the brokenhearted and mournful were left out, and the three referring to the liberation of the poor and prisoners were supplemented from elsewhere in Isaiah by another reference to release of the oppressed. Even if we are not yet ready to accept the kernel of Luke 4:16–21 as a tradition going back to Jesus, it is nevertheless clear that someone very early made a selection of clauses from Isaiah 61:1–2 and 58:6 to point out rather precisely the ways in which Jesus' practice and preaching were fulfilling long-standing expectations for social-economic liberation.

MUTUAL FORGIVENESS AND CANCELATION OF DEBTS

On the basis of texts such as Luke 4:16–21 it has been suggested that Jesus was proclaiming a long-awaited "jubilee," in which debts would be canceled, prisoners released, and people returned to their family inheritance, as provided for in Leviticus 25—in other words, the offer of a new life made possible by the chance to start over economically.[4] The term for "release" or "liberty" in Isaiah 61:1 is the same as that used in Leviticus 25:10 *(deror);* and Jesus, in fulfillment of the prophecy, would appear to be the "messenger" proclaiming the release decreed by the divine King now effecting his "kingdom." Because of the allusive character of the evidence in the gospel tradition, it would be virtually impossible to prove or disprove that Jesus was calling for or proclaiming the implementation of the explicit provisions of the Jubilee in Leviticus 25. What we can do, however, is note how seriously some of the traditional covenantal provisions for the protection of families' inheritance were taken and how others were compromised, in effect, at the time of Jesus. That should then provide a context for investigating how concretely Jesus speaks about forgiving debts.

Observance of the seventh or sabbatical year as a fallow year for the fields was officially organized and practiced. Josephus mentions several military crises in which the observance of the sabbatical fallow year was a serious factor in the outcome of a siege or a war (*Ant.* 12.378; 13.234; 14.475; 15.7). It had to be taken into account in the Romans' demand for tribute (*Ant.* 14.202,206). Although one of the original intentions of the sabbatical year may have been to help provide food for the landless (i.e., similar in effect to provisions for not completely harvesting a field so that some was left for gleaning by the poor), its actual effect could be disastrous for marginal peasant households. When it occurred during a crisis such as war or drought (which happened in 47–48 C.E.), severe famine, dramatic escalation in indebtedness, and loss of land were the results for the peasantry.[5]

The sabbatical cancelation of debts was taken seriously enough to require legal accommodation. Ostensibly in order to make credit available in the years just prior to the sabbatical release, when creditors would be reluctant to lend because of the prospect of immediately writing off the loan, the *prosbul* in effect bypassed the intent and effect of the original provision for cancelation of debts, which was to provide a fresh start for indebted peasant families. Thus the lawyers and apparently the priestly establishment took the provision in the Torah seriously enough to use a legal device to avoid actually implementing it. About the jubilee Josephus writes in grand terms in his account of Moses' lawgiving. In the fiftieth year "debtors are absolved from their debts and slaves are set at liberty. . . . Now too he restores estates to their original owners" (*Ant.* 3.282–383). Although King Zedekiah had proclaimed the release of debt-slaves in 588 B.C.E. as the Babylonian army prepared to attack (Jeremiah 34:8–22), it is doubtful whether the release of debt-slaves and of prisoners and the return of disinherited people to their ancestral lands was regularly or seriously observed.

Although we thus doubt that the wealthy and powerful who benefited from the people's indebtedness would have backed official observance of the provisions of Leviticus 25, the cancelation of debts and the release of prisoners apparently remained alive as a popular hope or yearning. From Josephus we know of two "revolutionary" implementations of these provisions of the Torah during the great revolt against Rome, which indicates that these hopes could inspire action. In the summer of 66 the popular forces, after setting fire to the house of the high priest Ananias and the palaces of Agrippa and Berenice, "carried their combustibles to the public archives, eager to destroy the money-lenders' bonds and to prevent the recovery of debts, in order to win over a host of grateful debtors and to cause a rising of the poor against the rich" (*War* 2.426–427). Despite, or rather directly through, the obvious biases of Josephus in that passage, we can discern both the intensity of the yearning for debt-relief and the serious scope of popular indebtedness. The popularly acclaimed king Simon bar Giora also implemented a Torah provision. As he built a broad following in the Judean hill country prior to his march on Jerusalem, he "proclaimed liberty for slaves and rewards for the free" (*War* 4.508), a phrase that surely points to the release of debt-slaves, according to the ideal derived from the Torah (Exodus 21:2–6; Deuteronomy 15:1–18; Leviticus 25:39–43) and kept alive in prophetic expectations (e.g., Isaiah 61:1–2).

Whether or not it was understood as a sabbatical or jubilee release, Jesus insisted upon the mutual forgiveness of debts in his followers' local communities. Indeed, this is one of the fundamental concerns of the "Lord's Prayer." Ironically the considerable attention biblical scholars have focused on this text because of its "religious" importance has led to the recognition of how concrete is its orientation and how complete its perspective. Scholarly reconstruction of a hypothetical original Aramaic prayer has served to highlight the considerable spiritualization and generalization it has experienced in the Matthean and Lucan versions.[6] Although Luke's length and form may be the more original, he has changed "debts" to "sins" to make this petition more intelligible to Hellenistic readers, a change that also supports his own soteriological understanding of Christ. Luke has thus also broken the parallelism of "debts" and "debtors." He has also made the petition and the whole prayer less concrete and more universal by changing the perfect "we have forgiven" to the present "we forgive" and the more particular "debtors" to the generalizing "everyone who is indebted to us." Matthew has often kept the more concrete wording but has provided a "spiritualizing" interpretation as well as supplementary liturgical phrases. It is significant that the only place in which the term "trespasses" occurs in the synoptics is in Matthew's interpretative addition of 6:14–15 and the parallel in Mark 11:25, clearly a late tradition.

Thus, it is only because of changes or interpretative additions by Luke and Matthew that the Lord's Prayer contains a petition about "forgiveness of sins."

The petition in the more original form of the prayer was clearly far more concrete: "release for us [forgive us] our debts, as we have released [forgiven] our debtors." Here as elsewhere in the gospel tradition the term *opheilo/opheilema* ("debts") refers to one's economic or other legal obligations (e.g., Matthew 18:24–33; Luke 7:41; 16:5,7). The verb *aphiemi* (as well as the noun *aphesis*) means "release" and is the same term as that used for the "release" of captives and the "setting at liberty" of the oppressed in Luke 4:18 (Isaiah 61:1; 58:6). The occurrence of this petition in the context of a prayer for the kingdom and parallel to the petition concerning bread only confirms the concreteness of the reference. Whether we read "give us today the bread of tomorrow" or "give us each day our bread for subsistence," the bread meant is that material bread that sustains human life, as the church fathers understood, despite their general tendencies toward spiritualization.[7] However much "forgiveness" of figurative "debts or other obligations" may be included, the petition is about release of debts. The Lord's Prayer, far from listing a number of possible concerns, focuses on those most fundamental for life. In the context of prayer for the coming of the kingdom and as a principal aspect of that kingdom, this petition asks for a release from debts along with the provision of subsistence bread—in many ways the two most serious problems for ongoing life faced by peasants in a traditional agrarian society.

Equally important, however, is the second half of the petition. The relationship of the two clauses is not "since, if, or when God forgives . . . , then or therefore we forgive." The imperative petition followed by the perfect "we have forgiven" makes it appear that the latter is the model for the former. However much it may have been in anticipation of God's liberation, the petition about "forgiveness" presupposes that the people had already forgiven one another in their local social-economic relations.

One of Jesus' major parables is also concerned with the release of debts in local community life. The actual parable of the kingdom, Matthew 18:23–33, should be understood apart from its application by

Matthew 18:34–35 (God's forgiveness as conditional on our forgiveness from the heart) as well as from the church's disciplinary concerns of Matthew 18. It has been claimed that the relationship between monarch and royal servant, particularly the absolute power wielded by the king over the servant, does not accord with "Jewish practice" or conditions. That may indeed be true, if the later, rabbinic literature is the principal comparative material used. But there is no need to reach as far afield geographically or chronologically as the Persian empire and its satraps for this imagery. Since at least the reign of Herod there had been extensive royal estates just to the south of Galilee, and Herod surely wielded a free and brutal hand with his royal servants as well as with his sons. In any case, the hearers of the parable would have been familiar with a figure such as a royal servant and very familiar with ordinary "servants" being indebted. As can be seen by comparison with the spiritualizing, almost allegorical interpretation provided by Matthew, the point of the parable is rather to call the hearer to recognize that release of the debts of those obligated to them is now in order. Such is the appropriate response to the presence of the kingdom of God.

LOVE YOUR ENEMIES: LOCAL COOPERATION

It has become a standard generalization of modern social science that subject peoples, whether in colonized countries or metropolitan ghettos, develop an anxious distrust even of their brothers and sisters. Indeed, since any active expression of resentment against the dominant system or society is blocked by institutionalized repressive measures, subject peoples tend to vent their frustration in attacks against one another. Feeling steadily under attack from the larger system, individuals, families, and villages become suspicious and defensive with regard to one another as well as outsiders. There is abundant general evidence of just such a situation in Roman-dominated Palestine of the first century C.E. Best known, because of Jesus' parable, was the chronic hostility between the Jews and the Samaritans. Although this conflict between historically related peoples had begun much earlier, it intensified under Roman rule, occasionally flaring into fratricidal violence, with villagers killing villagers, followed by masses of people aroused to retaliation.[8] Such disorders, of course, only brought the repressive rule of Rome down ever more sharply on the heads of both peoples. There were also periodic hostilities between Jews and Gentiles, particularly in the cities around the edges of the predominantly Jewish territory in Palestine. It would seem that we should also allow for the likelihood of local distrust and hostility within the villages and towns as well, considering such factors as the cumulative economic pressures of double taxation, widespread indebtedness, and potential loss of land. If such were the concrete context of the lives of the people to whom Jesus ministered, it must also be the context addressed in some of his "teachings."

SEEKING THE KINGDOM AND RELEASE FROM ANXIETIES

When Jesus is treated primarily as a teacher addressing the individual, then modern interpreters understand a passage such as Luke 12:22–31 (parallel Matthew 6:25–33) as an exhortation to avoid "worldly cares" that would distract one from truly trusting in God, or to realize that true life is of far greater importance than concern about material existence. If the core sayings in this passage, however adapted in transmission, stem originally from the context of Jesus' ministry, then we have to consider some connection with a more concrete context. Recently when the question of social context has been raised, "the lifestyle of the wandering charismatics" (rather than "telling Galilean farmers to worry less about their crops") has provided a cursory solution.[9] But such a suggestion fails to give serious consideration to the perpetually marginal situation of a peasantry (and it would be only the Lukan lead into the passage in 12:22a that would induce anyone to think the passage applied only to the disciples).

The core of the passage would appear to be Luke 12:22,24,27–28, with the climax or conclusion in 12:31:

"I tell you, do not be anxious about your life, what you shall eat, nor your body, what you shall put on. . . . (24) Consider the ravens: they neither sow nor reap, they have neither storehouse nor barn, and yet God feeds them. Of how much more value are you than the birds! . . . (27) Consider the lilies, how they grow; they neither toil nor spin; yet I tell you, even Solomon in all his glory was not arrayed like one of these. (28) But if God so clothes the grass which is alive today and tomorrow is thrown into the oven, how much more will he clothe you, O men of little faith! . . . (31) Instead, seek his kingdom and all these things shall be yours as well."

The passage had already undergone considerable development at or prior to the Q stage.[10] The key term "anxious" in Luke 12:22 (parallel Matthew 6:25) provided a link for the addition of Luke 12:25 (parallel Matthew 6:27); but worries about one's mortality widen the focus and do not appear to have belonged originally with the more fundamental focus on food and clothing. Even Luke 12:23 ("for life is more than food") generalizes and philosophizes the wisdom here, which was originally more concrete in its concern. Luke 12:29 is concrete, suitable to the core of the passage, and forms a transition to the comparison with the Gentiles and/or the concluding statement about "seeking first the kingdom," whether or not it was present in earliest transmission of the tradition.

Once the secondary elements are removed, what remains is a fairly compact exhortation focused concretely on the basic necessities of food and clothing. The point of Jesus' wisdom here was to address the intense and justifiable anxiety about simple survival that haunted many ordinary people. The comparisons with God's providential care of the ravens and lilies pushed the people toward a more ennobling image both of their own value and of God's active concern for them. Whether or not the saying about "seek first the kingdom" was an integral part of the early tradition, it merely made explicit what would already have been implicit insofar as Jesus' wisdom teaching had its context in his message that kingdom of God was at hand. Thus in these sayings Jesus was calling the people to place their justifiable anxieties about obtaining even basic necessities in the context and perspective of their overall longings and, now, God's overall care and renewing action. This teaching of Jesus is similar or parallel to that in Mark 10:29–30 in the social-economic concreteness with which it understands the commitment to and the result of the renewal to which he called his listeners: in return for commitment to the kingdom, even if it meant relinquishing house, family, or lands, they would receive houses, family, lands in abundance. The passage is also parallel to the "blessings" promising the poor and hungry sufficient food in the kingdom of God in Luke 6:20–21, and it was appropriate that Matthew included both the blessings and the exhortation about anxiety in the same "sermon." The more particular point of Luke 12:22–31 was to relieve the people's anxieties about subsistence in the light of the perspective or goal of the kingdom.

The story in Luke 12:16–20 may originally have had a similar application. Like the "prodigal son," it is really more of an example or illustration than a parable. The rich man in the illustration is not an extremely wealthy and powerful person far removed from the local scene, but more of a prosperous farmer still supervising and probably actively working in his own fields and barns. Moreover, if he is storing up his goods in anticipation of a pleasurable retirement, it is a very parochial, not a cosmopolitan, life he envisions (contrast the "prodigal son," especially Luke 15:13,30). The reckoning in vs. 20, finally, is not any sort of eschatological judgment, but simply his own sudden death. Thus the story would appear to be directed neither to nor against the wealthy. Nor is it a general warning against greed. It could originally have been a story directed to ordinary poor people illustrating the futility of building up a surplus that one holds onto for oneself. The story can originally have addressed the same anxieties that Luke 12:22–31 and Matthew 6:25–34 addressed, the same defensive, private, self-protective behavior that results from anxiety-producing deprivation. The "rich man" in the story would have been a familiar character, if not in one's own smaller village, at least in a nearby large village or town; and such a character would not have been very popular. The story thus may hold up an unpopular and resented character as an example to the hearers of their own self-protective tendency and its deleterious social effects.

NONDEFENSIVE SHARING AND MUTUAL ASSISTANCE[11]

Matthew 5:38–48	*Luke 6:27–36*
[43]You have heard that it was said, 'You shall love your neighbor and hate your enemy.'	
[44]But I say to you, Love your enemies	[27]But I say to you that hear, Love your enemies do good to those who hate you,
and pray for those who persecute you.	[28]bless those who curse you, pray for those who abuse you.
[38]You have heard that it was said, 'An eye for an eye and a tooth for a tooth.'	
[39]But I say to you, Do not resist one who is evil. But if anyone strikes you on the right cheek, turn to him the other also;	[29]To him who strikes you on the cheek offer the other also;
[40]and if anyone would sue you and take your coat, let him have your cloak as well;	and from him who takes away your cloak do not withhold your coat as well.
[41]and if any one forces you to go one mile, go with him two miles.	
[42]Give to him who begs from you, and do not refuse him who would borrow from you.	[30]Give to every one who begs from you; and of him who takes away your goods do not ask them again.
	[31]And as you wish that men would do to you, do so to them.
(cf. Matt 7:12)	
[46]For if you love those who love you, what reward have you?	[32]If you love those who love you, what credit is that to you?

Do not even the tax collectors
do the same?
⁴⁷And if you salute only your
brethren,
what more are you doing than
others?
Do not even the Gentiles do
the same?

⁴⁵so that you may be sons of
your Father who is in
heaven;
for he makes his sun rise on
the evil and on the good,
and sends rain on the just and
on the unjust.
⁴⁸You, therefore, must be
perfect,
as your heavenly Father is
perfect.

For even the sinners love
those who love them.
³³And if you do good to those
who do good to you
what credit is that to you?

For even sinners do the same.
³⁴And if you lend to those from
whom you hope to receive,
what credit is that to you?
Even sinners lend to sinners,
to receive as much again.
³⁵But love your enemies,
and do good, and lend,
expecting nothing in return;
and your reward will be great,

and you will be sons of the
Most High;
for he is kind to the ungrateful
and the selfish.

³⁶Be merciful,

even as your Father is
merciful.

There are a number of reasons to conclude that Matthew rather than
Luke has rearranged the order of these sayings found together in the
sayings source Q. Most obvious is the grand structural scheme of the
fulfillment of the Law exemplified in the six antitheses (Matthew
5:21–48) of the Sermon on the Mount. Matthew 5:38–39a and 5:43 are
thus Matthean additions under which headings Matthew has rearranged
the particular sayings. Hence the Lucan order is likely closer to what
stood in Q. Both Matthew and Luke, however, have apparently made

changes in the more original wording to fit their own concerns. Matthew had added "pray for those who persecute you," 5:44b, in pursuit of a concern evident already at 5:10 and 11–12. This Matthean specification of "the enemies" may be correlated with why Matthew would have deleted the other two parallel phrases still found in Luke 6:27–28, which, according to form-critical criteria, form a natural synonymous parallelism. Luke, however, must have altered the wording in 6:29b and 30b to produce more general illustrations and to change the situations portrayed to theft instead of borrowing and claiming the security on a loan. The parallels in Matthew 5:39b–40,42 retain the more concrete terms, for example, specific to borrowing and lending.

Problematic Presuppositions

No teachings of Jesus are more widely and variously used and abused than these sayings grouped with "love your enemies." Some of them have become widely recognized if not observed principles of Christian ethics. "Do not resist evil" and "turn the other cheek" are used in situations ranging from interpersonal quarrels to philosophies of absolute nonresistance to military power. These sayings, and particularly "love your enemies," have been the traditional basis of Christian pacifism and are the key biblical texts for the modern philosophy of nonviolence. "Love your enemies" is also the principal text seized upon in dealing with the issue of Jesus and violence, the conclusion drawn varying remarkably from nonviolence to nonretaliation to nonresistance.

All such ways of using these sayings, of course, however prominent, influential, and legitimate, take them utterly out of their original context, both literarily and historically. In attempting to deal with these important sayings in their more original context, however, we must cut through some of the more distracting presuppositions, although many others must remain unaddressed. Most easily dispensed with, after the presentation made in Part Two is the supposed "Zealot" movement or any other supposed "resistance fighters" who have been used as a foil more prominently in relation to this passage than any other. There is simply no evidence for any violent resistance movement at the time of Jesus.

Sayings such as "turn the other cheek" and "love your enemies" have often been understood as abstract universal ethical principles, whether this understanding is rooted in the modern quest for a secure transcendent basis for ethics or in the modern view of Jesus as primarily a teacher addressing individuals, or whether it is simply the traditional way of reading the scripture as propositional truth. But it is highly unlikely that Jesus was articulating abstract truths, and it remains to be established whether he or the gospel tradition understood his teachings as universal ethical principles.

Our understanding of these sayings individually and collectively has been decisively influenced by their Matthean rearrangement and setting, in which they are usually read, quoted, and studied. Not surprisingly, the Matthean version is then projected back onto Jesus and/or the earliest tradition.[12] Matthew seems to be moving from internal community relations in his earlier antitheses to relations with outsiders in the final antithesis ("love your enemies," etc., Matthew 5:43–47) in the Sermon on the Mount. Moreover, the "antithesis" form, by which Jesus calls for a "higher righteousness" ("you have heard that it was said ... but I say to you") is almost certainly the creation of Matthew and not original to Jesus or the early tradition. Thus both the apparent contrast between the *lex talionis* and the "do not resist" and "turn the other cheek" and the contrast between loving your neighbor (Leviticus 19:18) (while hating your enemies) and love of enemies are Matthean and not integral to the early tradition and are surely not from Jesus. It is only the Matthean setting, not the sayings themselves, that makes us think that the "enemies" were outsiders.

Partly because of the influence of the Matthean version of the sayings, it has usually been assumed that the "enemies" in the key saying "love your enemies" were political, particularly foreign, enemies. In the case of Jesus and his contemporaries, it is assumed that this would have been the Romans, while later in the development of the gospel tradition, the persecutors of the church would have been implied. This assumption is so solidly rooted that few recent studies of these sayings have even raised the issue of who the "enemies" may have been. One study that implicitly raises the question simply reverts to the view that "love your enemies" refers to foreign political enemies, particularly the Romans and their Jewish collaborators.[13] The Greek term *echthros* can mean foreign and/or political enemy, but that would have to be established in a given text as read in its literary and social context.

Closely related to the assumption that "enemies" refers to foreign or political foes outside the community are the assumptions that "love your enemies" is the same as nonviolence and that the issue in "love your enemies" sayings is violence/nonviolence or nonresistance or nonretaliation. Apparently such assumptions are simply the result of our applying modern questions to these sayings of Jesus. In contrast to the division into two antitheses in Matthew, the Lucan arrangement, which is surely closer to Q, has all the sayings grouped under "love your enemy." Yet none of the individual sayings in Luke (and presumably in Q) concerns nonviolence. It is only the Matthean addition of "do not resist one who is evil," in connection with his arrangement of the sayings into antitheses, that might suggest nonviolence as an issue. But even in Matthew's antitheses, Jesus' sayings are not the opposite of the old *lex talionis* but its fulfillment (Matthew 5:38–42); and "love your enemies," which does not appear until the following antithesis, is not directly related to the issue of "an eye for an eye," but to a separate issue.

Recent interpretations in particular assume that the issue in Luke 6:27–36 and parallel Matthew 5:38–48, is violence and nonviolence.[14] But there is nothing whatever in the passage in either Matthew's or Luke's version pertaining to the issue of political violence. The saying about going the second mile may have originated as a reference to the imperial requisition of labor. But Matthew uses it in the antithesis dealing with interpersonal relations (5:38–42), not in connection with love of enemies. Matthew does mention persecutors in 5:44b, which fits one of his themes (cf. 5:10, 11–12; 10:23). But persecution, however psychologically violent it may be, does not imply the overt physical violence often projected onto these sayings. In Luke the only violence is verbal, the cursing of 6:28. The taking away of one's garments or goods, understood as theft in Luke 6:29–30, of course, may suggest a kind of private interpersonal violence, but that concerns local village interaction and not hostility toward outside enemies. The only apparent violence in Matthew's antitheses appears in the framing of some of the other sayings with "an eye for an eye," but not even that necessarily refers to violence, as we will see. Thus besides the complete absence of political violence as an issue in these sayings, interpersonal violence is not even particularly prominent. Nonviolence is neither the issue nor the message of these sayings.[15]

Nor do these sayings deal with nonresistance to evil. This notion probably stems from the King James Version of Matthew 5:39a, "Resist not evil." Recent translations have the less ominous and somewhat more precise "one who is evil" or "the wicked man." Among all the sayings in the passage, only Matthew 5:39-41 and principally 5:39a could possibly be taken as focused on nonresistance to an evildoer. But, since the antithesis in Matthew 5:38-42 deals with local interpersonal relations, nonresistance to oppression or persecution is hardly the message. And the language used *(antistenai)* does not imply resistance in a physical sense but in the sense of "protest" or "testify against."[16] "Turn the other cheek" has taken on a proverbial meaning of its own in modern English-speaking societies. But it would hardly be sound procedure to project that back into the sayings of Jesus.

Nonretaliation comes closer to what at least some of the sayings in Luke 6:27-36 and Matthew 5:38-48 are about. Still it is primarily only Matthew's juxtaposition of some of the sayings with the *lex talionis* that suggests this. Of course Matthew 5:43-47 could perhaps be read as a prohibition of revenge, somewhat like Paul's advice in Romans 12:19-21. But even the sayings that Matthew juxtaposes with "an eye for an eye" do not really deal directly with nonretaliation. "Turn the other cheek" in Matthew 5:39b is the only saying whose content approaches nonretaliation. Yet even though the *lex talionis* originally may have dealt with cases of personal injury, it is doubtful whether, at the time of Jesus, Matthew 5:39b can be read as referring to "physical abuse" and "blows."[17] Neither in Luke nor, apparently, in Q was there any connection between turning the other cheek and the *lex talionis*.[18] Thus no more than nonviolence and nonresistance does nonretaliation appear to be the theme or message of the "love your enemy" set of Jesus sayings.

The Character and Concrete Context of the Sayings

These sayings did not constitute a new Law that replaced, let alone abolished, the old.[19] Even in the Matthean Sermon on the Mount there is no suggestion that Jesus was abolishing the old Torah. He was rather fulfilling it, restoring its proper functioning, insisting on the realization of true righteousness intended originally in God's giving of the Torah. Even less at the pre-Matthean level of the tradition or in the situation of Jesus' ministry should we be expecting to find new law. Jesus was clearly a wise man. Equally clearly he was not a lawyer.

Indeed, it is questionable whether any of the individual sayings in this complex can be understood as laws, commands, or rules. The ethical sections of the letters of Paul, the former Pharisee, provide an elucidating comparison. In Romans 12–14, for example, Paul lays out generally formulated ethical rules for behavior and social relations, with considerable explication at points. "The precepts in Romans are perfectly straightforward general maxims which you could transfer directly to the field of conduct. . . . That could hardly be said of the gospel precepts. . . . You could not possibly go about applying these precepts directly and literally as they stand."[20] To use the most vivid example from Luke 6:27–36—if not the one most evident from English translations and modern experience (hence the following paraphrase): to apply Luke 6:29 "directly to the field of conduct" would have been embarrassing if not downright absurd: "If anyone would sue you and take your outer garments, then give him your underclothes as well." If Jesus was advocating nudism, it must have been at least with a touch of irony or humor!

Such sayings, however, are not ethical precepts or commands for general implementation in conduct, and certainly not legal regulations to be dutifully carried out. Like Luke 6:29, most of the other sayings grouped with "love your enemies" are extreme in their demands, deal with specific situations, and have a very limited application if taken literally. Such sayings are not "commandments" but illustrations or "focal instances" of a certain spirit or orientation toward one's life circumstances.[21] In contrast to "legal rules," which deal with particular kinds of social relations or interaction, can be implemented in their literal sense, and allow clear deductions concerning the range of their application, "focal instances" are both specific and extreme, and they refer to general relations up to and including the literal one portrayed. "Focal instances" such as those in Luke 6:29–30 challenge the hearers to the indicated spirit or special orientation and behavior in a whole range of situations by giving a few vivid and extreme illustrations.

Of course, not all the sayings in Luke 6:26–37 are "focal instances," and no absolute contrast should be drawn between the ethical commands or precepts given by Paul and the teachings of Jesus. "Love your enemies," its repetition and variation in Luke 6:35a, the "golden rule" in Luke 6:31, and the concluding "be merciful" are all general exhortations regarding social relations. In form and content they are similar to the proverbial wisdom exhortation traditional in the ancient Near East.[22] The sayings that fill out the rest of the passage, Luke 6:32–34,35b, are further exhortations to loving and merciful social action. It is unclear whether the "golden rule" stood in Q or is added in Luke 6:31. It is likely, however, that it is meant to be transcended, not simply clarified, by the sayings in Luke 6:32–34,35b. The rhetorical questions clearly suggest that the love of enemies called for by Jesus goes beyond the reciprocity between those who simply love each other. The love of enemies passage is not "new law," but a call for a general orientation toward one's social relations illustrated by some extreme instances and further motivated by comparative exhortations.

The content of these sayings, particularly that of the illustrative instances, indicates the concrete social context presupposed and addressed by the sayings. Examination of the sayings, both individually at the earliest accessible stage of the tradition and at the Matthean and Lucan level, indicates that that context was local interaction with personal enemies, not relations with foreign or other political enemies.

Luke 6:27–28: In the Septuagint, which strongly influenced the Greek usage of the early churches, *echthros* can be used both for foreign, political enemies and for personal (and more local) enemies. More decisive for determining the meaning of this and other terms, however, is the usage in the individual gospel writers, in the synoptic tradition generally, and especially in the immediate context. In two passages in Luke (the Song of Zechariah, 1:71,74, and the lament over Jerusalem, 19:43) the term refers to national enemies. None of the other occurrences Matthew and Luke is a reference to foreign national or domestic political enemies. The "enemy" is rather a local adversary, e.g., one who sabotages a farmer's crop by sowing weeds among the grain (Matthew 13:25,28). The crucial decision required in response to Jesus' preaching of the kingdom (bringing not peace but a sword) means that the members of one's own household may become "enemies" (Matthew 10:34–36). Herod Antipas and Pilate had been personal enemies, although there may have been an element of political rivalry involved (Luke 23:12). Even Satan is conceived of as a personal enemy, especially in the analogy drawn from the parable (Matthew 13:39; cf. 13:25,28; cf. Luke 10:19). The other principal passage, Matthew 22:44 (and Luke 20:43), is a quotation from Psalm 110:1 and is formulaic. In the immediate context of the saying in Luke 6:27–28 and in Q, there is nothing to suggest that foreign or political enemies are referred to. Standing in isolation, "your enemies" is vague. Taken in connection with the parallel sayings in Luke (and in Q, probably), the phrase surely means those with whom one is in personal, local interaction. Although "those who hate" and "those who curse" could be anyone, whether local or distant, "those who mistreat [epereazo] you" would have to be local. But, with a few exceptions (song of Zechariah and synoptic apocalypse, Luke 1:71 and Matthew 24:9), "those who hate," although outside the community of Jesus' followers, are within the local sphere of social interaction. The "hatred" could even be between family members, precisely as the result of response to Jesus (Luke 14:26). Similarly, while one could bless and pray for people at a distance, "doing good" presupposes direct interaction. Even in Matthew's specification of enemies as persecutors, the latter appear to be in local interaction with the community members.

Luke 6:29a: Far from being a symbol for violence or evil (to which Jesus then counsels passive nonretaliation or nonresistance), the slap on the cheek was simply a formal insult, not a spontaneous act of violence.[23] It was a serious insult (as in Mishnah Bava Kamma 8:6), but there is only insult and "no damage to person."[24] If we also consider the principle of "focal instance," in which an extreme example is used to cover similar actions up to and including the literal case, then the insulting slap in the face (the formal insult) is the most extreme case envisaged in the saying. Thus, if the content of the saying concerns the insulting slap in the face and other lesser but similar actions, then the context is local village or town interaction.

Luke 6:29b (and Matthew 5:40): While Luke may be imagining a case of theft, Matthew's wording makes intelligible the case of the seizure of a garment in pledge. According to the Torah (Exodus 22:25–26; Deuteronomy 24:10–13; cf. Amos 2:8), "If ever you take your neighbor's garment in pledge, you shall restore it to him before the sun goes down; for that is his only covering . . . ; in what else shall he sleep?" The Torah thus covers the outer garment (cloak/*himation*), but not the undergarment *(chiton)*. The saying (in Matthew's wording) thus appears to envisage a situation in which the creditor seizes a person's undergarment, and Jesus counsels rendering up the outer garment (which cannot legally be taken away) as well—thus leaving the poor person in the ridiculous situation of standing naked before the unmerciful creditor and any onlookers. The content of the saying clearly indicates a local interaction between creditor and debtor over a loan.

Luke 6:30 (and Matthew 5:42): That these exhortations do "not fit the topic of non retaliation very well" indicates that nonretaliation is not the subject of the passage as a whole.[25] In 6:30b, Luke may have a situation of theft in mind.[26] In the more original wording (Matthew 5:42), the sayings are straightforward exhortations to give to one who begs and to loan to one who seeks to borrow. The exhortation to lend is repeated in Luke 6:34 and 35a. It thus has a certain prominence in the passage as a whole, at least in Luke, and perhaps in Q as well (depending on one's reconstruction). The context and the content of the sayings clearly presuppose local social-economic relationships. Only without this concrete social-economic context do the references to "lending" appear to be "somewhat clumsy illustrations."[27]

Luke 6:32–33 (–34) (and Matthew 5:46–47): In these sayings Jesus challenges his hearers to transcend reciprocal love, "doing good," etc. Matthew 5:46 may well reproduce the more original wording from Q; "sinners" occurs often in Luke, and Matthew has the term only where clearly following Q or Mark. But the "Gentiles" in Matthew 5:47 is clearly a distinctive Matthean term, occurring elsewhere only in another Sermon on the Mount text (Matthew 6:7) and in the church-discipline discourse (Matthew 18:17). Thus it is only Matthew who uses non-Jews (outsiders) as a contrast for the reciprocal relations Jesus is calling for. In Luke and Q the sayings draw their comparison and contrast within the broader Jewish community. And, in the case of either "sinners" or "toll collectors," the contrast is drawn from people with whom the hearers would have been familiar at least in the area if not in a given village.

Luke 6:36 (and Matthew 5:48): Luke's "merciful" is surely closer to Q (the term occurs only here; compare Matthew 5:48 with Matthew 19:21). As the concluding exhortations, both terms, "be merciful" and "be perfect," in imitation of God, however, indicate that the context of the whole group of sayings is the Covenant people who are called to practice justice in imitation of God's justice.

Thus far we have been dealing with the sayings in Q and in the social context indicated very early in the tradition, with occasional comparative comments regarding Matthew's or Luke's redactions. When we shift the focus to Matthew and Luke, we find little change from what we have seen. For Luke we have few cases of definite editorial changes, principally alterations in wording, on which to base deductions. We have already noted that there is no evidence that in 6:27–36 Luke has in mind only persecutors from outside the Christian communities. With "enemies," "those who curse," etc., he may have in mind either community members or noncommunity members or both. Especially if the formulation of 6:35 is Luke's and was not originally in Q, then his focus is clearly local intracommunity social-economic relations. In Luke 6:29b and 30b he appears to envision situations less specific than local borrowing and lending, perhaps situations of theft, but the context is still local social interaction. Certainly there is no indication of foreign enemies.

We must treat the Matthean interpretation according to the framing into two different antitheses. The saying in Matthew 5:41 appears to refer to relations between the occupying imperial power and the population subject to forced labor *(angariae)*. But the surrounding sayings, and especially the formulaic antithesis of Matthew 5:38–39a, force us to assume that this saying is subordinated to the editorial framing. The *lex talionis,* of course, referred not to imperial-subject relations but to domestic Jewish social relations. Moreover, by Jesus' time and certainly by Matthew's the *lex talionis* was interpreted not in terms of violence and personal mutilation, but "as signifying the claim to accurate, nicely calculated compensation" for personal humiliation.[28] Matthew's framing in terms of not opposing or going to court against an evildoer is appropriate to the sayings he used from Q, all but one of which refer to local personal social-economic relations. In Matthew 5:38–42 he has in mind the internal relations of members of the church.

With regard to Matthew 5:43–44a, which has so decisively influenced the interpretation of the whole passage, Jeremias, attempting to reconstruct the Aramaic behind the Greek, suggests that the original saying, 5:43, should read, "You shall love your compatriot, but you need not love your adversaries." The adversaries, however, are now persecutors outside the church communities. Moreover, perhaps precisely because the adversaries are now outsiders to the Christian community, Matthew backs away from suggesting any concrete social-economic responsibility as the meaning of "love." In the context indicated by Matthew's content in 5:43–47, the "enemy" may still be a local adversary, but the Christian has no specific duty to do good or to lend to that adversary.

Analysis of the sayings in Luke 6:27–36 and Matthew 5:38–48, whether in the Q form and earlier stages of the sayings tradition or in the Matthean or Lucan adaptations, suggests that the context indicated by the content of the individual sayings is that of social-economic relations in a village or town. It is easy to understand the "enemies, haters, cursers, abusers" in the context of local interaction, but difficult if not impossible to understand them as referring to national or political enemies. This interpretation is confirmed simply by the kinds of relationships assumed in the following sayings: the insulting slap in the face, the local creditor's seizure of the token pledge given by the debtor, borrowing and begging among local community members, or doing good and lending to those who may be local adversaries. Matthew evidently reinterpreted the thematic saying he found in Q, "love your enemies," to refer to persecutors of Jesus' followers. But he also took most of the other sayings to refer to the internal relations of the local community. Finally, in the Lucan Sermon on the Plain, as well as in the sayings source Q, whether in this passage or in the sermon as a whole, "Jesus' words . . . touch on the concerns of daily existence, poverty, hunger, grief, hatred, and ostracism."[29]

The Background of the Sayings and the Situation They Addressed

In addressing local social-economic relationships in these sayings and others, Jesus drew on long-standing Jewish (Israelite) covenantal Torah and wisdom teachings. Allusions to Leviticus 19 are even evident in the sayings themselves, as noted above: "Be merciful as God is merciful [perfect]" clearly is an allusion to and/or restatement of the principle found in Leviticus 19:2; and prior to Matthew's reformulation into a quotation in the antithesis of 5:43–44a, "love your enemies" was likely related to Leviticus 19:17–18. The immediate scriptural context, Leviticus 19:17–18—and perhaps other injunctions in Leviticus 19 as well (especially 19:9–16)—indicates the kind of covenantal concerns that Jesus is addressing (and intensifying or sharpening):

"You shall not hate your brother in your heart, but you shall reason with your neighbor, lest you bear sin because of him. You shall not take vengeance or bear any grudge against the sons of your own people, but you shall love your neighbor as yourself."

Mosaic covenantal Torah, moreover, was formulated not simply in terms of giving aid to one's brother or neighbor, but also in terms of aiding one's personal local "enemy":

"If you meet your enemy's ox or his ass going astray, you shall bring it back to him. If you see the ass of one who hates you lying under its burden, you shall refrain from leaving him with it, you shall help him to lift it up." (Exodus 23:4–5; cf. Deuteronomy 22:1–4)

The wisdom of ben Sirah is much closer to New Testament times and substantively similar to Jesus' teaching. It understands mercy as manifested concretely in local covenantal economic relations:

He that shows mercy will lend to his neighbor, and he that strengthens him with his hand keeps the commandments. (Sirach 29:1)

The sayings of Jesus, however, sharpen or intensify, as well as renew, such covenantal teachings and wisdom. It is well, therefore, to examine more carefully the general social-economic situation indicated by the content of "love your enemies" and by the related sayings along with the situation indicated by other aspects of Jesus' teachings.

The sayings in Luke 6:27–36 and Matthew 5:38–48 depict circumstances of severe economic hardship among those addressed. It assumes that some in the local village community are asking for loans for which they have genuine need. Some to whom the sayings are addressed, already in debt, are unable to repay, and fear that their creditors may seize the security they have posted. Still others have been reduced to begging. Not surprisingly, in such desperate economic circumstances some people are at each other's throats, hating, cursing, and abusing. The picture given by the blessings and the woes, which must have immediately preceded the "love your enemies" passage even in Q, is similar: those addressed are apparently poor, hungry, and in despair. What is more, they stand opposite others (their urban creditors?) who are wealthy, well fed, and satisfied with life. This picture of peasant village life in Galilee and Palestine generally accords with that depicted in other synoptic gospel material.[30] We have already observed, on the basis of Jesus' parables and other evidence (Matthew 18:23–33; Luke 16:1–7) that many of the peasants in Galilee were heavily in debt and that many had become day laborers, either because they found it necessary to supplement the inadequate sustenance gained from their own small parcel of land, or because they had already forfeited their land to creditors.[31]

These sayings of Jesus appear to address, as well as to presuppose, people caught in such severe economic circumstances. In those circumstances one would expect a high degree of resentment of the wealthy. Indeed, the woes against the wealthy earlier in the "sermon" (Luke 6:24–25) reflect just that. The sayings beginning with "love your enemies," however, do not have the exploitative ruling class in mind. These sayings of Jesus rather called people in local village communities to take economic responsibility for one another in their desperate circumstances. Those addressed may have had little or nothing themselves. But Jesus called upon them to share willingly what they had with others in the community, even with their enemies or those who hated them. They were not to seek damages from a formal insult. They were even to render up the pledge for a loan that the unmerciful creditor had no right to take. And, assuming that these sayings were only a few "focal instances," they illustrate a general orientation that Jesus was calling for among his followers. The messages and the new orientation were: take responsibility for willingly helping one another, even your enemies, in the local village community.

RECONCILIATION AND AUTONOMY

Jesus' insistence on egalitarian social relations both in the local community and in the society as a whole may have appeared to some —those with a vested interest in the established hierarchical political-economic-religious order—as naive anarchism. Both traditional peasant village communities and inspired movements of renewal, however, have their own nonhierarchical and more flexible ways of resolving social conflicts, and both characteristically attempt to avoid (if not even to subvert) the formal governing institutions that exploit as well as control the people.[32] Jesus and his followers would appear to have advocated just such a double strategy of resolving actual or potential conflicts in a direct and flexible way so as to maintain harmony within the local community while simultaneously avoiding contact and cooperation with the established institutions such as the courts and the Temple.

WORKING OUT CONCRETE CONFLICTS WHILE AVOIDING THE COURTS

Modern interpreters have no trouble imagining that the apostle Paul —despite his orientation toward and excitement about the fulfillment of history that he believed was happening in his own lifetime—was a very practical man. He instructed the Corinthian community in no uncertain terms to handle disputes between its members within the community and to avoid a situation of "brother going to law against brother" in the official court (1 Corinthians 6:1–6). It need not imply that Paul knew the sayings of Jesus to note simply that Jesus appears to give equally practical instruction in Luke 12:58–59 and Matthew 5:25–26:

"Make friends quickly with your accuser while you are going with him to court, lest your accuser hand you over to the judge, and the judge to the guard, and you be put in prison; truly I say, you will never get out till you have paid the last penny."

This passage provides another illustration of two problematic characteristics of modern biblical interpretation. Having seized upon what appears to be the dominant theme of the "teaching" of Jesus, the presence and/or imminence of the kingdom of God, and the most distinctive mode of that teaching, the parables, we have tended to read as much of the Jesus traditions as possible in those terms. Then we also have tended to understand Jesus, his mode of teaching, and the content of his message as primarily and even exclusively "religious." This saying of Jesus has thus usually been understood as a parable or simile calling for repentance in the face of the imminence of the kingdom.[33]

Yet it is unclear even in Luke 12:57–59, where Luke has supplied the setting and possible application, that the passage functions as a parable calling for recognition of the situation and repentance.[34] The passage simply does not make a very good parable. "With a certain infelicity, the accuser is imagined as a human creditor, and reconciliation (with God) becomes little more than common prudence"; hence it is necessary on such a reading to rescue Jesus from having "offered this rather sordid motive . . . for reconciliation."[35] Moreover, the supposed parable will not work on the basis of an analogy between the separate spheres of "civil life" and religious life, since "civil" and "religious" life were not separate in ancient Jewish society.[36] The wiser form-critical counsel in this and certain other cases would appear rather "to reckon on a certain amount of the stuff of the tradition having been secular in its origin."[37] Surely Jesus was capable of "secular prudential wisdom."

Read as a bit of prudential instruction, Matthew 5:35–36 (and Luke 12:58–59) requires little interpretation other than placing it in its concrete social context. The situation envisaged in the saying would appear to be one of local conflict, one peasant owing a relatively small debt to another (cf. the situation portrayed in Matthew 18:28–30). Were the debt of considerable size and the accuser a wealthy, powerful creditor, he would likely have formalized the loan beforehand and have simply come with court decision in hand and with sufficient force to execute the judgment (debt-slavery, forfeiture of land). There would be little point in attempting to "make friends with" or "to settle with" such a creditor, who would surely have been an absentee landlord living in Tiberias or Sepphoris if not in Jerusalem, while managing his estate(s) through "servants" or "stewards" (see, e.g., Luke 16:1-7).

The situation is rather that of one peasant needing, perhaps desperately, to be repaid, the other resisting and perhaps incapable of repayment—a situation similar to that imagined behind Luke 6:29b and Matthew 5:40. If the debtor were to end up in jail, a further breakdown of the village community would ensue, since the debtor's family would be even less able to survive because of reduced labor or earning power, and would likely have to forfeit the family's land eventually. The prudential wisdom oriented toward the survival and renewal of local communities advises the reluctant debtor to seek some resolution short of the court. The latter, not oriented to the renewal of the local community, was expected simply to imprison the indebted peasant— hardly a solution to the general problem of a heavily indebted peasantry.

CONFLICT AND RECONCILIATION IN THE LOCAL COMMUNITY

The egalitarian ethos encouraged by Jesus depended heavily but not exclusively upon assertive interaction among individual community members. There was apparently also provision for community sanction and participation in dealing with sustained or persistent interpersonal conflict. The sayings in Matthew 18:15-22—whose process of transmission and development is difficult to unravel—provide a window onto the way Jesus and his followers dealt with interpersonal difficulties within the community without recourse to either the traditional local patriarchal patterns or to the official governmental institutions.

Ancient Israel, a relatively simply structured agrarian society in which the vast majority of people lived in village communities, depended heavily upon traditional wisdom for maintaining social order. Israelites had long been well aware that offenses by one party and pent-up resentment by the offended party could lead to more and explosive conflict. We thus find exhortations regarding timely reproof and reconciliation and the avoidance of vengeance, such as in Leviticus 19:17–18: "You shall reason with your neighbor, lest you bear sin because of him. You shall not take vengeance or bear any grudge against the sons of your own people, but you shall love your neighbor as yourself." There must have been a long-standing tradition of further exhortation developing this theme (and this text, as well as similar themes and texts). Testament of Gad 6:1–7, a text closer to the time of Jesus, offers a glimpse of how such exhortation took literary form, testamentary advice from a revered father to his sons. The saying in Luke 17:3 and Matthew 18:15a, "if your brother sins, rebuke him," whatever its original form and context, is yet another bit of wisdom building on the same tradition expressed in Leviticus 19:17, perhaps even having that passage in mind. As was noted by early form-critics, the rest of Luke 17:3–4 could then have been an expansion on that saying.

The more complex parallel to Luke 17:3–4 in Matthew 18:15–22 has evoked a great deal of debate concerning the originality and development of its components, and some of the presuppositions of that debate may require updating. Because the parallels with Luke 17:3–4 are not close, it is by no means obvious that Matthew simply expanded a double saying from Q with his own special material. It has been argued that Matthew reproduced the more complete passage from Q, which Luke must have abbreviated.[38] It seems more likely, however, that Matthew drew on his own special material that had a partial parallel in Q (or Luke's special material), which now appears in Luke 17:3–4.[39] In analyzing the passage in Matthew, most critics view at least Matthew 18:18–20 as a secondary addition. The form of Matthew 18:21–22, Peter's question and Jesus' answer, is likewise clearly a secondary development. Probes into the basic content of Matthew 18:15–17 suggest that 16b may also be a secondary expansion. Even the initial form-critical judgments held the core of the passage to be a dominical saying reformulated by the early Palestinian church.[40] The principal reason why the core of Matthew 18:15–17 has been denied to Jesus has been the occurrence of "Gentile and tax collector" in 17b, on the grounds that Jesus actively associated with "tax collectors and sinners."[41] As was noted above, however, that is an unwarranted assumption, given the secondary and redactional character of the texts that so portray Jesus. Moreover, the term "Gentile" *(ethnikos)* occurs only in Matthew (5:47; 6:9; and 18:17). Hence it seems highly questionable to deny the core of Matthew 18:15–17 to Jesus yet to insist it must be Palestinian church or Q, principally on the basis of the occurrence of "Gentile and tax collector". In matters of community relations and discipline such as this, of course, it may be impossible in any case to distinguish between the practice of the "early Palestinian church" and the teaching of Jesus and the original preacher-healers in the villages. Compared with the sayings in Luke 17:3–4, Matthew 18:15–17,21–22 displays important additional dimensions, the very same dimensions found in two parallel passages from the Qumran community.

"If your brother sins against you, go and tell him his fault, between you and him alone. If he listens to you, you have gained your brother. But if he does not listen, take one or two others along with you, that every word may be confirmed by the evidence of two or three witnesses. If he refuses to listen to them, tell it to the church [assembly]; and if he refuses to listen even to the church [assembly], let him be to you as a Gentile and a tax collector." (Matthew 18:15–16a,17)

They shall rebuke one another in truth, humility, and charity. Let no man address his companion with anger, or ill-temper, or obduracy, or with envy prompted by the spirit of wickedness. Let him not hate him [because of his uncircumcised] heart, but let him rebuke him on the very same day lest he incur guilt because of him. And furthermore, let no man accuse his companion before the Congregation without having first admonished him in the presence of witnesses. (1QS 5:25–6:1; parallel in CD 9:2–8)

In both cases, the offended party is to proceed by personally reproving the offender, then by trying the reproof in the presence of witnesses, and only if that fails, to bring about reconciliation by bringing the problem before the whole "assembly" or community. Thus in both Matthew 18:15–17 and the Qumran texts, reproof and reconciliation are now placed in the context of the community's concern for relations among its members, and involvement by the whole community is the recourse if aggressive individual efforts at reconciliation fail. It has often been supposed, probably because of assumptions about the significance of "as a Gentile and tax collector," that "the church" was here being instructed to expel recalcitrant offenders from the community. The instruction throughout Matthew 18:15–17, however, is formulated in the singular, to the individual; thus "let him be to you as . . ." refers to the offended person's attitude, not to any church disciplinary action. The emphasis throughout is on working out reconciliation and, failing that, forgiveness: seven or seventy-seven times, in the continuing exhortation of Matthew 18:21–22. Whether or not "Gentile and tax collector" was in the original saying, and whatever it may have meant, no one was being thrown out of the community; the context was apparently a local village community, and the offender, like the offended person, lived there and was literally a neighbor. Given the complexity of Palestinian Jewish society and the possibility that the "Matthean community" was outside of Palestine, it seems inappropriate to proceed as if we could trace "sectarian" practices that were combined with "rabbinic usage" in Matthew.[42] It seems more likely that we must reckon with a practice already in existence in Jewish villages and adapted by both Jesus' communities and the Qumranites.

Perhaps also at Qumran, but at least in the practice delineated or reflected in Matthew 18:17, action is taken by the whole local community (*ekklesia* = assembly, in this context), and not by the local elders or officers (cf. Deuteronomy 19:17–18). The Qumran community, of course, had completely separated itself from the rest of the society, hence obviously required its own internal means of discipline and governance. Jesus and his followers, however, developed their communities directly within the traditional villages and towns. Thus it is all the more striking that they had a similar means of dealing with interpersonal conflict within their communities and, at least by implication, avoided the official established institutions for handling conflicts. Emphasis was laid explicitly on aggressive personal and interpersonal action; but the egalitarian community as a whole was concerned and ready to be involved as a recourse, in lieu of (and in opposition to?) the established institutions. In this connection it is worth noting that, regardless of how much later it may be (Matthean?), Matthew 18:18, which gives the power of binding and loosing (absolution) to the community collectively (note its granting to Peter individually in

Matthew 16:19), is a consistent perpetuation of Jesus' earlier instruction and practice.

"THE SONS ARE FREE:" THE HALF-SHEKEL TEMPLE TAX

Interpretation of the basic thrust of Matthew 17:24–27 depends upon how one views its context. Scholarly interpreters are divided on the degree to which some or all of the passage represents tradition from the ministry of Jesus. The passage contains some typically Matthean language, but principally in the framing of the brief dialogue that constitutes its core. As it stands, the passage is somewhat legendary. Yet it is equally possible to view the passage as a composite of the basic saying in vv. 25–26 and the additional folkloric motif of v. 27 held together with a suitable framing. The folkloric flavor of Matthew 17:27, of course, means that it could as easily be early instead of late in the development of the tradition. Even Bultmann, who does not even consider the possibility of a concrete context in the ministry of Jesus, concludes that the short dialogue of vv. 25–26, with its metaphor and application, is primitive tradition. The conception of God as analogous to a human king is typical of biblical traditions prior to and of midrashic traditions subsequent to Jesus in the Palestinian Jewish context. The form of the question parallels other sayings in the synoptic tradition that are commonly viewed as from Jesus himself. On balance, then, the most persuasive evidence and arguments point toward the conclusion that at least the brief dialogue at the center of the passage goes back to Jesus himself.[43] Whether to view v. 27 as originally linked or subsequently added may depend on how we view the context and thrust of vv. 25–26.

This passage was traditionally understood e.g., by Jerome, Ambrose, and Augustine as referring to the Roman tribute, whereas most modern scholars assume that the tax being collected was the "half-shekel" paid to the Temple by adult Jewish males.[44] Against the latter, it has been argued recently that the reference must have been to "civil taxes."[45] The latter argument, and many treatments of the passage, rest on the false assumption that a sharp distinction can be made between "religious" (i.e., Jewish or Temple) and "civil" (i.e., Roman) taxation. In the ancient world generally, and particularly in Jewish society, for which God was supposedly the true "king," such a distinction did not exist. Tithes, offerings, and other taxes paid to God or the Temple or the priests were indistinguishably both civil and religious. From Josephus, *Ant.* 18.312, we know that the half-shekel tax was understood as paid "to God" *(tō theō);* and we know from *M. Shekalim* 4:1–2 that the revenues were used for maintaining the Temple and the city of Jerusalem as well as for the sacrifices.[46] The analogy in the brief dialogue of Matthew 17:25–26, the core of the passage, makes sense only if the tax referred to is one levied by or in the name of God. This, along with the fact that the value of the coin to be found in the fish's mouth was precisley that necessary to pay the tax for two males, Jesus and Peter, clearly indicates that the issue in the passage was the half-shekel tax paid to the Temple by adult Jewish males.

The half-shekel tax was almost certainly a late development in second Temple times, and its payment was controversial at the time of Jesus.[47] But by that time the tax was clearly a standard institution, even in the diaspora, as is evidenced in both Josephus *(War* 6.335; *Ant.* 14.110; 16.28,163–173; 18.312–313; cf. 3.194–196) and Philo *(Spec. Leg.* 1.77–78; *Heres* 186). Also it was apparently vigorously collected: the tractate on *Shekalim* in the Mishnah speaks of tables of collectors and money-changers being set up in the provinces on the fifteenth of Adar and in the Temple itself on the twenty-fifth. From those too poor (or too recalcitrant) to pay, pledges would be exacted *(Shekalim* 1.3).[48] Yet this half-shekel tax is not mentioned in the Torah. An unspecified yearly offering is mentioned in 2 Chronicles 24:5, and a new yearly tax of one-third shekel is mentioned in Nehemiah 10:32. Yet subsequent texts that discuss Temple offerings, such as Tobit 1:6–8, Aristeas, and Jubilees do not mention any yearly half-shekel tax. The Pharisees understood Exodus 30:13 as instituting the annual dues whereby all Israel shared in the support of the Temple sacrifices *(Shekalim* 4.1). A halakic fragment from Qumran, however, can be understood as a polemic against such an understanding of the half-shekel tax: "As for the half- [shekel, the offering of the Lord] which they gave, each man as a ransom for his soul: only one [time] shall he give it all his days" (4Q159).[49] Priests apparently claimed immunity from the tax, as is evidenced in Yohanan ben Zakkai's sharp denial of such a priestly claim

(*Shekalim* 1.4). And the Palestinian Jewish people generally must have been lax in if not resistant to paying the annual half-shekel, judging from the lament of Yohanan ben Zakkai that the intensified subjection of the people following the revolt against Rome was due to their recalcitrance about the Temple tax and other Jewish duties before the revolt.[50] Thus, if the half-shekel tax was of recent institution, without the clear authority of the Torah, and its payment was disputed and resisted or even denied, this story about Jesus' stance toward this tax would have a highly credible historical context.

Before moving to analysis of Jesus' brief dialogue in Matthew 17:25–26 in response to the question, we should note the discrepancy between the narrower focus of the question regarding the half-shekel tax in particular and the broad, almost absolute, principle enunciated in Jesus' saying ("then the sons are free"). That is, the question focuses on a particular and relatively new tax, while Jesus' statement appears to cover taxation of "the sons" in general. We will not simply assume that the saying concerns all taxation (tithes, offerings, etc.) officially demanded by the Temple. But it would be good form-critical procedure to trust the saying itself as being the earlier, more reliable tradition, in comparison with the framing of the saying, which is often provided secondarily as its setting. Two other considerations may also be relevant. It is possible that the new tax became an occasion for voicing resentment at other taxes or at taxation in general. And it is possible that the Jewish peasants' views of tithes, offerings, etc., followed the principles of earlier layers of the Torah, in which taxes were directed more toward the general welfare of the people, as distinguished from later laws, in which taxation had been centralized for the benefit of the Jerusalem priesthood.[51] All considerations would incline us toward a broader construal of Jesus' saying in this case, even though the question focused on the relatively recent half-shekel tax.

Interpretation of the passage hinges on the analogy in Matthew 17:25–26 and its application. "The kings of the earth" surely referred to imperial powers, most obviously Rome at the time, which took tribute from subject peoples while avoiding taxing its own "sons." As was noted above, both prior to Jesus in biblical traditions and subsequent to his ministry in rabbinic traditions, God was understood as the king of Jewish society and compared with human kings.[52] By analogy, then, "the sons" would have been Israel. As was noted in chapter 7, Jesus' ministry must have been directed to Israel and its restoration, as suggested in Mark 7:27 and in traditions appearing only in Matthew, 10:5–6; 15:24. Application of the analogy to the situation of taxation set up in 17:24 thus indicates that Jesus was declaring that Jews (Israel) were not obligated to pay taxes to God, indeed that taxation in the name of God was illegitimate.[53]

Having established in principle that Jews were not *obligated* to pay the half-shekel tax to the Temple, however, did Jesus then turn around and instruct his followers to pay the tax anyhow, but voluntarily (Matthew 17:27)? This is the conclusion often drawn. In the context of Jesus' ministry and in that of his followers prior to 70 c.e., those "offended" would have been the collectors of the tax. The key to the way in which Jesus instructed his followers to "go ahead and pay anyhow" is the folkloric motif of the coin in the fish's mouth. The coin had obviously been lost. Thus the payment instructed here by Jesus obviously was made only on an ad hoc basis and by a remarkably coincidental means.[54] It can hardly have been unintentional that the instruction was to pay by such accidental means and not out of the hearers' own resources. Thus the instruction in Matthew 17:27 did not contradict or even seriously qualify the principle established in Matthew 17:25–26 that Jews were not obligated to pay the tax in the first place. It can hardly be said to have articulated a "policy of compliance."[55] Indeed, one might say that the coincidental means by which the payment was made in this instance only (to avoid giving offense) served to emphasize the absence of obligation, the freedom from the Temple tax.

Jesus' declaration that "the sons are free" thus appears to have provided an unmistakeable declaration of independence from the Temple and the attendant political-economic-religious establishment. It is apparently the usual situation for peasants to feel that their lords, the established government or religious hierarchy, do little for them while living off their labor and its products rendered up as taxes, rents, or tribute. Such typical resentment of the ruling groups and the feeling that their exactions were illegitimate and to be avoided if possible were probably exacerbated in ancient Palestinian Jewish society by the belief that God was the only true, legitimate ruler of the people. Such an idea was firmly grounded and explicitly expressed in the sacred biblical traditions of Israel—ironically standing side by side in the Torah with other traditions that legitimated the Temple establishment and the payment of tithes and offerings to the Temple and the priesthood. Yet however free the people felt they were in principle and wanted to be in fact, they were forced to deal daily with the concrete realities of the power of the establishment to enforce its demands or else execute sanctions on any recalcitrants. Hence the concern not to give offense —so that Jesus' ministry or his movement would be allowed to continue without the authorities' punitive intervention. The concern not to give offense, however, is not on a par with the declaration that "the sons are free" in Matthew 17:24–27. As was just noted, the whole manner and coincidental means by which payment is made reinforces in effect the main point: the absence of obligation to pay the Temple tax. Thus the passage is hardly an expression of "loyal and dutiful citizenship" and an endorsement of paying taxes, as it was ready by subsequent generations. It is rather an expression of a radical theocratic faith that the kingdom of God is now present.

Yet neither of those last two statements would be sufficient for an adequate understanding of "the sons are free" in the context of Jesus' ministry and the communities of his followers. Both "citizenship" and "theocracy" remain rather vague without further explication. We observed above in chapter 8 that it is a misunderstanding or a distortion of the issue to claim, on the basis of certain sayings, that Jesus was "antifamily." He was not antifamily but was against the rigid patriarchal forms of family and community. In the same way it would be distorting—it would not even comprehend the issue Jesus has engaged —to pose the issue as "loyal citizenship" (including payment of taxes) or the opposite ("disloyal" and nonpayment). As was argued in chapter 7 above, we can best understand Jesus' ministry as involving the renewal of the people, the restoration of Israel in its "twelve tribes." But we cannot automatically assume that the Temple, supported by the requisite taxes, tithes, and offerings, was expected to be a part of that restoration. The renewed people in "the kingdom of God," moreover, was surely a theocracy, a people living according to the will of God. But was it also to be a hierocracy, the rule of God being mediated by the rule of the high priests and their Temple establishment? Such issues require further exploration.

10. Judgment of the Ruling Institutions

With regard to the ruling institutions of his society Jesus went far beyond the typical peasant strategy of avoidance. Nor did he confine his activity to healing, preaching the presence of the kingdom, and catalyzing renewal of local community life in rural Galilee. Assuming yet another of the roles of a traditional Israelite prophet, he also pronounced oracles and parables of judgment against the ruling institutions of Jewish Palestine, the Temple and the high priesthood.

We thus come to the ostensible reasons for the arrest and execution of Jesus. However elaborated, embellished, and legendary the gospel passion narratives may be, it is clear that Jesus was executed by the Romans as a politically dangerous popular leader and that he was arrested by initiative of the priestly aristocracy. This would have been standard procedure in such a Roman province, where the local authorities were responsible for the arrest of troublemakers. However uncertain historically the trials before the Sanhedrin and Pilate may be, the principal charges brought against Jesus were that he had threatened destruction of the Temple, claimed to be a messianic king, and (in Luke) had stirred up the people and forbidden them to give tribute to Caesar. Examination of Jesus' sayings regarding the Temple and high priesthood thus also provide an occasion to analyze the validity of the charges on which he was crucified.

In the following discussion there is no attempt to explore Jesus' Jerusalem ministry in general. Because of the character of the gospel narratives about Jesus in Jerusalem, it may be impossible to reconstruct a reasonable picture of events in Jerusalem. We will simply focus on sayings of Jesus embedded in the Jerusalem narratives or occurring earlier in the Gospels in order better to assess Jesus' general stance toward the ruling institutions of Palestinian Jewish society.

PROPHECY AND DEMONSTRATION AGAINST THE TEMPLE

Before dealing directly with Jesus and the Temple it is necessary to address some standard assumptions or viewpoints that have limited our understanding of the subject.

PROBLEMATIC ASSUMPTIONS ABOUT THE TEMPLE

(1) It is often assumed that the Temple was only a religious institution. The "cleansing of the Temple" has become the keynote of much of the discussion of Jesus' relations with the Temple and the high priesthood. Jesus' action is then understood variously in terms of the establishment of "pure" (inner) worship of God vs. the mere externals of ritual, or of a religious reformer "purifying" current practice or opening the Temple to worship by the Gentiles, or "a demonstration intended to initiate a national renewal of prayer and dedication."[1] More recently it has been recognized, somewhat more concretely, that "the principal function of any temple is to serve as a place for sacrifice."[2]

The function of the Temple was far more extensive and central in Jewish society than the typical modern theological reduction to the religious dimension allows. Sacrifice was surely one of the functions of the Temple in Jerusalem. But sacrifices, whether the sin-offerings or the guilt-offerings or the offering of firstborn livestock, were consumed largely by the priests, as were the many other offerings, tithes, and duties.[3] Moreover, "the priests kept the hide of every animal they sacrificed, even if it was subsequently found unclean."[4] The Temple was clearly the basis of an economic system in which the agricultural producers supported the priests, particularly the priestly aristocracy who administered the system and were its chief beneficiaries. Besides its religious basis, the tithes and offerings ostensibly being given to God, the system had the political backing of the empire, Caesar having decreed shortly after Rome took control of Palestine that the tithes would be brought to the high priests (Josephus, *Ant.* 14.203). The funds of the Temple treasury, of course, were used to supply the needs of the Temple. But they were also used to finance the communal needs of

Jerusalem, as was noted above.[5] Administration of these funds and the uses to which they were put also required a staff of high-ranking officers, who clearly wielded considerable power in the city and the society. The supply of the special needs of the Temple's sacrificial system, for example, of doves or unblemished animals, was apparently also controlled by members of the priestly aristocracy.[6] The economy of the city of Jerusalem as a whole, finally, depended directly and indirectly on the Temple. Thus, the Jerusalem Temple was the basis of a whole political-economic-religious system headed by the priestly aristocracy, as was noted at the outset in chapter 1. It was the center of power in Jewish society in every respect, and it stood at the vortex of the imperial relationship between Rome and the Palestinian Jewish people. Besides the sacrifices called for in the Torah, sacrifices were offered also in honor of Rome and the emperor, and failure to perform them was tantamount to rebellion. The Temple was thus functioning as an instrument of imperial legitimation and control of a subjected people (*Ant.* 15.248).

(2) The second problematic assumption or viewpoint is that the people basically supported the Temple. This view has been explicitly and vigorously reaffirmed recently.[7] But it is clearly necessary to distinguish between the Temple as symbol and the actual Temple system, and to recognize the inadequacy of the view that popular discontent focused only on the particular high-priestly incumbents while the people remained basically loyal to the system itself. The Temple and its ruling high priesthood had surely suffered a diminution of both prestige and power since Hasmonean days by its subjection to the Herodian client kingship and then to the Roman authorities. The high priesthood was instituted in the Torah. But a gulf had developed between the legitimating ideals in the Torah and the actions of the actual high priests and their practices in the Temple. The Qumranites, of course, rejected the Hasmonean high priests as totally illegitimate. For Palestinian Jews, whether Jerusalemites or peasants, Herod's elevation of powerful families from Egypt and Babylon into dominance of the high-priestly offices must have seemed of doubtful legitimacy. The frequent depositions and new appointments, and the Roman control of the appointment of the actual High Priest, must have raised further

questions. Moreover, although the Temple and high priesthood had been an instrument of imperial rule of Jewish society since the restoration under Persian sponsorship, high-priestly collaboration with the sharply repressive Roman rule must have raised further questions of legitimacy in some circles. Surely the practice of offering Temple sacrifices on behalf of Rome and the Roman emperor must have appeared illegitimate (i.e., contrary to the Torah) long before their defiant cessation by the priests in 66 as a symbolic act of revolt. Such actions by the high priests surely undermined the people's confidence in the Temple system itself, and not merely in the incumbent of the moment. A good indication that the people may have been resisting the Temple and high priesthood as a system is their failure to pay the expected taxes. As we have mentioned, the fragmentary sources available indicate that there was a general laxity among Palestinian Jewish peasants in paying all the various tithes.[8]

The increasing illegitimacy of the high priests and the people's laxity in paying taxes does not, of course, mean that the people were wholly alienated from the Temple or Jerusalem as a symbol of their unity as a people and their relationship with God. But it is surely also important to recognize that the Temple-state was not the only model in the Jewish cultural tradition for organizing their existence as a people. The Torah provided an alternative model in the exodus and covenant on Sinai, with Mosaic-prophetic instead of high-priestly leadership. Indeed, the historical model of exodus-covenant stood in considerable tension with the Temple system, a tension that must have been compounded by the subordination of the people and the Temple to foreign rulers. Since the discovery of the Dead Sea Scrolls, we know that the use of that alternative model was more than a hypothetical possibility. The Qumranites provide an example of how even a priestly-oriented group could reject the established order of the Temple system and organize "Israel" according to the exodus-covenant model. The popular prophetic movements that emerged shortly after the time of Jesus indicate that large groups of peasants were ready to respond to somewhat the same model for liberation from their apparently intolerable situation. The very occurrence of popular revolts in the form of "messianic movements" indicates the existence of yet a third model from Israelite traditions for the organization of their existence as a people: the leadership of a popularly acclaimed king.[9] We should recall, finally, that there was also outright condemnation or opposition to the Temple and to the city in which the system was based. The solitary peasant prophet Jesus, son of Hananiah, repeatedly pronounced oracles of doom against both city and Temple in the years just prior to the revolt of 66–70.

(3) The older schematic Christian theological treatment of Jewish eschatology that gave an important place to a rebuilt Temple in the eschaton has recently been revived.[10] This has been used to make intelligible, and to soften the severity of, Jesus' sayings and actions against the Temple. Given the disillusionment over the Temple and high-priestly rulers, it would seem possible that the idea of a rebuilt and glorified Temple might have become a feature of Jewish hopes for the future. Judging from the late prophetic literature and Palestinian Jewish apocalyptic literature prior to 70 c.e., this did not happen.[11]

Far from a rebuilt Temple being an integral part of an apocalyptic scheme of eschatological restoration, closer examination of the textual evidence indicates that it was never very important either as part of such a scheme or by itself as an object of eschatological fulfillment. It is also evident that far from Zion's being a synonym for the Temple, it, along with its standard synonym Jerusalem, usually refers to the people of Israel generally as well as to its symbolic center and capital city. Indeed, even "house" and "house of God" often refer to the people along with or instead of the Temple or the city as the special place of God's dwelling.

In Second Isaiah (40–55) the rebuilding of the Temple, along with Jerusalem, is mentioned only once and almost in passing, in 44:28, in reference to a decree of the Persian emperor Cyrus, and seems otherwise incidental to the main concern: the redemption of the captive people and their return to their land in a new exodus. Zion and Jerusalem are almost always symbols of the people rather than (or in addition to) being place names. In Third Isaiah (56–66) the dominant concern is for the restoration of the people's life in peace and welfare on their land. Zion and Jerusalem are throughout symbols for the people of Jacob/Israel and their land (e.g., Isaiah 60:3; 65:18–19). The theme of the future glorification of the Temple does appear once, but only in chapter

60 and only as part of the overall concern for the future restoration of the people. Elsewhere, when the Temple or sacrifices are mentioned, the concern is with inclusion and acceptance in the community (Isaiah 56:3–8), or restoration to the community (Isaiah 66:20). Indeed Isaiah 66:1–6 is a sharp condemnation of sacrifices and offerings.

Similar conclusions emerge from a survey of Jewish apocalyptic and testamentary literature written prior to the destruction of Jerusalem and the Temple. Tobit 14:5–6 is the only text where a whole scheme can be found: the return of the exiles, a rebuilding of Jerusalem and a glorious rebuilding of "the house of God," followed by the Gentiles' praising God and God's exaltation of his people. Once we recognize that "Zion" does not mean the Temple and that God's "house" does not necessarily mean the Temple, however, then it is striking that the Temple is missing from many of the important visions of fulfillment in apocalyptic literature. In fact, the Temple was conceived of as coming to an end along with its profanation in such texts as 1 Enoch 89–90 (The Animal Apocalypse), the Assumption of Moses, and the Psalms of Solomon.

In the Psalms of Solomon, in particular, the Temple does not play any role in the portrayal of eschatological fulfillment. In fact, the Temple or its sacrifices are mentioned only twice in all of the eighteen Psalms. The trampling of the divine altar by alien nations (Pompey, in 63) is viewed as just punishment for the profanation of holy things by the (Hasmonean) "sons of Jerusalem" (Psalms of Solomon 2:2–3) in Psalms of Solomon 8:10–13,20–25, the alien (Pompey) captures Jerusalem and destroys its (Hasmonean) rulers as deserved punishment for blatant plundering of the sanctuary of God. In Psalms of Solomon 17 the Messiah is to liberate Jerusalem/Israel/the holy people from foreign domination and to purge them of domestic unrighteousness. But there is no indication that "the place" where the Lord is to be glorified is the Temple rather than Zion/Jerusalem/holy mountain, the broader symbol with which "the place" stands in synonymous parallel construction. It is relevant also to note that in the Psalms of Solomon the dwelling of God, far from being specially in the Temple, is portrayed as being in the midst of or near the people, the house of Jacob, who in turn constitute God's "holy inheritance" (Psalms of Solomon 7:1–2,5,9).

It is important, finally, to take the Qumran community and its literature into account in considering the supposed importance of the eschatological rebuilding of the Temple. The recently published Temple Scroll now confirms what previously appeared to be presupposed in the War Scroll: the community expected a restored or rebuilt Temple (see especially 11 QTemple 29:8–10). Far more prominent in the literature of the community, however, was the community's understanding of itself as the sanctuary of the Lord in Exodus 15:17 and the house promised in 2 Samuel 7—a "sanctuary of men" where the sacrifices were "the deeds of the law"—in contrast with the present Jerusalem Temple that had been profaned by the wicked Hasmonean priesthood. That is, the literature of the community may well attest the idea of a rebuilt or restored Temple. But far more significant (for comparison with Jesus' Temple action and sayings) would be the fact that a community that thought of itself as living in anticipation of God's salvation had both rejected the current Temple and its priesthood and had understood itself as the true temple of God indicated in such important texts as Exodus 15 and 2 Samuel 7.[12]

(4) The fourth questionable view that has played an important role in recent discussion of Jesus and the Temple is that after the resurrection Jesus' followers in Jerusalem were engaged in Temple worship. This belief is used to exclude the possibility that Jesus could have opposed the sacrificial system in his dramatic Temple demonstration. It has also become a key basis for the claim that Jesus prophesied the destruction of the Temple with the express expectation that the Temple would be rebuilt and the sacrificial system reconstituted.[13] The argument is that the supposed worship in the Temple by Jesus' followers as indicated in Acts 2:46 (cf. Matthew 5:23–24) would be inexplicable if Jesus had attacked the sacrificial system in the Temple demonstration.

But does Acts 2:46 provide solid evidence that the apostles were taking part in the sacrificial system? The parallel terms in Acts 1:14 ("all these with one accord devoted themselves to prayer") might lead one to think of Acts 2:46 also in terms of worship. Yet the presence of typical Lucan terms (*homothumadon* = 'with one accord" or "unanimously"; *proskartereo* = "attend to" or "wait upon") in what is a typical Lucan summary idealizing the piety and solidarity of the original community of Jesus' followers in Jerusalem suggests that this is a picture painted by Luke (see Acts 2:43–47; 4:32–35; 5:42; and Luke 24:52–53) rather than a reliable account of the precise activities of the early apostles. What is more, if the early community pooled their property and held all in common, as is indicated in these same summary passages in Acts, then what happened to the economic basis from which individuals or families would have made sacrifices and offerings?

Other passages early in Acts, however, indicate that the apostles were in the Temple mainly to spread the word about the fulfillment of history that they believed had begun with Jesus' actions, crucifixion, and vindication, to do healings and exorcisms, and generally to expand their movement (Acts 3:11; 5:12–16). The Temple courtyard was the principal public meeting place in Jerusalem, and the obvious place for such activities. According to Acts, many years later Paul went to the Temple for a purification rite and to make offerings as well as to pray (Acts 21:26; 22:17). But there is simply no clear indication in Acts 2:46, 3:1, or elsewhere that the early apostles in Jerusalem were in the Temple to bring sacrifices and offerings. Matthew 5:23–24, part of the special material Matthew weaves into the Sermon on the Mount, is an illustration assuming that offerings at the altar are a standard practice. It is difficult to see how it provides any evidence that the early apostles were regularly participating in the sacrificial worship or that Jesus himself approved of the sacrificial system.

JESUS' SAYINGS AGAINST THE TEMPLE

At two key points in the passion narrative Mark and Matthew report Jesus as threatening to destroy the Temple and to rebuild it. In the first case it is presented as the testimony of false witnesses at Jesus' trial before the Sanhedrin. "I will destroy this Temple that is made with hands, and in three days I will build another, not made with hands" (Mark 14:58). In the second it appears as common knowledge among the people who taunt Jesus on the cross, saying "Aha! You who would destroy the Temple and build it in three days, save yourself, and come down from the cross!" (Mark 15:29–30).

Now, although it is probably futile to attempt to reconstruct the original wording, it is generally accepted that Jesus must have uttered some such saying of judgment on the Temple, and even the double saying about the building of another Temple as well as the destruction of the old Temple. It is difficult to imagine why the early church would have invented a saying that was so awkward for them. Indeed, it is evident that the saying was the basis of a charge leveled at Jesus' followers after his death, as is indicated in the report of Stephen's martyrdom in Acts 6:13–14: "We have heard him say that this Jesus of Nazareth will destroy this place." The fact that the saying against the Temple, along with the attribution to "false witnesses," reads as an insertion by Mark into the account of Jesus' trial before the Sanhedrin suggests that the saying circulated as an independent unit prior to Mark's use of it in both 14:58 and 15:29. The tradition that Jesus prophesied or threatened the destruction and rebuilding of the Temple was so solidly embedded in the gospel tradition that John carefully explained rather than suppressed it: "Destroy this Temple, and in three days I will raise it up" (John 2:19). Moreover, although Mark also took pains to interpret the saying in a way that complicates his report of the trial before the Sanhedrin, he clearly accepts the testimony of the "false witnesses" as a true charge against Jesus, whose death inaugurated the destruction of the Temple, beginning with the rending of the veil (Mark 15:38).[14]

The only forms in which we know of Jesus' sayings against the Temple are secondary, either as a charge by others as in Mark and Matthew, or as transformed into a supposed threat against Jesus' person in John. Nothing in the gospel traditions themselves would suggest a scheme of eschatological fulfillment, just as there is little or no textual evidence for a rebuilt Temple as part of some supposed Jewish apocalyptic scheme into which Jesus' saying might have fit. The point of the saying, whatever its original form and wording, and the reason why it was problematic for the early church (as is attested in the report about Stephen and in John's major transformation and even Mark's "clarifying" alterations) was that the existing Temple was about to be destroyed. The saying must have been fairly clearly understood as a prophecy of destruction. The form of the saying in Mark 14:58 would most easily be understood then as Jesus speaking in traditional oracular prophetic style as the spokesperson of God, who is the first person in the saying ("I will . . ."). Regardless of how the second half of the saying (about the rebuilt Temple) is understood—whether as referring to Jesus' resurrection or to the new community—the severity of the first half cannot be mitigated. Jesus was clearly understood in the gospel tradition to have uttered a prophetic judgment against the existing Temple in Jerusalem.

The short saying "There will not be left here one stone upon another that will not be thrown down" in Mark 13:2b is usually connected with Mark 14:58 and 15:29 as an attestation of Jesus' saying against the Temple. Mark 13:2b, of course, is referred directly to the Temple only by Mark's editorial work in 13:1 in a passage that provides an occasion for the "synoptic apocalypse" of Mark 13. The stones' being thrown down could have broader reference than simply the Temple. But since the Temple was the most prominent as well as the focal building in the capital city, the reference would surely have been to the Temple as much as or more than to the rest of the city. Probably because the Markan setting of the saying is a discourse on future events, scholarly interpretations tend to understand Mark 13.2b as an eschatological prophecy. But surely the Markan context, clearly redactional, is not original. Hence there is no good reason to choose the eschatological interpretation over an understanding in terms of a historical prophecy in the style of classical prophetic oracles: because or since . . . (this part being missing in explicit words), therefore "there will not be left one stone upon another. . . ." Mark 13:2b would thus provide yet another attestation of Jesus' prophecy of judgment against the Temple.

If the claim to "build another temple" was part of Jesus' prophetic sayings on the Temple, then it seems best to understand it metaphorically, in terms of a new community of people (but not "spiritually" or allegorically, in terms of either a heavenly Temple or Jesus' resurrected body). Earlier treatments of the New Testament understanding of the Christian church as the "Temple" held that such a concept could have developed only on Hellenistic presuppositions. Since the discovery of the Dead Sea Scrolls, however, it is clear that the Qumran community provides a Palestinian Jewish precedent for a renewal community understanding itself as the "Temple." This latter is usually treated primarily in terms of a "spiritualization of the cult." However, this interpretation does not probe sufficiently into traditional Jewish-biblical linguistic usage and important facets of Jewish self-understanding.

The Qumranites not only viewed their community as the real or true Temple, the Temple in Jerusalem having become hopelessly evil and polluted by the wicked Hasmonean high priests; they elaborated this identification with reference to particular aspects of the Temple building and rituals. Their own community was now making atonement for Israel, their own prayers being "an acceptable fragrance of righteousness," their "perfection of way" a "delectable free-will offering," and their own deeds of Torah the true "smoke of incense" (e.g., 1QS 5.5–7; 8.4–10; 9.3–6; 4QFlor 1.1–13). This is a very understandable interpretation of their situation by a priestly-dominated community alienated from the Jerusalem Temple. It now looks likely, from the Temple Scroll, that at least some members of the community looked forward to being vindicated as the true and rightful leaders of Israel when God would finally reestablish the proper Temple. But what is most striking about the community's self-understanding is the almost complete assimilation of Temple and sacrificial symbolism into the alternate model for understanding Israel, i.e., the new exodus and covenantal community and its "perfect way" according to the Torah. The very symbols and biblical texts the community uses to make that assimilation or identification, however, suggest that less sacerdotally oriented Jews at the time might have understood themselves similarly as the true "Temple" while symbolically or concretely rejecting rather than assimilating particular facets of the Temple building and system.

The clue to this possibility is the variety of meanings of the term "house." In most instances we would be inclined to assume that "house of God" in biblical texts refers to the Temple. Even "house" by itself or "house of truth" or "house of holiness" in Qumran literature can be seen to refer to the Temple that is being identified as the community itself (cf. 1QS 8.4–10; 4QFlor 1.1–6). From the texts being interpreted in 1QFlor, however, we can see that "house" has a variety of interrelated and overlapping meanings that make possible some different and potentially conflicting understandings of the Jerusalem Temple. The promise to David in Nathan's oracle in 2 Samuel is, among other things, an extended play on the word "house." We can readily see that from a basic meaning of "family" and its land, dwelling, and other property the term can, depending upon its context and connections, mean lineage (house of Jesse), a whole people (house of Israel), a monarchy (house of David as the ruling house), a dynasty (house of David), an ordinary dwelling place, a palace (house of David), and/or a temple (dwelling place of God). As is readily evident, even though one meaning may be primary in a particular context, other connotations remain, as in "the house of David."

Now "the house of God," as sacred, is synonymous with the "sanctuary/Temple" and, in ancient Near Eastern mythic culture at least, is placed on and is synonymous with a sacred mountain, literally or symbolically. In Israel's biblical traditions, typically, such language was "demythologized" and used metaphorically, as in the Exodus passage cited in 1QFlor 1: the "mountain"/"abode"/"sanctuary" of God in Exodus 15:17 meaning the land into which Yahweh was bringing his people. The fact that God's abode or "sanctuary" and sacred "mountain" can mean the land of Israel in this important text, however, should make us all the more sensitive to biblical usage in which the "house of God" is not the Temple but the people of Israel. Moreover, the people could be God's house, and God could dwell among the people with or without connotations of a temple, as in Numbers 12:7. Particularly if the connotations of temple were present, however, there would hardly be need of a physical temple building if the people were God's real house, or else there could easily develop a conflict between the people as the real house of God on the one hand and the temple on the other.

If Jesus' prophecy against the Temple included the promise of a new "temple" or "house of God," then the most likely meaning was that God, while about to destroy the Jerusalem Temple, was building his *true* house, the renewed people of Israel. The renewed society or people, indeed, was one of the principal implications of "the kingdom of God," which Jesus had been proclaiming was now present and ready to be entered.

JESUS' PROPHETIC DEMONSTRATION IN THE TEMPLE

We can dismiss several previous interpretations of Jesus' action in the Temple (Mark 11:15–17 and parallels) as simply reductionist, failing to take into account dimensions other than the religious. Jesus' concern was almost certainly not simply to defend Gentiles' right to access to the Temple or to open the Temple eschatologically to worship by the Gentiles. The "court of the Gentiles" is the modern, not the ancient, name of the outer court where the incident supposedly took place, thus removing the usual point of departure for such an interpretation. This interpretation, moreover, owes too much to Christian theological interests to make it credible as a historical reconstruction. Similarly, Jesus' concern was almost certainly not to purify the Temple cult, as is suggested by the traditional title "cleansing of the Temple." No more likely is the seemingly opposite and equally reductionist interpretation that Jesus' action in the Temple was simply an attack on cult or ritual as opposed to more "spiritual" or ethical religion. Although this interpretation may contain some truth, it is not a sufficient explanation. The political-revolutionary interpretation of Jesus' Temple action, and its opposite, the denial of any and all political dimension to Jesus' action, take better into account the inseparable dimensions of ancient social life. These interpretations, however, are no more credible or rooted in the evidence than the others. Both of the latter have been premised on and have taken their cue from the supposed existence of "the Zealots" as a long-standing religiously motivated anti-Roman revolutionary party.

Despite the lack of any historical model such as "the Zealots" that Jesus could have been following, however, we could nevertheless pose the possibility that in the action in the Temple he was attempting a direct takeover of the religious-political-economic center of society. It is not an adequate or valid objection to this interpretation to argue that the Temple police or the Roman garrison on duty for the Passover festival would have intervened almost immediately if there had been any such serious challenge or commotion in the Temple area.[15] The events in the Temple area at Passover time under Archelaus and Cumanus provide no evidence for such an argument. In fact, they could be

used for exactly the opposite argument: that the very absence of intervention by the authorities for days indicates the considerable size and
seriousness of Jesus' action in the Temple. Neither Archelaus in 4 B.C.E.
nor Cumanus in the 50s sent in troops at the first sign of a disturbance.
Indeed, when the demonstration became large and vocal, they still did
not order the troops to set upon the crowds. Such restraint on their part
accords with the behavior of authorities in other preindustrial cities. It
appears that only after prolonged protest was under way did Archelaus
and Cumanus panic in these two cases. Thus the absence of intervention
by Pilate or the Temple authorities in the case of Jesus' action, combined with the clear evidence that the gospel writers, for their particular
concerns, would have reduced the scope of the event rather than have
blown it up, points to a more rather than less disruptive demonstration
led by Jesus in the Temple.

It nevertheless seems unsatisfactory to reconstruct this as an attempted takeover of the Temple by Jesus and his followers, despite the
fact that it would fit well with the "triumphal entry" and the subsequent arrest and execution of Jesus as a revolutionary leader. It would
mean that Jesus' actions were naïve and abortive. However shielded he
may have been temporarily, so that the authorities hesitated to intervene, he was eventually arrested by the officials, and without much
difficulty at that. He would appear to have had no sense whatever of
the actual power relations in the society, unless we imagine him trusting
in God's sudden apocalyptic intervention with legions of "heavenly
hosts." He apparently did believe in the existence of the latter, but
either refused to call for their "intervention" or thought of their role
as being a future one (see Matthew 26:53). The hypothesis that Jesus'
action in the Temple was an attempt at direct takeover of the religious-
political-economic center of the society (on the assumption that the
kingdom of God was at hand), although more likely than the usual
attempts to reduce the demonstration to a mere religious gesture of
"purification," is still not an adequate interpretation in the concrete
social-historical context.

It may be well to step back from the story in order to gain some
perspective, and this in three interrelated respects. (a) It may be well
to step back from the particulars of the interpretation of the action

offered in Mark 11:17 (the originality of which has been questioned by form-critics), for it has been phrases in these scriptural references that have triggered some of the reductionist interpretations. (b) As was noted above, it is difficult to guage the scope of the action, except insofar as it must have been more serious than the gospel writers indicate. And (c) we must keep in mind the overall, concrete, and multidimensional importance of the Temple in Jewish society of the time. Thus by stepping back somewhat from the particulars and examining an action that must have been more than a mere religious "purification" but less than an attempt at direct takeover of the seat of hierocratic government, we can view the action as a minimally violent prophetic demonstration symbolizing an imminent action by God.

It is highly unlikely that it would have been a symbolic act of destruction in preparation for the building of an eschatological temple.[16] As was noted above, the idea of a rebuilt Temple is unimportant in pre-70 C.E. Jewish literature, and there is no evidence whatever for the connection between a rebuilt Temple and the destruction of the old. Judging from the criticism and resistance of the Temple system evident in late second Temple times, a "gesture" indicating destruction of the Temple would have implied just that: the destruction of the Temple.

Thus perhaps Jesus' actions should be viewed against the background of the classical prophetic tradition, as well as against the background of the popular discontent with the Temple and ruling groups in first-century Palestine. The most prominent examples of symbolic prophetic protest from biblical history were pronouncements of judgment, usually addressed to the rulers of the people (e.g., Ahijah the Shilonite, 1 Kings 11:29–12:20; Isaiah 20). Most memorable, perhaps, were the many prophetic demonstrations by Jeremiah, such as the wearing of yoke bars around the city to symbolize submission to Babylon or destruction by her armies (Jeremiah 27–28). Jeremiah's deliberate smashing of the earthen flask in the presence of the elders and senior priests was the most vivid public demonstration symbolizing God's imminent judgment on the capital city and its inhabitants (Jeremiah 19). Along lines similar to these prophetic prototypes, Jesus' action in the Temple can be understood as a demonstration symbolizing destruction and directed against the high-priestly establishment. Assuming that the

gospel tradition would have softened rather than exaggerated the severity of the action, however, Jesus' demonstration surely did more than
symbolize an attack. It must also have been an actual attack involving
some violence against property if not against persons. Thus Jesus'
demonstration is an escalation over and above the biblical paradigms,
except for the insurrection attendant upon Elijah's direct symbolic act
of restoration of Israel in 1 Kings 18.

In attacking those who sold and bought and those who changed
money in the outer court of the Temple, Jesus was attacking, not things
peripheral to the system, but integral parts of it. Moreover, these
activities that were operated and controlled by the aristocratic priestly
families must have been points at which the domination and exploitation of the people was most obvious. That is, Jesus does not make a
direct attack upon the conduct of the actual sacrifices at the altar—
assuming he could have gained access to the altar area in order to bring
a sacrifice himself at Passover. Moreover, the Passover sacrifices, which
in contrast to nearly all other sacrifices were consumed by the people
themselves and symbolized the liberating exodus from Egyptian bondage, would hardly have provided an appropriate focus. Instead, Jesus
attacks the activities in which the exploitation of God's people by their
priestly rulers was most visible. Without undertaking the extensive
analysis of the details of the story in Mark 11:15–17 that would be
necessary to argue this interpretation more precisely, it seems possible
to conclude that Jesus' demonstration in the Temple was a prophetic
act symbolizing God's imminent judgmental destruction, not just of the
building, but of the Temple system.

RULING PRIESTS AND RULING CITY

The prophetic judgment announced by Jesus was not confined, however, to the Temple itself. It also included both the high-priestly rulers
and the capital city from which they ruled Palestinian Jewish society.

JESUS' LAMENT OVER JERUSALEM

Jesus' prophetic lament over Jerusalem is early tradition clearly taken
from Q by both Luke, where it appears in the middle of the journey

section Luke 13:34–35, and Matthew, where it is the conclusion of the harangue against the Pharisees (Matthew 23:37–38).

"O Jerusalem, Jerusalem, killing the prophets and stoning those who are sent to you! How often would I have gathered your children together as a hen gathers her brood under her wings, and you would not! Behold, your house is forsaken."

The linking of the lament with the other saying ("You will not see me until you say . . .") is secondary (i.e., in or before the setting in Q), since it is an obvious link with another piece of the gospel tradition (preserved independently and used in Mark 11:9 and parallels). Luke 13:34–35a (and Matthew 23:37–38) by itself then stands as a saying of Jesus strikingly similar to prophetic laments known from classical biblical traditions. Moreover, if the lament itself is examined apart from the saying attached to it in Q, Matthew, and Luke ("You will not see me until . . ."), then there is little or no reason to think that the "I" is Jesus himself. As in the related saying about sending them prophets whom they will kill (Luke 11:49–52 and parallel Matthew 23:34–36), in the lament over Jerusalem, Jesus would have been speaking as the mouthpiece for God or the "Wisdom of God" (as in Luke).

Central to the content of this prophetic lament is Jerusalem's long history of violent opposition to the prophets and resistance to God ("I"). Moreover, of course, the prophets were presumably sent by God. To understand the prophecy adequately it is necessary to determine more precisely the meaning of both "house" and "children." "House" has often been thought to mean the Temple; but there is no reason internal or external to the saying itself for this interpretation. As was noted above, "house" (especially when modified by "your") can as easily refer to the ruling house, i.e., the monarchy, dynasty, state, and even the whole governing apparatus. The term is used precisely in that sense in the passage in Jeremiah 22:1–9 to which the phrase "your house is abandoned" appears to be an allusion. In that prophecy, Jeremiah was proclaiming God's judgment (destruction) against the ruling "house of the king of Judah," i.e., "you [the king], your servants [government officials], and your people who enter these gates [other Jerusalemites]." When we recall also that most of those who lived in a governing seat of a monarchy or temple-state such as Jerusalem would have been directly or indirectly involved in the business of the capital city, then it is more easily understandable how the monarchy or the Temple establishment and their retainers and other dependents could all be referred to collectively as "the city" (or "Jerusalem"). Indeed, this is precisely the usage in Jeremiah 22:1–9: "This house shall become a desolation" means that Yahweh is about to destroy "this great city," the seat of "the house of the king of Judah."

"Children" in Luke 13:34 and parallels is often understood simply as the inhabitants of Jerusalem. The reference may be broader than simply Jerusalemites, however. Just as the term "daughters" refers in a number of biblical passages to the villages subject to a city, and just as "sons of Jerusalem" can mean the people of Judah/Israel generally (Isaiah 51:17–18), so the "children" of Jerusalem could be the people in general who are subject to and supposedly under the care of Jerusalem as the ruling city. This is particularly likely considering the context, i.e., a saying in which Jerusalem resists what God wills for the "children" and violently resists the prophets God has previously sent.

But why would Jerusalem or the governing "house" be about to become "desolate"? Or how would God have intended to gather the people governed by Jerusalem under his/her wings (for protection or nurture)? Again the passage in Jeremiah is suggestive: Yahweh was about to destroy the city "because they forsook the covenant." And this fits together perfectly with the explicit charge in Jesus' lament: that Jerusalem has killed the prophets, that is, those (such as Jeremiah himself) whom God had sent to call the ruling house back into observance of the Covenant. It is worth noting that the image of the hen gathering her young under her wings likely depends somehow on the traditional imagery visible in the "Song of Moses": God is "like an eagle that stirs up its nest, that flutters over its young, spreading out its wings . . ." (Deuteronomy 32:11; cf. further Psalm 36:7; 94:1). The Hebrew word there for "nest" was translated by *nossia,* the word used here in Jesus' lament. In the "Song of Moses" the image is used with reference to God's redemption of the people of Israel in the exodus. In Jesus' lament over Jerusalem, God is portrayed as intending or attempting to protect or redeem the people in some way from their own rulers. Jesus' lament states explicitly that the rulers have killed the prophets. But it also clearly indicates, as is implicit in the image of Jerusalem's opposition to the intention of the mother bird, that the ruling house has resisted God's redemptive efforts on behalf of the people. And that is the reason for the imminent destruction that is the burden Jesus' lament.

A related, more precise prophecy against Jerusalem comes from Luke's special material in 19:41–44. Despite suspicions of an Aramaic original, early form-critics considered the passage to be a "prophecy after the event" of the Roman destruction of the city in 70 C.E. Realizing that the details in the prophecy can all be accounted for from biblical prophecies, particularly those referring to the Babylonian conquest of Jerusalem in 587/86, critical interpreters now cautiously recognize that this oracle must go back to Jesus in some form. Its reformulation in the pre-Lukan tradition has then been affected by biblical prophecies or accounts of the Babylonian conquest, and its insertion into an otherwise Marcan context has been influenced by Luke's knowledge of the Roman conquest of Jerusalem.[17]

Even if the original kernel of the oracle is reduced to Luke 19:43–44a (on the grounds that 42 and 44b show signs of typical Lucan language), what remains is a sharp prophecy of total destruction of the city by its enemies, who, at the time of Jesus, would obviously have been the Romans. Although the destruction announced in this prophecy of Jesus is not as intense or severe as that announced in many of the biblical oracles of Micah, Jeremiah, and others, to which it is similar, Jesus' words condemn the capital in no uncertain terms. Moreover, there is no reason to interpret this oracle as eschatological rather than as a traditional prophetic oracle directed toward the historical situation. If the last clause, "because you did not know the time of your visitation" (Luke 44b), was part of the original oracle and not simply a Lucan addition, then the prophecy has a "warrant" as well as a "threat," and this constitutes yet another similarity to oracles of judgment on Jerusalem by earlier prophets such as Jeremiah (e.g., 22:8–9; 23:38). In the Lucan context, the "visitation" is focused on the crisis brought about by Jesus' imminent entry into the city. Originally, however, the "visitation" would more likely have been the general crisis or judgment created for the city and the rulers located there by the presence of God's kingdom as announced by Jesus. The time of decision and judgment was at hand, and they did not recognize it.

It should be noted, finally, that there are additional fragments of prophetic oracles of judgment against Jerusalem that have been transmitted through Luke's special material and that Luke has used to adapt and supplement Mark in the "little apocalypse" (Luke 21:20–24, especially 21b–22,24) and to expand the narrative of the crucifixion (Luke 23:28–31).[18] These prophetic fragments provide further evidence from the synoptic tradition that Jesus delivered prophecies of judgment and destruction against the city and the rulers based there.

We do not know whether there was any precedent for oracles against the city from some other rural prophet prior to the time of Jesus of Nazareth. But we do have a report from Josephus of another Jesus, son of Hananiah, a "crude peasant," who uttered similar laments of judgment against the city beginning four years before the outbreak of the great revolt: "A voice from the east, a voice from the west, a voice from the four winds; a voice against Jerusalem and the sanctuary, a voice against the bridegroom and the bride [cf. Jeremiah 7:34], a voice against all the people" (*War* 6.301). His prophetic cries, moreover, like those of Jesus of Nazareth, were highly threatening to the Jewish rulers in Jerusalem. They arrested him, chastised him, and attempted to get the Roman governor Albinus to condemn him, although the latter, after having him "flayed to the bone with scourges," simply dismissed him as a maniac (*War* 6.302–306). Josephus's report of Jesus, son of Hananiah, provides important comparative material for our interpretation of Jesus of Nazareth's prophecies against Jerusalem and the Temple. That is, it is not historically impossible at all that a rural prophet would utter nonapocalyptic oracles of divine judgment against Jerusalem, oracles oriented toward the concrete historical, not the eschatological, situation.

JESUS' PROPHETIC PARABLE AGAINST THE HIGH PRIESTS

In addition to his prophetic demonstration and oracles against the Temple and Jerusalem, Jesus at one point told a parable that points to God's rejection of the priestly ruling group (Mark 12:1–9 and parallels). This parable was clearly understood as directed against the rulers in

Jerusalem in the gospel tradition. As it stands in the synoptic Gospels, however, it is virtually an allegorical history of salvation as understood in early Christianity. Because the story of the vineyard and its wicked tenants in the synoptic Gospels is an allegory and not a parable in form, it was thought to be a creation of the Christian community. More recent critical analysis and the discovery of a parallel version not dependent on the canonical gospels in the Gospel of Thomas, however, have led to the recognition that Jesus must have told a parable about the vineyard and its tenants. The version in no. 65 is thought to be closer to the original:

There was a good man who had a vineyard. He leased it to tenant farmers that they might cultivate it and he might get its produce from them. He sent his servant so that the tenants might give him the produce of the vineyard. They seized his servant and beat him—a little more and they would have killed him. The servant went (back) and told his master (about) it. The master said: "Perhaps [they] did not recognize [him]." He sent another servant; the tenants beat him too. Then the master sent his son and said, "Perhaps they will respect my son." Since those tenants knew that he was the heir to the vineyard, they seized him and killed him. Let the one who has ears give heed.

Like other parables of Jesus, this story gives a credible picture of the sort of social-economic relations then prevailing in Palestine, particularly of large landed estates with absentee landlords and restive tenant farmers (who had perhaps only within recent memory lost their own family inheritance). Moreover, the trio of a servant, another servant, and the son in the Thomas version of the parable fits with the usual sequence of three found elsewhere in Jesus' teachings. The image of the vineyard, of course, had since Isaiah been a standing metaphor for the land and/or inheritance of Israel.

Placed in a concrete political-economic-religious context, this "extended metaphor" about wicked tenants entrusted with care of the vineyard and calling for a judgment by the hearers on their own situation would almost certainly have to point toward the priestly aristocracy entrusted with responsibility for God's people. Even without a concluding clause such as Mark 12:9a, the hearers would not have much difficulty drawing the appropriate conclusion as to what God would do to the priestly aristocracy: "he will come and destroy the tenants."

The continuation in Mark 12:9b, "and give the vineyard to others," may be part of the further development of the story toward an allegorical history of salvation in the early church. Of course, in comparison with other parables such as that of the great supper, in which other guests are invited after the original invitees do not attend, it is possible that the giving of the vineyard to others such as the poor and disinherited was the natural extension of the conclusion. It would be an illustration of the compact and appropriate character of the parable as extended metaphor, that the irresponsibility of the tenants to the landlord would point toward the priestly aristocracy's exploitation and dispossession of the poor in contradiction to the Covenant.

Regardless of how explicit the ending may have been, this parable constitutes a prophetic indictment and rejection of the high-priestly ruling group. It stands directly parallel with Jesus' lament over Jerusalem in which the ruling house was proclaimed to be "desolate."

THE THINGS THAT ARE CAESAR'S AND THE THINGS THAT ARE GOD'S

Caesar or Roman power and authority enter the gospel story only at the beginning and the end. Then, of course, the Roman governor Pilate and his soldiers crucified Jesus. But the only point at which Jesus says or does anything directly about Roman domination is his famous saying in response to the authorities' question, "Is it lawful to pay taxes to Caesar or not?" (Mark 12:13–17). The implications of Jesus' saying "Render unto Caesar the things that are Caesar's . . ." have generally been avoided in both ecclesial and scholarly interpretations. The saying has been used as a justification of general obedience to one's rulers. But it is possible that the original thrust of the saying, including ". . . and to God the things that are God's," was virtually the opposite.

The possible implications of the saying have been obscured by a heavy overlay of apologetic concerns in both the ancient and the modern traditions of interpretation. Even the gospel writers took steps to soften traditions that might suggest that Jesus was dangerous to the imperial order.[19] Moreover, the second-century apologist Justin Martyr uses the saying, dissolved from its original context in the ministry of Jesus and the earliest Palestinian churches, in defense of Christians' obedience and tranquility with regard to the Roman order (*Apology* 1.17). Modern biblical scholarship has displayed a similar concern to ward off any implication that Jesus was revolutionary.[20] Underlying modern apologetic interests, moreover, are such standard assumptions as the separation between church and state and the modern partition of reality into separate spheres of religion and politics.[21]

However, most recent interpreters recognize that in his ostensibly ambiguous response to the authorities' question, Jesus was asserting the absolute and exclusive sovereignty of God. The implications of Jesus' subtly stated answer emerge more clearly when we locate the issue in the imperial situation of Jewish Palestine and sharpen our sensitivity to the nuances of phrases such as "the things of God" and "the things of Caesar" according to the likely presuppositions of those who heard and transmitted Jesus' statement.

The saying in Mark 12:17 and parallels is intelligible only as part of the current setting, Mark 12:13–17. Early form-critics recognized that the passage as a whole is a unity, that it is not a product of the early church, and that it can easily have been orally shaped.[22] Thus we are dealing with a very early tradition that reflects a situation in the life of Jesus, even if the precise original situation is lost to us and impossible to reconstruct. The current setting as a conflict in Jerusalem corresponds to the historical situation in the early 30s, for Jerusalem, as part of the Roman province of Judea, was subject to direct Roman tribute, whereas Galilee, then still under the rule of Herod Antipas, was not.

Nearly all modern interpreters recognize that the question addressed to Jesus, "Is it lawful to pay taxes to Caesar, or not?" is a trick to induce him to say something that would provide a reason for his arrest. Matthew and Luke merely make more explicit what was already clear in Mark, that this question is addressed to Jesus as yet another device by the chief priests (scribes and elders, or Pharisees, in Matthew) designed to entrap Jesus. If that is the case, however, it means (a) that the payment or nonpayment of the tribute was already a well-defined issue of controversy in Judea, (b) that a no answer would have been grounds for arrest, and finally (c) that the officials expected that Jesus' stance was such that he might well answer that it was not lawful to pay the tribute. Otherwise the passage makes no sense: the motive and the question do not cohere.

The long-drawn-out statement that falsely flatters Jesus (like God, he "cares for no man," i.e., is not influenced by anyone's position in life; cf. Leviticus 19:15) is of course full of hypocrisy; after all, this is purposeful entrapment. More interesting are two clear implications in the flattery, both of which would contribute to trapping Jesus. First, the false compliment, "caring for no man," challenges Jesus, prior to hearing the tendentious question, not to defer to the position of any one, including in this context Caesar. Second, the questioners are not asking Jesus simply for his personal opinion, but for his understanding of "the way of God" on the issue of the tribute. That is, as portrayed in this controversy story, Jesus' opponents clearly expect that Jesus' understanding of "the way of God" is such that it would not be lawful to pay the tribute. One of the most exciting points of the story is thus how Jesus so skillfully wriggles out of the trap. But this should not prevent us from discerning also both the serious religious-political conflict engaged in the story and the subtle but dramatic way in which Jesus indicates that the claims of Caesar are illegitimate.

Certain elements in Jesus' counter-question and response provide evidence of such conflict. First of all, the coin was a highly controversial symbol in Jewish Palestine. The image of Caesar on the coin was an abomination to the Jews.[23] More important in connection with the question of the tribute, however, is that coinage in the ancient world was a symbol of sovereignty and independence and had long been a sensitive issue for Jews (e.g., 1 Maccabees 15:6; and in both 66–70 and 132–135 C.E. the Jews minted their own coins as symbols of their liberty). In the Roman empire, as in the preceding Hellenistic empires, "the coin was the symbol of the ruler's dominance."[24] It is likely that the coin that Jesus asks his questioners to produce, on which is the likeness and inscription of Caesar, was the denarius minted by the reigning emperor Tiberius. "Though perhaps the most modest sign, this *denarius* of Tiberias is the most official and universal sign of the apotheosis of power and the worship of the *homo imperiosus* in the time of Christ."[25]

Second, the verb *apodidonai,* "give back/render," in Jesus' reply, is the standard term used where people are obligated to recognize the rightful claims of others, as when a debtor "pays back" what was borrowed as rightfully belonging to the creditor (Matthew 5:26 and parallel Luke 12:59; Matthew 18:25,24; Luke 7:42).[26] Jesus' reply thus accords with the ancient understanding that tribute is owed to Caesar, who has a recognized claim on the land, people, and produce (cf. Romans 13:7). In "correcting" to "give back" the simple term "give" used by his Pharisaic questioners, Jesus is thus pointing out (and playing on) the understanding of tribute in ancient Roman imperial culture: duty is owed to the emperor because of his lordship. Even if we took a more sceptical attitude toward this tradition, i.e., that we cannot get behind its current form, even the story in Greek has Jesus draw out clearly the imperial situation of domination and subjection in which he, the questioners, and listeners all stand.

Finally, the phrases "things of Caesar" and "things of God" refer to far more than simply the coin. The phrase "the things of" in New Testament and *koine* Greek means basically "the things pertaining or belonging to" someone or something, but can also have the clear connotations of "the demands of" as in "the things of the Law" in Romans 2:14. When used in a contrast, as in "the things of the Lord" vs. "the things of the world" in 1 Corinthians 7:32–34 or "the things of God" vs. "the things of men" in Jesus' rebuke to Peter in Mark 8:33 and Matthew 16:23, two conflicting and irreconcilable concerns or orientations are involved. Used in connection with the verb "give back," the phrase "the things of" would refer clearly to all those things and duties to be rendered to one's religious-political lord, of which the material items such as the tribute would be only the most tangible manifestation.

It is thus clear that Jesus' response to the intended entrapment is to escalate and refocus the issue from that of the tribute to the broader issue of lordship. In a Palestinian Jewish context, however, virtually all would have held that God was the lord, if not exclusively, then at least

310 / JESUS AND NONVIOLENT SOCIAL REVOLUTION

ultimately. In the very structure of the Mosaic Covenant and Torah, God was the king. Psalms of the period began and ended with the proclamation of the kingship of God (e.g., Psalms of Solomon 17). Even scriptural texts expressing the interests of the monarchy held the view that "all that is in the heavens and in the earth is thine; thine is the kingdom, O Lord," and "all things come from thee, and of thine own have we given thee" (1 Chronicles 29:11,14). This same view of lordship and "what things are God's" still prevailed in scholarly circles shortly after the time of Jesus. A rabbinic teaching cites this very prayer of David (1 Chronicles 29:14) in a statement of the claims of God: "Give to Him of what is His, for thou and thine are his." (Avot 3.8).

The issue in Jesus' statement "render to Caesar . . ." is lordship, and the emphasis comes in the second half of the statement: "and to God the things that are God's." Yet many of those same interpreters hedge on the implications. Such interpretations are simply baffling. If, in Jesus' statement, "the second half has all the weight, . . . and the first half has its weight taken from it," then how can one conclude that Jesus is indicating that there is still an obligation to Caesar, however temporary?[27] Or, if "everything" or "the whole man belongs to God" and "that which is God's must not be given to Caesar," then how can Caesar still have rights or claims, however limited?[28] Similarly, it seems overly subtle and even somewhat incredible to determine, on the one hand, that the issue is not simply the tribute but Caesar, while determining on the other hand that although one cannot give Caesar divine honors, it is surely right to pay the tribute.[29] Many modern interpreters seem more concerned than the recognizedly apologetic gospel writers to extricate Jesus from the entrapment—and to avoid the obvious implication of their own exegesis: if Jesus is suggesting that everything belongs to God as lord, then Caesar has no legitimate claims as lord.

It is evident from the examples just cited that what many interpreters do to rescue Jesus or their own exegesis from such an implication is to conceive of some sort of subordination of the claims of Caesar to the overall or higher or "eschatological" sovereignty of God. But can Jesus' statement be read as somehow subordinating "the things of Caesar" to "the things of God," or must the two be understood rather as conflicting and irreconcilable? Subordinationist interpretation often appeals to other early Christian texts such as Romans 13:1–7 and 1 Peter 2:13–14. It may be inappropriate methodologically, however, to project such Pauline positions back into the Palestinian Jewish situation of Jesus and the earliest stages of the gospel tradition. Earlier biblical traditions may provide some broader and more appropriate perspective and context. In fact, there were two prominent and conflicting biblical traditions regarding the relation of human lordship to the lordship of God. In the one, stemming from more popular circles of early Israel— resistance to the monarchy, and prophetic criticism of monarchic exploitation—God was seen as the only lord, loyalty to whom excludes any human kingship (e.g., Gideon's comment, Judges 8:23; God's comment to Samuel, 1 Samuel 8:7; and Hosea 8:4). In the other tradition, stemming from monarchic and professional scribal circles, kings were seen as regents instituted by God (or as the historical instruments of God) and therefore legitimate overlords (e.g., Psalm 2; Proverbs 8:15–16; Wisdom 6:1–11; cf. Isaiah 45:1–4).

There might appear to be some support for the subordinationist interpretation of "render unto Caesar" in the context of this second tradition, specifically in discussions of the organization of the obligations due to God and the king respectively. In 2 Chronicles 19:11, "the things of God" and "the things of the king" appear to stand parallel, the people being subordinated to the chief priest and to the governor of the house of Judah respectively in the corresponding matters. In 1 Chronicles 26:32, "the affairs of the king" appear to be coordinated with and even somewhat subordinated to "the affairs of God," both being handled by the same officer and bureaucracy. During most of the second Temple period, the local government by the high priesthood was coordinated with and supposedly subordinated to "the things of God," both being supported by the people's rendering of tithes and other taxes to the Temple and priests. We have no evidence for what the vast majority of the people thought, but at least the high priests must have been reasonably comfortable coordinating "the things of" the Persian, Ptolemaic, and Seleucid emperor as well with "the things of God," for they functioned as the imperial tax collectors as well as the mediators with God.

It is difficult and perhaps impossible, however, to read Jesus' statement in this way, i.e., that "the things of Caesar" are somehow legitimately subordinated to and coordinated with "the things of God." It would appear rather that "the things of Caesar" stood in sharp conflict with "the things of God." This can be seen clearly (a) by placing this statement in the context of Jesus' other teachings and (b) by viewing this and other statements of Jesus in the context of contemporary Jewish resistance to Roman domination.

The fundamental reality manifested through Jesus' message and actions was the presence of the kingdom of God. Jesus and his followers clearly understood the rule of God as direct, unmediated by the traditional human institutions of government. Indeed, the latter were to be avoided (e.g., Matthew 5:25–26 and parallel Luke 12:57–59; see the last part of chapter 9). Most important with regard to the tribute question, Jesus seemed adamant that the rule of God was exclusive. The language of contrast, conflict, and decision is prominent in his prophetic sayings and parables. One must decide for "the things of God" and no longer be determined by "the things of men." Most striking perhaps is the saying: "No servant can serve two masters. . . . You cannot serve God and Mammon" (Matthew 6:24 and parallel Luke 16:13). Contrary to the misleading statements of some commentaries, this "illustration" is not taken from the institution of slavery; and "servant" (Luke 16:13) is probably the more original wording (simply deleted by Matthew, but retained in Gospel of Thomas no. 47).[30] In ancient Near Eastern societies, everyone was understood as the "servant" of the king or other ruler of society. In one biblical tradition mentioned just above, which is perhaps the dominant one and the one that has popular roots, God was understood as the king, the exclusive lord of Israel. This same basic belief is both assumed and articulated, for example, in Jesus' parable pertaining to the Temple tax: God is to Israel as a king is to another society (Matthew 17:24–26). For Luke and especially for Matthew, the saying that it is impossible to serve two masters points to both the exclusiveness of God's rule and the necessity of exclusive devotion to God.[31]

Throughout the ministry of Jesus, the kingdom of God appears to exclude any other lordship and loyalty. Moreover, as is often pointed out (and is argued again in chapter 7 above), given the defeat of Satan and the imminent fulfillment of the kingdom of God "with power" (Mark 9:1), the old political-economic-religious structures, including Roman rule, were about to be ended.[32] There is simply no evidence anywhere else in the gospel tradition that would lead us to believe that Jesus would compromise the lordship of God with regard to Caesar any more than he would with regard to the high-priestly aristocracy, Satan, or Mammon. Thus the key in the saying "render to Caesar what is Caesar's and to God what is God's" must lie in what is Caesar's and what is God's. Jesus would appear to be consistent with later rabbinic teaching in this regard—only more adamant about it—that everything is God's (cf. again Avot 3.8). Hence the implication seems obvious in the saying: that there is not much to be rendered to Caesar.

No more than the tradition of Jesus' sayings do the synoptic gospel writers give us reason to think that Jesus was ready to compromise or qualify the rule of God when it came to Caesar's claims. In Mark, and in Matthew and Luke as well, the controversy over the tribute question is presented as part of an intensifying climactic conflict between Jesus and the Jewish ruling groups in Jerusalem (Mark 11–12 and parallels). The face-off begins dramatically with the triumphal entry, and Jesus challenges the high-priestly government directly and sharply in his Temple action. He tells a parable that the high priests recognize as pronouncing their own rejection and replacement by God. The authorities are determined to arrest and execute Jesus, but they must move by means of entrapment because Jesus is protected by the crowds who are hostile to them. The controversy over the tribute to Caesar is part of the entrapment strategy, according to the Gospels. There is no indication that Jesus' answer on the tribute question in any way defused the conflict by indicating in effect that he accepted the lordship of Caesar. Jesus had wriggled his way out of the trap set up in the question. But part of his opponents' astonishment at his answer was that while not saying anything on the basis of which they could arrest him (i.e., though he did not explicitly forbid payment as they had hoped he might), he had also not said, "Yes, pay tribute to Caesar." It is generally pointed out that the Gospels tend to downplay the conflict between Jesus and the Romans.[33] Hence the conflict between Jesus and the authorities would likely have been at least as sharp as it is portrayed in the Gospels. The story about the tribute question is an integral part of that conflict.

Of direct relevance to the question of Jesus and the tribute to Caesar is the charge mentioned only in Luke that Jesus "was forbidding us to give tribute to Caesar." This and the other charges brought against Jesus in Luke 23:2 are often declared to be "deliberate falsehoods" uttered by the chief priests and elders as part of Luke's political apology.[34] Recent analysis of Luke and Acts, however, indicates that these charges are not at all presented as lies in Luke. It had been made abundantly clear in Luke that Jesus had indeed been "stirring up people . . . from Galilee even unto this place" (the Temple and Jerusalem; Luke 23:5) so that from the rulers' perspective he had indeed been "perverting the nation" (Luke 23:2; cf. 23:14).[35] Moreover, Jesus' followers had acclaimed him king, giving the rulers a basis for the accusation that Jesus had said that "he himself is the Christ, a king" (Luke 23:2).[36] The declaration that Jesus is "righteous" (*dikaios,* Luke 23:47, often translated "innocent") is a scriptural-Christological apology, not a political apology directly connected with the charges in Luke 23:2,5.[37] Are we to believe, then, that alongside these other two charges that according to Luke's own account have a clear basis in Jesus' ministry, Luke slipped in a third charge that he considers completely false? On the journey toward Jerusalem Luke (16:13, as already noted) has Jesus proclaiming that "no servant can serve two masters." And Acts 5:29, at a crucial point in the continuing conflict between Jesus' followers and the high-priestly rulers, has Peter declare: "We must obey God rather than men." It would appear that Luke's apologetic element (usually viewed as more pronounced that Matthew's and Mark's) was to downplay but not to deny that Jesus had opposed Caesar's lordship, perhaps had even opposed the payment of tribute.

To determine further how "render to Caesar the things of Caesar and to God the things of God" would likely have been understood by the hearers, or at least in the earliest Palestinian tradition, we can place the statement in the context of the resistance to Roman domination. As is evident from the persistent popular movements and demonstrations, the Jewish people generally resented their subjection to Roman rule. Active resistance or protest flared up particularly, however, when provoked by specific symbols of Caesar's lordship. For example, as discussed in chapters 3 and 4 above, the aggressive demonstration led by the two revered teachers at the time of Herod's death in 4 B.C.E. focused on the golden eagle over the Temple gate as a symbol of Rome's or its client Herod's domination. Then once just prior to the ministry of Jesus (during Pilate's administration) and again shortly after his ministry, the massive protest demonstrations erupted over the presence of symbols of Caesar's rule, the Roman army standards brought in by Pilate's troops and the bust of Gaius about to be introduced into the Temple.

The period of Jesus' life and that of his nascent movement in Palestine is significantly framed by two major incidents of resistance to payment of the tribute, in 6 and again in 66 C.E. Moreover, besides illustrating the general attitude toward the tribute, both incidents reveal the conflicting positions of the ruling groups and the people or popular leaders, respectively. The first major resistance to the tribute was the Fourth Philosophy led by the scholar-teacher Judas of Galilee and the Pharisee Saddok in reaction to the imposition of direct Roman rule in Judea. As was noted in chapter 3 above, from Josephus's reports it is clear that these Jews held that the lordship of God excluded that of Caesar or of any other human rulers and that acquiescence in the tribute was tantamount to acknowledging the lordship of Caesar. Over against the popular resistance led by intellectuals in 6 C.E. stood the high priest Joazar, who (says Josephus) was instrumental in persuading the Jews to submit to the assessment. There was serious popular opposition to Joazar, however, for he was eventually "overpowered by the multitude" (*Ant.* 18.26). Even if the issue of the tribute was not the only point of grievance, it is reasonable to conclude that it was involved in the popular action against Joazar, whose principal action mentioned by Josephus was to advocate compliance with the tribute.

The second major protest against the tribute occurred in the early summer of 66 C.E. when, after the steadily worsening conditions of the late 50s and early 60s, the Judean people were in arrears in their payment of tribute. This was a serious situation, since the Romans viewed nonpayment of tribute as tantamount to rebellion. The ruling aristocracy brought the Herodian king Agrippa II up to Jerusalem, where he exhorted the people to pay the tribute without delay, arguing (according to Josephus) that "there is nothing to check blows like submission" (*War* 2.345–404). The ruling group set out to collect the tribute. The people, however, exasperated at continuing abuse by the Roman governor and at Agrippa himself, "heaped abuse on the king and formally proclaimed his banishment from the city; some of the insurgents even ventured to throw stones at him" (*War* 2.406).

From these two major events involving the issue of the tribute it would appear that, during the decades around the ministry of Jesus, the payment of the tribute to Caesar was highly controversial: the Jewish people, understandably, generally opposed and even resisted payment, while their ruling aristocracy, equally understandably (because their own position depended on their cooperation with Rome), favored and indeed collected the tribute. Now, this would appear to be precisely the situation portrayed in the gospel story about the tribute question. The Jewish rulers (who sent "some of the Pharisees and Herodians" or "spies"), favored payment of the tribute, as is implied in their hope of entrapping Jesus by inducing him to utter a treasonable statement against the tribute. As is indicated in the other stories of conflict between Jesus and the ruling group in Jerusalem, however, they found it necessary to proceed cautiously and deceitfully because they were afraid of an uproar among the people, who viewed John the Baptist as a genuine prophet and who would supposedly support Jesus as well. In the case of the tribute question, in which so much depends on how the hearers would have understood each of the two halves of Jesus' double statement—"render to Ceasar what is Caesar's and to God what is God's"—this suggests that the people would almost certainly have understood that, since Caesar really has no legitimate claims anyhow, nothing need be rendered. All belongs to God, the true Lord.

Clever as he was, Jesus had uttered an utterly safe statement in the context, appropriately ambiguous and ostensibly noncommittal. He had not forbidden payment of the tribute in so many words. But by couching his statement in terms of what was owed to overlords by their servants, he had articulated the Jewish theocratic understanding in clearly intelligible terms, especially to those who shared that under-standing. The fundamental burden of Jesus' prophetic ministry was the presence of the kingdom of God. For those who responded to Jesus' call "to enter the kingdom of God" the implications for rendering unto Caesar were clear.

Conclusion:
Jesus and Social Revolution

Was Jesus a pacifist? We have no evidence that he ever directly or explicitly addressed the issue of violence. Certainly nonviolence was not a principal theme in his preaching and practice. Portrayals of Jesus as an advocate of nonviolence, particularly recent ones, have depended basically on "the Zealots" as a foil for Jesus' position and the sayings in Matthew 5:38–48 as an articulation of Jesus' pacifist, even non-resistant, stance vis-à-vis the Romans. It is increasingly recognized, however, that there was no sustained movement of violent resistance to Roman rule during the first century C.E. If the contention in chapter 9 above is correct, that the sayings grouped with "love your enemies" refer to local enemies and not to foreign political enemies, then both of the principal pillars of the portrayal of Jesus as a pacifist prove to be without historical basis. Some of the lesser components of that portrayal, dependent on one or another of the two principal pillars anyhow, themselves turn out to be unhistorical. For example, Jesus' supposed fellowship with tax collectors, further understood as "quisling" collaborators in Roman rule, was used as a key argument that Jesus could not have been a Zealot or otherwise an advocate of resistance to Roman rule. But it turns out that there is little or no evidence that Jesus in fact associated with tax collectors. Further arguments for an apolitical Jesus such as his being declared "innocent" in the crucifixion scene in Luke prove to be unfounded even at the level of the politically apologetic evangelists. However likely or attractive the claim may seem, we do not know that Jesus advocated nonviolence.

On the other hand, there is no evidence that Jesus advocated violence, either, at least not overt individual acts of violence. Jesus is portrayed as using moderate violence against property in the Temple demonstration. And he apparently announced a good deal of imminent divine violence, at least implicitly, such as the the woes he proclaimed over Jerusalem and certain unresponsive Galilean villages. But there is no indication that he advocated acts of violence, let alone any sort of armed revolution against Roman domination.

The way these questions have usually been posed, however, is inappropriate to the material we have from and about Jesus. In the society in which Jesus lived, no one ever posed an issue in such abstract reflective terms as whether one should act violently or nonviolently. Nor was there any movement engaged in violent opposition to Roman rule at the time of Jesus that posed the issue concretely in terms of overt acts of violence. The social-historical situation in which Jesus lived, however, was permeated with violence. We can thus take a step toward a more adequate understanding of Jesus and violence by noting that Jesus, while not necessarily a pacifist, actively opposed violence, both oppressive and repressive, both political-economic and spiritual. He consistently criticized and resisted the oppressive established political-economic-religious order of his own society. Moreover, he aggressively intervened to mitigate or undo the effects of institutionalized violence, whether in particular acts of forgiveness and exorcism or in the general opening of the kingdom of God to the poor. Jesus opposed violence, but not from a distance. He did not attempt to avoid violence in search of a peaceable existence. He rather entered actively into the situation of violence, and even exacerbated the conflict. Driving out the demons involved convulsions for the possessed, and the preaching and practice of the kingdom generally brought not "peace" but "a sword." Jesus and his followers, like Judas of Galilee and others of the Fourth Philosophy, were prepared to suffer violence themselves and to allow their friends to be tortured and killed for their insistence on the rule of God.

Toward a more precise sense of Jesus' opposition to and involvement with violence we can examine where his preaching and practice are situated in the spiral of violence in Jewish Palestine. Some fragments of the gospel tradition, such as the multiply attested saying about taking up one's cross and following him (Mark 8:34 and parallels; Luke 14:27 and Matthew 10:38), suggest that the opposition of Jesus and his followers to the system was sufficiently serious that they were likely to be executed as rebels. However, the saying linked with taking up one's cross in Mark 8:35 (although perhaps not in Q; cf. Matthew 10:39 and Luke 17:33: "Whoever seeks to gain his life will lose it, but whoever loses his life will preserve it") suggests that Jesus and his followers understood their opposition in terms of a protest or resistance for which the individuals would be vindicated by God, but not in terms of its being a serious revolt. Sayings such as these make Jesus' ministry and the actions of his followers appear similar to the protests led by the scholars in both 4 B.C.E. and 6 C.E., in which part of the motivation to protest against the forms of domination or exploitation was the participants' expectation that they would be vindicated by a future resurrection.

The expectation of a future vindication by resurrection, however, suggests that there is a broader perspective in which such resistance must be understood. In Josephus's opinion about Judas of Galilee and the Fourth Philosophy, they understood themselves as doing the groundwork for the future well-being of their society. In gospel passages such as Mark 8:38 and parallels and 9:1, whether these are from earlier or later in the tradition, it is clear that at least his followers, and probably Jesus as well, were confident of the imminent fulfillment of the renewal that Jesus had inaugurated in his ministry: God/the Son of man was to come in judgment, and the kingdom of God was to be fully realized. Perhaps Jesus' active opposition to the established order should be understood not simply as resistance or protest that he knew would result in repression, but as a more serious opposition, a revolt that would surely and imminently result in a transformed historical situation.

Jesus' actions and prophecies, especially those directed against the ruling institutions of his society, suggest that he was indeed mounting a more serious opposition than a mere protest. It is certain that Jesus was executed as a rebel against the Roman order. Our examination of Jesus' prophecies and actions, moreover, has shown that from the viewpoint of the rulers the crucifixion of Jesus was not a mistake. The charges brought against him, however apologetically handled by the gospel writers, were in effect true. He had definitely been stirring up the people. Herod Antipas was reportedly already hostile to Jesus, perhaps even plotting his arrest, simply because of the threatening effects of his healing activity; and, as can be seen in Jesus' insistence on local social-economic cooperation, his practice was far more comprehensive in social renewal than a few healing miracles. Jesus had almost certainly threatened the Temple. More particularly, he had pronounced God's judgment against the Temple and against the high-priestly rulers and the ruling city as well. It is unclear just how explicitly Jesus claimed to be or was acclaimed as a king; but from the viewpoint of the rulers, he clearly was a dangerous popular leader, and from the "messianic movements" of a generation earlier they were familiar with popularly acclaimed kings as a revolutionary threat. Finally, it is less certain but likely that Jesus had in effect taken the position not only that the people were "free" of illegitimate taxation by the Temple system, but that they were also not obligated to render up the Roman tribute, since all things being God's, nothing was really due to Caesar. Taken together, these sayings and prophecies begin to sound more systematically revolutionary than an unrelated set of incidental sayings juxtaposed with a protest or two.

Although it begins to appear that Jesus and his movement were engaged not simply in resistance but in a more serious revolt of some sort against the established order in Palestine, there is no evidence that Jesus himself advocated, let alone organized, the kind of armed rebellion that would have been necessary to free the society from the military-political power of the Roman empire. The solution to this apparent contradiction lies in taking more seriously than we have the social ambiance in which Jesus was working. As we ascertained in chapter 7, Jesus was engaged in direct manifestations of God's kingdom in his practice and preaching, and he was confident that God was imminently to complete the restoration of Israel and judge the institutions that maintained injustice. The power of Satan had been broken. According to the apocalyptic way of understanding reality, in which events could be happening on three "levels" simultaneously (the spiritual, the social-historical, and the personal), so that happenings on one level constituted evidence for happenings on the other levels, the implications were obvious for the historical situation.

Perhaps because the apocalyptic orientation is so foreign to our own modern "scientific" view of reality, we have tended to ignore or often actually "demythologize" the perspective in which Jesus and his followers were thinking and acting. For us, the fact that Jesus himself did not advocate or engage in violent actions becomes evidence that he had no relationship with any sort of violent response to the violence and oppression he opposed. The same approach has often been taken to Paul. Thus, for example, Paul's admonition to be subject to the governing authorities in Romans 13:1–7 is completely removed from its setting of his expectation of imminent eschatological fulfillment, which would put an end to the old structures of governing authorities. Similarly, Paul exhorts his readers never to avenge themselves. But there is no need for petty personal vengeance now, since God is about to bring wrath aplenty on the enemies (Romans 12:14–21). In order to understand adequately what Jesus, Paul, and others were saying and doing, we must take seriously what they understood God to be doing, for they understood their activities as part of God's action in history. At least since the time of the visions in the book of Daniel many Jews had believed that God was soon to judge the oppressive imperial regimes and give dominion to the people, as well as vindicate the martyrs who had meanwhile died for the faith. Jesus apparently shared this perspective, only he was convinced that God had already inaugurated the time of renewal and fulfillment. Jesus' prophecies and other sayings do not elaborate much on the violent character of God's judgment. But that component of the overall perspective is clearly present in his preaching. God was effecting the revolution that would end the spiral of violence as well as liberate and renew Israel and, assuming Jesus was cognizant of the promises to Abraham, through Israel bring salvation to the nations.

Lest we once again begin slipping into a certain spiritualization of concepts such as revolution or salvation, it is well to remind ourselves of the concrete historical conflict involved in the gospel tradition and Jesus' ministry (or God's salvation, for that matter). Rabbinic Judaism and Christianity have been described as "historical religions" that arose as part of the "axial age," meaning that these "religions" and this period of cultural history involved a crystallization of an "other" transcendent world above this world, among other features. It may be useful for understanding Jesus to examine briefly in concrete terms how that other, higher religious world emerged in the Hellenistic period.

The cultural traditions of ancient Near Eastern civilizations such as those of Babylon, Egypt, or Israel were originally symbols of reality in all its dimensions: political, economic, and physical as well as religious. As political and cultural imperialism intensified in the Near East in the transition from Persian to Hellenistic rule and imposed new political, cultural-religious (at least for the elite), and sometimes even new economic forms, what had been cultural systems providing symbolization for all dimensions of life became displaced, relativized, and spiritualized into otherworldly ideals appropriate only to individual souls. For example, the Isis-Osiris-Horus myth cycle, which had played a central role for the whole of Egyptian society, was transformed into individual rites of initiation (the "mysteries" of Isis) or became the subject of platonizing philosophical interpretation (e.g., Plutarch's treatise "On Isis and Osiris"). Hellenistic Jews, like other participants in Hellenistic culture, similarly narrowed and spiritualized their heritage in order to preserve it.

In this general Hellenistic historical context, Palestinian Jewish society was a special case: it held onto its cultural traditions and its political-religious forms by the special compromise arrangement described in chapter 1 above. Yet many Palestinian Jews, perhaps the vast majority, were not prepared to accept the compromise. The imperial situation was such, of course, that they had to make an adjustment. They did this by projecting the fulfillment of God's promises into the future: the current situation was ruled by the imperial as well as by the demonic forces; but God would soon assert divine sovereignty and liberate the people. Impatient Jewish groups, of course, made repeated attempts to insist on the comprehensive functioning of their own cultural traditions to the exclusion of the dominant imperial forms. Such Palestinian Jews understood the rule of God concretely. Thus, when Jesus preached and practiced the presence of the rule of God here and now, the clear implication was that imperial and high-priestly rule was excluded and was imminently to be judged by God. Jesus' conviction that the kingdom of God was at hand meant direct conflict with Roman imperial and Jewish high-priestly rule.

In order to comprehend how Jesus was involved in a "revolution" and not simply resistance against the Roman imperial order in Palestine, we have made a distinction similar to that made by some political scientists: between a *political* revolution and a *social* revolution. Modern revolutionary parties have often thought that it is necessary to take political control of a society in order that they can then begin seriously to transform the social relationships of power and production. Jesus and his followers obviously did not think in such terms. But they appear to have worked with a similar distinction. Adapting the modern terms somewhat to the pattern of Jewish apocalyptic understanding, Jesus would appear to have believed that God had already begun, as it were, to implement the political revolution, even though it was hardly very far along. But in the confidence that it was under way, it was his calling to proceed with the social revolution thus made possible by God's rule, to begin the transformation of social relations in anticipation of the completion of the political revolution.

We have examined here how social relations were to be transformed. First and perhaps most important as a way of holding together the other aspects, the kingdom of God in Jesus' preaching and practice, while indeed an assertion of divine rule, was concerned with persons, individually and socially. The kingdom meant wholeness of life. Moreover, as can be seen particularly in the sayings about entering or being in the kingdom, it was a society, a people, although not a place or a realm. That the kingdom of God was "in the midst of" or "among" the people says somewhat the same thing. Preaching and manifesting the kingdom of God thus also involved the restoration of the people, Israel. More particularly, the renewal of the life of the people meant renewal of the fundamental social-political form of traditional peasant life, the village. Within the local communities, however, in an apparent break with the traditional patriarchal forms that had either broken down or become oppressive, Jesus called for new "familial" but egalitarian relations. He also insisted on an egalitarian principle in relations going beyond the local community as well—relations with no authority figures. Indeed, there would have been little need for authority figures and roles in the egalitarian local communities, which could handle their own conflicts without resort to official institutions such as the area courts. Jesus affirmed that, with the kingdom now at hand, it was no longer necessary to remain divided against one another in anxiety and defensiveness. Instead the people were to enter a new spirit of cooperation and mutual assistance, even in relation to their local enemies, responding to one another's needs despite or rather because of the economic pressures most of them faced.

There is no indication in the gospel tradition that Jesus saw any role for the ruling institutions of his society. In fact the evidence points in the other direction. Given the appearance of prophecies or a demonstration against the Temple at four different points in the gospel tradition, paralleled by solid traditions of his lament over the governing city and the parable told in judgment against the high-priestly rulers, it would appear that he did not simply condemn the present incumbents of those ruling institutions but rejected the institutions themselves. That is, Jesus rejected the institutions by which the priestly ruling class controlled and extracted its living from the vast majority of the people. There is certainly no indication that Jesus himself posed as a monarchic ruler, for the traditions that portray him as a "messianic" king can best be understood in terms of popular, not monarchic, kingship. In this it appears that he worked out of the central biblical traditions of a covenantal society without the special power and privileges that went with an institutionalized ruling class such as a monarchy or a high priesthood, for which there were also legitimating biblical traditions. The kingdom of God apparently had no need of either a mediating hierocracy or a temple system.

The social revolution that Jesus catalyzed in anticipation of the political revolution being effected by God also created a crisis and entailed a severe discipline. Response to the kingdom by some and rejection by others created divisions within families, often apparently between the generations. Other divisions provoked by the *crisis* or judgment that had come into the present situation with the coming of the kingdom of God constitute a prominent theme in Jesus' sayings and parables. Those too busy attending to their worldly security would find themselves excluded from the great banquet to which they had been invited. The wealthy would find it impossible to enter the kingdom. Judgment that had been thought to be in the future had suddenly come into the present, for people's future was being determined by the way they responded to Jesus and his offer of the kingdom. The woes Jesus pronounced on unresponsive Galilean villages indicate the seriousness with which collective as well as individual response was taken.

Response to the kingdom, moreover, required utter dedication, particularly for those called to leadership roles. "No one who puts his hand to the plow and looks back is fit for the kingdom of God" (Luke 9:62). "Leave the dead to bury the dead; but as for you, go and proclaim the kingdom of God" (Luke 9:60 and Matthew 8:22). Of course, if such sayings are understood merely as radical ethics addressed to a few wandering charismatics, conceived of after the model of Cynic philosophers, then they can be dismissed as irrelevant for the vast majority of people and do not express a revolutionary ethos at all. But many of these "hard sayings" are clearly addressed to the people generally; and the "charismatics," quite unlike the Cynics, were catalysts of a broader movement based in the villages of Galilee.

It would be difficult to claim that Jesus was a pacifist. But he actively opposed violence, particularly institutionalized oppressive and repressive violence, and its effects on a subject people. Jesus was apparently a revolutionary, but not a violent political revolutionary. Convinced that God would put an end to the spiral of violence, however violently, Jesus preached and catalyzed a social revolution. In the presence of the kingdom of God he mediated God's liberation to a discouraged Jewish peasantry and offered some fundamental guidance for the renewal of the people. "Love your enemies" turns out to be not the apolitical pacific stance of one who stands above the turmoil of his day, nor a sober counsel of nonresistance to evil or oppression, but a revolutionary principle. It was a social revolutionary principle insofar as the love of enemies would transform local social-economic relations. In effect, however, it was also—even if somewhat indirectly—politically revolutionary. That is, when the people have achieved solidarity with regard to the basic values of life focused on concrete social-economic relations, it has usually been threatening to the ruling groups. The communities of Jesus' followers appear to have been such a threat.

ABBREVIATIONS

CBQ	*Catholic Biblical Quarterly*
HJP	Emil Schuerer, *The History of the Jewish People in the Age of Jesus Christ: A New English Version*, 3 vols. Revised and edited by G. Vermes and F. Millar (Edinburgh: Clark, 1973–1986)
HTR	*Harvard Theological Review*
HUCA	*Hebrew Union College Annual*
IDB	*Interpreter's Dictionary of the Bible*, 4 vols. (Nashville: Abingdon, 1962). Suppl. vol. (1977)
IEJ	*Israel Exploration Journal*
JAAR	*Journal of the American Academy of Religion*
JBL	*Journal of Biblical Literature*
JJS	*Journal of Jewish Studies*
JPFC	*The Jewish People in the First Century*, 2 vols. Edited by S. Safrai and M. Stern (Assen: Van Gorcum, 1974–1976)
JQR	*Jewish Quarterly Review*
JR	*Journal of Religion*
JRS	*Journal of Roman Studies*
JSJ	*Journal for the Study of Judaism*
JSNT	*Journal for the Study of the New Testament*
JTS	*Journal of Theological Studies*
LCL	Loeb Classical Library editions of classical texts
Nov T	*Novum Testamentum*
NTS	*New Testament Studies*
TDNT	*Theological Dictionary of the New Testament*, 9 vols. (Grand Rapids: Eerdmans, 1964–1974)
WHJP	*The World History of the Jewish People. First Series: Ancient Times*, edited by A. Schalit. vol. 6: *The Hellenistic Age*, edited by A. Schalit; vol. 7: *The Herodian Period*, edited by M. Avi Yonah (New Brunswick: Rutgers University Press, 1972–1975)
Q	*Quelle* (sayings source) Jesus sayings common to Matthew and Luke.

NOTES

INTRODUCTION:

1. E.g., V. P. Furnish, *The Love Command in the New Testament* (Nashville: Abingdon, 1972), ch. 1.
2. E.g., J. Riches, *Jesus and the Transformation of Judaism* (London: Darton, Longman & Todd, 1980); E. P. Sanders, *Jesus and Judaism* (Philadelphia: Fortress, 1985).
3. E.g., see now the substantial analyses in *JPFC*.
4. E.g., see the discussions in as well as the titles of the books in n. 2 above.
5. K. Lake, "Appendix A: The Zealots," in Lake and Foakes Jackson, *The Beginnings of Christianity*, 5 vols. (New York: 1920–1933) I, pt. 1.421–425; S. Zeitlin, "Zealots and Sicarii," *JBL* 81 (1962):395–398, review of the highly synthetic reconstructions by M. Hengel, *Die Zeloten* (Leiden: Brill, 1961).
6. E.g., O. Cullmann, *Jesus and the Revolutionaries* (New York: Harper & Row, 1970); the two tracts by M. Hengel, *Was Jesus a Revolutionist?* (Philadelphia: Fortress, 1971) and *Victory over Violence* (Philadelphia: Fortress, 1973).
7. Y. Yadin, *Masada: Herod's Fortress and the Zealots' Last Stand* (New York: Random House, 1966).
8. M. Stern, "Sicarii and Zealots," in *WHJP* vol. 8, 264; G. Theissen, *Sociology of Early Palestinian Christianity* (Philadelphia: Fortress, 1978), 50–51,61.
9. R. A. Horsley, "Josephus and the Bandits," *JSJ* 10 (1979):37–63; "The Sicarii: Ancient Jewish 'Terrorists'," *JR* 59 (1979):435–458; "Ancient Jewish Banditry and the Revolt against Rome, A.D. 66–70," *CBQ* 43 (1981):409–432; "Popular Messianic Movements around the Time of Jesus," *CBQ* 46 (1984):471–495; " 'Like One of the Prophets of Old': Two Types of Popular Prophets at the Time of Jesus," *CBQ* 47 (1985):435–463; "The Zealots: Their Origin, Relationships and Importance in the Jewish Revolt," *Nov T* 27 (1986):159–192; Horsley and J. S. Hanson, *Bandits, Prophets, and Messiahs* (Minneapolis: Winston-Seabury, 1985).
10. E.g., see Hengel, *Was Jesus a Revolutionist?;* Riches, *Jesus* (n. 2 above); S. G. F. Brandon, *Jesus and the Zealots* (Manchester: Manchester University Press, 1967).

CHAPTER 1: THE IMPERIAL SITUATION OF PALESTINIAN JEWISH SOCIETY

1. M. Smith, "Palestinian Judaism in the First Century," in *Israel: Its Role in Civilization*, Ed. M. Davis (New York: Harper & Row, 1956).
2. G. Balandier, "The 'Colonial Situation' Concept," *The Sociology of Black Africa* (New York: Praeger, 1970), ch. 1, pp. 21–56; G. Balandier, "The Colonial Situation: A

Theoretical Approach," in *Social Change: The Colonial Situation,* ed. I. Wallerstein (New York, London: Wiley & Sons, 1966), 34–61. P. Worsley, *The Third World* (London: Wiedenfeld & Nicolson, 1964), 21–49. The rest of this section consists of the application of Balandier's and Worsley's discussion to Palestian Jewish history from the Babylonian to the Roman empires.

3. Worsley, *Third World,* 26.
4. Ibid., 30.
5. Ibid., 36.
6. Ibid., 38.
7. Ibid., 38.
8. Ibid., 42.
9. On Judea during the Persian period, see E. Bickerman, *From Ezra to the Last of the Maccabees* (New York: Schocken, 1962); N. K. Gottwald, *The Hebrew Bible: A Socioliterary Introduction* (Philadelphia: Fortress, 1984) ¶44; S. K. Eddy, *The King Is Dead* (Lincoln: University of Nebraska Press, 1961).
10. On Jewish Palestine under the Hellenistic and Roman empires, see V. Tcherikover, *Hellenistic Civilization and the Jews* (New York: Atheneum, 1970); M. Hengel, *Judaism and Hellenism* (Philadelphia: Fortress, 1974); and articles in two multi-volume surveys: *WHJP* vol. 6, and vol. 7; and *JPFC*.
11. Balandier, *Sociology,* 27–28.
12. J. Jeremias, *Jerusalem in the Time of Jesus* (Philadelphia: Fortress, 1969), 105; M. Stern, "The Province of Judaea," in *JPFC* vol. 1, 324–335.
13. A. N. Sherwin-White, *Roman Law and Roman Society in The New Testament* (Oxford: Oxford University Press, 1963), 139.
14. Worsley, 39.
15. Balandier, *Sociology,* 45.
16. Balandier, *Sociology,* 24,45.
17. Worsley, 29–30,36.
18. I.e., by the work of J. Neusner; e.g., *From Politics to Piety* (Englewood Cliffs, NJ: Prentice Hall, 1973); and A. Saldarini, *Pharisees, Scribes, and Sadducees* (Wilmington, DE: Glazier, 1987).
19. See G. Lenski, *Power and Privilege* (New York: McGraw-Hill, 1966), 243–248.
20. See Tcherikover, *Hellenistic Civilization and the Jews,* 125–126, 196–198.
21. F.M. Cross, *The Ancient Library of Qumran* (Garden City: Doubleday, 1961), ch. 3; G. Vermes, *The Dead Sea Scrolls in English,* 2nd ed. (Harmondsworth: Penguin, 1975), ch. 3.

CHAPTER 2: THE POLITICS OF VIOLENCE

1. R. M. Brown, *Religion and Violence* (Philadelphia: Westminster, 1973), 7.
2. J. G. Gray, *On Understanding Violence Philosophically* (New York: Harper & Row, 1970), 14.
3. J. G. Davies, *Christians, Politics and Violent Revolution* (Maryknoll, NY: Orbis, 1976), 128–129.

4. W. R. Miller, *Nonviolence: A Christian Interpretation* (New York: Association Press, 1964), 33.

5. R. M. Brown, *Religion and Violence*, 7–8.

6. T. Merton, *Faith and Violence* (Notre Dame: University of Notre Dame Press, 1968), 7–8.

7. *Summa Theologica* Ia, IIae, q. 96.4.

8. Davies, *Christians, Politics*, 131.

9. J. Galtung, "Violence, Peace, and Peace Research," *Journal of Peace Research* 3 (1969): 171.

10. Report of the Consultation on "Violence, Nonviolence and the Struggle for Social Justice" (Geneva: World Council of Churches, 1972), 6.

11. H. Camara, *Spiral of Violence* (London: Sheed & Ward, 1971; orig. 1970), 29–30.

12. R. M. Brown, *Religion and Violence*, 9.

13. Camara, *Spiral of Violence*, 30–31.

14. Brown, *Religion and Violence*, 9.

15. Camara, *Spiral of Violence*, 34.

16. R. M. Brown, *Religion and Violence*, 10.

17. P. Berryman, *The Religious Roots of Rebellion* (Maryknoll, NY: Orbis, 1976) 109–110.

18. See, e.g., H. Edward Price, Jr., "The Strategy and Tactics of Revolutionary Terrorism," *Comparative Studies in Society and History* 19 (1977):52–65; T.P. Thornton, "Terror as a Weapon of Political Agitation," in *Internal War* (ed H. Eckstein; New York: Free Press, 1964), 71–99; B. Crozier *The Rebels: A Study of Post-War Insurrections* (Boston: Beacon, 1960); e.g., 170.

19. On both, see Brown, *Religion and Violence*, 11.

20. Brown, 10.

21. B. Lomar, *Hungary 1956* (London: Allison and Busby, 1976); P. Windsor, *Czechoslovakia 1968: Reform, Repression, and Resistance* (New York: Columbia University Press, 1969); P. Gleijeses, *Dominican Crisis 1965: Constitutional Revolt and American Intervention* (Baltimore: Johns Hopkins University, 1978); S. Kinzer, *Bitter Fruit* (Garden City, NY: Doubleday, 1982).

22. W. R. Miller, *Nonviolence*, 34 (citing Boulding).

23. V. Tcherikover, *Hellenistic Civilization and the Jews* (New York: Atheneum, 1970).

24. J. Jeremias, *Jerusalem in the Time of Jesus* (Philadelphia: Fortress, 1969), 105; M. Stern, "The Province of Judaea," *JPFC*, 1.586.

25. Jeremias, *Jerusalem*, 134.

26. Merton, *Faith and Violence*, 8.

27. C. Arnson, *El Salvador: A Revolution Confronts the United States* (Washington, D.C.: Institute for Policy Studies, 1982), 11.28.

28. M. Goodman, "The First Jewish Revolt: Social Conflict and the Problem of Debt," *JJS* 33 (1982):422–434.

29. On the prosbul, see J. Neusner, *The Rabbinic Traditions about the Pharisees before 70*, 3 vols. (Leiden: Brill, 1971), 1.217–220.

30. G. d'Arbousier, "Les problemes de la culture," in *Europe*, special African number: *Afrique noire*, May-June 1949; G. Balandier, *Sociology*, 30.

31. Cited from the translation in *Marx and Engels on Religion*, intro. by Reinhold Niebuhr (New York: Schocken Books, 1964), 41–42.

32. R. A. Horsley, "Like One of the Prophets of Old: Two Types of Popular Prophets at the Time of Jesus," *CBQ* 47 (1985):435–463; Horsley and J. S. Hanson, *Bandits, Prophets, and Messiahs,* ch. 4, from which the following translations of Josephus passages are quoted.

33. R. E. Brown, *The Semitic Background of the Term "Mystery" in the New Testament* (Philadelphia: Fortress, 1968).

34. R. A. Horsley, "Josephus and the Bandits," *JSJ* 10 (1979):37–63.

35. E. J. Hobsbawm, *Bandits,* rev. ed. (New York: Pantheon, 1981), 23,26.

36. Hobsbawm, *Bandits,* 18. The pattern of "social banditry" sketched by Hobsbawm, however, may not be universally valid. Chinese banditry, as portrayed in the Water-Margin novel, is clearly an exception. Yet the pattern of "social banditry" in Roman antiquity and in Jewish Palestine does appear basically the same as that found by Hobsbawn in early modern European folklore. See further R. A. Horsley, "Josephus and the Bandits," *JSJ* 10 (1979):37–63.

37. Cf. Hobsbawm's comments, *Bandits,* 89.

38. Hobsbawm, *Bandits,* 55.

39. Hobsbawm, 101. The same is true of the great Cossack leaders of peasant rebellions in Russia.

40. Hobsbawm, 26–29.

41. R. A. Horsley, "Ancient Jewish Banditry and the Revolt Against Rome, A.D. 66–70," *CBQ* 43 (1981):409–432.

42. On the Sicarii see further R. A. Horsley, "The Sicarii: Ancient Jewish Terrorists," *JR* 59 (1979):435–458.

43. E. N. Luttwak, *The Grand Strategy of the Roman Empire* (Baltimore: Johns Hopkins University Press, 1976) esp. 25–26,32–33,41–42,46–47.

44. On Herod's repressive policies and practices, see further A. Schalit, *König Herodes: Der Mann Und Sein Werk* (Berlin: de Gruyter, 1969); M. Smallwood, *The Jews Under Roman Rule* (Leiden: Brill, 1976); M. Stern, "The Reign of Herod," in *WHJP* 7.71–117.

45. J. Neusner, *From Politics to Piety* (Englewood Cliffs, NJ: Prentice Hall, Inc., 1973).

46. See further R. A. Horsley, "Popular Messianic Movements around the Time of Jesus," *CBQ* 46 (1984):471–493.

47. See H. de Jonge, "The Use of the Word 'Anointed' in the Time of Jesus," *Nov T* 8 (1966):132–148; and now J. Neusner, *Messiah in Context* (Philadelphia: Fortress, 1983).

48. See R. A. Horsley, "Popular Messianic Movements," 471–493; vs. J. S. Kennard, "Judas of Galilee and His Clan," *JQR* 36 (1945–1946):281–286.

49. R. A. Horsley, "The Zealots, Their Origin, Relationships and Importance in the Jewish Revolt," *Nov T* 28 (1986):159–192.

50. On Simon bar Giora, see further O. Michael, "Studien zu Josephus," *NTS* 14 (1967–1968):403 and R. A. Horsley, "Popular Messianic Movements," 471–493.

CHAPTER 3: FROM REBELLION TO TAX-RESISTANCE

1. See references in n. 9 of the introduction, above.

2. E.g., O. Ploeger, *Theocracy and Eschatology* (Richmond, VA: John Knox, 1968), 7–9,23–24; W. R. Farmer, "Hasidim," *IDB* 2.528; F. M. Cross, *The Ancient Library of*

Qumran, rev. ed. (Garden City, NY: Doubleday, 1961), 72,131–141; G. Vermes, *The Dead Sea Scrolls in English*, 2nd ed. (Harmondsworth, England: Penguin, 1975, repr. 1981), 62–66.

3. See ch. 1, n. 19, above.

4. E.g.,J.Jeremias,*Jerusalem at the Time of Jesus* (Philadelphia: Fortress, 1969), 111–115, and at points in chs. 10 and 11.

5. J. J. Collins, *The Apocalyptic Vision of the Book of Daniel* (HSM 16; Missoula: Scholars Press, 1977), 211–215; and *Daniel, 1-2 Maccabees* (Old Testament Message 16; Wilmington, DE: Glazier, 1981), 111–113. The *maskilim* who produced Daniel were apparently not the only intellectuals engaged in such resistance, despite the repressive consequences. The *Testament of Moses*, like the visions in Daniel, exhibits a willingness to suffer martyrdom rather than abandon the Torah.

6. Collins (previous note) concludes that the *maskilim* were advocates of nonviolent resistance.

7. G. W. E. Nickelsburg, "Social Aspects of Palestinian Jewish Apocalypticism," in *Apocalypticism in the Mediterranean World and the Near East*, ed. D. Hellholm (Tübingen: Mohr, 1983) 645–650; P. Davies, "Hasidim in the Maccabean Period," *JJS* 28 (1977): 127–40, a critique of previous reconstruction of the Hasidim.

8. E.g., V. Tcherikover, *Hellenistic Civilization and the Jews* (New York: Atheneum, 1970), 198; cf., Collins, *The Apocalyptic Vision*, 202–205. Tcherikover's reconstruction would be strongly reinforced by another possible reading of 1 Maccabees 7:12–13: the first among the Israelites to seek peace were the Hasidim. That is, the latter were basically a *scribal group*, and 1 Maccabees 7:12–13 refers explicitly to them.

9. J. J. Collins, *The Apocalyptic Imagination* (New York: Crossroad, 1984), 55–56.

10. Collins, *Apocalyptic Imagination*, 62–63.

11. Collins, *Apocalyptic Imagination*, 56.

12. Davies, "Hasidim in the Maccabean Period," 137–138.

13. J. Neusner, *From Politics to Piety* (Englewood Cliffs, NJ: Prentice-Hall, 1973).

14. Neusner, *Politics to Piety*, 66; on the Pharisees in the Roman period, see further G. Allon, "The Attitude of the Pharisees to the Roman Government and the House of Herod," *Scripta Hierosolymitana* (Jerusalem: Magnes Press) 7 (1961):53–78.

15. It is not clear that Josephus intends to be as sarcastic or denigrating with the word *sophistēs* as Thackeray's translation suggests at *War* 2.118 in the Loeb ed.

16. Neusner, *Politics to Piety*, 65, citing at length M. Smith, "Palestinian Judaism in the First Century," in *Israel: Its Role in Civilization*, ed. M. Davis (New York: Harper & Row, 1956), 75–76.

17. Neusner, *Politics to Piety*, 95–96, 121–122.

18. E. M. Smallwood, *The Jews Under Roman Rule* (Leiden: Brill, 1976), 99, cites some refined points of religious law; these, however, must have been symbolic of broader concerns as well.

19. G. W. E. Nickelsburg, *Resurrection, Immortality, and Eternal Life in Intertestamental Judaism* (HTS 26; Cambridge, MA: Harvard University Press, 1972), 19; cf. 94–95 on 2 Maccabees 7.

20. Nickelsburg, *Resurrection, Immortality* 42.

21. Nickelsburg, 172.

22. Thackeray's unfortunate translation "zeal for the law" in *War* 1.654 only provides more

fuel for the fires of those who find "the ideal of zeal" and "the Zealots" behind every incident of resistance to Roman or Herodian tyranny.

23. M. Hengel, *Die Zeloten* (Leiden: Brill, 1961), 107–108 (with references).

24. M. Hengel, *Victory over Violence* (Philadelphia: Fortress, 1973), 31–32; similarly in *Die Zeloten*, 89; D. M. Rhoads, *Israel in Revolution* (Philadelphia: Fortress, 1976), 55.

25. M. Stern, "Zealots," *Encyclopedia Judaica*, suppl. vol. 1972, 136, 140.

26. Vs. Hengel, *Zeloten*, 86.

27. M. Stern, "Sicarii and Zealots," in *WHJP* 8:268. It would seem to be a rather questionable approach (considering what needs to be proven) to "attempt to extend our knowledge of Judah of Gaulanitis . . . by identifying him with Judah son of Hezekiah. . . ."

28. On Menahem and the Sicarii and their relation with Judas and the Fourth Philosophy, see R. A. Horsley, "Menahem in Jerusalem: A Brief Messianic Episode among the Sicarii —not 'Zealot Messianism,' " *Nov T* 27 (1985):334–348.

29. I.e., against L. H. Feldman's translation of *Ant.* 18.4, etc., in the Loeb ed.

30. Translation taken from Horsley and Hanson, *Bandits, Prophets, and Messiahs*, 191–192.

31. See, e.g., Neusner, *From Politics to Piety;* and Tcherikover, *Hellenistic Civilization and the Jews.*

32. Hengel, *Victory over Violence*, 30–33; *Zeloten*, ch. 3; Stern, "Sicarii and Zealots," 266–268.

33. Hengel, *Zeloten*, 108,94.

34. Hengel, *Zeloten*, 120. Hengel's further discussion of the eschatological liberation-hope of the Zealots et al. is all based on historically false presuppositions; e.g., 123,127,128.

35. Hengel makes too much of "emperor worship" in Jewish Palestine under Herod, since most of the imperial temples were in locations with heavy Gentile populations such as Caesarea. Nevertheless, see further Josephus, *War* 1.403–416; *Ant.* 15.262–275,292–299, 331–341,363–364.

CHAPTER 4: POPULAR MASS PROTESTS

1. H. Taine, *Les Origines De La France Contemporaire. La Revolution*, 3 vols. (Paris: 1897) 1.18,53–54,130,272, etc.; G. Lebon, *The Crown: A Study of the Popular Mind* (London: 1909).

2. E. J. Hobsbawm, *Primitive Rebels* (New York: Norton, 1965; orig. 1959), ch. 7, "The City Mob"; E. P. Thompson, "The Moral Economy of the English Crown in the Eighteenth Century," *Past and Present* 50 (1971):76–136; G. Rudé, *The Crowd in History* (New York: Wiley, 1964); *The Crowd in the French Revolution* (Oxford: Clarendon Press, 1959).

3. Hobsbawm, *Primitive Rebels*, 111.

4. Hobsbawm, *Primitive Rebels*, 111.

5. Hobsbawm, 113–114; Rudé, *The Crowd in History*, 61,198,204–205.

6. Rudé, *Crowd*, 61; Thompson, "Moral Economy," 115–119.

7. "The popular ethic sanctioned direct action by the crowd." Thompson, 98; see further Thompson, 98–101,131–136.

8. Hobsbawm, *Primitive Rebels*, 111.

9. Rudé, *Crowd,* 62.
10. Rudé, *Crowd,* 60; Thompson, 107–112,114–119.
11. Rudé, *Crowd,* 228–229.
12. Hobsbawm, 114.
13. Hobsbawm, 115.
14. Rudé, *Crowd,* 217–219,61–62.
15. See further Thompson, 78–79.
16. Hobsbawm, 117.
17. Rudé, *Crowd,* 49–51.
18. Rudé, *Crowd,* 49–61,220–221.
19. G. Rudé, *Paris and London in the Eighteenth Century,* 87.
20. Hobsbawm, 116.
21. Hobsbawm, 119.
22. Rudé, *Crowd,* 55–59,22,28,261.
23. V. Tcherikover, "Was Jerusalem a 'Polis'?" *IEJ* 14 (1964):61–78.
24. This corresponds with the portrayal of Jerusalem by J. Jeremias, *Jerusalem in the Time of Jesus* (Philadelphia: Fortress, 1969).
25. Vs. M. Hengel, *Victory over Violence* (Philadelphia: Fortress, 1973), 32,37–38; E. M. Smallwood, *The Jews Under Roman Rule* (Leiden: Brill, 1976), 155.
26. P. W. Barnett, "Under Tiberias All Was Quiet," *NTS* 21 (1974–1975):569–570; M. Stern, "The Province of Judea," *JPFC* 1:358
27. *HJP* 1.379–381; M. Stern, "The Province of Judea."
28. E. M. Smallwood, "Some Notes on the Jews under Tiberius," *Latomus* 15 (1956):327.
29. C. H. Kraeling, "The Episode of the Roman Standards at Jerusalem," *HTR* 35 (1942): 263–289.
30. So Kraeling, "Roman Standards," *HTR* 35 (1942):274.
31. Cf. what may have been behind Jesus' saying about "oaths" in Matthew 5:34–35.
32. Cf. J. Gutmann, "The Second Commandment and the Image in Judaism," *HUCA* 32 (1961):169–174; E. R. Goodenough, *Jewish Symbols in the Greco-Roman Period* (New York: Pantheon, 1953–) vol. 8, 121–141; because Goodenough's approach is so general and synthetic, it is difficult to apply his conclusions to any specific Jewish community in particular, such as first-century Judea.
33. Kraeling, "Roman Standards," 275–277.
34. A. D. Nock, "The Roman Army and the Roman Religious Year," *HTR* 45 (1952):239, is characteristically cautious on this matter; but he does allow that "to Tacitus and Tertullian the Roman army standards appear to be the gods of the army."
35. C. Roth, "An Ordinance Against Images in Jerusalem, A.D. 66," *HTR* 49 (1956):170, mentions in passing "political resentment" as a factor.
36. A. V. Domaszewski, *Die Religion des Romischen Heeres,* 1895, as cited by Kraeling, "Roman Standards," 275.
37. So J. P. Lémonon, *Pilate et le gouvernement de la Judée* (Paris: Gabalda, 1981), 152–153; and Gutmann, "The 'Second Commandment' . . . ," 170–175. Josephus explains apologetically: "Our legislator [Moses!], not in order to put, as it were, a prophetic veto upon honours paid to the Roman authority, but out of contempt for a practice profitable to neither God nor man, forbade the making of images, alike of any living creature, and much more of God . . ." (*Ag. Apion,* 75).

38. G. Sharp, *The Politics of Nonviolent Action* (Boston: Porter Sargent, 1973), 547.

39. Cf. the similar passive resistance in 1959 in Ixopo, South Africa: when ordered to disperse by police prepared to make a baton charge, African women demonstrators went down on their knees and began to pray; the baton charge was not made, and "police hung around helplessly." From Sharp, *Politics of Nonviolent Action*, 550, n. 109.

40. If the date of 3 Chislev in Megillat Taanit, as the day on which "the images were removed from the Temple-court," refers to Pilate's removal of the Roman army standards (instead of to the rededication of the Temple in 164 B.C.E. after the profanation by Antiochus IV Epiphanes), it indicates how profound an impression was made in Jewish society by these events. See Kraeling, 283; Smallwood, *The Jews*, 161–162, n. 62.

41. *HJP*, vol. 1, ch. 2, par. 24.

42. *HJP*, 1.379.

43. So also P. L. Maier, "The Fate of Pontius Pilate," *Hermes* 99 (1971):364.

44. Statements in Mishnah *Shekalim* 4.2–3 would appear to authorize expenditure of surplus "shekalim" on public projects.

45. So Colson, in LCL edition, vol. 10, xxiii; followed by P. L. Maier, "The Episode of the Golden Roman Shields at Jerusalem," *HTR* 62 (1969):120.

46. Maier, "Golden Roman Shields," 113–115.

47. R. A. Horsley, "The High Priests and the Politics of Roman Palestine," *JSJ* 17 (1986) 23–55; cf. E. M. Smallwood, "High Priests and Politics in Roman Palestine," *JTS* 13 (1962) 14–34.

48. Smallwood prefers Philo's *Legatio ad Gaium* to Josephus' two accounts as the more historically and chronologically reliable. Her reasons, however, are unconvincing and problematic. Philo, who was in Rome during the events surrounding the plan to place Gaius's statue in the Temple, may have been familiar with affairs in Rome, but this does not mean he had reliable information on the sequence of events in Palestine. Some elements of Josephus's accounts may well appear as "fairy tale," yet Philo's whole treatise is "essentially a Philippic and not a sober history," and includes "heavy-colored emotion and lyricism, rhetoric, and exaggeration" throughout (see Maier, "Golden Roman Shields," 120). The chronology at the beginning of Josephus's report in the *Antiquities* is problematic, but this does not discredit his whole account, and the chronological difficulties of Philo's report for the later part of the sequence of events are far more problematic. Little weight, in any case, should be placed on the speeches put in the actors' mouths by either Philo (vs. Smallwood) or Josephus. The latter's account in the *Antiquities* appears to be the most satisfactory source with regard to the sequence of *events*. Any historical reconstruction of the events, of course, must depend upon critical examination and comparison of all source materials. The chronology of events as reconstructed by J. P. V. D. Balsdon in *JRS* 24 (1934):19–24 appears to be the most satisfactory. With Josephus it places the Jewish demonstrations in the late fall of 40 C.E. during the sowing season, vs. Philo and Smallwood, who prefer to place them at the harvest season in early summer.

49. Some scholarly reconstructions of the events, with little attempt at source-criticism, merely conflate Philo's and Josephus's accounts or, in effect, add the variants in one to the variants in the other; e.g., *HJP*, 1.389–397.

50. Smallwood, "High Priests and Politics," 23.

51. Hengel, *Victory over Violence,* 37; Smallwood, *The Jews,* 176; *Legatio,* 275; Stern, "Province of Judea," 356.
52. Is this reflected in Tacitus, first account, *Hist.* 5.9? "Then, when Caligula ordered the Jews to set his statue in their Temple, they chose rather to resort to arms; but the emporor's death put an end to their uprising." In his later account, *Annals* 12.54,2 he mentions only "rioting" and "disaffection," no "resort to arms."
53. See G. Sharp, *Politics of Nonviolent Action,* 261–262 on "peasant strike."
54. Cf. G. Rudé, *The Crowd in History* (New York: Wiley, 1964), 23–31.
55. Cf. Sharp, *Politics of Nonviolent Action,* 737,745,746.
56. J. V. Bondurant, *Conquest of Violence: The Gandhian Philsophy of Conflict* (Berkeley: University of California Press, 1969); and Sharp, *Politics of Nonviolent Action.*

CHAPTER 5: APOCALYPTIC ORIENTATION AND HISTORICAL ACTION

1. See M. Hengel, *Was Jesus a Revolutionary?* (Philadelphia: Fortress, 1971), 10–11; and *Victory Over Violence* (Philadelphia: Fortress, 1973), 30,35; O. Cullmann, *Jesus and the Revolutionaries* (New York: Harper & Row, 1970), 1–5; Kohler, "Zealots" (in Cullmann, 73); W. R. Farmer, *Maccabees, Zealots, and Josephus* (New York: Columbia University Press, 1956), 49,52,56,83,123.
2. E.g., K. Kohler, "Zealots," *Jewish Encyclopedia* (New York: Funk & Wagnalls, 1905); M. Hengel, *Die Zeloten* (Leiden: Brill, 1961).
3. E.g., in a standard introductory textbook, R. A. Spivey and D. M. Smith, *Anatomy of the New Testament,* 3rd ed. (New York: Macmillan, 1982), 31, we find, almost casually in passing: "The Zealots sought to realize their hope by the recovery of national autonomy, under God, through armed rebellion."
4. M. Stern, "Sicarii and Zealots," *WHJP* 8:263–297.
5. Stern, 265.
6. Stern, 266,299, acknowledges that there is only scanty evidence for "the ideology of Jewish freedom" in the first place and virtually no evidence that would connect it with "the extremist movement and its factions," yet insists on perpetuating the fictional ideology.
7. Vs. Farmer, *Maccabees, Zealots,* 124.
8. Hengel, *Zeloten,* 232; Stern, "Sicarii and Zealots," 266; Stumpff, art. on *"zelos, zelotes,* etc.," *TDNT* 2:879–883.
9. Even Hengel points this out; *Zeloten,* 154.
10. M. Smith, "Zealots and Sicarii, Their Origins and Relations," *HTR* 64 (1971):9; B. Salomonsen, "Some Remarks on the Zealots with Special Regard to the Term 'Qannaim' in Rabbinic Literature," *NTS* 13 (1966):168–169,175.
11. Hengel, *Zeloten,* 178–180.
12. Hengel, 157.
13. Hengel, 172.
14. R. Hayward, "Phineas—the Same Is Elijah: The Origins of a Rabbinic Tradition," *JJS* 29 (1978):22–34.

15. H. C. Kee, "Testaments of the Twelve Patriarchs," in *The Old Testament Pseudepigrapha*, 2 vols. (Garden City: Doubleday, 1983–1984), 1.777–778.

16. Hengel, *Zeloten*, 181–188; Farmer, *Maccabees, Zealots*.

17. Hengel, *Zeloten*, 187–188.

18. Vs. Hengel, *Was Jesus a Revolutionist?*

19. Considerable advances have been achieved in the last decade or two with regard to our understanding of apocalyptic *literature* and of the particular historical contexts in which particular apocalypses have been written. See especially J. J. Collins, *The Apocalyptic Imagination* (New York: Crossroad, 1984); and G. W. E. Nickelsburg, *Jewish Literature Between the Bible and the Mishnah* (Philadelphia: Fortress, 1981). Such advances may not be directly useful for understanding the motivations of Jewish resistance groups or incidents. But by providing a clearer picture of the circles that produced the earlier apocalyptic texts, they do enable us to reconstruct a more precise sense of the possible orientation of later groups involved in similar circumstances.

20. P. D. Hanson, "Apocalypticism," *IDB* suppl. vol., 28–34.

21. Hanson, "Apocalypticism," 30–32, while an important modification of earlier treatment, still overplays the differences.

22. S. Niditch. *The Symbolic Vision in Biblical Tradition* (Chico, CA: Scholars Press, 1980).

23. On Daniel 12:1–3 and related texts, see further Nickelsburg, *Jewish Literature*, 11–33.

24. Hanson, 30.

25. Hanson, 30.

26. It is extremely unfortunate that biblical scholars did not follow the lead of Amos Wilder, who combined an appreciation of the distinctive apocalyptic use of language with an attention to concrete historical circumstances and who steadfastly resisted the willful literalism and metaphysical tendencies of the hostile German (Lutheran) theologians. Apropos of the issue at hand:

> Biblical theologians tend to create too great a disjunction between the transcendental imagery and the historical process. They see the reality conveyed as belonging to the sphere of sheer idealization and fantasy. Or they allow a metaphysical or theological dualism to obscure the concrete meaning of the texts. Too often they fail to enter into the late Jewish and early Christian mythical [his unfortunate term for apocalyptic] frame of mind. ("Eschatological Imagery and Earthly Circumstance," *NTS* 5 [1959]:232)

27. W. Schmithals, *The Apocalyptic Movement: Introduction and Interpretation* (Nashville: Abingdon, 1975), 108.

28. It bespeaks a misunderstanding of and lack of sympathy with the persecuted *maskilim* when the distinguished Old Testament scholar von Rad accuses them of "a great loss of historical sensitivity," in *Theologie des alten Testaments* II, 4th ed. (Munich: Kaiser, 1966), 320–321.

29. Hanson, 28,30–31.

30. Vs. Hanson, 30–31; see rather Collins, *Apocalyptic Imagination*, 56–63; G. W. E. Nickelsburg, "Social Aspects of Palestinian Jewish Apocalypticism," in D. Hellholm, ed. *Apocalypticism in the Mediterranean World and the Near East* (Tübingen: Mohr, 1983), 650–654.

31. See Horsley and Hanson, *Bandits, Prophets and Messiahs*, ch. 4.

32. The remembering and the creative envisioning functions of the apocalyptic imagination are embodied in the very literary forms of the apocalypse and the testament insofar as both are revelations about the course of history given to or by revered figures of the past, such as Enoch, Moses, or Daniel.

CHAPTER 6: ABANDONING THE UNHISTORICAL QUEST

1. See R. A. Horsley, "Ethics and Exegesis: 'Love Your Enemies' and The Doctrine of Non-Violence," *JAAR* 54 (1986):3–31.

2. R. Bultmann, *Jesus Christ and Mythology* (New York: Scribners, 1958); *Jesus and the Word* (New York: Scribners, 1958, orig. 1926).

3. See W. C. Smith, *The Meaning and End of Religion* (New York: Mentor, 1964), ch. 2.

4. See, e.g., the influential books, G. Bornkamm, *Jesus of Nazareth* (New York: Harper, 1960, etc.), e.g., 66–67,121–123; J. Jeremias, *New Testament Theology* (London: SCM, 1971), e.g., 71–72,122–123,228–229. Proclaimed explicitly by O. Cullmann, *Jesus and the Revolutionaries* (New York: Harper & Row, 1970), 1–10. More critical historical awareness, e.g., in W. D. Davies, *The Gospel and the Land* (Berkeley: University of California Press, 1974), 344.

5. J. Weiss, *Jesus' Proclamation of the Kingdom of God* (Philadelphia: Fortress, 1971; orig. 1892); A. Schweitzer, *The Quest of the Historical Jesus* (New York: Macmillan, 1961; orig. 1906), esp. ch. 19.

6. R. Bultmann, *New Testament Theology*, 2 vols. (New York: Scribners, 1951–1955), 1.4.

7. Bultmann, *Jesus and the Word*, 35–37.

8. See ch. 5, nn. 19 + 30.

9. Illustrations of such a less literalistic doctrinal and more concrete contextual reading of key apocalyptic texts could be multiplied. For example: in The Apocalypse of Weeks, 1 Enoch 93 and 91, the "new heaven" of the tenth week seems subordinate to the real fulfillment, the perpetuation of "goodness and righteousness" (i.e., societal life the way God wills it) during "weeks without number forever"; in Assumption of Moses 10 the imagery of "cosmic catastrophe" and the elimination of Satan used in connection with God's kingdom appearing throughout all the creation serves as a vivid expression of how fantastic will be God's vindication and restoration of his people against their oppressive enemies, probably the Romans.

10. See, e.g., D. Juel, *Messiah and Temple* (SBLDS 31; Missoula: Scholars, 1977) 122–123,138,212–213; J. R. Donahue, *Are You the Christ?* (Missoula: Scholars, 1973), 73–75.

11. A. N. Wilder, "Eschatological Imagery and Earthly Circumstance," *NTS* 5 (1959): 229–245.

12. J. Weiss, *Jesus' Proclamation of the Kingdom of God.*

13. J. H. Yoder, *The Politics of Jesus* (Grand Rapids: Eerdmans, 1972).

14. Bultmann, *History of the Synoptic Tradition* (London: Blackwell, 1963); and more recently, see esp. E. Güttgemanns, *Candid Questions Concerning Gospel Form Criticism* (PTMS 26; Pittsburgh: Pickwick, 1979); W. H. Kelber, *The Oral and Written Gospel* (Philadelphia: Fortress, 1983); J. G. Gager, "The Gospel and Jesus: Some Doubts about Methods," *JR*, 54 (1974):244–272. Further references in Kelber.

15. Kelber, *The Oral and Written Gospel*, 15.

16. Kelber, *The Oral and Written Gospel*, 19.
17. H. Koester, "One Jesus, Four Primitive Gospels," *HTR* 61 (1968):203–247.
18. Kelber, *The Oral and Written Gospel*, 20–24; and contra G. Theissen, *The Sociology of Early Palestinian Christianity* (Philadelphia: Fortress, 1978) and "Itinerant Radicalism: The Tradition of Jesus' Sayings from the Perspective of the Sociology of Literature," *The Bible and Liberation: A Radical Religion Reader*, ed. N. Gottwald and A. C. Wire (Berkeley: 1976), 73–83.

CHAPTER 7: THE KINGDOM OF GOD AND THE RENEWAL OF ISRAEL

1. Esp. R. Bultmann, *History of the Synoptic Tradition* (Oxford: Blackwell, 1963); N. Perrin, *Rediscovering the Teachings of Jesus* (New York: Harper & Row, 1967); and *Jesus and the Language of the Kingdom* (Philadelphia: Fortress, 1976).
2. On this and the following paragraph, see Perrin, *Rediscovering the Teachings of Jesus*, 54–63.
3. As Perrin himself has argued, *Rediscovering*, 173–185.
4. Perrin, *Rediscovering*, 60.
5. See esp. W. G. Kümmel, *Promise and Fulfilment* (London: SCM, 1957).
6. Vs. B. D. Chilton, *God in Strength: Jesus' Announcement of the Kingdom* (Freistadt, West Germany: Ploechl, 1979), 287.
7. Vs. Perrin, *Rediscovering*, 67.
8. Perrin, *Rediscovering*, 59.
9. *Rediscovering*, 203.
10. *Rediscovering*, 173–185.
11. Bultmann, *History of the Synoptic Tradition*, 109.
12. Perrin, *Rediscovering*, 163.
13. Cf. Perrin, *Rediscovering*, 102–104.
14. J. Jeremias, *The Lord's Prayer* (Philadelphia: Fortress, 1973).
15. Perrin, *Jesus and the Language of the Kingdom*, 28–29,47.
16. For fuller analysis behind the following interpretation, see Perrin, *Rediscovering*, 165–191.
17. Of uncertain date, but most recently thought to have been written at least by the first-century c.e.; J. J. Collins, *The Apocalyptic Imagination* (New York: Crossword, 1984), 143; J. H. Charlesworth, *The Old Testament Pseudepigrapha and the New Testament* (Cambridge: Cambridge University Press, 1985), 89.
18. Perrin, *Rediscovering*, 195–197, apparently reverting to the parousia of a divine-figure reading of these texts, which he had earlier rejected in favor of the variant use of Daniel 7 interpretation, denies authenticity to these sayings, against Bultmann and Colpe.
19. Kümmel, *Promise and Fulfilment*, 43–44.
20. The Aramaic term behind "son of man" in this and similar cases could apparently be used as a circumlocution for "I," as in the English "yours truly." Also, Perrin's treatment of Jesus' "table fellowship" as being primarily with "tax collectors and sinners," in *Rediscovering* 102–106, distracts attention from the general sense of renewal celebrated in Jesus' table fellowship and misrepresents the issue of "sinners" as well. On the latter

issue, see E. P. Sanders' critique of Perrin in *Jesus and Judaism* (Philadelphia: Fortress, 1985), esp. 200–203, and chapter 8 below.

21. J. A. Sanders, "The Ethics of Election in Luke's Great Banquet Parable, *"Essays in Old Testament Ethics: J. Philip Hyatt, in memoriam,* ed. Crenshaw and Willis (New York: KTAV, 1974), 257–258, interprets it thus in Luke.

22. This is true once we recognize and peel away the Lucan interest in who turned out to be included, with "the poor and maimed and blind and lame" of vs. 21 repeating the list in 14:13 of the previous story.

23. Jeremias, *New Testament Theology,* 86–92, provides a concise treatment of the situation. For a recent critical reconsideration of the oral transmission and shaping of the healing and exorcism stories, see W. Kelber, *The Oral and Written Gospel,* 46–55; cf., other recent literature in his notes.

24. It is impossible to develop this line of analysis of Jesus' healings and exorcisms (and the sickness and demonology to which they respond) more fully in the context of this book. However, I hope to elaborate such an analysis in the near future. The groundwork has been laid by much recent literary and historical examination of the "miracle stories." See esp. G. Theissen, *The Miracle Stories of the Early Christian Tradition* (Edinburgh: T. & T. Clark, 1983); and H. C. Kee, *Miracle in the Early Christian World* (New Haven: Yale, 1983).

25. E.g., Jeremias, *New Testament Theology,* 114–115, and Perrin, *Rediscovering,* 102.

26. See, e.g., Martin Buber, *The Prophetic Faith* (New York: Harper & Row, 1960), 188–197.

27. On how some healing stories thus expose the restrictions of the religious authorities, see further A. C. Wire, "The Structure of the Gospel Miracle Stories and Their Tellers," *Semeia* 11 (1978):92–96; and on the purposeful challenge posed in the healings on the sabbath, see Elisabeth Schüssler Fiorenza, *In Memory of Her* (New York: Crossroad, 1983), 124–126.

28. Matthew must have changed "finger" to "spirit," since "spirit" is a favorite Lucan term (see esp. 4:18).

29. See n. 24 above.

30. R. A. Horsley, "Who Were the Witches? The Social Roles of the Accused in the European Witch Hunts of the Sixteenth and Seventeenth Centuries," *Journal of Interdisciplinary History* 9 (1979):689–715; and "Further Reflections on Witchcraft and European Folk Religion," *History of Religions* 19 (1979):71–95.

31. See further Perrin, *Rediscovering,* 66.

32. Perrin, still working out of the modern individualistic orientation, argues just the opposite; *Rediscovering,* 67.

33. Perrin, *Jesus and the Language of the Kingdom,* 46.

34. E.g., Perrin, *Rediscovering,,* ch. 2; Chilton, *God in Strength,* "Conclusions," 275–298.

35. Recent critical reconstruction based on Luke 16:16 in Chilton, *God in Strength,* 203–230.

36. B. F. Meyer, *The Aims of Jesus* (London: SCM, 1979); J. Riches, *Jesus and the Transformation of Judaism* (London: Darton, Longman & Todd, 1980); E. P. Sanders, *Jesus and Judaism* (Philadelphia: Fortress, 1985). C. H. Dodd had made the point in his 1954 Evans Lectures, *The Founder of Christianity* (New York: Macmillan, 1970), ch. 5, as had G. B. Caird a decade later, *Jesus and the Jewish Nation* (London: Athlone, 1965).

37. Respectively, for example, J. Riches, *Jesus and the Transformation of Judaism;* G. Theissen,

The *Sociology of Early Palestinian Christianity;* and E. P. Sanders, *Jesus and Judaism.*

38. See Jeremias's arguments against Bultmann's doubts in *Jesus' Promise to the Nations* (London: SCM, 1958), 27.
39. Sanders, *Jesus and Judaism,* 106–117.
40. These prophetic woes are surely from Jesus, not from early Christian prophets, with Fitzmyer, *Luke* 2.852. In their current setting in Matthew and Luke these woes may be anti-Jewish, as older form-critics suggested; but that simply means that the early church, in carrying the words of Jesus over into a changed context and perspective, failed to maintain Jesus' hermeneutics, a prophetic critique of his own community, as explained by J. A. Sanders, "The Ethics of Election . . . ," 251–253.
41. See R. P. Meye, *Jesus and the Twelve* (Grand Rapids: Eerdmans, 1968), 192–193; Sanders, *Jesus and Judaism,* 98–106, arguing against Bultmann, Vielhauer, and others.
42. See further the arguments in Meye and Sanders.
43. Bultmann, *History of the Synoptic Tradition,* 158–159.
44. W. D. Davies, *The Gospel and the Land* (Berkeley: University of California Press, 1974), 364–365.
45. E.g., M. Trautmann, *Zeichenhafte Handlungen Jesu* (Würzburg: Echter, 1980), 199; but far from a contradiction, judgment includes redemption as the alternative to its opposite, punishment.
46. Davies, *The Gospel and the Land,* 365.
47. Herntrich, *"krinō,"* *TDNT* 3.923–932.
48. We should also note that the description of this function of the Council flows directly into the description of the Council as 'a House of Holiness for Aaron, . . . precious cornerstone, . . . Most Holy Dwelling for Aaron, . . . an agreeable offering atoning for the Land. . . ." Jesus may have understood the new community he started in parallel terms as the new Temple. See below, ch. 10.
49. It is worth noting also that the social-economic content of justice or deliverance to be looked for among the peoples in the [last?] judgment in Matthew 25:31–46 (probably a later tradition) is the same as that initiated by Jesus' ministry, continued in the disciples' mission, and to be established in their eschatological role of delivering and establishing justice for the twelve tribes of Israel.

CHAPTER 8: THE RENEWAL OF LOCAL COMMUNITY, I: EGALITARIAN SOCIAL RELATIONS

1. See, e.g., G. Aulen, *Jesus in Contemporary Historical Research* (London: SPCK, 1976), 87; E. Schweizer, *Church Order in the New Testament* (London: SCM, 1961), 20,25.
2. It is "a well-defined fellowship" in Jeremias, *New Testament Theology,* 170; but the proof text, Luke 11:1, is clearly redactional. The church is then seen to be "the successor of the group of disciples," in Schweizer, *Church Order,* 28.
3. E.g., Schweizer, *Church Order,* 20–22, 29–31,47.
4. M. Hengel, *Was Jesus a Revolutionist?* (Philadelphia: Fortress, 1971), 23–25; O. Cullmann, *Jesus and the Revolutionaries* (New York: Harper & Row, 1970).
5. Perrin, *Rediscovering the Teaching of Jesus* (New York: Harper & Row), 102–103.
6. E. Schüssler Fiorenza, *In Memory of Her* (New York: Crossroad, 1983), 126–129; L.

Schottroff and W. Stegemann, *Jesus of Nazareth: Hope of the Poor* (Maryknoll: Orbis, 1986), 6–13.

7. J. R. Donahue "Tax Collectors and Sinners: An Attempt at Classification," *CBQ* 33 (1971):51–52.

8. E.g., Perrin, *Rediscovering;* Schüssler Fiorenza, *In Memory of Her;* E. P. Sanders, *Jesus and Judaism* (Philadelphia; Fortress, 1985).

9. E.g., Schüssler Fiorenza, 127; Perrin, 102.

10. For a more detailed and documented analysis, see W. O. Walker, "Jesus and the Tax Collectors," *JBL* 97 (1978):221–238.

11. Jeremias, *New Testament Theology,* 109.

12. Sanders, *Jesus,* 174.

13. Bultmann, *History of the Synoptic Tradition* (Oxford: Blackwell, 1963), 18.

14. Sanders, *Jesus,* 207.

15. See further Bultmann, *History of the Synoptic Tradition,* 28,56.

16. Walker, "Jesus and the Tax Collectors," 234–236.

17. Sanders, *Jesus,* 326 and passim. The book also contains a sharp critique of how earlier interpreters have understood the term "sinners" (ch. 6).

18. E.g., Perrin, *Rediscovering,* begins his discussion of the issue by calling attention to "the frequently recurring 'tax collectors and sinners' in the gospel tradition" (90), then acknowledges that Jesus' table fellowship with 'tax collectors and sinners' "has all but disappeared from the gospel tradition" (102), only to reiterate his actual working assumption a few pages later: that "the emphasis upon 'tax collectors and sinners' . . . is so widespread in the tradition" (106). Sanders, *Jesus,* similarly acknowledges the problematic character of the gospel passages mentioning Jesus' association with sinners (174–175) but then argues that Jesus understood his own mission as primarily to "the lost" and the "sinners" (179) and offered the kingdom to the wicked even though they did not repent (e.g., 207,319,322,340).

19. With Sanders, *Jesus* 175, vs. Perrin, *Rediscovering,* 121–122.

20. This is deliberate and habitual breaking of the Torah, as explained by Sanders, *Jesus;* cf. Jeremias, *New Testament Theology.*

21. This is something not apparently done in the secondary literature.

22. Jeremias, *New Testament Theology;* E. P. Sanders, *Paul and Palestinian Judaism* (Philadelphia: Fortress, 1977), 142–143; *Jesus,* ch. 6, esp. 177–178. Perrin, *Rediscovering,* 90–94, follows Jeremias on this meaning, but realizes there are others as well.

23. J. Jeremias, *Jerusalem at the Time of Jesus* (Philadelphia: Fortress, 1969), ch. 14.

24. Sanders, *Jesus,* 178.

25. Jeremias, *New Testament Theology,* 109.

26. M. Jastrow, *A Dictionary of the Targumim, the Talmud Bibli and Yerushalmi, and the Midrashic Literature,* 2 vols. (New York: Pardes, 1950), 1.537–588.

27. One thinks of the character "Sportin' Life" in Gershwin's *Porgy and Bess* or the terms "playboys" or "partyboys"; cf. W. O. Walker, "Jesus and the Tax Collectors," 237. It is worth noting that both Luke 18:9–14 and Matthew 21:31–32 would make more sense if the original tradition had an Aramaic term meaning something like "playboys" instead of the Greek translation (a misunderstanding?) of "toll collectors."

28. Recently, see L. Schottroff and W. Stegemann, *Jesus of Nazareth: Hope of the Poor,* 16–28; E. Schüssler Fiorenza, *In Memory of Her,* 122–130.

29. E.g., Bultmann, *History of the Synoptic Tradition,* 126; Kümmel *Promise and Fulfilment* (London: SCM, 1957), 109–112.

30. Jeremias, *New Testament Theology,* 113.

31. See further G. Theissen, *The Miracle Stories of the Early Christian Tradition* (Edinburgh; T. & T. Clark, 1983), 129–140.

32. G. Theissen, *Sociology of Early Palestinian Christianity* (Philadelphia: Fortress, 1978), 8–14.

33. K. Kohler, "Abba, Father," *JQR* 23 (1901):567–580.

34. Bultmann, *History of the Synoptic Tradition,* 154–155.

35. Perrin, *Rediscovering,* 141; Bultmann, 161–162 vs. 163.

36. Bultmann, 49–50, vs. the argument but not the evidence in A. J. Hultgren, *Jesus and His Adversaries* (Minneapolis: Augsburg, 1979), 121–122 and notes.

37. But not certainly; see Bultmann, 136,146; and Hultgren, 124–125.

38. See further Schüssler Fiorenza, 143–145.

39. Bultmann, 29–30, vs. 143.

40. Bultmann, 129–130.

41. Bultmann, like many other scholars of his generation, assumed that this later, rabbinic pattern of "eschatological" thinking was also current much earlier, as in his comments on Mark 10:29–30, *History of the Synoptic Tradition,* 110–111.

42. Bultmann, 125.

43. Cf. Perrin, *Rediscovering,* 141.

44. Perrin, *Rediscovering,* 145; cf. Bultmann, 103; Fitzmyer, *The Gospel According to Luke* 2 vols. (Anchor Bible vols. 28 and 28A; Garden City, NY: Doubleday, 1981–1985) 2:1044.

45. Bultmann, 144.

46. Schüssler Fiorenza, *In Memory of Her,* 149–150.

47. See further J. Neusner, *First Century Judaism in Crisis* (Nashville: Abingdon, 1975), ch. 2; A. Saldarini, *Pharisees, Scribes, and Sadducees* (Wilmington, DE: Glazier, 1987).

48. See J. B. Frey, *Corpus Inscriptionum Iudaicarum* I (Rome and Paris: 1936), 95–96, no. 494, 509, 511; B. Lifshitz, *Donateurs et fondateurs dans les Synagogues juives* (Paris: 1967), no. 9, 10; J. D. M. Derrett, "Matthew 23, 8–10, a Midrash on Isaiah 54, 13 and Jeremiah 31, 33–34," *Biblica* 62 (1981): 379–380.

49. J. Jeremias, *New Testament Theology,* 68; K. Kohler, "Abba, Father," *JQR* 23 (1901): 567–580.

50. See further Jeremias, *New Testament Theology,* 62–68,179–182.

51. Ironically, within a few generations the church, having fully reverted, was appealing to the Father as sanction for submission to patriarchal-monarchial authority, the bishop being a type of the Father (Ignatius of Antioch, *To the Trallians* 2.1,2; 3.1). Yet this serves to illustrate just how radical Jesus' opposition to patriarchal hierarchies was even at the local level, the hierarchies that maintained the structural injustice that the kingdom of God would overcome and replace with egalitarian social relations in accordance with the will of God.

52. Fitzmyer, *Luke,* 2.1414.

53. E.g., F. W. Beare, *The Gospel According to Matthew* (Oxford: Blackwell, 1981), 428.

54. W. Bauer-Arndt-Gingrich.

55. Fitzmyer, *Luke,* 2.1414.

CHAPTER 9: THE RENEWAL OF LOCAL COMMUNITY, II: SOCIAL-ECONOMIC COOPERATION AND AUTONOMY

1. Luke 8:18 indicates precisely what position a rich person was likely to hold in such a society: that of a government officer.
2. Fitzmyer, *Luke*, 2.1109.
3. Particularly by H. Schürmann, *Das Lukasevangelium*, on which see Fitzmyer, *Luke* 1.527, and S. H. Ringe, *Jesus, Liberation, and the Biblical Jubilee* (Philadelphia: Fortress, 1985), 43; and B. Chilton, *God in Strength*, 123–178.
4. See esp. J. H. Yoder, *The Politics of Jesus* (Grand Rapids: Eerdmans, 1972), chs. 2–3, who drew on the earlier work of André Trocmè, *Jesus and the Nonviolent Revolution* (Scottdale, PA: Herald, 1973), Part 1; and, more cautiously, Sharon H. Ringe, *Jesus, Liberation, and the Biblical Jubilee*, chs. 3–6.
5. See Jeremias, *Jerusalem*, 143.
6. The following analysis relies heavily on the work of Jeremias, *New Testament Theology*, 193–203; and Fitzmyer, *Luke*, 2.896–907.
7. With Origen and Fitzmyer, *Luke*, 2.900.
8. The most explosive incident with repercussions for both Samaritan and Judean ruling classes is recounted in Josephus, *War* 2.232–246; *Ant.* 20.118–136.
9. E.g., David Mealand, *Poverty and Expectation in the Gospels* (London: SPCK, 1980), 85.
10. The parallels in Gospel Thomas no. 36 and OxyP 655:1–17 do not provide access to an earlier stage of the tradition in this case.
11. The following discussion builds upon and uses material from my essay "Ethics and Exegesis: 'Love Your Enemies' and the Doctrine of Non-Violence," *JAAR* 54 (1986): 3–31.
12. This is done even by biblical scholars, e.g., J. Piper, *Love Your Enemies* (Cambridge: Cambridge University Press, 1979), 96–99.
13. O. J. F. Seitz, "Love Your Enemies," *NTS* 16 (1969):43–44,46,48,50,52.
14. R. J. Daly, "The New Testament and the Early Church," *in Non-Violence Central to Christian Spirituality: Perspectives from Scripture to the Present*, ed. J. T. Culliton (Toronto: Edwin Mellen, 1982), 41,52; M. Hengel, *Victory over Violence* (Philadelphia: Fortress, 1973); L. Schottroff, "Non-Violence and the Love of One's Enemies," *Essays on the Love Command* (Philadelphia: Fortress, 1978), 9–39.
15. See also S. C. Mott, *Biblical Ethics and Social Change* (Oxford: Oxford University Press, 1982), 171–173.
16. S. D. Currie, "Matthew 5:39a—Resistance or Protest," *HTR* 57 (1964):140–145.
17. J. Piper, *Love Your Enemies* (Cambridge: Cambridge University Press, 1979), 58; and F. W. Beare, *The Gospel According to Matthew*, (Oxford: Blackwell, 1963), 158.
18. Cf. Fitzmyer, *Luke*, 1.638.
19. Vs. J. Piper, *Enemies*, 89,90,95; V. P. Furnish, *The Love Command in the New Testament* (Nashville: Abingdon, 1972), 56.
20. C. H. Dodd, *Gospel and Law* (New York: Columbia University Press, 1951), 51–52.

21. See R. Tannehill, "The 'Focal Instance' as a Form of New Testament Speech: A Study of Matthew 5:39b–42," *JR* 50 (1970):377–382.
22. W. Klassen, *Love of Enemies* (Philadelphia: Fortress, 1984), 34–35.
23. N. Perrin, *Rediscovering the Teachings of Jesus* (New York: Harper, 1967), 147.
24. D. Daube, *The New Testament and Rabbinic Judaism* (London: Athlone, 1956), 257.
25. V. Furnish, *The Love Command,* 56.
26. Fitzmyer, *Luke* 1.639.
27. Vs. L. Schottfoff, "Non-Violence," 25.
28. D. Daube, *The New Testament and Rabbinic Judaism* (London: Athlone, 1956), 255–258.
29. Daube, *The New Testament,* 255–258.
30. And with the conclusions of scholarly analyses, such as A. N. Sherwin-White, *Roman Society and Roman Law in the New Testament* (Oxford: Clarendon, 1963), 139–142, who found in the Galilee portrayed by the Gospels a society characterized by the extremely poor masses over against the extremely wealthy upper class.
31. See further S. Applebaum, "Economic Life in Palestine," *JPFC* 2.657–667; M. Goodman, "The First Jewish Revolt: Social Conflict and the Problem of Debt," *JJS* 33 (1982): 417–427.
32. This is a frequent generalization about peasant societies. See, e.g., E. Perry, *Rebels and Revolutionaries in Northern China 1845–1945* (Stanford: Stanford University Press, 1980).
33. E.g., J. Jeremias, *Parables,* 43–44,96,180; *New Testament Theology* 134–135,152.
34. Fitzmyer, *Luke* 2.1002.
35. Beare, *Matthew,* 151.
36. As proposed by Bultmann, 172.
37. Bultmann, 99.
38. D. Catchpole, "Reproof and Reconcilation in the Q Community: A Study of the Tradition-History of Matthew 18, 15–17, 21–22/Luke 17,3–4," in *Studien zum Neuen Testament und seinen Umwelt* 8 (1985), 79–90.
39. T. W. Manson, *The Sayings of Jesus* (London: SCM, 1949), 139; B. H. Streeter, *Four Gospels* (London: 1926), 257,281.
40. Bultmann, 141.
41. See esp. Catchpole, 85.
42. Davies, 220–226.
43. See further esp. the arguments in Bultmann, *History of the Synoptic Tradition,* 34–35; H. Montefiore, "Jesus and the Temple Tax," *NTS* 12 (1965–1966):65,67–68,71; and W. Horbury, "The Temple Tax," in *Jesus and the Politics of His Day,* ed. E. Bammel and C. F. D. Moule (Cambridge: Cambridge University Press, 1986), 266–273.
44. References in Horbury, "The Temple Tax," 265, n. 2.
45. R. J. Cassidy, "Matthew 17:24–27—A Word on Civil Taxes," *CBQ* (1979):571–580.
46. See S. Safrai, "The Temple," in *JPFC* 1.879–884.
47. J. Liver, "The Half Shekel Offering in Biblical and Post-Biblical Literature," *HTR* 56(1963):173–198.
48. See J. D. M. Derrett, "Peter's Penny: Fresh Light on Matthew XVII: 24–27," *Nov T* 6 (1963):3.
49. See Allegro and Strugnell, in Horbury, 279, n. 75.
50. Horbury, 280; J. Neusner, *A Life of Yohannan ben Zakkai* . . . , 2nd ed. (Leiden: Brill, 1970), 185–187.

51. *HJP,* 2.257–274.
52. C. H. Dodd, *Historical Tradition in the Fourth Gospel* (Cambridge: Cambridge University Press, 1963), 381–382; A. Schlatter, *Der Evangelist Matthaeus,* 5th ed. (Stuttgart: 1959), 540.
53. So also Cassidy, 575; Derrett, 11; Horbury 282–285; Montefiore, 69–70; and D. Daube, "Responsibilities of Masters and Disciples," *NTS* 19 (1972–1973):14–15.
54. Similarly Daube, 14–15; Derrett, 12–13; Horbury, 283; Cassidy, 576.
55. Vs. P. Perkins, "Taxes in the New Testament." *Journal of Religious Ethics* 12 (1984):190.

CHAPTER 10: JUDGMENT OF THE RULING INSTITUTIONS

1. The last phrase is from J. Riches, *Jesus and the Transformation of Judaism* (London: Darton, Longman, 1980), 141–142; Sanders, *Jesus,* 61–63, provides a sharp critique of such interpretations.
2. Sanders, *Jesus,* 63–64.
3. *HJP,* 2.257–270.
4. Jeremias, *Jerusalem at the Time of Jesus,* 6, citing R. Hananiah, M. Eduy. ii.2; *HJP,* 2.261.
5. S. Safrai, "The Temple," 881, 879.
6. S. Safrai, "The Temple", 881.
7. S. Freyne, *Galilee, From Alexander the Great to Hadrian, 323* B.C.E. *to 135* C.E.: *A Study of Second Temple Judaism* (Notre Dame, IN: Notre Dame Press, 1980), ch. 7.
8. S. Freyne, *Galilee,* 283–286.
9. See R. A. Horsley, "Popular Prophetic Movements at the Time of Jesus, Their Principal Features and Social Origins" *JSNT,* 26 (1986): 3–27; and "Popular Messianic Movements around the Time of Jesus," *CBQ* 46 (1984):471–495.
10. Sanders, *Jesus,* chs. 2–3.
11. L. Gaston, *No Stone on Another* (Leiden: Brill, 1970), 102–128. Gaston's earlier critical survey of the sources should be given precedence to Sanders' recent revival of the old schematic treatment.
12. D. Flusser, *IEJ* 9 (1959):99–109; Gaston, 126–128.
13. Sanders, *Jesus,* 67,76, and the argument in chs. 1–2; Davies, *The Gospel and the Land,* 349, n. 45, ≠1.
14. Juel (see ch. 6, n. 10) 123,138.
15. This same objection has been made to the interpretation of Jesus on the model of "the Zealots."
16. Vs. Sanders, *Jesus,* chs. 2–3.
17. Fitzmyer, *Luke,* 2.1254–1255.
18. Fitzmyer, *Luke,* 2.1328.
19. "That the Gospel tradition has undergone a process of depoliticization has to be recognized"; W. D. Davies, *The Gospel and the Land* (Berkeley: University of California Press, 1974), 344.
20. See the recent survey by E. Bammel, "The Revolutionary Theory from Reimarus to

Brandon," in *Jesus and the Politics of his Day*, ed. E. Bammel and C. F. D. Moule (Cambridge: Cambridge University Press, 1984), 11–68. G. Petzke, "Der Historische Jesus in Der Sozialethischen Diskussion: Mark 12,13–17 par," in *Jesus Christ in Historie und Theologie: Festschrift Conzelmann*, ed. G. Strecker (Tübingen: Mohr, 1975), 223–235, contains some critique of the many apologetic nonpolitical interpretations.

21. More particularly, use of "the Zealots" as a foil for interpretation of Jesus has reinforced the obscuring effects of both the apologetic concerns and the false presuppositions in the quest for an apolitical Jesus. E.g., J. Jeremias, *New Testament Theology I* (London: SCM, 1971), 228–230; M. Hengel, *Was Jesus a Revolutionist?* (Philadelphia: Fortress, 1971); O. Cullmann, *Jesus and the Revolutionaries* (New York: Harper & Row, 1970); D. R. Griffiths, *The New Testament and the Roman State* (Swansea: John Perry, 1970), 56–62; C. H. Giblin, S. J., " 'The Things of God' in the Question Concerning Tribute to Caesar," *CBQ* 33 (1971):510–527; G. Petzke (see n.2); and F. F. Bruce, "Render to Caesar," in *Jesus and the Politics of His Day* (see n. 20), 249–264.

22. E.g., R. Bultmann, *The History of the Synoptic Tradition* (Oxford: Blackwell, 1963), 26,48. The recent work on oral transmission, with its emphasis on the social context of origin and memory and their transmission, e.g., W. H. Kelber, *The Oral and Written Gospel* (Philadelphia: Fortress, 1983), while generally critical of the older form-criticism, serves in fact to reinforce the conclusions of Bultmann in a passage such as this.

23. Fitzmyer, *Luke* 2.1296.

24. E. Stauffer, *Christ and the Caesars* (London: SCM, 1955), 125. A recent treatment of the coin involved in Mark 12:13–17 is H. St J. Hart, "The Coin of 'Render unto Caesar . . .' " in *Jesus and the Politics of his Day* (see n. 2), 241–248.

25. Stauffer, *Christ and the Caesars*, 127.

26. Similarly F. F. Bruce, "Render to Caesar," in *Jesus and the Politics of His Day*, 258: "The action amounts to giving back someone property to which he is entitled."

27. Vs. G. Bornkamm, *Jesus of Nazareth* (New York: Harper, 1960), 122–123.

28. Vs. R. Pesch, *Das Markusevangelium*, 2 vols. (Freiburg/Basel/Vienna: Herder, 1976–1977), 2.224–228; R. Schnackenburg, *The Moral Teaching of the New Testament* (New York: Herder & Herder, 1965), 117–118; and D. R. Griffiths, *The New Testament and the Roman State*, 61–62. J. D. M. Derrett, "Render to Caesar," in *Law in the New Testament* (London: Darton, Longmann and Todd, 1970), 313–338, is similar, in effect, by understanding the saying in terms of the subordination of Caesar to God.

29. H. G. Klemm, "De Censu Caesaris: Beobachtungen zu J. Duncan M. Derretts Interpretation der Perikope Mark 12:13–17 par.," *Nov T* 24 (1982):254; it is difficult to imagine that the issue in Mark 12:13–17 might actually have been, in effect, "Who is God"?

30. E.g., F. W. Beare, *The Gospel According to Matthew* (Oxford: Blackwell, 1981), 183.

31. Fitzmyer, *Luke* 2.1297, maintains that the Lucan Jesus "does not forbid the use of material possessions to pay taxes to a secular ruler," dismissing Luke 16:13d. Other recent interpretations find Luke less politically defensive; e.g., D. L. Tiede, *Prophecy and History in Luke-Acts* (Philadelphia: Fortress, 1980); W. M. Swartley, "Politics or Peace *(eirene)* in Luke's Gospel," 18–37, and D. Schmidt, "Luke's 'Innocent' Jesus: A Scriptural Apologetic," 111–121, in *Political Issues in Luke-Acts*, ed. R. J. Cassidy and P. J. Scharper (Maryknoll: Orbis, 1983).

32. E.g., H. W. Bartsch, *Jesus, Prophet und Messias aus Galilee* (Frankfurt: 1970), 53; E.

Lohmeyer, *Das Evangelium des Markus,* 17th ed. (Göttingen: Vandenhoeck und Ruprecht, 1967), *ad loc.*

33. E.g., Davies, *The Gospel and the Land* (see n. 1 above), 344.
34. H. Conzelmann, *The Theology of St. Luke* (New York: Harper, 1960), 85,140.
35. See further Luke 5:1–3,15,17; 6:6–7,11; 11:29,53–54; esp. 19:47–48 and 21:37–38.
36. See further Luke 1:32–33; 3:21–22; 22:67–70; 23:36–37.
37. See further Tiede, *Prophecy and History;* and Schmidt, "Luke's Innocent Jesus" (see n.31).

Subject Index

Index to Passages